D1190146

Karen Horney

Karen Horney

A Psychoanalyst's Search

for Self-Understanding

Bernard J. Paris

Yale University Press   New Haven and London

#3015557₄

Published with assistance from the Kingsley Trust
Association Publication Fund established by the Scroll
and Key Society of Yale College.

Set in Times Roman text and Insignia display type by
Marathon Typography Service, Inc., Durham, North Carolina.

Printed in the United States of America by Vail-Ballou Press,
Binghamton, New York.

Library of Congress Cataloging-in-Publication Data
Paris, Bernard J.
Karen Horney : a psychoanalyst's search for self-understanding /
Bernard J. Paris.
p. cm.
Includes bibliographical references and index.
ISBN 0-300-05956-6
1. Horney, Karen, 1885–1952—Psychology.
2. Psychoanalysts—United States—Biography.
3. Psychoanalysis. I. Title.
RC438.6.H67P37 1994
616.89'0092—dc20
[B]   94-14935
CIP

A catalogue record for this book is available from the
British Library.

The paper in this book meets the guidelines for permanence
and durability of the Committee on Production Guidelines for
Book Longevity of the Council on Library Resources.

10 9 8 7 6 5 4 3 2 1

For Hinda and Harvey

Contents

Contents

Part 2

The Freudian Phase and Feminine Psychology 53

Part 3

The Break with Freud and the Development of a New Paradigm 97

Part 4

Horney as an Adult 135

Part 5

Horney's Mature Theory 179

Appendix A

Appendix B

Acknowledgments

I have been fortunate to have had the assistance of many people in the preparation of this book. My greatest debts are to Marianne Eckardt and Renate Patterson, Karen Horney's surviving daughters, who have not only patiently answered my questions but have made the originals of their mother's diaries available to me and given me permission to quote from their own and their mother's unpublished writings. I could not have completed the biographical parts of this book without their generous help.

Renate Patterson alerted me to the fact that fifty letters from Karen Horney to her eldest daughter, Brigitte, were in the possession of Brigitte's friend and biographer, Gerd Høst Heyerdahl, who has made them available to me. I appreciate not only Professor Heyerdahl's cooperation but also that of her publisher, Scherz Verlag of Berne, who sent me proofs of her book on Brigitte Horney before its publication.

"Woman's Fear of Action" (Appendix B) was part of a collection of unpublished Horney material that I discovered in Harold Kelman's papers at the Postgraduate Center for Mental Health in New York. I was led to this collection by Natalie Jaffe, Kelman's niece and executor, who has kindly placed it in my possession. I hope to publish the rest of this material at a later date in a volume of Karen Horney's unpublished and uncollected essays.

Among the most valuable sources of which I have made use are the files that the late Jack Rubins, Horney's first biographer, had given to the American Institute for Psychoanalysis. These included notes from the more than one hundred interviews that Rubins conducted for his book, memoirs of Horney written at his request, and his extensive correspondence. I am grateful to Jeffrey Rubin, dean of the American Institute, for allowing me to transport this material to Florida, where I could process it, and for working with me to find a permanent repository for these files. They are now part of the collection of Karen Horney's papers that has been established in the Manuscript and Archives division of the Yale University Library. The Horney Papers also include Horney's diaries and notebooks, family photographs, Renate Patterson's unpublished writings about her mother, copies of Horney's letters to Brigitte, and personal documents, such as Horney's transcripts, marriage license, and immigration papers. I wish to thank Sam Gowan of the University of Florida Library for advising me on the establishment of the Karen Horney Papers.

The American Institute for Psychoanalysis was most cooperative in giving me access to Horney documents in its possession and to records concerning the history of the institute and of the Association for the Advancement of Psychoanalysis. These are now also part of the Karen Horney Papers. I am grateful to the archive of the A. A. Brill Library of the New York Psychoanalytic Institute for sharing with me its file on Karen Horney's relations with the institute and her departure in 1941, and to the Rare Books and Manuscript Library at Columbia University for sending me photocopies of Horney's correspondence with her publisher, W. W. Norton.

My work has been greatly facilitated by my research assistants. Usha Bande helped me to compile an initial bibliography and to secure the books and essays I needed from a variety of libraries. Her work laid the foundation for my research. Carolyn Geertz deciphered the shorthand in which Jack Rubins took his interview notes and provided me with easily readable transcripts. This required ingenuity and perseverance. Andrea Dlaska and Christa Zorn-Belde, both native speakers of German, have helped me in many ways, especially by translating the unpublished portions of Horney's diaries, her notebooks, her hitherto untranslated writings in German, her letters to Brigitte, and various German texts. All translations from the German of previously untranslated materials are by them, with my occasional editing. Their efforts to solve the puzzles of Horney's German script have been heroic. My deepest thanks to all my research assistants.

The work of Usha Bande, Carolyn Geertz, and Christa Zorn-Belde was supported by grants from the Division of Sponsored Research of the University of

Acknowledgments

Florida. The Department of English made the services of Andrea Dlaska available to me. My chair, Patricia Craddock, was most helpful in arranging this and in agreeing to a schedule that provided the maximum amount of uninterrupted time for writing.

My work has benefited greatly from the feedback of friends and colleagues. I have discussed Horney over the years with many analysts associated with the American Institute for Psychoanalysis—most notably, Harold Kelman, Alexandra Symonds, Andrew Tershakovec, Helen De Rosis, Mario Rendon, and Jeffrey Rubin—and I have learned much from questions and comments when I have lectured at scientific meetings of the Association for the Advancement of Psychoanalysis. I have tried out portions of this book at a Journal Club at the American Institute, at the inaugural conference of the International Karen Horney Society, and at several meetings of the Group for the Application of Psychology (GAP) at the University of Florida. I am grateful not only for the exchange of ideas but also for the encouragement I have consistently received from Horneyan analysts and GAP colleagues.

A number of people have had the kindness to read and critique portions of my manuscript. These include Edward Clemmens, Patricia Craddock, Jack Danielian, Franz Epting, Andrew Gordon, Molly Harrower, Nathan Horwitz, James Huffman, Isidore Portnoy, Michelle Price, Jeanne Smith, Maureen Turim, and Christa Zorn-Belde. In addition to reading an early version of the introduction, Phyllis Grosskurth has shared her experiences as a biographer and given me wise advice. Norman Holland and Peter Rudnytsky, colleagues in the Institute for Psychological Study of the Arts at the University of Florida, read the entire manuscript (in a much longer version) and responded with encouraging support and helpful comment. I have followed many of the suggestions for revision that I have received from friends and colleagues, but I bear sole responsibility for the flaws that remain.

This book has also greatly profited from the ministrations of my editors at Yale University Press. Gladys Topkis encouraged the project from the beginning, and I am grateful for her unflagging enthusiasm. It has been a great stimulus to have had Gladys for whom to write. When the time came for her to put on her critical hat, she overcame my resistance and showed me how the book could be made better by being made shorter. My manuscript editor, Susan Laity, has suggested significant improvements in organization and has scrutinized every sentence with impressive care and intelligence. I thought I had submitted a highly polished manuscript, but working with these editors has taught me a great deal about writing. A problem that neither they nor I could solve is that Karen Horney, following the practice of her time, almost always used the masculine pronoun. I have had to follow Horney's usage when integrating quotations from her works into my prose.

Acknowledgments

My very first reader, as always, has been my wife, Shirley. She read Horney a year before I did, in 1958, and has maintained an interest in Horney's theory through the years. I cannot adequately acknowledge how much I have gained from having her to share and enrich my mental universe. Her emotional support has been unfailing and her insights astute. I have also learned a great deal from discussing Horney with my son, Mark, whose reservations about her theory have helped enlarge my perspective. I have gone through some difficult times while writing this book and have been sustained by Shirley and Mark. I went through an even more trying time in 1985, when I had a brain tumor that was diagnosed as malignant but turned out to be benign. I was helped through that ordeal by the love and support of my sister and brother-in-law, Hinda and Harvey Cohen. I dedicate this book to them in gratitude.

Introduction

Karen Horney (1885–1952) is at once one of the most important and one of the most undervalued psychoanalytic thinkers of the twentieth century. She was well known during her lifetime, but her work gradually receded from view until 1967, when *Feminine Psychology,* a collection of her early essays, was published. Only in recent years has she begun to receive the attention she deserves.

Two biographies have largely established the public record of Horney's life— Jack Rubins' *Gentle Rebel of Psychoanalysis* (1978) and Susan Quinn's *A Mind of Her Own* (1987). In this book, I tell the story of her inner life and relate it to the evolution of her ideas. Horney's thought can be divided into three stages. During the 1920s and early 1930s, in a series of brilliant essays, she tried to modify orthodox ideas about feminine psychology while staying within the framework of Freudian theory. In the late 1930s, however, she published two books that rejected some of the basic premises of Freudian psychoanalysis and replaced its biological orientation with an emphasis on culture and interpersonal relationships. In the 1940s, she developed her mature theory, in which she postulated that individuals cope with the anxiety produced by the frustration of psychological needs by disowning their real feelings and developing elaborate strategies of defense. I believe that Horney's mature theory makes a major contribution to psychological thought—particularly the study of personality—that deserves to be more widely known and applied than it is.

Although this book has a large biographical component, it is not a conventional biography. Through bringing together Karen Horney's personal history, her conflicts, and her evolving ideas, I shall examine how her inner struggles both inspired her writings and are revealed by them. Horney's personal problems induced her to embark on a search for self-understanding, the record of which is contained first in her diaries and then in her psychoanalytic writings. That quest is evident in her auto-biographical essays on feminine psychology, and it at least partly inspired her development of a new psychoanalytic paradigm. It eventually led her to the original insights into human behavior that are most fully unfolded in her mature theory. The personal sources of the mature theory will be clear in my portrait of the adult Horney, but the value of the theory is independent of its creator, and I shall present it without biographical reference. Although this theory has not been properly appreciated, many of its concepts have been absorbed into psychological thought, and it has had a considerable impact on clinical practice.

Born Karen Danielsen in a suburb of Hamburg in 1885, Horney studied medicine at the universities of Freiburg, Göttingen, and Berlin. She married Oskar Horney in 1909, entered analysis with Karl Abraham in 1910, and became a founding member of the Berlin Psychoanalytic Institute in 1920. Having separated from Oskar in 1926, she emigrated to the United States in 1932, when Franz Alexander invited her to become associate director of the newly formed Chicago Psychoanalytic Institute. She moved to New York in 1934 and became a member of the New York Psychoanalytic Institute. In 1941 she founded the American Institute for Psychoanalysis, of which she was dean until her death in 1952. During the last fifteen years of her life she published five major books: *The Neurotic Personality of Our Time* (1937), *New Ways in Psychoanalysis* (1939), *Self-Analysis* (1942), *Our Inner Conflicts* (1945), and *Neurosis and Human Growth* (1950). Two additional books were published after her death: *Feminine Psychology* (1967) and *Final Lectures* (1987). A version of her *Adolescent Diaries* edited by her daughter Marianne Eckardt appeared in 1980.

Despite the fact that she was ostracized by the psychoanalytic establishment because of her iconoclasm, Horney experienced great success during her lifetime. Her books sold extremely well, her institute flourished, articles about her appeared in newspapers and magazines, and she was in great demand as both a speaker and an analyst. She and her fellow neo-Freudians were regarded by many as providing the leading challenge to orthodox, Freudian theory.

Introduction

After Horney's death, her work was given a good deal of space in textbooks and histories, and she was treated as a major figure, but over time she received less and less attention. This is not to say that she was forgotten. After going through numerous printings in their original editions, her books were all reissued in paperback and have sold more than half a million copies. They are still in print. Her institute continues to train analysts, while her ideas have influenced the course of psychoanalysis and her theories have been employed in other disciplines. But the degree of recognition she has received has not been commensurate with her importance. In the words a current writer used to describe her own situation, Horney's work "lacks cultural presence: no one has to know about it or take it into account to appear less than ignorant; no one will be held accountable for ignoring it" (Dworkin 1989, 110). Although things have begun to change, this still holds true for the most significant and distinctive parts of Horney's contribution.

The revival of interest in Horney began with the publication of *Feminine Psychology*. Because these early essays took issue with Freud about penis envy, female masochism, and feminine development, they created controversy on first appearance, but they were largely ignored thereafter, as Freud and his more faithful followers sought to silence the disputes they had aroused. Horney's essays on feminine psychology were far ahead of their time, but today there is a growing consensus that Horney was the first great psychoanalytic feminist. Although in *The Reproduction of Mothering* (1978) Nancy Chodorow cites Horney mainly to disagree with her, the work of Zenia Odes Fliegel (1973, 1982, 1986) and Marcia Westkott (1986) and Susan Quinn's biography elicited from her the following tribute in *Feminism and Psychoanalytic Theory* (1989):

> Psychoanalytic feminism has a rather complex and sometimes underground prehistory which recent work on early woman psychoanalysts helps us to excavate. I locate its political and theoretical origins with Karen Horney, a second-generation analyst whose early essays on femininity forcefully challenge Freud. Horney asserts a model of women with positive primary feminine qualities and self-valuation, against Freud's model of women as defective and forever limited, and she ties her critique of both psychoanalytic theory and women's psychology to her recognition of a male-dominant society and culture. Horney's theories, and indeed the early psychoanalytic debates about femininity, do not seem to have made a major impact on mainstream psychoanalysis for many years, indeed, until the current revival of interest in female psychology sparked by the feminist movement and challenge. However, her theories form the basis, acknowledged or

unacknowledged, for most of the recent revisions of psychoanalytic understandings of gender and for most psychoanalytic dissidence on the question of gender in the early period as well. (2–3)

Ironically, Horney herself turned away from the topic of feminine psychology in
the mid-1930s and began to develop a theory that she considered gender-neutral (see
Westkott 1986 for dissent). She increasingly focused her attention on psychological
defenses and conflicts that occur in both sexes, while recognizing that culture induces
a greater frequency of some defenses in men and of others in women. In her essays
on feminine psychology she emphasized the influence of culture upon our conceptions of gender, and in an unpublished paper entitled "Woman's Fear of Action"
(1935; see Appendix B) she made it clear that one of her reasons for turning away
from the topic of feminine psychology was the impossibility of distinguishing what
is essentially "feminine" from culturally induced behavior and gender identity. In
addition, she considered defining the feminine to be the political strategy of a patriarchal society that wanted to exclude women from male-dominated spheres of
activity.

The revival of attention to Horney's ideas about feminine psychology, while
welcome in itself, threatens to identify her too strongly with the earliest stage of her
thought and to obscure the importance of her later work. This has been an effect of
Susan Quinn's biography. Quinn genuinely appreciated the early essays, which she
discussed at length, but she apparently lost interest in Horney's ideas as they moved
away from feminist concerns. For the most part, Quinn's reviewers have followed
her lead, saying little or nothing about Horney's later, major books.

In the second stage of Horney's thought, culture and disturbed human relationships, which had been increasingly emphasized in her essays on feminine psychology,
replaced biology as the most important causes of neurotic development. As the
author of *The Neurotic Personality of Our Time* (1937) and *New Ways in Psychoanalysis* (1939), Horney is often thought of primarily as a neo-Freudian member of
"the cultural school," which also includes Erich Fromm, Harry Stack Sullivan, Clara
Thompson, and Abraham Kardiner. *Neurotic Personality* had a tremendous impact in
its day, and it is still the work for which many know Horney. It has produced a
heightened awareness among clinicians of cultural factors in mental disturbance and
has inspired studies of culture from a psychoanalytic perspective.

The Neurotic Personality of Our Time made Horney famous in intellectual circles. *New Ways in Psychoanalysis,* a systematic critique of Freud, made her infamous among classical analysts. Although it pays tribute to Freud's genius and the
importance of his contribution, it vigorously rejects many basic premises of psycho-

analysis. Horney's first book made her colleagues at the New York Psychoanalytic Institute uncomfortable; the resentment aroused by her second forced her to resign, and anger underlies the dismissive attitude toward her that persists in many quarters.

In her first two books, Horney proposes a model for the origin and structure of neurosis in which adverse conditions in the environment—especially in the family—create a basic anxiety against which the child develops strategies of defense that are self-defeating and in conflict with each other. The child's sexual development is but a small part of this picture; sexual difficulties are the *result* of character problems rather than their cause.

Perhaps Horney's most significant modification of Freud in these two books is her emphasis on the present rather than the past. She advocates focusing on current defenses and inner conflicts rather than on the past, and she explains behavior in terms of its function within the present constellation of defenses. Past experiences produce a character structure that can be understood without reference to infantile origins. Horney sees adult behavior as an evolved product of the past rather than as a repetition of early fixations or relationships. Horney's emphasis on the present has made it almost impossible for orthodox analysts to assimilate her thought.

Horney's third book, *Self-Analysis* (1942), presents her most detailed account of how the psychoanalytic process works in terms of her new paradigm and contains her only extended case history: that of her patient "Clare." The book was not well received in analytic circles, where there was much skepticism about Horney's optimistic assessment of the possibilities of self-analysis; but it, too, has been widely read, and it helped inspire the Institute for Self Analysis in London.

Our Inner Conflicts (1945) and *Neurosis and Human Growth* (1950) describe the defenses against basic anxiety much more fully than the earlier books and develop a far more sophisticated taxonomy. *Self-Analysis* simply lists ten neurotic trends. The mature theory divides defenses into interpersonal and intrapsychic. *Our Inner Conflicts* focuses on the interpersonal: moving toward, against, and away from other people (compliance, aggression, and detachment). It also begins to explore intrapsychic defenses, which are then examined systematically in *Neurosis and Human Growth*. Here Horney describes what she calls "the pride system": people compensate for feelings of worthlessness and inadequacy by developing idealized images of themselves that generate neurotic pride, neurotic claims, tyrannical "shoulds," and self-hate. The neurotic project is a search for glory in which we attempt to actualize our idealized image. Since this is impossible, we intensify the self-hate we were attempting to assuage. This is one of the "vicious circles" that figure prominently in Horney's thought.

Horney is often perceived as having developed a culture-bound theory that describes only the neurotic personality of her time. The emphasis on culture in *Neurotic Personality* and *New Ways in Psychoanalysis* has no doubt created this impression, but her theory evolved to encompass defenses that are present in many societies, both Eastern and Western, from ancient times to the present day. Aggression, withdrawal, and compliance are complex human versions of the basic mechanisms of defense in the animal kingdom—fight, flight, and submission. The instinctive basis of these strategies may be one reason we find them in such a variety of manifestations. The wide applicability of Horney's theory has been shown by its use in literary criticism, biography, and cultural studies (see Appendix A).

But if Horney's mature theory has such range, power, and applicability, why are more people not using it? This is a difficult question. Without delving too deeply into the sociology of thought, I shall offer a few suggestions.

In the first place, after Horney resigned in protest from the New York Psychoanalytic Institute, many orthodox analysts saw her as a presumptuous woman who had attacked their hero, Freud (probably because of penis envy and unresolved resentment toward her father), and who was out to overturn the theory that sanctioned their professional practice and their whole way of thinking. As we have seen, a dismissive attitude toward Horney developed that continues to affect the reception of her work. Quinn reports that "one prominent psychoanalyst, on hearing at a conference that I was writing the Horney biography, asked archly, 'Is she worth a book?'" "Because Horney left the psychoanalytic establishment as a rebel," Quinn found, "there is a continuing myth in some circles that 'she was a nobody'" (Dinnage 1987, 11).

Another reason for Horney's lack of cultural presence is that her writing is so clear and commonsensical. Reviewing her *Adolescent Diaries* in the *New York Times Book Review,* Edgar Levenson observed that her "viewpoints, once taken, seem apparent. Reading Freud, one thinks, 'Who would have thought. . . .' Reading Horney, one thinks, 'Yes, of course'" (1980, 16). I wrote a reply to the *Book Review* that still expresses my sentiments: "It is true that Horney's ideas, unlike Freud's, seem like simple common sense, something that could have occurred to anyone. They did not occur to anyone, however, before Horney. Too often people do read her thinking, 'Yes, of course,' and then forget that they had not known it all before" (18 January 1981). If clarity was unfashionable in 1981, it is almost fatal today, in the age of Lacan, Derrida, and postmodernism.

There is something limiting, to be sure, about Horney's clarity and common sense. Her work has little in it of poetry or myth. It is not full of mysterious, recondite terminology, as are the writings of Freud, Jung, and Lacan, and it does not have the aura of being secret knowledge possessed only by the master. It does not provide an elaborate analogical or mythological system that appears to explain the obscure or the ineffable. Much of it deals with what we can learn through self-observation rather than with highly inventive hypotheses about infantile and unconscious experience. Horney explores unconscious motives and conflicts, but she makes them readily accessible to conscious understanding. Many find it difficult to believe that such an intelligible theory can be deep—and, indeed, there are depths that Horney does not explore.

The mysteries her work does explain are of the kind we do not normally perceive to be mysterious. They are the enigmas of ordinary behavior, the common neuroses of mankind. Horney's mature theory defamiliarizes the psychopathology of everyday life, allowing us first to recognize and then to understand it. I should add that it is also capable of explaining extreme behavior, like that of Iago, King Lear, Raskolnikov, or Cathy and Heathcliff in *Wuthering Heights* (see Paris 1982, 1991a, 1991c). Horney's theory has, as Rosemary Dinnage puts it, "a certain dimension missing" (1987, 11), but so does every theory. Horney's theory is not all-encompassing, nor does it pretend to be, but it explains a great deal.

The neglect of Horney is in part a matter of resistance. She tells us too many things about ourselves that we cannot reject but do not want to know. Most other psychoanalytic theories have much greater deniability. Horney teaches that health is a possibility but makes us feel neurotic—a threatening combination. The fact that she holds out the prospect of growth makes her insights more challenging: she wants us to try to change and will not allow us to adopt a consolatory pessimism, like Freud's. For her, neurosis is widespread, but it is not inevitable, and she believes in therapeutic possibilities. Such hope can be inspiring, but it can also be oppressive, conducive to self-criticism. It is sometimes easier to believe that civilization has doomed us to discontent.

Perhaps the most important reason for the lack of cultural presence of Horney's mature theory is its explanation of human behavior in terms of currently existing constellations of defenses and inner conflicts. In our culture, the analysis of human behavior has been dominated by an emphasis on its origins, and a theorist who focuses on the present is bound to be shunted aside. Psychoanalysis has tried to advance by searching farther and farther back into preoedipal experience. People who have been conditioned to think about human motivation in terms of origins do not find Horney's structural explanations satisfying.

The shift from the first to the second stage of Horney's thought was a product in part of her coming to America, where she encountered new intellectual influences, a different culture, and a patient population that made her aware of how much Freud's theory had been affected by its origin in a sexually repressive society. A close reading of her writings of the 1930s shows, however, that although her ways of thinking changed, the problems in which she was most interested did not. She was still struggling with issues she had focused upon in her essays on feminine psychology, issues that the biographical material reveals to have been her own. In her diaries, in her analysis with Karl Abraham, in her essays on feminine psychology—indeed in all of her psychoanalytic writings—Karen Horney was struggling to make sense of herself and to obtain relief from her own difficulties. Her thought kept evolving not only in response to external influences but also because her earlier efforts to comprehend herself had failed and she needed a different approach in her quest for self-understanding.

Jack Rubins and Susan Quinn—and Harold Kelman before them (1971)—have pointed to connections between Horney's life and her writings but have not explored them in detail. Rubins had only limited access to Horney's adolescent diaries, which enable us to see the suffering and inner conflict that inspired her interest in psychoanalysis and that generated many of her later insights. Quinn used the diaries mainly to reconstruct the events of Horney's adolescence and the early years of her marriage. Without the work of Rubins and Quinn, I could not have written this book, since a good biographical record had to be established before it was possible to concentrate on the relation between Horney the person and her ideas. But I have much to add to the biographical record, for in the course of my research I have discovered a great deal about Horney's life that was hitherto unknown.

I am indebted to the work of Jack Rubins in yet another way. In preparing his biography, he corresponded with and interviewed well over a hundred people, most of whom have since died, and he collected and commissioned reminiscences of Horney. This material was available to Susan Quinn, and it is now in the Karen Horney Papers at Yale. When I began my research, I did not anticipate its richness since there was much that Rubins and Quinn did not use in their books. Although Rubins claimed to be showing his subject "warts and all," he was a Horneyan analyst who wished to protect the image of his mentor. His interviews revealed Horney not only as an admired, charismatic person who helped many people but also as a ruthless, competitive individual who sometimes behaved destructively and was full of contradictions. She had difficulty relating to others, and her sexual behavior was compulsive and often unprofessional. Quinn revealed more unpleasant truths about Horney than Rubins; still, she left a good deal of material unused that I shall employ here, not for sensational purposes but because it helps us to see the connection between Horney's struggles and her insights. I have conducted numerous interviews myself but without those of Rubins there is a great deal about Horney that we would never know.

Other primary sources include unpublished writings by Marianne Eckardt and Renate Patterson, Horney's surviving daughters, as well as audio- and videotapes with a number of Horney's contemporaries that were recorded for historical purposes. A problem for the biographer is that Horney was a very reserved person who rarely told others much about her feelings and experiences. Both Marianne and Renate say that they did not know their mother well. The diaries that Horney kept between the ages of thirteen and twenty-six tell us a great deal about her inner life; but the only personal documents surviving from her later years are fifty letters she wrote between 1945 and 1951 to her oldest daughter, Brigitte, who had remained in Germany to pursue a film career. Toward the end of her life, Horney was closer to Brigitte than to anyone else, and these letters, which have become available only recently, give us an intimate view of their relationship.

Is this enough, we might ask, to provide a picture of Karen Horney's personality and experience that is sufficiently detailed to reveal how they affected her ideas? Possibly not—but this information enables us to recognize how self-revealing Horney's psychoanalytic writings are. This extremely private person wrote about herself constantly, revealing her inner life to anyone able to recognize this. Horney spent an enormous amount of energy analyzing herself, but according to Renate she did not share her self-insight with others. Renate observes, however, that "she couldn't keep it suppressed, entirely to herself"; her books were "covert autobiography."[1]

I came to recognize Horney's self-revelation when, in rereading her writings, I noticed many parallels between Clare in *Self-Analysis* and the Karen of the diaries. The story of Clare contains information about Karen's childhood that throws an entirely different light on the relationship with her mother depicted in the diaries. With the knowledge of Horney gained from *Self-Analysis* and the diaries, the autobiographical features of the essays on feminine psychology became clear, as well as those of all her later writings.

We have, then, an abundance of information about Karen Horney's development, self-perceptions, and conflicts. Her writings are fascinating not only because of the value of their ideas but also because of the human story they tell, the insight they give us into the personality and quest for self-understanding of this extraordinarily complicated person. Being able to trace Horney's search in detail contributes to our understanding of the subjective component in psychological theory, an issue that has been raised in a number of biographies and that is the focus of two important books, *Faces in a Cloud: Subjectivity in Personality Theory,* by Robert Stolorow and George Atwood (1979), and *Makers of Psychology: The Personal Factor,* by Harvey Mindess (1988). It also sheds light on aspects of the creative process, particularly the relation between emotional suffering and insight.

The relation of Clare to Karen Horney has long been a subject of speculation. The psychoanalyst Harold Kelman, who knew Horney well, concluded that although "Clare was a composite of many people . . . she did reveal many of Horney's own character problems—problems with which she was acutely and painfully struggling from the time she finished *New Ways* to the completion of *Self-Analysis*. Her later works reveal the continuation of that struggle illuminated out of her own pain and her work with people with similar problems" (1971, 23). Rubins also describes Clare as a "semifictitious patient" and points to details suggesting that Horney "may have been partly referring to herself" (1978, 16). He draws upon Clare in his account of Karen's relationships with her mother and brother but without citing his source or assessing the degree to which the Clare story is autobiographical.

Susan Quinn does not consider the Clare case at all for biographical purposes, and as a result she sometimes presents a misleading picture of Horney's relationship with her family. Although she describes *Self-Analysis* as one of Horney's "most personal books" (1987, 419), she tacitly rejects the account of Karen's family situation that Rubins had derived from Clare's story. Whereas Rubins reports that Karen "questioned whether she had really been wanted" and felt "from as far back as she could remember . . . that her brother had been treated differently than she" (1978, 11, 10), Quinn claims that "in another family she might have grown up in the shadow of her brother. . . . But in the Danielsen household Karen seems to have been almost equally prized from the start" (19). As I shall show, Rubins is correct.

In reconstructing the process by which Horney sought to understand herself, I shall begin by presenting a picture of the young Karen as she appears in the diaries and in *Self-Analysis,* concentrating for the most part on her pre-psychoanalytic perspective. While writing in the diaries Horney felt that she was engaged in self-exploration, but I think she came to see that although she had honestly recorded her experiences of others and of herself, she had not penetrated "beneath the conscious level" or arrived at an understanding of her motivations that she could later endorse (*SA*, 188).

The diaries reveal many of the difficulties with which Horney grappled throughout her life, and they show us her first efforts to comprehend them. Toward the end they become an adjunct to her analysis with Karl Abraham. In later writings she repeatedly looked at the family history and psychological problems revealed in the diaries but from different analytical perspectives. The essays on feminine psychology and *Self-Analysis* are the most transparently autobiographical of her works, but she is still quite recognizable in later writings, even her last two books, although as she developed her new paradigm for the structure of neurosis and her taxonomy of defenses, her insights drew on more sources and became more broadly applicable.

When Susan Quinn's biography revealed that Horney had a compulsive need for men that persisted to the end of her life, some readers, dismayed by the inability of the physician to cure herself, saw this revelation as a threat to Horney's stature. I see Horney's difficulties—which were not only sexual—as a source of her insight rather than as something that diminishes the value of her work. Renate has argued that her mother's "childhood problems with her family, her deep depressions and neurotic trends, were her greatest blessing in disguise. How else would she have developed her theories, her deep understanding of human nature?"[2] I agree. Horney's insights were derived from her efforts to relieve her own pain, as well as that of her patients. If her suffering had been less intense, her insights would have been less profound. James Hillman urges us to read the biographies of artists because they "show us what they did with their traumas" (1992, 137). I shall try to show what Karen Horney did with hers.

Part 1

The Making of a Psychoanalyst

Chapter 1

"Never-Ending Self-Analysis"

We can observe the beginnings of Karen Horney's search for self-understanding in the five diaries she kept between the ages of thirteen and twenty-six and in her letters to Oskar Horney, most of which were written when she was twenty-one. These remarkable documents reveal the problems, the qualities of mind and temperament, and the ways of coping with her difficulties that led Horney to become a psychoanalyst.

The diaries begin on a note of youthful exuberance: "How I come to be writing a diary is easy to explain: it's because I am enthusiastic about everything new, and I have decided now to carry this through so that in later years I can better remember the days of my youth" (*AD,* 3). But the last item in the published collection is a letter to Karl Abraham, who had been her psychoanalyst, expressing a need for further treatment: "Won't I ever be getting well, completely well? I am beginning to despair of it. Most of the time it is not so bad, but I often feel as though I were paralyzed—there is a general disinclination in me. When I waken in the morning, I wish the day were already over" (270).

In the intervening pages there is a good deal of enthusiasm—about school, teachers, family, friends, lovers, nature, and the study of medicine—but also much suffering and anxiety about herself: "Hornvieh [her pet name for Oskar], do help me—I believe I am wandering in a special labyrinth and shall never get out, and see only my own picture everywhere, but always so extremely different." She can "hardly manage to clothe in words" what is oppressing her. She has everything "that a person could ask in order to be happy—satisfying work, love, home, natural surroundings," but "the feeling comes creeping up more often than ever, what is all this for?" (186–87). In addition to suffering from "many changes of mood" (118), depression, inability to function, and feelings of futility, she often has a sense of inner emptiness, a desperate need for love, and longings for death.

In order to cope with her difficulties, Karen engaged in self-analysis, she underwent psychoanalysis, and she became an analyst herself. Before she had heard of psychoanalysis, she used Oskar as a therapist; she had "a burning wish" for him to know her "wholly, wholly" and wondered why it was "so unutterably beneficial, the thought that somebody besides myself knows me??" (212). In her second letter to Oskar, she describes herself as engaging in an "unremitting, ever more refined self-observation that never leaves me, even in any sort of intoxication—then, if I have butted up against some problem . . . I gather some 'thoughts' together until I am in the clear with the affair" (*AD*, 156). In the entries preceding this letter we can see Karen trying to work through a variety of disappointments in others and discomforts with herself. After her marriage she used her diary as an adjunct to her sessions with Karl Abraham or, when she was not seeing him, as part of her effort to cure herself: "If I am taking up my diary again it is from the ardent endeavor to master this illness at last" (247). She intermittently underwent analysis with Abraham (between 1910 and 1913, and again in 1918) and with Hanns Sachs in the early 1920s, but she later felt that these experiences were not of great help. She eventually wrote a book on self-analysis because this was the process on which she had relied most heavily for relief from her difficulties.

Indeed, Horney engaged in self-analysis throughout her life. At the age of fifteen, she wrote in her diary: "I don't understand myself, am dissatisfied with myself and everyone else. In the condition I am in now, I am absolutely good for nothing. I can only work hard 1 to 2 days a week, and for that I am mortally weak the next day. I constantly have the feeling that I'm going to collapse." Her speculations about the possible causes of her condition included longing for her old teachers, the "daily excitements with Father," sympathy for her mother, and not being "quite at home" in the gymnasium (roughly equivalent to high school), which she had been attending for two months (43).

Once Horney became a psychoanalyst, she developed additional motives for seeking self-understanding. It was important to analyze countertransferences, to recognize how her own character influenced interactions with her patients, and above all to keep herself as mentally healthy as possible so as to be a reliable source of guidance. She observes in *New Ways in Psychoanalysis* that as long as the analyst "harbors certain pretenses himself, he is bound to protect them in the patient too." Not only must he undergo a thorough didactic analysis, "but he must also subject himself to a never-ending self-analysis," since "self-understanding is . . . an indispensable prerequisite for analyzing others" (303). In her final lectures, delivered in the last few months of her life, she emphasized what she elsewhere characterized as "the analyst's personal equation" (Azorin 1957) and the way his or her "remaining personal neurotic difficulties" handicap analytical work (*FL*, 17). If self-analysis cannot free the analyst of personal problems, it can facilitate taking them into account.

Horney's efforts at self-understanding began with her adolescent diaries. The first four, along with the letters to Oskar Horney, tell of her troubled relationship with her family, of her enthusiasm for school and "crushes" on her teachers, of her intellectual and sexual awakening, and above all of her relationships with the first five men in her life: Ernst Schorschi, who introduced her to love and with whom she was infatuated for several months; Rolf, a "languishing Jewish youth" (175) who was her mentor and to whom she was deeply attached; Ernst, a boarder, toward whom she felt a strong physical attraction and for whom she abandoned Rolf; Losch (Louis Grote), a fellow student and her lover during two terms in medical school; and Oskar Horney, her future husband and Losch's friend, with whom she corresponded while she was involved with Losch. My object in the chapters that follow is not to reconstruct her milieu and the details of her life but to focus on her inner world as revealed by her own words.

Chapter 2

Family Troubles

Karen Danielsen was born in a suburb of Hamburg on 15 September 1885. Her father, Berndt Henrick Wackels Danielsen—Wackels—was a sea captain of Norwegian origin; her mother, Clothilde, known as Sonni, was of Dutch-German extraction. This was the second marriage for Wackels, a widower with four nearly grown children. He was the son of a watchmaker, while Sonni's father, Jacob Joseph van Ronzelen, was the architect who had overseen the construction of the port of Bremerhaven, which meant that there was a social as well as an age difference between husband and wife.

There were tremendous tensions between the Danielsens. Karen and her brother, Berndt, who was four years her senior, lined up with Sonni against Wackels, whose children from his first marriage incited him against his second wife. Karen's reactions to these tensions were manifested most visibly in her solicitude toward her mother and her hostility toward her father. After a quarrel between her parents at Christmas, she lamented: "Mother is ill and unhappy. Alas, if only I could help my 'dearest in the whole world.'" She hoped that Sonni would be "spared" so that "later on she can lead a friendly life" with Karen and Berndt (AD, 19). Evidently Sonni reacted to marital stress by becoming ill, and Karen feared for the life of the parent on whom she depended for love and security. Her concern for her mother runs like a refrain through her first two diaries. She describes herself as "often quite sad and discouraged. For things are bad at home, and Mutti, my all, is so ill and unhappy. Oh, how I would love to help her and cheer her up" (45).

There is a revealing picture of mother and daughter in Karen's account of Sonni's visit to a fortune teller. According to the diary, the fortune teller divined that Sonni had a fifteen-year-old daughter whose "only passion [was] for books and study," and she predicted that this girl would "take a much respected, special place . . . in the world and . . . belong to a very fine circle" (32). This prophecy reflected Sonni's desire that her daughter achieve an unusual degree of academic success and assume a position appropriate to her van Ronzelen heritage. Sonni seems to have been afraid that Karen would be deflected from her destiny by the ordinary desires of womanhood. The fortune teller also foresaw "some battles" for Karen between the ages of seventeen and eighteen over the issue of marriage but assured Sonni that academic goals would win out. That Karen was excited by the fortune teller's predictions suggests that at this point she and her mother had similar hopes for her future.

The fortune teller told Sonni what she wanted to hear about herself as well. She confirmed the sense of martyrdom that Sonni had conveyed to her daughter—"You have been through so many difficulties in the last 7 to 10 years that you could write a book about it"—and predicted that Sonni's "hot-tempered, nagging" husband would die "in the next 3 1/2 years." After rejecting a proposal of marriage and the offer of "a brilliant position," Sonni would live for the most part with her daughter (32).

While Karen idolized her mother, hovering about her with tenderness, care, and anxiety, she scorned her father as a hypocrite who made demands upon others that he did not live up to himself. His lofty religious sentiments were belied by his behavior. She wished for a father she could "love and esteem," as prescribed by the fourth commandment, but she could not respect "that man who makes us all unhappy with his dreadful hypocrisy, selfishness, crudeness, and ill-breeding" (21). Karen's principal charge against her father was that he made her mother unhappy, and she was apparently able to stand up to him on her mother's behalf. One day when he complained about Sonni, Karen gave him "a piece of [her] mind," telling him that they were all "unspeakably happy" when he was not there: "Mother is our greatest happiness, our one and all" (36).

Karen's contempt for her father made her antipathetic toward the religiosity he endeavored to impose upon the family. She complained about his "conversion sermons" and the "endless, rather stupid, prayers" he said every morning (28). Renate reports that her mother wanted to give her own children "all the spiritual freedom she had missed as a child under the shadow of her Bible-throwing father, to whom the Bible had really become a deadly weapon, not only in words but physical weight."[1] The children used to call Wackels *"der Bibelschmeisser"* (Bible-thrower) behind his back (Rubins 1978, 11). Although the fifteen-year-old Karen does not seem to have been afraid of her father, she may have felt threatened when she was younger. She later told Franz Alexander, her colleague in Berlin and founding director of the Chicago Psychoanalytic Institute, that she often recalled "the frightening gaze of [her] father's blue eyes" (Natterson 1966, 451).

If Karen was Sonni's ally, Sonni was Karen's. The girl's desire for a professional career could never have been fulfilled without Sonni's support. When Karen decided at the age of thirteen that she wanted to study medicine, there was no gymnasium for girls in Hamburg, and Sonni immediately wrote to Hannover to ask for a prospectus for the gymnasium there. When she was fifteen, in December 1900, Karen complained that her " 'precious Father' " had forbidden her "any such plans once and for all" (*AD,* 19). Within a few weeks of this entry, however, a gymnasium for women was announced in Hamburg, and Sonni, Karen, and Berndt mounted a successful campaign to win Wackels' consent. Karen was bitter at her father's reluctance: "He, who has flung out thousands for my stepbrother Enoch, who is both stupid and bad, first turns every additional penny he is to spend for me 10 times in his fingers." Unlike her mother, her father had no dreams of Karen's attaining a special position in society. Rather, he wanted her to stay at home and take over the work of the housemaid: "He brings me almost to the point of cursing my good gifts" (26).

Most of the entries concerning her father were written in 1900–01, when Karen was fifteen, during one of his longer stays at home. After that, he almost disappears from her diaries. He and Sonni separated in 1904, and from this point on, he seems virtually to have disappeared from his daughter's life. There is no indication that she ever visited her father or had any desire to do so. Karen's hostility toward her father was replaced after the separation by condescension: he was, she wrote, "a big child, whose world of ideas revolves around a strong, touchingly naïve belief in the Bible" (169). He seems to have given her a lifelong distaste of the Bible: "I know the Bible very well, as my father was a strict Christian (or is), but for that very reason it is unsympathetic to me" (198). We have no direct information about how she reacted to his death in May 1910 because she had taken a break from writing in her diary, and there is no mention of the event when she resumed. There are anguished entries after the death of Sonni in February 1911.

Karen's conscious feelings toward Sonni underwent a great transformation over the course of the diaries. Whereas she had adored her mother during her teen-aged years, in her entry for 5 January 1911, for example, when she was six months pregnant, she professed such a "deep aversion to Sonni" that she wondered whether she had an unconscious "resistance against finding myself in a situation that makes me resemble her: becoming a mother as she is my mother" (254). In her next entry, she identified Sonni as one of the causes of her recurring bouts of fatigue. Sonni was so "annoying with [her] hysterics" that Karen wished she were not around (258).

It was now Sonni toward whom Karen was critical and by whom she felt oppressed. On 20 January she reported having felt "well and lively yesterday morning" but she began to feel fatigue following a visit from Sonni; "Today it is so bad I can't work. All the old heaviness and weariness." Sonni also felt victimized by Karen. Each blamed the other for her suffering. Karen had some sympathy with Sonni as an aging, frustrated woman who was "morbidly seeking for expressions of affection from those nearest to her—insatiably"—but Sonni's discontent made her "an almost intolerable burden to everybody" (260). This complaint occurs in the last diary entry before Sonni's death.

In the first entry after it, Karen feels great remorse for having "failed so badly, so badly," to give Sonni "all the happiness in [her] power." She interprets her current lethargy as a desire to be "dead like Sonni" (263). With husband Oskar's help, she analyzes her "distaste for everything" as a result of feeling guilty because she had unconsciously wished for her mother's death. Now she wants to "atone through an exaggerated grief." In the last entry she wrote about Sonni, Karen describes a dream that she interprets as an expression of her wish to die "together with Sonni. For Sonni was my great childhood love. If the wish for her death was there on the one hand, on the other there was my strong love for her, which cannot let her go, and if she dies it wants to die too" (265–66).

What transformed Sonni from Karen's great childhood love, her one and all, into someone whose very presence seemed to make Karen ill? The diaries do not explain why Karen had originally idealized her mother, but they do indicate what precipitated her disillusionment. In a letter to Oskar she wrote: "The tension between Mother and me is getting unbearable. Though nothing, nothing at all special has come up, she treats me like air. . . . And the injustice makes me so *angry* that I wish she were dead or far away. . . . And the reason? 'Alienation,' we are told. But she lost my confidence and friendship 3 years ago—so why suddenly now?" (224). Karen was twenty-one when she wrote the above letter; therefore the precipitating events must have occurred when she was eighteen. At that time she was in the early stages of her relationship with Rolf, her first great love, who received a "frosty" reception from Sonni and Berndt because he was Jewish: "The boy was as good as outlawed by our family. And as I was on his side, this . . . placed me in sharp opposition to the others, so that I drew closer and closer to Rolf" (124). Her family's bigotry toward Rolf made her angry and ashamed, and in order to continue seeing him, she started living a secret life that required constant lying to her mother.

Although Karen claimed three years later that nothing at all special had occurred to cause her anger, this is not true. She had received a letter from Rolf about a month earlier, and both Sonni's opposition and Karen's bitterness were reactivated. She found her mother's behavior "contemptible and unworthy" and had to think steadily about Oskar and Rolf "not to drown in my own anger": "It's a long time since I've been so truly furious" (224).

Karen's rage at Sonni seems to have been largely repressed for most of the period between her mother's initial rejection of Rolf and her reaction to his letter three years later. She made no negative entries about her mother during her relationship with Rolf, and when Sonni moved to Freiburg in 1906 and took in Karen's friends Losch (Louis Grote) and Idchen (Ida Behrmann) as boarders, Karen wrote of her most affectionately.

The resentment that emerged after the arrival of Rolf's letter must have been present all along beneath the surface. There is evidence of it in a letter written to Oskar about two weeks before Karen heard from Rolf. In an earlier letter she had been critical of her "entire entourage" as "thoroughly amoral" (207); in reply to Oskar's observation that she deserved "another entourage," Karen gave examples of her mother's hypocrisy and lack of moral idealism. Her most serious complaint was that Sonni "silently overlooks my brother's meannesses, while at an unfriendly word from me she loses her temper. Incidentally: I am *really not* of a lovable nature" (216).

The sense of injustice that made Karen "so *angry*" had been generated in part by her feeling that Sonni had treated her unfairly in relation to Berndt. That Karen is not of a lovable nature was Sonni's view of her, which she seems to have accepted. We know this from Karen's letter of 1 July 1907, in which she describes how she thinks that Sonni perceives her: "On the whole good at the core, but extravagant ideas and rather cold-hearted, lack of self-control, not likable, exaggerated feeling of independence" (227). If we imagine the consequences of feeling unfairly treated in relation to one's brother and being regarded as unlikable by one's mother, we can begin to understand the deeper sources of Karen's anger.

The change in Karen's feelings toward her brother followed a similar pattern to that in her feelings toward her mother. The few mentions of Berndt before Rolf's appearance were all positive. Berndt really was "a fine fellow," when he helped her with a theological issue (23). He supported her academic and theatrical ambitions, and when he entered military service, Karen described him as "our dear boy," whom she missed "very much" (39). But Karen was disgusted by Berndt's prejudice in opposing her relationship with Rolf, and she began to compare him unfavorably with her high-minded mentor. Berndt was a "cool skeptic and cynic" (169), whereas Rolf was an idealist with a "rigorous morality." Karen felt that Berndt's "utilitarian morality" (125) was "beginning to infect" her before Rolf provided an "effective counter-balance" (98).

Karen's anger with Berndt was not expressed in her diary until three years after the event. About a month before she received Rolf's letter, she confessed to "an act of vengeance" against her brother. Berndt had wanted her to write to his girlfriend "so that she should feel free to make a trip with him at Whitsun"; but, even though she had no moral objection, Karen refused his request because at the time of her friend-ship with Rolf, Berndt had maliciously "gummed up a meeting with him" (207).

Karen's anger toward Berndt, like her anger toward Sonni, has deeper sources than Rolf: "He has always behaved unfairly toward me. . . . And now the whole old grudge awoke that had slowly but surely been storing itself up, and—yes—I took a grim pleasure in his hellish anger at my attitude" (207). The *Adolescent Diaries* pro-vide no information about the unfair treatment of which Karen complains, other than in the matter of Rolf, but later writings will shed light upon this. Whatever the cause, there was a powerful, long-standing "grudge," largely repressed, the emergence of which is triggered by Berndt's request. As was the case in relation to Sonni, Karen feels that in the past she had been taken in—Berndt had "always behaved unfairly," and she had been "stupid enough" to cooperate (207)—but that now she sees the truth. And as is also the case with Sonni, the *Adolescent Diaries* shed more light upon what precipitates Karen's disillusionment than upon what led her to idealize Berndt in the first place.

Chapter 3

Karen and Clare

In spite of the generally held impression that as a psychoanalyst Horney neglected the importance of childhood, she wrote about it often, insisting that its effect on psy-chological development could not be overestimated. Her discussions of childhood frequently seem autobiographical, especially in the light of her diaries, and reflect a continuing preoccupation with her own formative experiences.

Take, for example, her description of the typical history of the self-effacing per-son in *Neurosis and Human Growth* (1950), written when she was over sixty: "The

self-effacing type . . . grew up *under the shadow* of somebody: of a preferred sibling, of a parent who was generally adored (by outsiders), of a beautiful mother or of
a benevolently despotic father. It was a precarious situation, liable to arouse fears.
But affection of a kind was attainable—at a price: that of a self-subordinating devotion. There may have been, for instance, a long-suffering mother who made the child
feel guilty at any failure to give her exclusive care and attention. Perhaps there was
a mother or father who could be friendly or generous when blindly admired, or a
dominating sibling whose fondness and protection could be gained by pleasing and
appeasing" (221–22). Many of the details in this passage parallel Horney's own situation. She grew up under the shadows of a preferred sibling and a beautiful mother,
who was adored by outsiders and demanded blind admiration. She could gain their
affection only by pleasing and appeasing. Her father was despotic, and her long-suffering mother required a great deal of care and attention.

On 2 April 1912, Karen wrote: "I still can't recover from my oppression as a
child" (UD), and in her later writings, she painted many dark pictures of childhood
that have an autobiographical flavor. In "The Distrust between the Sexes" (1931),
for example, she proclaimed that "the paradise of childhood is most often an illusion with which adults like to deceive themselves." For children "this paradise is
inhabited by too many dangerous monsters," such as "unpleasant experiences with
the opposite sex," difficulty in expressing their desires, dismissal of their feelings by
adults, or having to take second place to a parent or sibling (110). In *New Ways in
Psychoanalysis* (1939), she observed that the child who develops "basic anxiety"
feels the environment to be "unreliable, mendacious, unappreciative, unfair, unjust,
begrudging and merciless." It is "a menace to his entire development and to his most
legitimate wishes and strivings. He feels in danger of his individuality being obliterated, his freedom taken away, his happiness prevented." His "self-esteem and self-
reliance are undermined" and "fear is instilled by intimidation and isolation" (75).

From what we know of Karen's childhood, it is difficult to see where such
intense feelings of injustice, oppression, and humiliation originated. We can make
sense of these feelings, however, if we reinterpret the diaries in light of the story of
her patient "Clare." Versions of Clare's history appear most fully in *Self-Analysis*
(1942), but they are also present in *The Neurotic Personality of Our Time* (1937),
New Ways in Psychoanalysis (1939), and "The Overvaluation of Love" (1934). Clare
is named only in *Self-Analysis,* but the similarities between her and the patients
described in these other works are too striking to be coincidental, and I shall draw on
all the accounts in my discussion of her.

According to Horney's account in *Self-Analysis*, Clare was a patient with whom
she worked on and off for four-and-a-half years. During a period when she was not

in analysis, Clare successfully worked through her morbid dependency on Peter, her lover, and freed herself from the compulsive reliance on idealized figures that had long driven her. She employed techniques of self-analysis—especially free association, which she recorded through the use of key words and phrases—that are described in the book. According to *Self-Analysis*, Clare has made her records available to Horney and granted permission for her story to be published.

It seems highly unlikely that Horney could have understood notes that consist "mostly of catchwords" (*SA*, 192) well enough to have told another person's story with such precision and detail. According to Harold Kelman, Horney was "in the throes of self-analysis" (1971, 23) between *New Ways* and *Self-Analysis*, and it seems much more credible that she was describing her own self-exploration and drawing on her own notes.

There are a number of striking parallels between Clare's family situation and Karen's. Like Karen, Clare has a beautiful mother who is "the dominating spirit in the family," a brother who is four years older than she, and a distant father who is "openly despised by the mother." The mother's "undisguised hatred and contempt" for the father make Clare feel that it is "much safer to be on the powerful side." The father is "absent most of the time" because he is "a country doctor" (*SA*, 49), a detail that seems to be a rather unskillful attempt at fictionalizing. A country doctor would not be absent most of the time, though a sea captain would.

Clare was an unwanted child who was the product of an unhappy marriage: "After having one child, a boy, the mother did not want any more children. Clare was born after several unsuccessful attempts at an abortion" (*SA*, 48). We have no way of ascertaining whether Sonni attempted to abort Karen, but given her unhappiness in her marriage she may well have been dismayed at the thought of having another child. Karen seems to have believed that she was an undesired addition to the family. In her unpublished introduction to her mother's diaries, Renate refers to Karen as Sonni's "unwanted child."[2] The feeling of being unwanted is a recurring motif in Horney's accounts of pathogenic childhoods: "A child can stand a great deal of what is often regarded as traumatic . . . as long as inwardly he feels wanted and loved" (*NP*, 80).

Clare's brother is four years older than she, which is also the age difference between Karen and Berndt. Like Karen, Clare felt that her brother received preferential treatment. References to the preferential treatment of siblings, usually brothers, are sprinkled throughout Horney's writings, often as part of a litany of pathogenic factors (see *NHG*, 18). In "Inhibited Femininity" (1926–27) Horney explains that "gross favoritism of a brother" can "contribute a great deal toward establishing strong masculinity wishes in the little girl" (78). She makes the same point in "Psychogenic Factors in Functional Female Disorders" (1933b, 168) and "Maternal Conflicts" (1933c, 179). In *New Ways,* Horney complains that one of the cultural factors to which Freud does not give sufficient importance is that "a brother in the family is preferred to the sister" (170; see also 178, 218). I am not suggesting that all Horney's references to brothers are autobiographical, but she mentions the brother-sister relationship far more frequently than her psychoanalytic contemporaries do.

Although Clare felt that her mother was partial to her brother, the girl "was not badly treated or neglected in any coarse sense: she was sent to schools as good as those the brother attended, she received as many gifts as he did, she had music lessons with the same teacher, and in all material ways was treated as well." Karen also went to a good school, and both Karen and Berndt had piano lessons. It was in "less tangible matters" that Clare "received less than the brother, less tenderness, less interest in school marks and in the thousand little daily experiences of a child, less concern when she was ill, less solicitude to have her around, less willingness to treat her as a confidante, less admiration for looks and accomplishments" (*SA,* 48–49).

Clare is particularly bitter about not being treated as her mother's confidante: "There was a strong, though for a child intangible, community between the mother and brother from which she was excluded" (48). The version of the Clare story in *Neurotic Personality* also dwells on this sense of exclusion: "The mother discussed all her troubles with the brother," and "the girl felt completely left out" (165). In *Self-Analysis* Clare reports that in the eyes of her mother and brother she was "only a nuisance" (243).

The young Clare had had a "fighting spirit": during analysis early memories emerge of "opposition, rebellion, belligerent demands, all sorts of mischief." Her aggressiveness had subsided when she lost her "fight for a place in the sun," but after "a series of unhappy experiences, this spirit reemerged . . . in the form of a fierce ambition at school" (84–85). In *Neurotic Personality* Horney introduces the Clare story to illustrate how "the neurotic striving for power . . . is born out of anxiety, hatred and feelings of inferiority," as well as how "such a striving can develop, in the form of ambition, when the need for affection is thwarted." It is her brother from whom the girl needs affection and by whom she is rejected: "A girl was strongly attached to her brother who was four years older than she. They had indulged in tenderness of a more or less sexual character, but when the girl was eight years old her brother suddenly rejected her, pointing out that they were now too old for that sort of play. Soon after this experience the girl developed a sudden fierce ambition at school" (164). Kelman reports that "moving apart had always been deeply painful to Horney, beginning with what she experienced as her brother's rejection" (1971, 31).

It is impossible to know whether "tenderness of a more or less sexual character" had also been part of Karen's relationship with Berndt. There are a number of references to the effects of early sexual stimulation in Horney's writings during her Freudian phase, but these may reflect her theoretical orientation and the kinds of details she elicited from her patients rather than her personal experience. There is one passage in Karen's diaries that seems to indicate an almost complete ignorance of sexual matters until the age of seventeen, when she describes biting into "the apple of knowledge" and finding it "very sour" and difficult to "digest" (*AD,* 60). In another passage, written soon after her sexual awakening, she writes that although in her imagination "there is no spot on me that has not been kissed by a burning mouth," in reality, "not even the tips of my fingers have been kissed": "There is nothing in the world more immaculate than I" (64).

In "The Overvaluation of Love" Horney describes seven women patients who have problems in relating to men and to work that are similar to hers and Clare's. One of these subjects sounds like Clare and may have been Karen herself. All of the women "had come off second best in competition for a man (father or brother)" as children. In one case "the still young and unusually beautiful mother was the absolute center of attention on the part of the father as well as of the sons and the various men who frequented the house." A "complicating factor" in the girl's psychological development was that from her fifth to her ninth year she "had had a sexually intimate relationship with a brother some years her senior, although the latter was the mother's favorite and had continued to be more closely tied to her than to his sister. On account of his mother, moreover, he suddenly broke off the relationship with his sister, at least as regards its sexual character, at the time of puberty" (193–94).

If there had been some sort of sexual relationship between Karen and Berndt, she may have been repressing the memory of her earlier experience in describing herself as immaculate. Horney introduces the concept of repression in "The Overvaluation of Love." Some of the women there recall "experiencing in early childhood sexual excitation similar to orgasm." This excitation "was terrifying either because of the specific conditions under which it was experienced or simply on account of its overwhelming strength relative to the subject's immaturity, so that it was repressed" (204).

Sexual contact between Karen and Berndt—perhaps in the form of manual stimulation—would have figured as one of those "dangerous monsters" that inhabit the seeming paradise of childhood. The Clare figure in *Neurotic Personality* "felt definitely stigmatized by the experience with her brother" (165–66), and the women discussed in "The Overvaluation of Love" are harmed by their "exaggerated early experience of sexual excitation" (195), which generates problems ranging from "frigidity" to female Don Juanism.

Regardless of whether there was a sexual component to her relationship with Berndt—and I think there probably was—it seems likely that Karen experienced what she felt to be a rejection by her brother and that this had a traumatic effect. This is supported by the Clare story, by Harold Kelman's independent report, and by references in Horney's writings to girls being disappointed in childhood in their relationship with a beloved male. In "Psychogenic Factors in Functional Female Disorders," Horney notes that in the history of women with such disorders, "There may be deeply engraved disappointments in their early love life: a father or brother to whom they felt tenderly attached and who disappointed them" (1933b, 167–68; see also 1933c, 179).

In *Self-Analysis,* we are told that Clare's academic ambition emerges after a series of unhappy experiences, and if we draw upon the version of the story in *Neurotic Personality,* we can determine what these experiences were. After feeling rejected by her brother, the girl makes "one more attempt to get the affection she need[s]" by falling in love with a boy whom she meets on a trip. She begins "spinning glorious fantasies about this boy," but when he drops out of sight, she reacts to "the new disappointment" by becoming depressed. The family physician ascribes her condition to her being in too advanced a class at school, so her parents take her out of school, send her away to a summer resort for recreation, and then put her in a class a year below the one she had been in before. It is at this point, at the age of nine, that the girl shows "an ambition of a rather desperate character. She [cannot] endure being any but first in her class" (*NP,* 165).

There is no conclusive evidence that these events occurred in Karen's life, although she did feel rejected by her brother, she was very ambitious in school, and being first in her class was extremely important to her. But was she taken out of school, sent to a summer resort, and then put into a lower class? It may be that this is a fictionalized version of real events.

We can find evidence in the diaries of a concern for Karen's health. In the very first entry, written at the age of thirteen, she reports that she has been "excused from technical subjects at [her] doctor's wish" (*AD,* 3). At fifteen, after three weeks at the gymnasium, her "objective is still medicine—if my powers hold out (pecuniary, mental, and physical)" (41). Six weeks later she complains of being able to work hard for only one or two days a week and of constantly feeling that she is about to collapse. She speculates on the possible psychological causes of her state but reaches no conclusion, "for I have not overworked myself *as yet*" (43). These passages suggest that Karen both recognized that her weakness may have had emotional sources and thought of herself as a fragile person to whom hard work posed a threat.

The most pertinent document available is a letter Karen sent to Oskar five years later, when she was in medical school. "Just think," she wrote, "I had gone through a metamorphosis in the last 6 days, I had become an old professor with spectacles, a bald pate, and wrinkles, and studied from early morning to late evening and had no thought for anything but my work" (179). This was an unusual state of affairs, for Karen seems to have gone through medical school without consistent application. She was enjoying her work, but "Sonni naturally saw the matter with concern—and I was at once transported hither [to the Black Forest for a holiday]. For Sonni operates with the word 'healthy' a great deal. . . . 'Only nothing too much!'—a little friendship, a little work, a little of idling, etc." (180). It is significant that Sonni became alarmed about Karen's health when she applied herself to her schoolwork and that Karen found this reaction natural, if somewhat irritating. Karen's letter confirms my sense that for a number of years her family had been worried about her overworking and that Karen at once acquiesced in, shared, and rebelled against this anxiety. This picture (if correct) is compatible with the history of the Clare figure in *Neurotic Personality,* whose family attributed her depression to academic stress and took her out of school.

Also compatible with that history is a story Horney told a *New York Post* reporter of traveling to South America with her father when she was nine years old (12 December 1945, Daily Magazine section, 41). She related versions of this story to her daughters as well and also to Harold Kelman, who dates the trip instead to her middle teens (1971, 1). Jack Rubins reports several trips with her father (1978, 12), as does Renate in her unpublished introduction to the diaries. Susan Quinn, however, doubts that Horney ever made such a journey: "There is no mention of such a trip in her diaries, even though it would have lasted six months and caused a major interruption in her schooling" (1987, 36).

Quinn's objection is precisely what makes the trip seem probable to me, since such an interruption occurs in the life of the Clare figure at about the same age. In my view, the detail of the summer resort in the story of the Clare figure may have been Horney's way of fictionalizing the trip so as to make it less transparently autobiographical. There is no reason for Karen to have mentioned the trip in her diary, since she did not begin keeping it until four years later. If she did not make the trip, moreover, we must account for her saying that she did. Quinn's explanation is that "for all of her anger at [her father], there was a part of her that wished to be close to him and to see the wide world he knew" (1987, 37). Perhaps, but I am not sure that this accounts for Horney's repetition of the story as an adult, both to family and friends and to a reporter—unless she had developed not simply childhood fantasies, as Quinn suggests, but a fixed delusion.

The father in the Clare story that is reported in *Neurotic Personality* and *Self-Analysis* occupies much the same position that Wackels did in the Danielsen household. He is absent most of the time and is "indifferent to his children" when at home (*NP*, 164). He is regarded as a "bumpkin" by the mother, who gets the children to take her side. The daughter, preoccupied with mother and brother, gives little thought to her father. In the version of the Clare story found in *New Ways*, however, the father is an intimidating figure. The girl develops "an attitude of compulsory unobtrusiveness," in part because there were "several frightening instances" that "made her afraid of being actually killed if she did not behave" (143–44). Karen may have felt a similar fear of her Bible-throwing father with the steely blue eyes. For the most part, however, Clare's father is presented as a disappointing figure who is unresponsive to his daughter's "pathetic attempts to get close to him" (*SA*, 49).

In "The Distrust between the Sexes," Horney concluded her account of the dangerous monsters of childhood by observing that "children will undergo painful and humiliating experiences of being rebuffed, being betrayed, and being told lies" (1931a, 110). If the account of Clare's childhood is autobiographical, it suggests that Karen felt rebuffed by her father and lied to and betrayed by her brother, who awoke illusions that were shattered when he distanced himself from her. Her beautiful mother dominated the situation erotically, making her feel that she would never be able to attract a male.

As she is in Karen's diaries, the mother is the central figure in the Clare story, and the history of their relationship is presented in some detail. Because Clare felt unwanted, discriminated against, and excluded from the community between mother and brother, "she became discontented and cross and complaining." Since it did not occur to members of her family that Clare was being treated unfairly, they blamed her "ugly disposition" and teased her "for always feeling herself a martyr." At first Clare "had a native assurance that she was as good as the others," but she could not bear her exclusion and gave up her fight for justice. Yielding to "the majority opinion about herself," she began to feel that everything was her fault. She shifted from "essentially true and warranted accusations of others to essentially untrue and unwarranted self-accusations" (*SA*, 49–50). The complaining, discontented child became excessively considerate and self-sacrificing.

Instead of feeling resentment, Clare took all blame on herself and joined the group of those who admired the mother. She had a strong incentive to do this, for if she, too, praised the mother she "could hope to receive some affection, or at least to be accepted." Although she did not receive the affection for which she hungered, her "mother, like all those who thrive on the admiration of others, was generous in giving admiration in turn to those who adored her" (*SA*, 49–50). Contributing to her mother's change of attitude was Clare's fierce ambition at school, which was now "loaded with repressed hostility" (85). By thus displacing her aggression, Clare defused her mother's resentment and gained her support. She was "no longer the disregarded ugly duckling, but became the wonderful daughter of a wonderful mother" (50).

"By admiring what in reality she resented," Clare "became alienated from her own feelings. She no longer knew what she herself liked or wished or feared or resented" (51). This was Karen's state, I believe, when she was writing her diaries. The diaries begin after Karen has repressed her hostility toward mother and brother and has become one of mother's admirers. She idolizes her mother, hovers about her with tenderness, care, and anxiety, and empathizes with her suffering. She confirms, in effect, Sonni's view of herself as the ideal, self-sacrificing mother and long-suffering, victimized wife. In return, Karen is taken into the mother-brother community and receives admiration and support.

Karen's repressed hostility finds an outlet in her academic ambition, which involves not merely being first in her class but also pursuing the grandiose dream (for her time and place) of becoming a physician. Her lofty goals and achievements make her a wonderful daughter, and Sonni's support of her ambitions makes her a wonderful mother. Karen has been forced to repress her resentment toward mother and brother, but it is allowable, even virtuous, to feel anger and contempt toward her father, and so she displaces much of her bitterness onto him. This generates inner conflict because such feelings violate the commandment to honor her parents, but they are encouraged by Sonni. Indeed, Karen's condemnation of her father is an act of loyalty toward her mother and makes her feel part of the dominant alliance. Horney will later cite as a pathogenic factor in childhood "marital conflicts between the parents, which forced the daughter to side with one or the other parent" (1935b, 240).

Earlier I observed that we could not understand from the diaries alone what led Karen to idealize her mother and brother. We now see that she needed to admire them in order to gain their acceptance. Drawing upon the Clare story, we can also understand Karen's grudge against Berndt. It arose from being left out of the mother-brother community, from being rejected by the brother after they had developed an affectionate relationship, and perhaps from being sexually exploited by him. It is no wonder that she took a grim pleasure in having finally hurt him back.

The awakening of Karen's grudge against her brother seems also to have revived negative feelings toward her mother. As Karen became critical of her mother, Sonni became critical of her, and the alliance based on Karen's being the wonderful daughter of a wonderful mother began to fall apart. The message that she was not of a lovable nature must have revived bitter memories of having been made to feel unlovable throughout her childhood. Karen's position in the household was now similar to what it had been before she joined the circle of her mother's admirers. She felt that everyone was against her.

When the letter from Rolf arrived in June 1907, Karen's resentment toward Berndt and Sonni had already risen to the surface, and she was in a volatile state. What made her so angry was not simply Sonni's opposition to Rolf but the revival of childhood resentments. She felt that Sonni treated her "like air"—that is, like someone with no weight or significance. Karen responded as she must have done in childhood, by feeling that her life was miserable and wishing that Sonni were dead. Sonni reverted to her earlier treatment of Karen by turning around "every word" Karen said and "falsely interpret[ing]" everything she did (AD, 224). Karen found Sonni's behavior "contemptible and unworthy" and became afraid of drowning in her own anger. These powerful emotions are difficult to understand solely on the basis of the diaries, but if we supplement the information there with the Clare story, we can see them as the return of feelings she had repressed.

Clare's life is similar to Karen's in other ways as well. When Clare goes to college at the age of twenty, she is at first overwhelmed by loneliness, writes "desperate letters to her mother," and feels "like a feather blown around in the universe" until she is saved from her homesickness by finding male companionship (81). Karen went to Freiburg at the age of twenty and had a desolate first semester until she met Oskar and Losch: "never will I forget those first days here, days full of desperate loneliness, of the disconsolate feeling of being forsaken" (AD, 147). Clare marries at the age of twenty-three, as did Karen, but her husband dies after three years. That is a longer period of time than Karen and Oskar had a satisfactory marriage.

One of the most arresting parallels between Karen and Clare—the one that first convinced me that the Clare story was autobiographical—is Clare's difficulty freeing herself from her lover, Peter, because she has a long-standing fantasy of "a great and masterful man whose willing slave she [is] and who in turn [gives] her everything she want[s], from an abundance of material things to an abundance of mental stimulation, and [makes] her a famous writer" (SA, 82). She has "a strong interest" in not recognizing Peter's deficiencies because she does not want anything to "prevent her from seeing in Peter the realization of the great man of her daydream" (219). Horney describes this dream as "a kind of Pygmalion fantasy, created from the point of view of the girl to be developed." The great man makes advances to Clare because beneath her "inconspicuous exterior" he senses "her great potentialities." He devotes all his

time and energy to her development, making "a beautiful swan out of an ugly duckling." Under his guidance, Clare works hard "not only at becoming a great writer but
also at cultivating mind and body." She needs to be "devoted to her master exclusively" (203).

Karen too felt like an ugly duckling, and there is considerable evidence that the
dream of a great and masterful man to whom she would be a willing slave was a frequent fantasy of hers. The search for such a man and her subsequent disappointment
were recurring motifs in her life. The great-man fantasy was first recorded in her
diary on 26 February 1904, when she copied a passage she had found in a book:
"Always, you dearest, keep on impressing me—let me grow small alongside you—
oh, be the strong man, the big man, the healthy man, the superior human being in
whom I can lose myself completely, before whom I gladly and willingly kneel. Force
me to my knees, dearest. For I am a woman. No good, shy little girl of the humble
womanliness described in books—no, on the contrary. But just for this proud, free,
independently thinking woman there is no sweeter lot than to be allowed to worship,
to bow down in love. Oh, dearest—will you be my master?" (AD, 73). Almost two
years later she had an intense reaction to a passage in a book by Renate Fuchs about
"woman, searching for the one, the only one, to whom she belongs": "It has set all
the strings in me vibrating. The searching—the erring but still searching—searching ceaselessly" (116).

By this time Karen had had relationships with both Rolf and Ernst and had
found the men wanting. In her diary she describes Ernst as "not the man to whom I
belong," and although she longs for Rolf, she knows that "neither is he the one who
must come." She is "tired," wishing that "everything would stop," and, much like
Clare, she feels her life to be "frightfully purposeless and without content" because
she does not have the "One person!" for whom she hungers (116–17).

Karen did not consider her next lover, Losch, to be the one, either, but during the
year she was living with him and corresponding with their friend Oskar, she idealized
Oskar and perceived him as capable of being her savior. This feeling did not long
survive their marriage in 1909. Little more than two years later—and less than a
year after the birth of Brigitte, their first child—Karen was having an affaire with
Walther Honroth, the husband of her best friend, Lisa. As this relationship deteriorated, she had to "make do with remembering that my dream of a noble man's love
came true once. Walther isn't a person, after all, who will help me on. I will find a better one yet. But I have never been able to wait" (UD, 2 April 1912). Her attitude is
strikingly similar to that of Clare, who fears that she will "immediately try to replace
the lost pillar with a new one" (SA, 228, 231).

In addition to having a compulsive need to merge with a great man, both Karen and Clare complain of having remarkably little self-confidence and are "easily over-come by a paralyzing fatigue" that interferes with their work and their social life (*SA*, 76). Both feel lost when they are alone (81) and are insecure about their phys-ical attractiveness and intellectual ability. Clare wants to write plays and stories but feels inhibited about trying to do so because of "her probable lack of talent" (76), while Karen feels "frightfully stupid" despite having received the highest marks in school (*AD*, 47). Both impress others as "haughty" while inwardly feeling "quite timid" (*SA*, 83).

Both Karen and Clare have suicidal tendencies. When Peter tells Clare that it would be better for them to separate, the idea of suicide keeps recurring to her; she "had indulged in suicidal notions at previous times" (*SA*, 227, 231). In the published portion of the diaries, Karen longs for extinction on more than one occasion, and in an unpublished entry she reports being suicidal over the separation from Walther: "I went in Oskar's open car, recovering from influenza, in thin clothes and cold weather, hoping that I should catch a severe pneumonia" (7 April 1912).

Although Clare is the editor of a magazine, her inability to do "productive work" could easily be a fictionalized version of Karen's, especially during her early years as a psychoanalyst. In her diary for 4 January 1911, Karen wrote: "I really have almost never worked productively, and I am afraid of it, too. This fear comes from mistrust of my own capacity" (*AD*, 250). By productive work she meant doing some-thing creative, making a distinctive contribution. In spite of Clare's self-doubts and inhibitions, notes Horney, "it was attainable for her, as her later life showed, to be liked by many people, to look attractive, to write something that was valuable and original" (*SA*, 78). The pattern ascribed to Clare fits Karen's career very well. Horney achieved much, but she began late. She published her first important essay ("On the Genesis of the Castration Complex in Women") at the age of thirty-eight, and all her books were written during the last fifteen years of her life. For much of her early adult life she probably experienced frustration similar to Clare's. She had a satisfac-tory career as an analyst despite her inner difficulties but wanted to do something original and felt that she could not.

Thus, many of Clare's presenting symptoms were the same as Karen's were when she entered analysis with Karl Abraham, Clare's professional frustrations resembled those of the early years of Karen's career, and Clare's morbid dependency upon Peter reflected a long-standing problem of Karen's. These parallels between Clare and Karen—especially with respect to the inner life—lead me to believe the Clare story to be autobiographical. It tells us things about the young Karen that we can learn nowhere else and gives us a different picture of Karen's family history than can be derived from the diaries alone.

Chapter 4

School and "Times of Transition"

School provided a refuge for Karen from the unhappiness of her home. She wrote that even though she often left for school "with tears in [her] eyes," she always came back cheerful. In her first two diaries, expressions of enthusiasm for school are frequent, and they are still present after she became preoccupied with her love life. Karen's passion for school derived in part from her ambition, in part from her love of learning, and in part from crushes on her teachers.

Karen was so ambitious because she needed to compensate for feelings of rejection by her family, and she "struggled to make up in wits what she felt she lacked in beauty."[3] By the time she began keeping a diary, she had entered into her mother's dream of glory through academic achievement. She had a need to feel herself an exceptional person with a special destiny. In an entry entitled "Unsteady," dated 1903, she spoke of often feeling that she was sinking into a "bottomless abyss" and wondered whether every young person had "to take such a plunge": "Oh, dear Karen, delusions of grandeur again? You any more than the average? Strange, that it is so infinitely difficult for me to convince myself that I am something ordinary, an average person, one of the herd. O *Vanitas*!!" (*AD*, 65). Later, when she was in analysis with Abraham, she related her chronic fatigue to a need to be "above average": "The reproach I was always most anxious to avoid in any field was to be judged ordinary, average" (250–51).

Karen had doubts about her intellectual ability that made her need for academic success a source of painful anxiety. She suffered whenever she had to take an important examination, and she was in panic at the beginning of her last term at the gymnasium, for it ended with the *Abitur,* which would qualify her for the university. Her anxiety made her "desperately dull-witted" (116), and she had recurring spells of lassitude, paralysis, and loss of concentration. Her difficulties sometimes made school an ordeal, but she was gifted enough to do well and was almost always enthusiastic about her studies.

Karen's enthusiasm for school was inspired in part by her attachment to her teachers. This was especially true in convent school, before she became involved with young men. Just as she idealized Sonni and Berndt, she glorified her teachers, especially a Herr Schulze, who became a major figure in her life from the time she began her diary until she went to the gymnasium two years later. He was her "adored," her "idolized teacher" (18); when she visited him in Reinbeck it was "lovely," "heavenly," "just like Paradise" (11). There was clearly a sexual component to her attraction: "Oh, that feeling, as he stepped into the room! What bliss to look into his beautiful eyes. I believe I won't forget that moment very easily" (5).

If Herr Schulze was a substitute for a romantic interest of her own age, he was also a substitute for the father she was unable to "love and esteem" (21) and a much-needed source of authority and support. As her religion teacher, he answered her questions from a liberal point of view and served to counteract the negative feelings aroused by her father's dogmatism. Because he was the person to whom she looked for guidance, the thought of leaving him when she went to the gymnasium was "dreadful": "He is my inner God. I am afraid that when I no longer have him as a teacher, I may go astray" (29, 33). Herr Schulze reinforced Karen's self-confidence by reciprocating her admiration and confirming her sense of being special. When she thanked him for everything he had given her, he replied: "It gave me much pleasure to work with you, and I learned a lot in the process" (38–39). Such praise must have been intoxicating, coming from her idol. Given her insecurity, Herr Schulze's support was invaluable.

Karen was very fond of women teachers as well. There was Fräulein Banning (for French), who was "angelic, charming, interesting, clever, lovable," and Fräulein Emmerlich (for English), who was "clever, interesting, obliging . . . the nicest classroom teacher one could imagine" (20). Karen developed a full-fledged "crush" on Fräulein Banning: "I think I shall die of enthusiasm. Frl. Banning has been added to Herr Schulze. But she really is charming" (28).

Perhaps because of a need to test her special status, Karen precipitated conflicts with both Herr Schulze and Fräulein Banning, from which she suffered great anxiety. When she voiced skepticism about the reliability of Paul's vision of the risen Christ, Herr Schulze delivered a "severe sermon." Karen was deeply shaken: "If I were not still totally dumbfounded, I should long ago have despaired, for the . . . feeling that he is angry with me is terrible" (25–26). After failing to persuade Fräulein Banning to change the topic of an in-class assignment, Karen manifested her pique by making no effort to write the composition. She felt "deeply hurt" when she was accused of being "obstinate" and found herself "getting quite desperate" when Fräulein Banning was "cool" toward her the entire following week (29–30). Like Herr Schulze, Fräulein Banning treated Karen with a special interest and affection that she could not bear to forfeit.

Karen's crushes on her teachers are noteworthy because, as Jack Rubins has pointed out, "however much we might be inclined to dismiss these sentiments as only teen-age puppy love . . . the attitudes involved—intense adulatory affection, idealization, fear of invoking rejective anger—seemed to presage similar attitudes later on toward . . . men" (1978, 16). And, of course, she displayed the same attitudes toward her mother.

Karen was at times uncomfortable about her propensity toward adulation. Of Fräulein Banning she wrote, "I'm afraid I have adored her terribly" (*AD,* 34). She had thought that she would "always and always be fond" of Herr Schulze, "even if other crushes command[ed her] emotional energies" (38); but after attending the gymnasium for less than two months, she found him boring and was "ecstatic" about some of her new teachers. This made her feel like "a weakling." She firmly resolved "to go in for no more enthusiasms," but she could not help herself: "Yes, I confess it honestly—I am a stupid *Backfisch* [adolescent girl] with my eternal crushes." In December 1901 she announced, with a good deal of self-mockery, that she had "entered into a state that you [Kitten, her diary] will hardly understand. I haven't a crush on anybody. That would be miraculous?—But it's true. Perhaps it comes from the beneficent influence of mathematics or maybe I'm already so old and sensible? For I am already 16" (46–47).

We hear little about crushes after this. In 1902 there was a Herr Schrumpf, an actor from whom she received declamation lessons and under whose influence she considered abandoning school for the stage, but the next major crush (if that is still the right word) was on a young man named Schorschi who appears in a diary entry entitled "Awakened to Life," from December 1903, when Karen was eighteen.

Between the summer of 1902, when the second diary ends, and the winter of 1903, when the third diary begins, a major change took place in Karen. The first entry in the published version of the third diary is entitled "Times of Transition": "Everything in me is storming and surging and pressing for light that will resolve this confusion" (55). The entry "I Myself" makes clear the nature of Karen's inner "chaos" (57). Now seventeen, she has been attending the gymnasium since the previous March and has been exposed to new people and ideas. "In consequence," she writes, "I have developed with uncanny rapidity from an intellectual and moral point of view" (58). By the winter of 1903, her religious doubts have intensified and her ideas about sexual morality have undergone a revolution.

Harold Kelman asserts that Karen went through an intense religious period in her early teens, and there is a seemingly autobiographical passage in *Neurosis and Human Growth* (1950) where an eleven-year-old girl tries "in her childish way for a kind of mystic surrender in prayer" (20; see also Rubins 1978, 13). Karen's loss of orthodox belief occurred when she was fourteen. In December 1900, she looked back to "the true (devout) Christmas joy" that she used to experience and recalled the "pious enthusiasm" with which she had entered that year. On New Year's Eve she felt "bitter self-reproaches" because of her lack of belief and because she had made fun of "the holiest things." She resolved "to stop mockery, even if I unfortunately don't possess a child's faith any more and no other faith has taken its place" (*AD*, 22).

Karen's contempt for her sermonizing father's hypocrisy and dogmatism was no doubt partly responsible for her mockery of religion, but she developed intellectual doubts as well. On Christmas Day 1900 she wrote, "My religion is in a desperately sad state at the moment. I am stirred by questions and doubts that probably no one can solve for me. Was and is Christ God? Is there resurrection? Is God personal? Is he a God of love?" (18). Confirmation lessons from her father's hated ally, Pastor von Ruckteschell, did not "make it any clearer" for her (18). She thought that St. Paul was in "an overwrought nervous condition" when he had his vision of Christ (25); she looked for naturalistic explanations of miracles, doubted Christ's divinity, and took comfort in statements by Berndt and Herr Schulze that enabled her to view Christ as a symbol of the divine in all people (23, 33). Her confirmation in March 1901 was a painful experience, for she no longer believed the doctrines she was asked to profess and was too full of rage at her father to be able to imitate Christ as an ideal of human love (37–38).

Two years later, at the age of seventeen, Karen had settled into her skepticism but was still uncomfortable with the absence of authoritative answers. At the time of her confirmation, she had longed for "the faith, firm as a rock, that makes oneself *and others* happy" (38), but in the poem she wrote to celebrate times of transition she describes the ability to sustain uncertainty as heroic. "Does one have to believe anything at all? Obsolete!" Still, she was not content with uncertainty: "I have to analyze and explain everything in a nice clean-cut way—'I can't do otherwise'" (66). The effort to analyze and explain everything in a clean-cut way certainly characterized her work as a psychoanalyst.

There is little mention of religion in the rest of the published diaries, but the unpublished portions, especially of the third diary, suggest that Karen became a confirmed unbeliever. A voracious reader, she began in the winter of 1903 to make notes on books and to transcribe favorite poems into her diary. There are fifty pages of such notes and transcriptions preceding the "Times of Transition" entry with which the published version begins and at least as many more in the remainder of the diary, as well as some in the fourth diary.

Many of Karen's entries are antireligious. A poem entitled "Religious Education" by Rehtz displays a satirical attitude toward revealed religion. As a teacher reads the biblical account of creation, the narrator exclaims, "Away with the old book of myths!" In another poem, one entitled "Books," Rehtz writes that "The Bible itself did not suspect / that it should stand as knowledge forever. / What childlike thinking once invented / they now regard as revelation." In September 1904, Karen read Spinoza's *Tractatus-Theologico-Politicus* and took notes on his arguments against miracles and against the Bible as "supernatural illumination."

The erosion of Karen's religious belief came gradually, but her attitudes toward sexual morality changed rapidly during the winter of 1903. In "I Myself," she locates the beginning of the process in a conversation with a friend named Alice on a Monday in February. In response to Karen's indignation at having been followed by "an impudent gentleman," the amused Alice told her about an encounter she and another friend, L., had had the evening before with a man named B. When Alice said that L. would probably have sex with B. if he asked her, Karen was "dumbfounded": "You mean L. would do the worst thing a girl can do?" (59). Having thought that "such things didn't happen at all in our circles," she was "speechless with horror" when Alice assured her that they happened "in masses": "A girl in our class did it—and even with her father." After a conversation that covered lesbianism, promiscuity, prostitution, incest, and where babies come from, Karen was exhausted: "The whole dreadful knowledge all at once. It was too much" (60). Soon afterward Alice confided to Karen that L. had become B.'s lover and that she saw nothing wrong with the affaire. At this, "little Karen, naturally, burst into excited moral sermons: 'How *can* you, Alice, it really is the worst thing one can do'" (61).

Within a period of months Karen had moved from sermonizing to vacillating over whether it was wrong to give oneself to a man outside of marriage to a conviction that "it is never immoral to give oneself to a man one really loves, if one is prepared to also bear all the consequences." She was not sure how she arrived "at this joyously triumphant certainty," but Shakespeare had helped her: "'For there is nothing either good or bad but thinking makes it so.'" She felt that "every consideration of things human" should be judged on this basis. Marriage was not an absolute but "something only external." It was not a bad institution in theory, but women often married for the wrong reasons: money or the "desire for a home" (61), which resulted in unhappy relationships and unloved children. (Karen was no doubt thinking of her mother, who had married for a home.) Free love was morally superior to a marriage without love. "All our morals and morality are either 'nonsense' or immoral" (62). Karen had developed with uncanny rapidity, indeed, in terms of her intellectual and moral perspectives.

The notes in the unpublished portion of her diary clarify some of Karen's ideas. Probably because of her family history, she was vehement on the topic of marriage without love. She wrote at length about Madame Roland in Guy de Maupassant's *Pierre et Jean*. The wife of a goldsmith, Madame Roland "does not find gratification in her marriage with a narrow-minded and philistine man." This passage could be describing the marriage of Sonni and Wackels. A few years after the birth of her first son, Pierre, Madame Roland "begins a passionate relationship with another man" by whom she has a second son, Jean. She does not consider this love "a lapse on her side." "Why," Karen asks, "does society consider it a sin to give oneself entirely to a man one loves, while it promotes the colossal immorality of a marriage without love?"

Karen's loss of religious belief prepared the way for her moral transformation, which clashed with everything she had been taught. In order to educate herself on sexual matters, she read books about prostitution, Emile Zola's *Nana,* the novels of de Maupassant, and the erotic poems of Marie Madeleine. She was "tortured by pricks of conscience" because of the sensual pleasure she derived from her reading (61), for her ingrained values were in conflict with her liberated attitudes. More than three years later she told Oskar that "perhaps the concept 'morality' unconsciously combines for me with . . . an antithesis to Nature and instinct. Rudiments perhaps of my Christian period" (*AD,* 172–73). She proclaimed conventional morality to be either nonsense or immoral, but she could not be entirely comfortable with the liberation of nature and instinct sanctioned by her new philosophy. Hence her sense of confusion despite her joyously triumphant certainty.

Her confusion is evident in an entry on the poems of Marie Madeleine. At times, she writes, they intoxicate her "through the glowing sensuality and passion they breathe out," but she often turns from such arousal with aversion. She describes these times as her "Philistine hours, or perhaps the hours in which the intellect preponderates. . . . One's senses exult at her poems in unbridled delight. One's intellectual nature turns away in disdain." It is difficult to determine the intellectual basis for such disdain, since Karen rejects conventional morality, with its emphasis upon repression and abstinence. She believes that "a *spiritualized great sensuality* is a sign of a great personality," that "limited people will show themselves to be limited in sensuality too." So sensuality is a mark of distinction, but it must be spiritualized to be a sign of greatness. This clearly represents an attempt to reconcile her definition of morality as a triumph over nature and instinct with her celebration of the erotic. Some "great personalities" combat desire "because they think it is wrong," and they achieve a great victory, "but is the battle against these natural instincts and desires right at all?" Karen invokes the "riotous sensual exuberance" of the Greeks, with their Dionysian festivals and Mysteries, and rejects the asceticism of the "petty bourgeois" (63–64).

Karen was in a highly eroticized state even before she became involved with young men, and she had a vivid idea of the kind of experience she was looking for.

She was drawn to the poems of Marie Madeleine because they dealt with "desire, sensuality, the torments of love" (64). Such themes occurred in many other poems as well. From "Tannhäuser," by Julius Wolff, Karen copied a passage that expresses the fantasy of possession from the male point of view: "To conquer you / is my desire, / swaying and yielding / in hot embraces." In an unattributed poem entitled "Spring of Love," the lovers feel that they are "king and queen" because they have each other and their "blissful lust." In "Evening," by Grete Massé, the girl responds to her lover's "consuming desire," which "lay there like the fear of having to die one day / without knowing love and happiness." She will "gladly bear the torture of hell" for having sinned if this means that she has opened "heaven on earth" for him. The motif of sacrifice for the beloved recurs in Massé's "Girl's Song," in which the girl wishes she were a butterfly that had fallen "shining but exhausted" into her lover's hands and "died in utmost bliss" (UD).

The novels of Clara Viebig also appealed to Karen because they dealt with the heroine's yearning "to surrender herself entirely to the man to whom she is the dearest in the world." She identified especially with Nelda Dallmer in *Rheinlandstöchter:* "The one yearning cry for a great love, this sensual exuberance that often seizes me too and tumbles me about" (*AD,* 72). Like Nelda, Karen yearned for love but was not beautiful. Karen desired Nelda's fate—to find *the man* and to give herself to him without regard for custom. Nelda encounters many frustrations before she and her lover are finally united, but pain was part of Karen's ideal scenario, for it spiritualized sensuality.

Along with the fantasy of finding one great love with whom to experience a spiritualized sensuality, Karen also had fantasies of sexual degradation. She was drawn to the masochistic component of Marie Madeleine, whose "Three Nights" is "a book of fables that tells of those who are 'crucified because they love'" (64). Karen had "a preference for walking in the streets of the prostitutes" (61) and wrote that in her "own imagination" she was "a strumpet." There is "no depravity [she has] not tasted, to the dregs." Unlike her fantasies about a great love, which were accompanied by a sense of righteousness, she regarded these fantasies as "mental sins, which are the worst because . . . they are a sin against holy life!" (64).

Chapter 5

"Awakened to Life":

Schorschi and Rolf

In 1903, when Karen was eighteen, a young man named Ernst Schorschi visited the family for a few days over Christmas, and by the end of his brief visit, Karen felt that she had been borne "into a white temple with high columns" and set down "at the feet of a young spring god" (*AD,* 91). On New Year's Eve, she wrote a poem, "Awakened to Life," in which she celebrated her "exultant happiness"—her "heavenly joy" at having been given "the highest and best we human beings can have—love" (67–68). Her relationship with Schorschi was over by March 1904, but it is significant for what it reveals about her personality and patterns of behavior.

From the time Karen met Schorschi, she idealized him, investing him with the attributes of the hero of her dreams. He was "my love, my Baldur, my joy" (69). In both her perceptions of Schorschi and her own feelings, she was faithful to her previously imagined scenario: "I experienced the supreme happiness of being in love. It came over me like an elemental force, like a storm. There was no reflection . . . upon what I was doing and ought to do, only total giving to an immense emotion" (88). After Schorschi left in December, Karen went through weeks of agonized waiting, first for his letters and then for his return, fueling her imagination with more romantic literature.

When Schorschi arrived for a four-day visit in early March, he was "indifferent" (74), and Karen became depressed. She had a great deal of youthful resilience, however, and her depression was considerably less severe than later ones would be. Although everything seemed colorless now that Schorschi no longer loved her, she was happy to have had the experience, and she felt a continued "thirst for life . . . for love." Her fluctuations continued for several months. After forgetting her woes in the joy of dancing, she was visited again by "the grey ghost, that crushes the nerves of my life with its bony hand" (76). At times she wanted to cry aloud, for she felt that she could no longer endure her depression.

There are two features here that became typical of Karen's relationships: an idealization of the male—who was then expected to transform her life—followed by a depression when her hopes were disappointed. As Schorschi's ardor cooled, Karen's walk grew "heavy and dragging," the "sunny gleam" in her eyes disappeared, and she cried herself to sleep every night (74, 83). Whereas she had recently been seized by "a morbid fear of death," death now lost its terrors (74).

Also typical of Karen's relationships was that her "desperate pain" was followed by an effort to obtain relief through making sense of the affaire: "And I was always brooding: why? how could it happen? Until I understood. Then I grew calmer" (83). The record of Karen's relationship with Schorschi is the first instance we have of such a process, the Clare story the last, although I think all of Horney's writings were part of her effort to gain relief through understanding.

There is a vast difference, of course, between the insight at which Clare arrived and Karen's explanations of what happened with Schorschi, which were more defensive than self-analytic. Karen wanted to regard Schorschi as a superior being as long as she could feed her pride by merging with him, but this view of him became threatening when she felt that he had used her as a "plaything" and then cast her "carelessly aside" (*AD*, 76). Gradually Karen created an image of Schorschi that allowed her to feel better about both him and herself and to retain a positive attitude toward her experience. He was one of those people, she decided, who "does everything instinctively," who "doesn't reflect about himself, not about his actions, still less about the effect his actions may work on others. A big child?" (80). This both made him less culpable and salved her hurt pride, for she could claim that he had not meant to show her disrespect and could not help not being one of the superior people who reflect about themselves. He was no longer a "mean man" against whom Karen wanted to take revenge but a "sunny creature of the moment, only led by his instincts in barbaric health," who had lost sight of her "image among new impressions" (89). He was not a god, although he remained a "creature divinely endowed" whom Karen could thank for having lifted her out of childhood and opened her eyes to "the puzzling labyrinth" of her own being (83).

There is a somewhat similar pattern in the way Clare processes her painful experience with Peter. When Peter rejects her, she sees his faults and recognizes the "unconscious inflation of her feelings" toward him (*SA*, 244). With the deflation of her feelings, she achieves a sense of "serenity": "Instead of wavering between longing for Peter and wanting to take revenge," she can take "a calm stand toward him" and appreciate his good qualities (245). Because it has heightened her self-awareness, she feels that her experience has left her stronger.

We do not know how many times the pattern of idealization, expectation, disappointment, depression, and analysis was repeated in Karen's life, for we have no detailed information—with the exception of that inferred from *Self-Analysis*—about her relationships once she stopped keeping her diaries. I suspect that the pattern occurred frequently. Karen's yearning for love seems to have reasserted itself despite her disappointments, as it did after she decided that Schorschi was just a healthy but cruel child:

> Now the ardent longing for love is in me again:
> Pray with fervor on your knees:
> give us love, Aphrodite. (80)

On a Sunday in April 1904, one month after the break with Schorschi, Karen met Rolf, a young Jewish music student who came to the house in search of a room to rent. (Sonni, as noted above, took in boarders after her separation from Wackels). Her relationship with him developed far more slowly than her explosive romance with Schorschi and was never very physically passionate, but she described it as a decisive event in her life and brooded about it for the next several years. Rolf left Hamburg in early October, which meant that he and Karen were together for only six months, but there were letters and visits to Berlin, and they seemed committed to each other until Karen became involved with a boarder named Ernst in July 1905. Karen told Rolf about Ernst, hoping to maintain both relationships, but Rolf would not tolerate such an arrangement and they became estranged.

Karen's off-and-on relationship with Ernst lasted for about a year, and in the midst of it she began to write a detailed account of her experience with Rolf. She left for the university at Freiburg in late March and was very lonely until she met Losch and Oskar, who later became her lovers, in July. She spent time with Losch at the end of the term, saw Ernst again when she returned home, and began living with Losch and corresponding with Oskar when she returned to Freiburg in the fall. She began writing the third installment of the Rolf story in her diary during January 1907, and in May she reported to Oskar that she had completed it and that it had "come to over 70 closely written quarto pages" (*AD*, 201). In June she experienced "*boundless* joy" when she heard from Rolf again, nearly two years after their break-up (222).

What was it about Karen's relationship with Rolf that made it so important to her, and why did she devote so much time and energy, in the midst of other relationships, to writing about him? There are no simple answers to these questions, but, as we shall see, Karen felt that Rolf was in many respects a soul mate, and she was profoundly uncomfortable about having abandoned him for Ernst. She described her account of their relationship as a confession that needed to hurt her self-love with its honesty for it to have any value (120). Karen had tried to assuage her injured pride by analyzing Schorschi after he rejected her. After she rejected Rolf, she tried to alleviate her guilt by analyzing herself and their relationship.

Karen was confused about her relationship with Rolf. As a human being she was powerfully drawn to him, but as a woman she was not, despite her longing for sexual experience and a great passionate love. She was bewildered by the split in her feelings, which occurred again in her relationship with Oskar. Reviewing the previous year on her birthday in September 1904, she recalled the waverings "between indifference, friendship, and love" in her feelings toward Rolf and concluded that she did in fact love him. He gave her "a feeling of deepest security, of rest": "I have infinite confidence in him. He is true through and through, and I must be true toward him too. I can give myself to him quite openly, just as I am. He is my friend. He confides his cares and plans to me and I my worries to him" (95). This passage gives us a good idea of the nature of the relationship, which was more than friendship but less than romantic love, and of the reason for Karen's guilt when she rejected him.

Karen's initial impression of Rolf was unfavorable. He was "a slim boy," about a year older than she, "with dark brown, curly hair, snow white teeth, and such a pretty face" that she dismissed him as a dandy (120). Rolf rented a room in Reinbeck, and he and Karen found themselves taking the same train to Hamburg, where Rolf had a job and Karen was attending gymnasium. During those trips their friendship slowly ripened. Their initial rapport was emotional, but Karen soon found in Rolf a source of intellectual and moral elevation. Through his companionship and his circle of friends, he offered her an escape from the stultifying atmosphere of her middle-class home. When Rolf was rejected by Sonni and Berndt, Karen and he became coconspirators pursuing a noble but clandestine relationship in defiance of bourgeois society.

"It was sympathy," wrote Karen, "that first compelled me to be fond of Rolf" (95). The "melancholic" Rolf had an "unhappy temperament" that was "tearing him to pieces" (96). Like Karen, he had endured a miserable home life, lacked self-confidence, and was often in low spirits: "He told me about his depressed moods and was glad that I understood him well because I knew the condition myself" (122). Karen became his confidante, "the good companion who wanted only to help and to comfort him" (137): "He often laid his head on my shoulder and lamented about the suffering the encounter with a cold, mendacious world caused him, and about the deep *Weltschmerz* that filled his young soul. And I tried to drive away the black shadows. Often I talked about one thing or another, and often just let him weep in my arms" (150). Rolf was a fellow sufferer, unhappier even than she, for whose well-being she came to feel responsible.

The relationship was by no means one-sided. Karen confided her worries to Rolf and felt free to speak openly with him. This was tremendously important to a young woman who was full of turbulent emotions that she could otherwise express only in her diary. Rolf lifted the burden of hypocrisy from her, and she no longer felt alone. As she tried to help Rolf understand himself, so he encouraged her "search within" (149). The romantic aura of their relationship derived from their desire for each other's happiness: "If that is love, we fulfilled it perfectly in all its glory" (150–51).

Rolf was also a kindred spirit intellectually. He was the first person with whom Karen could discuss her new ideas, and because she considered his thinking to be more advanced than hers, she adopted him as her mentor. Through Rolf and his circle of friends Karen received "tremendous intellectual stimulation" (98), while he fed her pride by regarding her as a "big-thinking" person (122). His description of his friends as "a lot of respectable people who left conventionality aside and only sought the truth" evoked "a powerful echo" (125), for this is precisely how Karen saw herself—free-thinking and unconventional, but respectable.

Through her relationship with Rolf, Karen escaped her emotional and intellectual isolation and gained entrée into "a life of a higher sort" (175). She was deeply impressed by Rolf's "rigorous morality" (125). He represented "a new and more noble view of the world" in which "you must always do what you think is right, disregarding the outward disadvantages." Whereas Karen kept her ideas to herself and acted on her beliefs surreptitiously, Rolf and his friends were in open rebellion against convention and orthodoxy. Karen sought to remain on good terms with her family, but Rolf refused to accept presents from his mother, to whose "superficiality and falseness" he objected. This seemed "quite odd" to Karen but was also impressive. Rolf was her teacher, her "better self": "his idealism . . . awakened everything that is good in me" (98).

Rolf's idealism made him superior in Karen's eyes to the hypocritical Sonni and to Berndt, who was engaged in the calculated pursuit of selfish objectives. In Karen's surroundings, "higher things were not placed above practical ones" (122), but Rolf "unconditionally" put what he held "to be right above practical utility" (125). Rolf's efforts to influence Karen to the good made her take a dislike to herself, but she welcomed them nevertheless, for she wished to change. In her diary entry for 29 April 1904, she noted: "Nobody will declare that I am immoral—and yet I could drown in the ocean of my lies." *The first moral law,*" she proclaimed, is *"thou shalt not lie!"* (81–82). Her assessments probably do not reflect the influence of Rolf—they had just met—but they reveal the conflict within her between wanting to be honest and practicing subterfuge. She saw Rolf as her better self because he chastised behavior for which she felt guilty and reinforced her desire to reform.

The diaries do not indicate what Karen had been lying about, other than truancy, but she grew up in an environment that bred unconscious self-deception and conscious mendacity, and it is evident that she dealt with her hypocritical family by being dishonest herself. Her hostility toward her mother did not emerge in her diaries until June 1907, but it was manifested indirectly in her constant lying. After her family rejected Rolf, Karen calculated "with the greatest craftiness" how she was to see him (129). Karen's lying was a sign of fear, anger, and disrespect, and the fact that her family forced her to engage in an activity for which she disliked herself intensified her rage and contempt. This alienated her still further and bound her the more to Rolf, who was at once her moral guide and her fellow conspirator.

It is not difficult to see why Karen felt that there was an "unbreakable bond embracing" her and Rolf (154). When he left she experienced a "desperate longing": "I flung my arms around the wooden beam in my attic room and sobbed, I lay before my bed and buried my head in the down comforter to choke my sobs. Paralyzing fatigue and apathy." She was grateful to Rolf for his mental and moral influence, for giving her "the infinite happiness of loving and being loved," and above all for arousing her senses (98).

But the sensual part of the relationship was never very intense. Although the mystery of sexual attraction cannot be fully explained, we may be able to identify some of the factors that made Rolf less erotically exciting to Karen than either Schorschi or Ernst. This is a significant issue, since her choice of Ernst over Rolf troubled Karen for years.

The physical side of the relationship with Rolf developed very slowly indeed. Whereas Karen fell in love with Schorschi overnight and was kissing him passionately the next day, she met Rolf sometime in April, and they did not kiss until 13 July. After the kiss, she felt "disconcerted and sad," while he was "depressed." A boarder told her that she called out that night in her sleep, "No, I don't want to, I don't want to!" and Rolf reported that "he had had fearful qualms of conscience that evening" (133–35). A great deal of fuss about a kiss! Instead of bringing them closer, the introduction of a sensual element had an estranging effect. At their next meeting she called him "Sie" again rather than the familiar "Du," and although she allowed him to kiss her, she felt "nothing, not the least bit, save for displeasure at my uncomfortable position and his too vehement passion" (136). When Alice came to visit for a week, Karen's passions were aroused by her friend's "glowing sensuality" and she became "half sick with longing" for Rolf; but when she was with him, "his amorous attentions were simply repugnant," and she found that "his behavior disturbed the beauty of the evening" (138–39).

After a while, Karen grew "accustomed" to Rolf's kisses, but for the most part they left her cold (137). When she was with him she was "cool and not at all in love," but desire arose when they were apart, and her "doubts" vanished "before the one elemental feeling" (136). Except for a few rare occasions, the elemental feeling seems to have disappeared when Rolf was actually there.

In spite of her highly eroticized state, then, Karen was not physically attracted to Rolf. We have seen that she had a fantasy of being swept off her feet by a great man, a big man, a healthy man, with whom she could merge and who would transform her life. She wanted to submit to such a masterful figure in an orgy of unthinking, ele-mental passion. She could project this fantasy onto Schorschi, whom she hardly knew, but she could not project it onto Rolf. He was too slender, too pretty, too cere-bral, and too emotionally troubled to trigger the desired response. He wanted Karen to regard him as her "Lord and God" but that was "something very far from my thoughts" (137). She looked up to him as her mentor in moral and intellectual mat-ters, but he was otherwise too insecure to inspire submission. That they shared so many problems created a strong emotional rapport, but it also made Rolf seem unex-citingly weak.

Karen wanted to see herself as a strong, independent-minded woman who would kneel to a stronger man, but Rolf was not that man. He needed her even more than she needed him. He constantly reproached himself for being "inept and depraved by inheritance and upbringing" and was so miserable that "Berndt says the most consistent thing he could do would be to put a bullet through his head" (96). Karen felt that with "a little bit of lightheartedness" and "rough vitality" Rolf "could lead a happy life," but instead he was one of those Jews with a "fine-feeling sensi-tivity" who were a "vanishing small number among their own race" because they were "too weak for the battle of life" (183).

Rolf's insecurity carried over into his lovemaking, which was awkward: "He did not kiss well, he was at bottom such a chaste nature that he too found himself in strange waters. And certainly the man must take the sure lead. Only then, when he is able to, does the woman have full enjoyment. He must not feel hesitant, he must proceed, calm and sure" (143). Karen was living with Losch when she wrote this. Poor Rolf waited two months to steal a kiss, and when he took it, he was shy, gen-tle, and uncertain. Afterward he felt depressed, guilty, and full of self-reproach. On a later occasion, he asked Karen whether he could kiss her breast. When, "quite astonished and embarrassed," she said no, Rolf became "deeply melancholy" because nobody loved him: "Gone was any being in love—and I was once more the good companion who wanted only to help and to comfort him" (137). His sad-ness quenched all erotic feeling in Karen. After he left Hamburg, Rolf wrote Karen a letter in which he expressed the feeling that "my loving him was an undeserved gift for which he could never, never thank me enough" (151). By kneeling, as it were, in this way, Rolf was playing the woman's part in Karen's scenario. Gratitude for the love of a superior being was what she was supposed to feel toward a great man.

Chapter 6

Rolf and Ernst

Karen fell in love with Ernst almost as precipitously as she had with Schorschi. Although there were temperamental affinities, the attraction was predominantly sexual. Sometimes she felt that Ernst was the one for whom she had been waiting, while at other times she thought him distinctly inferior to Rolf. Reviewing the course of events in a letter to Oskar in December 1906, Karen described her relationship with Rolf as "an infinitely meaningful friendship that brought us both a deep, pure happiness," which was disrupted when "out of the blue I was seized by a senseless passion for someone else, who was built of a coarser stuff" (*AD*, 176). Karen was troubled not only by guilt for having rejected Rolf but also by a sense of bewilderment at her preference for Ernst.

Karen was convinced that she would have remained faithful to Rolf had he remained in Hamburg, but in his long absence her senses "at last awaken[ed]," she yielded to them, and, as a result, she strayed (*AD*, 153). Her erotic awakening began well before she met Ernst, with a Herr Matthaes, an actor from the German Theater who served as coach for a graduation performance in which Karen participated. Although he was "fat and homely," his acting was "elegant and clever," and Karen noted that as a man he exerted "a charm on [her] stronger than [she] had ever felt." When he sat beside her, her blood boiled so that she was "scarcely clear in the head" (153), and when he pulled her into a theater box and kissed her, she returned to her dressing room "in a feverish glow." Her "passion for the fat M." was soon over, but it had a "critical effect" on her relationship with Rolf. When she told him of it, Rolf replied that he had no right to reproach her, and his "mild judgment" led her to deceive him from then on "without any qualms of conscience" (154). Apparently, she wanted Rolf to assert his claim to possession, and his failure to do so aroused her contempt.

In November 1905, Karen wrote that "from April till August I had my fling. All calmed down. Perhaps it was good that everything wild in me found an outlet." In July and August she was involved with Ernst, but in April, May, and June she did a lot of "bumming around" (107), about which she deceived Rolf. We do not know the extent of her sexual activities or the identities of her partners, since she recorded only the incident with Herr Matthaes.

Her diary reflects a discomfort with her sexuality and efforts to repress it. She felt that a woman could have power and independence only by being free of sensuality. Otherwise, she would always be longing for a man, "and in the exaggerated yearning of her senses she will be able to drown out all feeling of her own value. She becomes the bitch, who begs even if she is beaten—a strumpet." Karen was afraid of her masochistic impulses. In spite of her belief that love sanctified sex without the need for marriage, her old Christian attitudes toward nature and instinct were still in evidence: every "victory of the senses" became a "Pyrrhic victory" bought with "ever deadly loathing afterwards." Karen wished to be free from "the war . . . between sensuality and intellect." In June she recorded "a hard battle between reason and senses. Reason has triumphed. . . . 'And I am so quiet after the wild play.'" The quiet did not last long. Eleven days later she celebrated casual dalliance: "Kisses and caressings without love, inspired only by animal sensuality, are like champagne out of a golden crystal glass in the blazing light of a festive hall" (104–06). Karen alternated between wanting to transcend sensuality and wanting to enjoy it.

While engaging in her "fling," she tried to understand her relationship with Rolf in a way that would allow her to preserve it. An ideal friendship such as theirs "does not exclude one or the other 'falling in love' with a third person, for the senses and all the lower instincts too want their full right." Indeed, it might be better "if these demands are satisfied elsewhere, so that the one relationship is kept more immaculate" (106). She was not betraying Rolf, therefore, but was preserving the purity of their relationship by looking elsewhere for the satisfaction of her physical needs. Hers sounds like the kind of rationale a male of her culture might use to justify sexual relationships with women other than his beloved.

Karen had conflicting needs. She wanted the emotional rapport, intellectual stimulation, and moral elevation that Rolf provided, but his very sensitivity and similarity to herself made him sexually unexciting. The men who appealed to her physically did not interest her as human beings, and her encounters with them passed "without leaving a trace" (106). She tried to justify the division in her love life by arguing that it was better to engage in both kinds of love simultaneously. She wanted most of all to heal the division by finding a masterful man with whom she could merge morally, emotionally, and intellectually, and to whom she could abandon herself. Her search for her one and only love was a driving force in her life, and her image of this man was the measure by which she judged all other men.

A few days after meeting Ernst, Karen visited Rolf in Berlin. She protested that she loved him, "could never, never do without him," and that her feelings for Ernst were still uncertain (156–57). She did not wish to give up either man, but Rolf would not wait until her emotions had clarified. He demanded her "full, undivided" love— and that she could not give him (108). He followed her to Hamburg, where she found him at the station, "beside himself, sobbing, his whole body trembling," asking for her love and threatening "to kill both Ernst and himself." Despite Rolf's desperation, Karen spent the next afternoon "laughing and kissing with Ernst": "not a thought of Rolf. Feelings become shallow? Or deep, very deep love that pushes all, all else aside?" (108–09).

Rolf made one more attempt to win Karen back, but when she could not promise to love him wholly, he withdrew, letting her know in December that she was "nothing to him any more." Karen found this a "bitter" experience, even though she was now hotly in love with Ernst. Writing in 1907, she spoke of her love for Rolf as her "holiest memory" and complained that he could not even summon up "a feeling of piety toward what was once sacred" (159).

Troubled by her abandonment of Rolf, Karen tried to make sense of her behavior, citing Rolf's awkwardness in sexual matters, her immaturity, and the overwhelming force of her love for Ernst. But "something unresolved still remain[ed] in spite of these explanations," and she concluded that "the *fundamental tone*" of their relationship "was that of friendship and not love, that it was spiritual and not sensual" (143). She explained to Oskar that "grieving over times past is useless." Instead it was important to "conjure up how everything had to happen as it did, just as it did. Belief in the necessary in life calms me" (175–76). Even before she knew anything of psychoanalysis, Karen instinctively pursued one of the goals of therapy: to defuse self-hate and promote self-acceptance by understanding the inevitability of our past behavior.

Karen could not make much sense of what had happened, however, and she continued to reproach herself, especially when she received a report that Rolf was quarreling with his friends: "Why didn't I stand by him in those days? I was very fond of him and knew what I meant to him. I believe it is the only step in my life that I sincerely regret" (201). She concluded her lengthy diary account of the Rolf episode with the hope that she would "be able to do him some kindness once more, to help him, to recompense him for what he was to me, and to atone for what I did to him" (160). But since he wanted to have no dealings with her, this seemed impossible.

When Karen received a "kind letter" from Rolf at the end of June, less than two months after expressing her hope for a chance to atone, she felt that her "most ardent wish" had been fulfilled (160). As we have seen, however, the letter provoked Sonni's renewed hostility, which enraged Karen. Her anger stemmed in part from the reawakening of past resentments, but it was also triggered by the threat Sonni posed to her chance of redemption. Her reconciliation with Rolf did not restore their intimacy, but it seems to have freed Karen from her preoccupation with him. She no longer dwelt upon him in her diaries or letters to Oskar. They saw each other occasionally after she moved to Berlin with Oskar in 1909.

Karen's relationship with Ernst consisted of four brief but intense episodes, with long periods of suffering in between. They met in July 1905. In mid-August a series of misunderstandings led Ernst to go away. She saw him again in early December, at the end of January, and in August, after she had met Oskar and fallen in love with Losch. When she reviewed the preceding year in January 1907, she proclaimed herself free of Ernst, and we hear little about him thereafter.

Although Karen reported that her "senses ran ahead of love" and that her relationship with Ernst was primarily one of physical passion (*AD*, 107), there was more to her feeling for him than sexual attraction. Unlike Rolf, Ernst was a candidate for the role of "the one." He was not as much of a soul mate, but they had temperamental and intellectual affinities that, combined with his physical appeal, made it seem possible that he was her great love. Karen was puzzled by the fact that Ernst had great power over her despite his neglect and his coarser nature. She needed to make sense of her feelings for Ernst all the more because she had sacrificed Rolf for him.

Looking back on the relationship, Karen wondered how she could have ever loved Ernst "so deeply, so passionately": "Forever an open question. And yet, I know why: he is of the same mixture as I am, the mixture of Rolf and Berndt, only in different proportions" (149). Like Rolf, Ernst was a conscientious intellectual who tended to be serious and who appreciated poetry. Like Berndt, he was "clever" and "sensible" (107). In many ways Karen found "a remarkable agreement" between herself and Ernst: they both had "strong moods" and "a similar mixture of naughtiness and usefulness or, let us say, of a tendency to an ordered life and bohemianism." Ernst reflected her own inner conflicts, and this gave them a rapport that complemented his sexual attractiveness. Karen felt that he was the man she had been looking for, and she often lay awake in bed "transfigured by the bliss of a wishless happiness" (156).

But the idea of Ernst was more satisfying than his actual presence, for Karen was not content when they were together. As with Rolf, the major source of tension was sexual, although her complaint about Ernst was that he demanded not too much but too little. She toyed with the idea of marriage, which would satisfy conventional morality, but she feared that it would prevent her continued development. What she really wanted was a physical affaire with Ernst, but he was too full of conflict between bourgeois and bohemian values to propose it. She longed for him to say, "Come, we two, you and I, we just can't do without each other!" But Ernst could not take this decisive step, and Karen was full of contempt: "He sits inside his armor of conventionality and talks of 'walls' against which he cannot bang his head. So small!" (110–11). Karen thought herself capable of living by her own romantic values, in defiance of the world, but Ernst was still a slave to middle-class morality.

In spite of Karen's belief that she was much freer than Ernst, both were paralyzed by the same inner conflict, from which each hoped to be released by the other. Ernst desired Karen intensely, but instead of taking her, as she wished, he needed her to offer herself to him. Quite early in their relationship, he gave her "a sheet of paper with two of [Richard] Dehmel's poems on it. . . . Poems all about impetuous loving. I understood, had to understand from the whole solemn way in which he gave me the paper" (108). Impetuous loving is precisely what Karen wanted, but Ernst, she concluded, was a coward: "He gave me the Dehmel poems—I know he waited for me to come and say: here I am—but he didn't want the direct, inevitable responsibility for it himself" (115).

What Karen did not perceive was her own dependence upon socially prescribed gender roles. Had she offered herself to him, she might have liberated his passion, just as he might have liberated hers by greater aggressiveness; but she was afraid that he would then be able to say that "she threw herself away upon me—or something of the sort" (116). Because Ernst did not want to behave like a cad and Karen was afraid of being perceived as an easy woman, neither could make the first move. Karen felt that Ernst would either bind her to him before she went out into "the big world" (112) or she would get over him. It was up to him; she could not act independently.

Karen's relationship with Ernst was as unworkable as that with Rolf, although for different reasons. Each episode followed the same pattern. When she and Ernst were together, they were tormented by unsatisfied desire, but when he went away, Karen suffered "unspeakably": "A leaden weariness lies upon me— / and no desire to live" (114). There was a masochistic component in Karen's attraction to Ernst. He meant "so infinitely much more" than the others because he was "the only one for whom I can suffer." By the bitterness of her suffering, she recognized "how great my love is for him" (146).

When she looked back on the year in January of 1907, there was a sense of relief that she was "free" of Ernst. As she had done with Schorschi, she salved her feelings

by seeing the man who had injured her "clearly for what he is. Him in his good-cit-
izen's pettiness and cowardice, in his mendacity, in his brutality and his egoism"
(149). Beginning with Rolf and Ernst, Karen's pattern was to move from one man
directly to another, engaging in several relationships, often of different kinds, at the
same time. When she was unattached, she would experience the same sense of being
lost, empty, and desperate that Clare fears at the thought of losing Peter.

Karen's preparations for the Abitur and medical school during this period
received remarkably little attention in her diary. Her "feminine" needs, as she understood them, were paramount, and she feared that they might prevent her from
achieving her full potential. She did not want to marry yet because she believed there
was "something more" in her that should be developed, but when she saw "how
dependent I am in my intellectual and moral life on my physical condition, and how
I lose my self-control, I think that this belief, too, amounts to nothing" (110). She
wanted to consummate the relationship with Ernst not simply to satisfy her sexual
desires but also to be free of them.

Chapter 7

Losch and Oskar

Karen was "mortally unhappy" during her first semester at Freiburg (*AD*, 127), but on
14 July 1906 she met Louis Grote (Losch) and Oskar Horney (Hornvieh) at a dinner of the academic-social society. By the next day she was in love with Losch, who
was her constant companion for the last two weeks of the term. The affaire seems to
have been consummated before she returned to school. In early September she spent
a few days in Fallingbostel with him, during which their "bond" became "stronger,
more intimate" (149). In mid-September Sonni moved to Freiburg to set up a board-
ing house, and when Karen arrived in October, Losch joined the household as
Karen's lover. The other boarder was Ida Behrmann (Idchen), a friend of Karen's
from the gymnasium.

From the beginning the relationship between Losch, Karen, and Oskar was tri-
angular. On the day after their meeting, Karen awoke from a nap on Oskar's sofa to
find Oskar gently stroking her cheeks. She was annoyed because she was "in love

with the tall fellow who had fallen asleep among cigarettes and books on the balcony" (148). During the next couple of weeks Karen was amused by the jealousy of the two men, which must have been gratifying in view of her previous feeling of abandonment. On 26 July she sent an invitation for a musical evening to Oskar in which she addressed him as "Dearly beloved sweet Hornvieh" (163), and the year-long correspondence that began in September was both intimate and full of affection. Losch was apparently jealous of their correspondence, but Karen tried to convince him that Oskar was "taking nothing from him": what Oskar was to her Losch could "not be at all" (182). A frequent topic in the correspondence was "exclusivity": "Does a collision always have to enter into it, even if one is close to only 2 people?" (201).

As was the case with Rolf and Ernst, Karen wanted to maintain her relationship with both men because each offered something she profoundly desired. She never entertained the thought that Losch might be her one love, however, and recognized his limitations from the start. In trying to sort out the relation between love and friendship, she rather wistfully referred to the myth of the hermaphrodite: "If one understood 'love' the way the wonderful Greek story pictures it, how human beings were halved at the Creation and now everyone seeks his complementary half, then of course there would be only one love for every person" (177). That was her ideal, but it was not the way things had worked out. Losch was more sexually appealing than Oskar, who was not only less physically prepossessing but was also too gentle. But what Rolf had awakened in her was brought to life by Hornvieh, "the search within" that she could not share with Losch (149).

Karen became enamored of Oskar's mind almost as quickly as she was physically attracted to Losch. In her first letter to Oskar, she reminisced about the time they had spent on his balcony in Günthersthal "when you explained to me how you had come to an understanding with those various big question marks. You know, I have found so few people with whom I could have conversed about deeper-lying things, and therefore I am the less likely to forget those hours" (165). Losch was a masterful lover, but Oskar had read a great deal of philosophy, and she thought that perhaps he was the one who could lead her out of her intellectual confusion. In her second letter, written a few days after her twenty-first birthday, she described the "unremitting, ever more refined self-observation" that never left her. Oskar was to be the confidante with whom she could share her self-observation and think through her problems until she was "in the clear" (166). In her third letter, she announced that "Little Hornvieh" was "functioning as Karen's diary!" (169), and indeed, her diary was suspended during their correspondence except for her New Year's entry in 1907 and her completion of the story of Rolf. We learn about her relationship with Losch mostly through her letters to Oskar.

Things went well between Karen and Losch for a few months, but by the beginning of 1907 there were signs of tension. Karen found in Losch's "strong love" for her "something infinitely calming, making for happiness" (149). It gave her a measure of freedom from her feelings of loneliness and insecurity and from her anxiety about finding a man. Moreover, Losch was a wonderful playmate for Karen, who had a great appetite for "lighthearted" pleasure (230). There was a childlike freshness about him that Karen found immensely attractive but that never completely satisfied her. As she later wrote to Oskar, her "longing for higher things" had little to do with Losch (210).

Late in March Karen reported to Oskar that she and Losch had been on the point of breaking up. Losch had begun frequenting the cafés day and night "and in consequence was quite utterly limp in his non-café life" (189). Perhaps his sexual attentions had fallen off, as Susan Quinn suggests (1987, 119–20). Karen went on to explain that she and Losch had become "very much accustomed to each other" and that it would be stupid at present to let "the whole thing go to the devil." She knew this sounded "awfully unloving, this intellectual weighing of For and Against—but love—I do not love Losch. I believe one can only love that which one recognizes as superior" (189). Quinn feels that Karen's "haughty claim" that she could love only what she recognized as superior had "a hollow ring" and suspects that Losch was in fact moving away from Karen, who was "trying not to care" (1987, 119). Karen's claim does not ring hollow to me. We have seen that she was looking for a great man who would be her Pygmalion and that Losch was never a candidate.

The rift between Karen and Losch corresponded to an internal division in Karen, and some of the things she disliked in him she also disliked in herself. In early February she wrote to Oskar that she was wandering in a labyrinth in which she saw her "own picture everywhere, but always so extremely different." In her next letter she had come to the conclusion that probably not much was the matter with her, but there was still something: "Perhaps I'm a genius at bumming around." She and Losch had been going to the Festhalle, where there was drinking and kissing and "frightfully common" behavior: "It intoxicated me, infected me—and I was not better than all the others." As a result of this experience, she became "all confused again": "Don't know what to think of myself, whether I am really serious about striving for knowledge, my striving to become something" (186–88).

On 22 February Karen lamented "the yawning emptiness in me and the disgust." She believed that she "*could* amount to something pretty good" but that she was going in the wrong direction: "I now understand the one drive in monasticism— the pathos of distance—not making oneself common with others." She admonished herself never to "give in to mediocrity" and pleaded with Oskar to write to her "so that I have someone once more to whom I can look *up*" (188). The reference to monasticism suggests that her feelings of commonness and self-disgust were at least partly sexual in origin.

There is evidence that while living with Losch, Karen was involved with other men. In a letter in which she imagined how others perceive her, she identified "*Various*" as saying, "Careless, tendency to 'bum around'" (227). This ended at least temporarily when she settled down with Oskar in the fall of 1907. Sonni is described as relieved that her flirting has stopped. In response to her depression after their marriage in 1909, Oskar suggested that she leave for a semester, and she immediately thought of Freiburg but decided against going there because she did not wish "to think on every path I take: I used to walk here with this one or that one, here we kissed, here we picked raspberries, here we drank a wine punch" (240).

Karen could not help seeing that Losch was inwardly divided, like herself. He seemed in his own way to be a combination of Berndt and Rolf. He had a "keen mind," "an immense realism," and "an instinctive aversion to philosophy." He was also a musician, like Rolf, and had "a rich emotional life" that was partly expressed through his art (211, 181). He was torn between the bohemian life of music and cafés and the more regulated existence of his studies in science and medicine. Karen attributed his dissipation to his inner division, and she became disturbed when he leaned toward becoming an artist. At this point, Oskar represented wholeness, wisdom, stability, and the serious, intellectual side of her nature, while the wild and frivolous Losch mirrored and perhaps exacerbated her own inner conflicts and her confusion about her identity.

Karen and Losch spent one more term together, during which she experienced growing contempt for the members of her household, quarreled with her brother, heard from Rolf, quarreled with her mother, and fought to keep Losch from going into "a restaurant life" again (218). Her spirits fluctuated, as did her relationship with Losch. The only constant factors were love of her work and a growing intimacy with Oskar. To Oskar's admonition that she help Losch "and be his friend," Karen replied, "That I am doing, can be, and am. It is probably the maternal element, which so often lies in a woman's love, that comes strongly to expression in our relationship" (210). This echoes her maternal feelings toward Rolf. She was initially attracted to Losch because she thought that he was strong, but she now saw that he was a weak figure who needed her support and whom she tried to keep out of trouble through her "petticoat government" (218). His love for her was "touching" and, given her needs, "of incalculable worth" (211), but she was clearly disenchanted and ready for another relationship.

Sometime between August and October 1907 Karen stopped living with Losch and began living with Oskar, but we do not know the details of the transition. Losch did not disappear from Karen's life. He and Idchen had become friends while he was with Karen, and when Karen and Oskar married on 30 October 1909, they were the witnesses. He remained in the house in Freiburg after Oskar moved in, which may be when his relationship with Idchen developed. Both boarded with Sonni again when she moved to Berlin to be near Karen and Oskar, and they married two years after their friends and remained in touch with them. Renate Patterson recalls that when she was growing up "there were father's friends and mother's friends and a few that came under the heading of 'family' like Losch and Idchen and their three daughters."[4]

A philosophical man three years older and more highly educated than she, Oskar impressed Karen with his knowledge and sophistication and became her intellectual companion and guide. They recommended books and articles to each other and exchanged ideas on free will, ethics, the indissolubility of marriage, the role of women, the nature of artistic value, and egoism. Karen developed great confidence in Oskar's empathy and insight, his "capacity for spiritual gropings" (*AD*, 211). She entrusted him with her joys, frustrations, and sorrows, discussed her feelings toward the important people in her life, and told him about her psychological problems. Her dependency on Oskar grew as she became increasingly dissatisfied with Sonni, Losch, and Idchen and had more frequent spells of depression.

Karen dwells so much in her diaries and letters on her difficulties that the enthusiastic girl who began the diary at the age of thirteen sometimes seems to have disappeared. But she can still be found in selected passages. We see the enthusiastic side of her personality during the first several months of her correspondence with Oskar, when her relationships with Losch and Sonni were going well. In one of the early letters, she speculated that perhaps everything "turned into enjoyment in my hands" because "everything I do—or almost everything—I attack intensively. Whether learning chemical formulas or making a pudding or reading something beautiful or being out in the open—profligate epicure, eh?" (168–69). A capacity for throwing herself with great intensity into whatever she was doing was also a characteristic of the mature Karen Horney, who has been described by those who knew her as a person who put as much effort into her pleasure as into her work and who had a gift for enjoyment.

One of the pleasures Karen celebrated in her letters was the study of medicine. She had a particular relish for dissection. On 12 November 1906 she wrote that she was "thrilled" to be in the dissecting room (173), and a month later she announced that Losch had come home "with the happy message that we shall have a new corpse on Thursday. You know that is such real work, it gives me tremendous joy" (175). As her personal life began to sour, Karen's mood darkened, but her undiminished enthusiasm for medicine gave her a source of strength in her "abysmally black states of mind." Chemistry was "enchanting," and she experienced the "pure joy of discovery" as she studied the brain (208–09). She had "a rapturous feeling" when "some bit of knowledge" really became her "possession," and she asked Oskar, "My dear, what do your studies mean to you?" (219).

Another of Karen's lifelong enthusiasms was for scenic beauty. She loved the mountain settings of Freiburg and Feldberg, where she went to ski and enjoy views of the Alps: "Nine hours to get up there. Danced in the evening. Oh Hornvieh, were those the days! How lovely to be young" (178). During her stay in the Black Forest, she wrote that she had "been skiing all day, just a brief break for lunch. Hornvieh, my dear, how I *love life!*" (182). Her vivid descriptions of scenery suggest the intensity of her response. Like medicine, nature was a refuge from unsatisfactory human relationships. Despite tensions with her companions during a trip to the Vosges, Karen informed Oskar that her soul was "filled with beautiful pictures" that gave her "a feeling of secret joy, as though I carried a talisman with me" (206).

Among Karen's enthusiasms none was more intense than her admiration for Oskar, which steadily increased throughout the year. In her early letters she expressed a longing to philosophize with him, and she regarded him as an expert on love. He reawakened in her the longing for a higher life that had faded since her separation from Rolf. She had, she mourned, adapted herself "to the coarser way of thinking of her surroundings," but in Oskar's letters she found "the finer language again." She compared her feelings toward Oskar to those of a pious Catholic who "goes to the priest for confession" (175–76). From the Black Forest she wrote, "You would certainly laugh at my having so much respect for you" (179). She wrote in a letter from Laufenburg am Rhein that she wished she were "sitting on a stool at your feet with you reading aloud something beautiful to me" (196). It would be, she assured him, like being in church.

Karen's letters to Oskar reveal not only her enthusiasms but her difficulties as well, for they often have a confessional quality. She brought Oskar her problems with others and her worries about herself, in search of comfort, guidance, and understanding. Although she had a "fear" of "spiritual undressing" (186), she found it "unutterably beneficial" to reveal herself to him (212) and instinctively employed Oskar as a therapist. She complained of being tired, depressed, and apathetic, so emotionally fatigued at times that she could summon up "no strong feelings" and her "senses seem[ed] to be dead" (228). She could feel nothing when Losch kissed her. Lamenting her ridiculous shyness, she dreaded "already [having] spoiled a great deal with this not-being-able-to-get-out-of-myself" (198; see also 182, 220, 225).

These were remarkable revelations for a "frightfully shy" (198) young woman to make to a man she knew so slightly, and they suggest the degree to which Karen invested Oskar with traits she needed him to have. Oskar sensed this and protested her idolization, but she persisted in regarding him as her guru. She felt in danger of being corrupted by the amorality of her entourage—in part because she herself had been "thoroughly unscrupulous in ethical matters"—and she feared that there was "some truth in *semper aliquid haeret* [something always persists]." Oskar was her "moral alarm clock" (208). She relied on him to save her from the effects of her early conditioning, much as she had relied on Rolf.

As the year 1907 progressed, Oskar and Karen became increasingly eager to see each other, but they also had anxieties. Oskar was afraid of failing to measure up to Karen's idealized picture of him, and Karen also felt insecure: "Hornvieh, good Lord, how I look forward to seeing you. And yet I am afraid, always thinking you must then notice how silly-stupid and giddy-tomfoolish I am" (189).

We have no records of the relationship until Karen began her fifth diary in April 1910, but they seem to have been happy during the year they lived together in Freiburg and during her two clinical semesters in Göttingen, when Oskar was completing his doctoral research in nearby Braunschweig. Sonni's letters to Berndt during the Freiburg period depicted the couple as extremely devoted, so much so that Sonni felt left out. We know nothing of the time in Göttingen, except that when she resumed her diary Karen referred to having been "well" during her first clinical semester, in contrast to her present state.

By April 1910, not quite six months after they were married, the relationship was clearly in trouble. Oskar was kind and intelligent but too self-controlled: "Even when he forces me to submit to him—it is never savagery or animal brutality . . . he is never elemental. For living together, certainly ideal—but something remains in me that hungers" (239). We have seen Karen's conflicting needs before, and now that she was married to Oskar, she found that he was not enough; she craved a more forceful and brutal man. With Oskar, she frequently found herself frigid. The spiritual and intellectual qualities that drew her to him had lost much of their importance, for Dr. Abraham had, "so to speak, taken Oskar's place" (244). Now that she was married to the man she had venerated, Karen was unhappier than ever. All her symptoms reappeared, especially the paralyzing fatigue of which she complained repeatedly for the two years during which she kept the diary.

At this stage, Karen thought a lot about extramarital affaires, but there is no direct evidence that she acted on her fantasies. When she was pregnant with Brigitte, she wondered whether she had an unconscious resentment of the baby because her condition made her "less desirable to other men" and because having a child forced repression of her "prostitution drive" and restricted "vagabonding." A woman without children "can give herself to many men" with no burdensome consequences (253). She tried to explain her renewed attraction to Losch, concluding that because he had provided clitoral stimulation, whereas Oskar did not, he meant more to her "sexually than Oskar." But she considered it "immoral" to find another man more attractive than Oskar (UD, 3 January 1911), so perhaps she was still monogamous.

In January 1911 Karen recorded that analysis had helped her to overcome her frigidity and to achieve a more harmonious relationship with Oskar. As she lay in his arms in the morning, she thought, "How wonderful it is to have such a lovely husband" (UD, 9 January 1911). She reasoned that Sonni's desire for another husband had increased "through seeing our married happiness" (AD, 256). She was gratified by Oskar's financial prospects, which were greater than those of Losch and Rolf and was proud that he had achieved so much (UD, 13 January 1911).

The first affaire we know about was with Walther Honroth, husband of Karen's close friend. When the Honroths first appear in Karen's diary, on 23 January 1911, it is because Oskar is attracted to Lisa, and Karen is recounting a dream that reveals her jealousy. She has had trouble waking up and concludes that Lisa is the reason she feels "battered and tired, incapable of anything" (AD, 261). Brigitte was born on 29 March 1911, and in May, Oskar told Karen that what appealed to him about Lisa was "the motherliness in her." Since Karen most valued motherliness at this time, "a remark like that was the very thing to arouse feelings of insufficiency" (268).

The published version of the fifth diary concludes on 29 June 1911, but in fact Karen's diary continued for another year, with a hiatus between July 1911 and April 1912. When Karen resumed writing, she was in the midst of an affaire with Walther that seems to have been going on for some time. Both Lisa and Oskar were aware of the relationship, but while Oskar gave his blessing, Karen worried that Lisa was trying to influence Walther against her by describing her special sexual cravings (which are never specified) "in a harsh light" (UD, 2 April 1912). Although the relationship was clearly not working, it continued for several months as Karen tried to assure herself that, despite all appearances, Walther did indeed love her.

In June 1912, Karen began a relationship with a man named Carl while continuing to see Walther. In her entry for 20 June, she complained that her inability to detach herself from Walther "prevents me from surrendering myself to this relationship entirely, the way I normally do." This suggests that such affaires had been a common occurrence. In her entry for 24 June, she recorded that "Artur's latest tenderness did me good," but that "Walther wasn't tender" and now she will be able to free herself of him. She intended to make her relationship with Carl "the finest and most beautiful," and in her final entry she wrote that he gave her "a calm, strong feeling of happiness": "When I think 'the two of us,' I feel pride and strength" (UD, 7 July).

By early 1912, Oskar had ceased to play an important role in Karen's life. She felt that the great tensions and emotions were missing in their marriage and sought satisfaction of her needs elsewhere. Analysis and self-analysis had replaced Oskar's guidance in her search within, and she looked to her lovers for erotic satisfaction (which she rarely found with Oskar) and for feelings of strength and pride. Within two years of their wedding, Karen and Oskar appear to have agreed on an open marriage, in which each pursued other relationships without concealment or deceit. Renate recalls that her father "was always busy with his short, brilliant career and his secretary. Mother must have known about this liaison that had started as early as 1911. But my Father was just. Every trip he took with his secretary he would take again with Mother at another time."[5] Karen and Oskar conducted their liaisons discreetly and maintained the appearance of being a conventional family as their three daughters were growing up, but the vitality went out of their relationship within a year after Brigitte's birth.

We can only speculate about how the open marriage arrangement came about. In her "Recollections of Karen Horney," Rita Honroth-Welte, the daughter of Walther and Lisa, wrote that "during their student days and in their early years of marriage," Oskar and Karen, as well as her parents, "belonged to a group of couples who, in today's terminology, would probably be called 'swingers.' Girlfriend and wife swapping was very much en vogue, thus antedating a similar social phenomenon in this country by some sixty years."[6] We know from Karen's letters that Oskar had two women friends while he was writing to her (that is, during the period from September 1906 to September 1907), that he regarded the claim to exclusivity as primitive, and that he had once said something that prompted Karen to reassure him, "I 'do not demand you for myself alone'" (AD, 209). There are also indications that Karen had casual relationships while she was living with Losch and that she felt uncomfortable about "bumming around." Although the extramarital affaires probably did not begin until after the birth of Brigitte, they may have started earlier. Karen's diary for 28 April 1910 contains a poem she wrote after a session with Abraham, the gist of which is that her instincts have driven her to betray her ideals. She had hoped to give her body only when her "soul agreed to it," but instead she yielded "to nature's deeply rooted drives" (243). We cannot tell whether she was referring to recent behavior.

Honroth-Welte's observations suggest that the extramarital relationships continued a pattern established during student days, that Karen and Oskar's behavior was typical for their circle, and that a casual attitude toward such behavior was rather widespread "in the upper middle-class milieu": "It was almost taken for granted that married men had their extra-marital affaires—perhaps as a proof of their virility. This certainly held true for the men in my family and it came as no surprise to me that Oskar belonged in the same group. The mistresses often were relatives or close friends of the wives and there was a certain amount of openness, tolerance, and laissez-faire; friendships continued, appearances were observed, and social intercourse did not seem to be interfered with by any other kind. The wives, by and large, were not as active sexually, but they too had their flings and no one got too much upset about that. (I am speaking here more or less for the larger cities, especially Berlin.)."[7] To a certain extent, then, Karen and Oskar's marriage reflected the norms of their social group, which undoubtedly influenced them.

Whatever the social influences, however, the open marriage arrangement was one that suited Karen's sexual predispositions and psychological needs. She had "polygamous prostitution desires" (UD, 11 April 1911) and dreams that expressed a craving "for many! robust! men" (13 January 1911). Oskar was not "elemental" enough for her, and she was attracted to men who had more of "the beast of prey," just as she had been drawn to the "coarsely sensual" Ernst while still involved with Rolf. Rolf could not bear to share her with another man, but the far more worldly Oskar was apparently agreeable as long as he was given comparable freedom.

It is important to recognize that although Karen undoubtedly wished for this arrangement, she was not truly happy in it. Perhaps as a residue of her Christian upbringing, she felt guilty about her wild desires, imploring Abraham in a poem to "lift my sin and make it light" (AD, 244). The same poem expressed disappointment in herself because she has failed "to win the noble prize / to be the master of my whims" (243). Although her behavior may have been sanctioned by Oskar and her friends, she was aware of its compulsiveness and it disturbed her.

She was disappointed, moreover, in Oskar. While genuinely admiring his "generous way of allowing [her] freedom," she nonetheless demanded "to be enslaved." Her "subconscious," she decided, wanted "a man who beats me if I only consider unfaithfulness." Her old friend Rolf thought that she needed "a man to brutalize" her, and Karen agreed. She was forced to look for such a man outside marriage, and Walther seemed at first a good prospect: "Lisa is brutalized by Walther, she can never be sure of his love, she constantly has to court him—and doesn't want things any other way." Karen at once despised the Honroths' marriage and saw her "ideal in it. Isn't there a compromise between all this, a harmony?" (UD, 16 April 1912). The harmony for which she longed was internal, of course, and she spent the rest of her life searching for it.

Karen hoped to save her marriage through her analysis with Karl Abraham but did not succeed. While their daughters were growing up, she and Oskar maintained the appearance of a normal family life, but they went their separate ways, consoling themselves with affaires. Her fifth diary will continue to give us an intimate view of their relationship, especially during her analysis. We shall gradually learn more about it from her psychoanalytic writings, which are often autobiographical, the recollections of her daughters, and the testimony of those who knew her.

Karen and Oskar remained together, rearing their three daughters, until 1926. They did not obtain a divorce until 1938. During the first fourteen years of their marriage, Oskar was a great success. After completing his studies in law, economics, and political science and earning a Ph.D., he joined the Stinnes Corporation, which became an industrial and financial giant during World War I. He quickly rose to a lofty executive position. As he prospered, the family lived in the fashionable suburb of Zehlendorf, where they had a large house, three acres of garden and grounds, and an impressive motor car. During the inflation of 1923, Stinnes collapsed, leaving Oskar without a job. He almost died of meningitis that same year. He never recovered his fortunes or his full mental vigor: he went bankrupt in 1926 and became enamored of a succession of get-rich-quick schemes. Karen and Oskar remained friends even after her move to the United States in 1932, and she gave him occasional financial assistance, especially after World War II. Oskar died in 1948.

Part 2

The Freudian Phase and

Feminine Psychology

part 3

Chapter 8

"The Given Task for a

Woman Psychologist"

After completing her studies at the universities of Göttingen and Berlin, Karen Horney passed her state medical examination in 1911—the year Brigitte was born—and did an internship and a psychiatric residency. She was licensed to practice medicine in 1913, completed her dissertation under Karl Bonhoeffer in 1914, and received her M.D. in January 1915. Daughter Marianne was born in 1913, and Renate in 1916. Horney pursued her interest in psychoanalysis through extensive reading, as well as through analysis with Karl Abraham and participation in the Berlin Analytical Society, of which she became secretary in 1915. During World War I she worked in a military neurological hospital (Lankwitz Kuranstalt), afterward opening her analytic practice, although she had begun seeing patients in 1912.

Horney was a founding member of the Berlin Psychoanalytical Institute, in which she was active during the 1920s, especially in screening candidates and training analysts. She served on the institute's board of education from its inception. She also served on the board of directors of the German Psychoanalytical Society from 1925 to 1930. In his letter to the American Consulate supporting Horney's application for immigration, Max Eitingon testified that her technical seminars were the "most highly appreciated" of those given at the institute, her lectures had "the largest attendance," and her papers at meetings and congresses were "among the most valuable."[1]

During this period, Horney developed a sense of her special mission as a woman psychologist and published a series of ground-breaking essays. In the "Educational and Scientific Record" she prepared as part of her application for immigration, she wrote: "My scientific interest concentrated more and more on female psychology and connected fields such as the differentiation between masculine and feminine psychology, general disturbances in the relationships between the two sexes, marriage problems. As psychology has been until now mostly worked at from the side of men, it seems to me to be the given task for a woman psychologist—or at least I think it to be mine—to work out a fuller understanding for specifically female trends and attitudes in life" (Horney Papers). By the time she left Germany in 1932, Karen Horney had established an important place for herself in the history of psychoanalysis.

First as a neophyte and later as an apprentice, Horney was too preoccupied with mastering psychoanalytic theory to think critically about it. In her diary she generally analyzed herself along orthodox lines, taking Abraham as her authority. In "The Technique of Psychoanalytic Therapy" (1917), her first published essay, she defended Freudian theory and practice against the Zurich School, "which, without justification, continued to call its method 'psychoanalysis' in spite of its basic differences" (9). (Horney also continued to call her theory psychoanalysis after she developed basic differences with Freud.) In her second essay, however, "On the Genesis of the Castration Complex in Women" (1923), she proposed a significant modification of the psychoanalytic account of female development, and in subsequent essays she made frequent efforts to revise psychoanalysis from within. Horney's essays eventually began to challenge basic features of the psychoanalytic paradigm and hence anticipated her break with Freud, but for the most part they employed the orthodox model and sought to replace the prevailing phallocentric version of female psychology with one constructed from a woman's point of view.

Although Horney's version of feminine psychology has come to be widely respected, there are still questions about the factors that led her to quarrel with her mentors. In the 1920s, after all, few women analysts objected to the orthodox account of femininity. In an essay on "Freud and Horney" (1986) William Grossman observes that "the possibility that an emotional issue about female sexuality" initiated Horney's dissent "awaits careful historical investigation" (67). I shall undertake that investigation here.

It is not difficult to see why Horney was attracted to psychoanalysis. She suffered many mysterious complaints, she was unhappy, and her ability to function was impaired. Of an introspective, analytical temperament, she had been in the habit of seeking relief by trying to understand herself and those with whom she had relationships. Psychoanalysis offered the most powerful tools available for self-exploration. Moreover, Freud's account of human motivation and development fit Horney in many ways; she frequently recognized her own situation in his description of women's problems. The idea of working with an analyst would not have seemed forbidding to her: she was accustomed to using Oskar as her therapist, and took great comfort in exposing herself to a person who might understand her. Given her suffering, her temperament, and her craving for explanation, psychoanalysis as a theory and as a therapy must have seemed to be exactly what she was looking for.

While some aspects of orthodox theory fit her experience well, others did not. By the early 1920s she began to propose modifications to Freud's theory in light of her self-understanding, her observations of her patients, and her experiences as a woman. Perhaps the most important factor in Horney's dissent was that she came to see psychoanalytic theory as reproducing and reinforcing the devaluation of the feminine from which she had suffered in childhood. The male bias of psychoanalysis, to which she was sensitized by having encountered similar attitudes within her family and culture, was certainly one of the "emotional issues" underlying her quarrels with Freud and Abraham.

Not surprisingly, Horney came to feel it to be her "given task" to understand female psychology: to explore the differences between men and women and the disturbances in relationships between the sexes from the woman's perspective. She had a personal stake in making psychoanalytic theory less threatening to her dignity and more useful as a tool of self-exploration and growth.

Beginning with her analysis, Horney's Freudian phase lasted approximately twenty-five years. Much of her thinking about feminine psychology was governed by orthodox theory, but her dissent on crucial issues eventually led to her break with Freud. Her essays on feminine psychology have made an important contribution to psychoanalytic and feminist thought. For that reason alone they are worthy of study, but they also tell us much about Horney's search for self-understanding and the evolution of her ideas. When we view them in light of her diaries and the Clare story, we can see that they are often autobiographical—or at least focused on problems that resemble her own.

Chapter 9

Analysis and Self-Analysis,

1910 – 12

In her fifth diary Karen began a process of self-analysis that continued for the next forty years. As she searched for self-understanding, she generated a multitude of explanations that were often inconsistent and that failed, by and large, to provide much relief.

The fifth diary records a very bad period for Karen, which began in April 1910, in the midst of her first analysis with Karl Abraham, and ended on 7 July 1912.[2] In the first entry she complains of "exhaustion, the inclination to passivity that increases to a longing for sleep—even for death" (*AD*, 238). Exactly two years later she reports "a strong tendency away from life into sickness and death. I considered the possibility of suicide yesterday. Absolute inability for self-control. Strong emotions against Oskar. Inability to work" (UD, 18 April 1912). There are repeated references to fatigue, inability to concentrate, compulsive behavior, frigidity with Oskar, and wishes for death.

At times Karen felt that her first analysis did her good, and when she took up her diary to try to complete her cure through self-analysis in January 1911, she listed her "new achievements": "the predominance of an equable, gay mood, the even tenor of my love for Oskar, and that of my capacity for sexual enjoyment, a definitely increased self-assurance in comparison to before, together with less shyness and less tendency to defensiveness toward others" (AD, 247). Unfortunately, these gains were transitory, and she was soon reporting severe symptoms again. On 9 January she complained of tiring easily, of feeling restive, anxious, and oppressed, and of being "totally incapable of concentrating . . . on work." She experienced chills, rapid heartbeats, and a tightness in her throat (AD, 255).

A few days later, Karen expressed the fear that her illness was "cyclical" (AD, 257); and it is clear that she oscillated between relatively brief episodes of well-being and long stretches of "listlessness," "tiredness," and "weariness of life" (UD, 20 April 1912). She wondered constantly whether she would ever get well. Although she often thought about returning to Abraham, she found little relief when she did and became skeptical of his ability to help her. She felt that she "really should be able to handle this" herself (16 April).

Karen began her diary because analysis had hit a snag: "Till now ideas have come with such playful ease. Now we must wait because the resistances are too great" (AD, 238). In the first half-dozen entries, she explored some familiar themes—fatigue, shyness, masochistic tendencies, polygamous leanings, and sexual guilt. She also tried to interpret her ambivalent feelings toward Abraham. In subsequent entries she sought to make sense of her feelings toward the important people in her life: Oskar, in whom she was losing interest; Sonni, toward whom she felt anger and then guilt; her baby Brigitte, who was a source of both joy and resentment; and Walther Honroth, who disappointed her as a lover but from whom she had difficulty freeing herself. I shall concentrate on how she analyzed her primary symptom—fatigue—and her struggle to understand her compulsive attraction to Walther. Much in the fifth diary reminds us of Clare, whose presenting symptom was "a paralyzing fatigue that interfered with her work and her social life" (SA, 76), and the goal of whose self-analysis was to free herself from her compulsive need for her lover.

In her first entry, Karen wrote that Abraham had given her many possible explanations for her states of exhaustion. As we might expect, he suggested a sexual etiology, comparing her state with the postorgasmic exhaustion of onanists. Karen tried to make the connection, even though she felt that masturbation played "no great role" in her life. As a child she "probably did it freely," and later she stimulated herself mentally by telling herself stories, which had an effect "comparable to the physical stimulation" (AD, 238–39). Although she no longer consciously told herself stories, her unconscious now created fantasies in order to satisfy her instinctual desires (UD, 18 April 1910). These fantasies were a form of onanism that left her in a state of exhaustion.

Karen considered other possible connections between her fatigue and autoerotic satisfaction. Perhaps she needed her exhaustion so that she would not have to work and thus would have the leisure to pursue erotic fantasies that provided "everything life denies" (AD, 246). The unconscious was an "enemy within" (AD, 268), which, in its pursuit of what our "darkest instincts desire" (UD, 18 April 1910), frustrates our conscious objectives and undermines our will. But what were these unconscious sexual desires that needed to be repressed?

Abraham saw Karen's longing for sleep and death as an expression of "the desire for physical and spiritual martyrdom" that led her to be attracted to brutal and forceful men, "the wanting to blend in with the will of a man who has set his foot on my neck." He traced the attraction of such men to Karen's "first childhood impressions, [to] the time when I loved my father with all the strength of my passion. I got my erotic ideal from that time." Her "conscious I" sought "a man of fine intelligence and discerning kindness," but her "instincts" wanted a brute. In Oskar, she had found everything she consciously wished for—"and behold: my instinctual life rebels. It feels itself drawn to a Karl U. because it scents the beast of prey in him, which it needs" (AD, 238). She interpreted threatening male figures in a dream as expressions of "the desire for many! robust! men. Robust—'like my father,' it occurs to me in this context" (UD, 13 January 1911).

Karen's attraction to brutal men was not entirely unconscious, although she felt it to be instinctually motivated and in conflict with her ideals. She was quite aware of her desire for Karl U. and, indeed, flirted with him so conspicuously that Oskar complained. When Karen reacted with depression, Oskar was apologetic, but Karen felt "deeply hurt" and went into "spasms of sobbing": "It was an outburst of such vehemence, such despair to the point of mortal weariness, that I could not believe it was explained simply by hurt feelings." In the afternoon, "great exhaustion" followed. "Dr. A. found that I had taken it so hard because the rebuke had hit upon a repressed wish, namely the very wish to throw myself away, prostitute myself—give myself to any man at random. Consider the polygamous leanings and stimuli in my dreams, the pleasure it gives me to be spoken to on the street, etc. In the prostitution wish there is always a masochistic wish hidden: to relinquish one's own personality, to be subject to another, to let oneself be used by the other. Hence again and again the drive away from marriage to the simple surrender, no matter to whom" (*AD,* 242). What her "darkest instincts" desired, then, was masochistically to prostitute herself with brutal and forceful men who resembled her father. Oskar's complaint about her flirting reminded her that she could not realize her desire, and this filled her with "despair to the point of mortal weariness."

Although she often saw her fatigue as the product of repressing her instincts, on one occasion Karen related it to having acted out some of her sexual desires. After a discussion of how "the conscious and the unconscious are at war," she composed some verses addressed to Abraham, the burden of which was that she could not "win the noble prize" because of the irresistible strength of her sexual impulses. She had "striven for the human good / in ardent honest measure" but was ruled by "another will / that scorns the world and labor." She was profoundly uncomfortable because of her inability to live up to her conscious ideals, and she wondered whether her enervation was the product of guilt over engaging in sex without love and over her "wild wishes" and "daring dreams." Her "soul's torment" had "gnawed away [her] vital strength," leaving her subject to terrible weariness (*AD,* 243). In this scenario, it was the conscious rather than the unconscious side of her psyche that was producing fatigue.

Another hypothesis was that her fatigue derived from her reluctance to terminate analysis. Perhaps her transference was so strong that she wanted "to uphold this relationship at any price" and so deployed "the whole corona of old symptoms to show that I am still far from well" (244). Why, she asked, was the analysis "so indispensable to the subconscious?" In addition to "the attachment to Dr. A," there was the pleasure of being the center of his undivided interest, at least during the sessions. This pleasure was partly exhibitionistic and partly masochistic. Her "spiritual disrobing" gave her "the sensual pleasure of shy embarrassment and submission." Her relationships with others had always been dominated by a desire for attention. This was combined with "an urge to martyrdom": "one puts oneself forward just as much through one's bad as through one's good characteristics" (245). By refusing to become well and by telling Abraham that the analysis was doing her no good, Karen prolonged the analysis, heightened Abraham's concern, and satisfied her need for martyrdom.

There was another primitive need at work as well—"the old childish 'megalomania,'" the urge "to be something quite special." The thought of "disappearing quietly in the great mass of the average" was "unbearable," yet standing out through "intellectual work" was "thoroughly repugnant to the unconscious because it dis-tract[ed] it from its activity in sexual life." Karen's "megalomania" made her want to be of special importance to Abraham, both personally and as an object of scientific interest. Her analysis was "of no overwhelming interest," however, and she could make herself "more important in Dr. A.'s eyes [only] by getting worse." Her weari-ness was a means of showing Abraham that she was unique and not easily cured. She recognized that she had felt well one week when Abraham was away because she had had "no possibility of making [herself] interesting to him" (245–46).

When Karen terminated her analysis, however, her exhaustion did not disap-pear, and she continued to speculate about its causes. She wondered whether she was producing fatigue "in order to induce myself to go back" to Abraham (*AD*, 255). Other possibilities were that she was oppressed by Sonni's influence upon her, and that she woke up feeling "battered and tired" because Oskar had flirted with Lisa Honroth (*AD*, 261). After Sonni's death, she reasoned that her longing for sleep expressed a desire to be dead like her mother. She also blamed such autoerotic expe-riences as nursing, afternoon naps, and unconscious fantasies. On one occasion when she felt better, she asked herself, "Why am I well again now?" (UD, 18 April 1912), and was as unable to explain her good health as she was her fatigue. Toward the end of her diary she wrote, "Both the sudden improvement and deterioration I cannot understand" (20 April). After more than two years of analysis and self-analy-sis, Karen was as baffled by her condition as she had been at the outset.

Although Karen's and Clare's symptoms were similar, there is little resemblance so far between Karen's diaries and *Self-Analysis* in how their difficulties are explained. One entry in the diary, however (4 January 1911), anticipates Horney's analysis of Clare, which will be discussed below. Inspired by the psychoanalyst Alfred Adler rather than by Freud, it reveals the seeds of Horney's dissent from orthodox psychoanalysis and anticipates her mature theory.

Karen's topic once again is fatigue, which set in soon after she began to study for her examination. She wonders whether her fear of productive work derives not only from her mistrust of her own capacity but also from "the tendency Alfred Adler con-siders characteristic of neurotics: 'Always wanting to be first' . . . Or rather from both tendencies together: from a feeling of uncertainty and inferiority, I am afraid that I will not be able to do anything first class, above average, and therefore prefer not to attempt it at all, perhaps trying to create a special position for myself through this exaggerated refusal." Her resistance to work, apparently even to "receptive or mechanical work" like preparing for examinations, derives from her fear that she will not excel (*AD*, 250–51).

Karen believed that this might explain both her "disproportionate anxiety about exams" and her shyness. She recalled her experience with the Abitur, when she was "quite sure of getting through" but "wanted to do particularly well, became anxious, nervous, and in consequence, when the exam actually came, [was] unable to do anything." She had suffered from fatigue a good deal while preparing for the exam, and her performance did not measure up to her abilities.[3] She accounted for her shyness in the same terms: a combination of insecurity and a need to excel. "Perhaps this also gives rise to my fear of social gatherings," she writes, "because I am afraid I won't be able to play first fiddle." She was always on guard against other people and could not give herself "naturally" because she wanted to conceal her "feelings of inferiority" from both herself and others (AD, 251–52).

While in analysis, Karen had attributed her need to be something quite special to "childish 'megalomania'" (245). Under the influence of Adler, she now saw it as a need to compensate for feelings of inferiority. Later, in her mature theory, she also identified such needs as compensatory. Adler mentions ugliness as one of the deficiencies that gives rise to the need for superiority (Ansbacher and Ansbacher 1956, 46–47), and Karen wrote that because she was "in no position to shine through beauty," she "wanted at least to look 'interesting'" or "uncommonly intelligent." She was especially intrigued by Adler's account of the masculine protest, which develops in every woman in response to her sense of inferiority to men. Feelings of inferiority in girls stem from their relative physical weakness and, according to Freud, from the lack of a penis. The girl "sees her father as the stronger, controlling partner," but "she identifies early on with her mother," thus reinforcing her sense of subordination. As a protest, "She tries to adopt as many masculine traits as possible or to stand out in some other form" (AD, 251–52).

Karen had no difficulty in identifying the masculine protest in herself. As a child she had wished to be a boy. She "envied Berndt because he could stand near a tree and pee," she liked wearing pants, she played the prince in charades, and at the age of twelve she cut her hair off to the neckline, "thus being the curly haired prince again." Although she loved to play with dolls, she "didn't like small children at all," a "rejection of specifically feminine motherliness." She compensated for her physical inferiority by academic achievement: "It was always my pride that in school I was better than Berndt" (AD, 252). A week after the Adlerian entry in her diary, she dreamed "that Oskar had a big vagina and that I put my finger in it." She argued that because she was imagining herself "as a man and Oskar as a woman," the dream revealed homosexual tendencies and her "wish to be a man" (UD, 11 January 1911). In the terms of her culture, Karen was behaving like a man by studying medicine and by indulging in a promiscuous sexual life.

According to Karen's Adlerian self-analysis, she needed to feel superior because of her lack of beauty and sense of inferiority as a woman, which led to her masculine protest. She wanted to "conceal [her] inferiority through excelling" in a male domain, but her feminine lack of self-confidence made her afraid she would fail, so she avoided productive work, as do "women in general" (*AD,* 251–52), and experienced disproportionate anxiety over exams. Her fatigue was at once a product of her anxiety, an excuse for withdrawing from the competition with men, and a means of creating a special position for herself. She could not conceal her inferiority by excelling, but she could by being unable to function. Clare's lack of self-confidence is attributed to her experiences in her family rather than to her gender, but the analysis of her fatigue is broadly similar to Karen's Adlerian self-analysis.

Most of Clare's history is presented in a chapter of *Self-Analysis* entitled "Systematic Self-Analysis of a Morbid Dependency." Karen also attempted to understand what she later called morbid dependency in her fifth diary, especially in the entries concerning her affaire with Walther Honroth. As in her efforts to comprehend her fatigue, she relied primarily on Freudian theory to understand her difficulty in freeing herself from Walther, but here too one entry anticipates her later ideas.

The affaire with Walther probably began in the second half of 1911 and seems to have come to an end in June 1912. The first mention of it was on 2 April 1912, when Karen reported problems because Walter was "scared" of her sexual wishes and seemed to prefer "peace" with his wife, Lisa, to Karen's demands (UD). Karen felt that it was "necessary for my development to detach myself from him" and admonished herself "to be persistent." She was "cold and offensive" toward him on the telephone that evening ("Revenge for my hurt pride"), but then she begged him to be "good and loving" toward her: "So I didn't get any further, can't get away from him." In spite of his characterization of their lovemaking the previous Sunday as "'a relapse'" that she had provoked, she was still "working on winning him back": "Is a man still in love if he can talk like that?! And if it is Lisa's doing, do I want a man who is another woman's creation? Don't I have any pride in me?" (UD, 3 April 1912).

Karen analyzed her relationship with Walther and Lisa as a repetition of her relationship with her parents. She was bound not just to Walther but to Lisa as well and was ambivalent toward both, "passionate affection" being followed by "an equally passionate rejection." She tried "to interfere with this marriage, one moment helpfully, the next destructively. Then these two people: Lisa, standing so much higher intellectually, hysterical, blinding, trying to 'dominate,' 'self-sacrificing,' morally defective; Walther, the simpler, stronger nature, more brutal but essentially inferior, dominated; my god, I must have been blind: that is Sonni-father and my attitude toward them" (UD, 7 April 1912).

Again Karen tried to explain behavior that was in conflict with her conscious judgments and objectives in terms of unconscious motivation—reconstructed with the aid of psychoanalytic theory—and again she found that such understanding did not alleviate her problem. Because she was reliving "the infantile constellation," she could not "get away" from Walther and Lisa. That was why "the separation from Walther hit me so hard that I was suicidal. . . . And all for Walther, Walther who means so little for my conscious life" (UD, 7 April 1912). The next day she experienced a "terrible desire for Walther" and wondered "what good is the insight that this is a repetition of the infantile constellation" (9 April). She had a keen awareness of both Walther's limitations and the compulsiveness of her own behavior: "Walther, you tall lout: it's only neurotic Karen who loves you; the healthy, free one despises you thoroughly" (18 April). In this context, the neurotic Karen was the Karen who was compulsively reenacting the infantile constellation under the domination of unconscious oedipal and homoerotic drives.

Another explanation for her morbid dependency on Walther anticipates the analysis of Clare. Karen saw herself as bound to Walther by her "dream of a noble man's love," much as Clare was bound to Peter. Her inability to free herself from Walther or, more generally, from her need for a man in whom to submerge herself, filled her with self-hate. She felt that Walther could not be in love with her, given his behavior, but because of her "oppression as a child" she had "no pride," "no self-confidence" (UD, 12 April 1912). Clare too was trying to "free herself from the aftermaths of an unfortunate childhood" that had left her desperate for love, devoid of self-confidence, and in need of salvation by a man (SA, 296).

Horney seems to have felt as far back as 1912 that there was a causal connection between her oppression as a child, her dream of a noble man's love, and her tendency to become morbidly dependent on males. (I shall examine her development of this connection when I return to the Clare case at the end of Part 3.) Throughout the 1920s, she continued to analyze herself in terms of classical theory, a process that is reflected in her essays on feminine psychology.

Chapter 10

The Masculinity Complex: "On the Genesis of the Castration Complex in Women" and "The Flight from Womanhood"

As we have seen, Nancy Chodorow locates the political and theoretical origins of psychoanalytic feminism with Karen Horney and feels that her theories "form the basis, acknowledged or unacknowledged, for most of the recent revisions of psychoanalytic understandings of gender" (1989, 203).[4] William I. Grossman observes that Horney's "feminist critique of psychoanalysis and of the influence of male-oriented culture on feminine mental life is the source, often unacknowledged, of some of today's most cogent feminist writings" (1986, 73). Janet Sayers names Karen Horney, along with Helene Deutsch, Anna Freud, and Melanie Klein, as one of the four mothers of psychoanalysis (1991).

Between 1923 and 1935 Horney published a total of nineteen essays on feminine psychology, more than a third of which deal with aspects of the masculinity complex in women. She seems to have been trying to comprehend herself in terms of this complex and to free herself from the male ideology she felt it reflected. Her analysis of the male view of women inevitably involved a critique of psychoanalysis, which had justified that view. Horney also devoted a number of essays to the relationships between the sexes in which she endeavored to combine orthodox modes of thought with insights derived from her own experience. She at first tried to modify psychoanalytic theory in a way consistent with its underlying premises, but she eventually came to question those same premises and rejected their dependence on sex and gender as explanatory principles.[5]

Horney's first four essays on feminine psychology—"On The Genesis of the Castration Complex in Women" (1923), "The Flight from Womanhood" (1926), "Inhibited Femininity" (1926–27), and "The Masculinity Complex in Women" (1927)—were focused on the masculinity complex, defined as "the entire complex of feelings and fantasies that have for their content the woman's feeling of being discriminated against, her envy of the male, her wish to be a man and to discard the female role" (1926–27, 74). Horney also discussed the female preference for the masculine role in several subsequent essays and in lectures on female psychology given in Chicago in May 1933. Her later treatments of the topic tend to be more autobiographical than her earlier ones.

Horney began to write about the masculinity complex in response to Karl Abraham's "Manifestations of the Female Castration Complex" (1920), an essay that recapitulated the psychoanalytic view of women and provided a rich array of illustrations. In her rejoinder, "On the Genesis of the Castration Complex in Women," Horney did not take issue with Abraham's description of the masculinity complex as such, but she was uncomfortable with his explanation of its origin and began to evolve her own "theory of feminine development" in which women would not be seen as inherently defective and inferior to men (1923, 69).

According to Abraham, most women wish to be men because in the early stages of their development they feel at a disadvantage "on account of the inferiority of their external genitals." Because of her narcissism, the young girl does not have a "feeling of inferiority in regard to her own body," so that when she becomes aware of her lack of a penis, she interprets it as "a secondary loss" resulting from castration rather than as "a *primary* defect" (1920, 339–40). She looks upon her genital as a wound and is reminded of her castrated state by such later events as menstruation, defloration, and childbirth.

Once she becomes aware of her lack of a penis, the girl's development is governed by her efforts to compensate for her deficiency. She tells herself that she will eventually be given a penis by her father; when this does not happen, she hopes to receive a child from her father as a substitute. In the oedipal stage, she identifies with her mother, develops an erotic attachment to her father, and becomes envious of her mother's possession of children. After the latency period, her oedipal desires are revived and, in an ideal development, she detaches her wish for a child from her father, seeks a new object for her libido, and becomes reconciled to her passive sexual role. This "normal" development is rare, however, because the woman's sense of having been castrated is reawakened by the vicissitudes of female experience. Most of Abraham's essay discusses the various forms the castration complex takes, both conscious and unconscious.

Horney's quarrel is not with Abraham's account of the forms of the castration complex, but with his contention that it is based solely on the woman's desire for a penis. He assumes, she argues, "that females feel at a disadvantage because of their genital organs," because "to masculine narcissism this has seemed . . . self-evident." For her, his conclusion that the girl *has* a "primary defect" because her external genitals *are* inferior to those of the male amounts "to an assertion that one half of the human race is discontented with the sex assigned to it." This view is "decidedly unsat-isfying, not only to feminine narcissism but also to biological science" (1923, 38). Horney does not question the existence of the female castration complex or of penis envy, but she denies the inherent inferiority of the female sex and the causal relation posited by Freud and Abraham between penis envy and the castration complex.

In explaining why penis envy is common among girls, Horney contends that although the young girl's sense of inferiority is "by no means primary," she is more restricted than boys in "gratifying certain instinct-components that are of the great-est importance in the pregenital period." These include urethral eroticism, the scop-tophilic instinct, and onanistic wishes. Because boys can urinate in a more satisfying way, can see their sexual organ, and are allowed to handle it, the difference "in bod-ily formation may easily give rise to a bitter feeling of injury" and envy of the male in young girls. Their later "repudiation of womanhood" on the ground that "men have greater freedom in their sexual life" is "really based upon actual experiences to that effect in early childhood" (1923, 41–42).

But Horney does not think that penis envy is the true source of the female castration complex. She points instead to identification with the father as a means of resolving the Oedipus complex. Women whose desire to be men is "glaringly evident" have "passed through a phase of extremely strong father fixation" dur-ing which they have taken the father as a love object and desired a child by him. Indeed, these women have fantasized "full sexual appropriation by the father" as a defense against their actual disappointment in him when he does not reciprocate their love. This results in even more bitter disappointment, since they feel that "their fathers had actually once been their lovers and had afterward been false to them or deserted them" (1923, 43–44). Disappointment leads the girl to relinquish the father as a love object and to identify with him instead. Horney explains this process most clearly in a lecture called "Common Deviations in Instinct Develop-ment" (1933),[6] citing the example of a child who dealt with the loss of her pet by pretending to be a kitten herself. In psychoanalytic terms, she made up for her loss by incorporating the lost love-object and playing its role. The girl handles her grief at the loss of her father in a similar way, by identifying with him and pretending to be a male.

When she gives up the father as a love object, the girl also relinquishes her desire for a child by him, and now the pregenital "demand for the penis" is revived in intensified form. The penis envy involved in the castration complex is not the pri-mary penis envy of the pregenital stage but a much stronger one that is the product of the oedipal girl's disappointment in, renunciation of, and subsequent identifica-tion with the father.

Horney posits two "primal" or "basic" feminine fantasies that contribute to the genesis of the castration complex. One is that of having been sexually possessed by the father, the other, of having lost the male genital through a sexual act with him. The fantasy of castration gives rise to the feeling of having been wounded and to anxiety about not being "normally made in the genital area" (1923, 50). In conjunction with the girl's disappointment at having been deserted, this fantasy provides a more powerful explanation of "the revengeful attitude toward men" that characterizes the castration complex than does penis envy and the disappointment of the "expectation that her father would give her the penis as a present" (52).

So far in this essay, Horney has not refuted the idea that one half of the human race is discontented with the sex assigned to it or shown this theory to be incompatible with biological science. Indeed, she presents a dark picture of women's lot. Women are at a disadvantage not only because they suffer from penis envy—both pregenital and postoedipal—but also because they must resolve the Oedipus complex in a way that damages their femininity, whereas men can resolve it so as to reaffirm their gender identity. After feeling deserted by the father, the girl suffers from frustration of her "feminine love attachment," from "feelings of vehement anger and of revenge" directed against her father, and from "feelings of guilt" produced by her "incestuous fantasies" (1923, 50). The boy who identifies with the mother and the girl who identifies with the father both repudiate their sexual roles, but there are powerful forces working against the boy's identification and in favor of the girl's. The boy's identification with the mother is "at variance with his conscious narcissism" and implies the realization of his fears of castration, but the girl's identification with the father "is confirmed by old wishes" for a penis and carries with it "a sense of acquittal" in that it is a defense against oedipal guilt. Females want to be like the opposite sex because "being a woman is in itself felt to be culpable" (53).

Although Horney's rhetoric at the beginning of the essay leads us to expect a version of female development that is more satisfying to feminine narcissism, her account seems bleaker than either Freud's or Abraham's. We must ask what Horney gains by her theory. How has it made her feel better about being a woman and served her own psychological needs?

Horney restores some feminine pride by arguing that at the oedipal stage the girl is disappointed not by the father's failure to give her a penis or a baby but by the frustration of her *feminine* love attachment—by her "wounded womanhood" (51). While the lack of a penis may constitute a real disadvantage in the pregenital phase, it is the frustration of the feminine love attachment to the father that most seriously impairs women's development. Their masculinity complex derives not from a biological inferiority to men but from a state of affairs at the oedipal stage that dooms them to disappointment, regression, and feelings of guilt. They are injured women, not defective males.

There is little doubt that Horney often saw herself in psychoanalytic accounts of the masculinity complex. She considered herself one of those women described by Abraham who sublimated the wish to be male by engaging in "masculine pursuits of an intellectual and professional character" (1920, 347). Horney did not quarrel with the idea that almost all women have some form of masculinity complex but rather showed why this was bound to be the case. She comforted herself, I suspect, by depicting hers as the common lot. She made that fate more romantic and less humiliating by depicting women as victims of disappointment in love rather than inherently defective.

What is most striking about "The Genesis of the Castration Complex" is the emphasis Horney places in it on the father-daughter relationship. This is partly a reflection of standard psychoanalytic ideas about the female Oedipus complex, but there are distinctive features of Horney's version that may have autobiographical significance. While it is true that in her diaries, Horney gives no evidence of a love attachment to her father—although there is plenty of vehement anger and disap-pointment—"The Genesis of the Castration Complex" may take us back to a time in Karen's life when she had "an extremely strong father fixation," such as she ascribes to women whose desire to be men is glaringly evident.[7] She describes the notion of having been sexually possessed by the father as a "primal feminine fantasy"—which suggests that it was a fantasy of hers The fantasy is especially difficult to give up when "the real relations with the parents are . . . unhappy," as they were in her case (43–44).

Horney's essay strongly expresses feelings of having been betrayed, deserted, and grievously injured by the father. Although these feelings are based on the *fantasy* of having had sex with the father, Horney observes that her patients experience the emotions as if a real wound had been inflicted. Karen herself was wounded by her father in an emotional, if not a physical, way. He did not love her when she was a lit-tle girl, he did not help her when she felt excluded by Sonni and Berndt, he discrim-inated against her in favor of Berndt and his sons from his previous marriage, he opposed her academic aspirations, and he made her miserable in countless small ways when she was an adolescent. Even though her patients have not had incestuous relations with their fathers, Horney still holds the fathers responsible for their daugh-ters' wounded state. The complaint of those patients who believe they were raped by their fathers is not that they were sexually abused but that they were deserted.

Is the subtext of the essay Horney's feeling that she would not have developed her masculinity complex, with its concomitant disturbances in her relationships with men, if her father had responded to her need for his love? Did lack of adequate warmth from her father lead to fantasies of incest and damage to her genitals? Is the pessimism that pervades the essay, despite its stirring introduction, a reflection of Horney's feeling that she can find no way out of her difficulties? Is she consoling herself by depicting her plight as the common lot?

In "The Flight from Womanhood: The Masculinity-Complex in Women as Viewed by Men and by Women" (1926), Horney tries once again to modify the psychoanalytic view of women as inherently inferior to men. This time she is both more aggressive and more successful, although her view of the female condition remains bleak. Her argument here is primarily with Freud, although she also takes issue with Helene Deutsch and Sandor Ferenczi. The psychoanalytic view of woman's nature and development is the product of a male genius and a male-dominated culture, she asserts; if we "free our minds from this masculine mode of thought, nearly all the problems of feminine psychology take on a different appearance" (59).

As Zenia Odes Fliegel (1973) has observed, Freud's "Some Psychological Consequences of the Anatomical Distinction between the Sexes" (1925) seems to be a response to Horney's "On the Genesis of the Castration Complex in Women," and Horney's "The Flight from Womanhood" is a reply to Freud's essay.[8] Freud accepts part of Horney's argument in "The Genesis of the Castration Complex," agreeing that "if the girl's attachment to her father comes to grief later on and has to be abandoned, it may give place to an identification with him and the girl may thus return to her masculinity complex and perhaps remain fixated in it" (1925, 195). But he argues for the primacy of penis envy in the girl's development by insisting that her wish for a child is a response to her disappointment at not having a penis and that it is this wish that leads her to take her father as a love object. For Freud, as for Abraham, women are castrated creatures whose development is determined by their need to compensate for the lack of a penis. He further devalues women by arguing that they show "less sense of justice than men" and are "more often influenced in their judgments by feelings of affection or hostility" because they are not forced by the threat of castration to abandon and desexualize their oedipal desires and incorporate them into the superego, as are males. He insists that "we must not allow ourselves to be deflected from such conclusions by the denials of feminists who are anxious to force us to regard the two sexes as completely equal in position and worth" (196–97).

In "The Flight from Womanhood," Horney indignantly maintains that the psychoanalytic view of women is the product of a one-sided male perspective and is therefore distorted and untrustworthy. Citing Georg Simmel, she argues that "ours is a masculine civilization" not because of inferiority in women but because of a "preponderance of force in men"; "the very standards by which mankind has estimated the values of male and female nature" are "themselves essentially masculine." Because of "the man's position of advantage," his conceptions of women have been regarded as objectively valid and adopted by women themselves (55–56).[9]

Not only do women have a tendency to see themselves as men want them to, but they adapt themselves to the wishes of men and then feel "as if their adaptation were their true nature." This adaptation takes place "at so early a period and in so high a degree that the specific nature of a little girl is overwhelmed by it." Women are infected with a masculine point of view, which gives them no chance to develop in accordance with their true natures (56–58).

Analytical psychology is also "under the spell" of the masculine mode of thought. Analytical research prides itself on having been founded upon "the sure ground of experience," but "all experience by its very nature contains a subjective factor." Clinical experience is influenced by the material supplied by patients and the analyst's interpretations of it. Interpretations of feminine psychology have been determined by masculine standards and therefore fail "to present quite accurately the real nature of women" (57–59).

The masculine mode of thought stresses the difference between the male and female genitals but ignores "the other great biological difference," namely the different roles played by men and women in reproduction. Women's capacity for motherhood gives them "a quite indisputable and by no means negligible physiological superiority," and men have a corresponding "envy of pregnancy, childbirth, and motherhood, as well as of the breasts and of the act of suckling." The male envy of motherhood gives rise to an unconscious "tendency to depreciation" that is reflected in Ferenczi's genital theory and in psychoanalysis in general. Men assuage their sense of inferiority by believing that the desire to have a child is really a desire for the penis and that motherhood is a burden they should be thankful they do not have to bear. As long as it is assumed that women actually are defective, we cannot see that "the dogma of the inferiority of women ha[s] its origin in an unconscious male tendency" (59–62).

In response to Helene Deutsch's contention that the masculinity complex in women is much stronger than the femininity complex in men, Horney points out that the "tremendous strength" of men's "impulse to creative work in every field" is "precisely due to their feeling of playing a relatively small part in the creation of living beings, which constantly impels them to an overcompensation in achievement" (61). In spite of their greater ability to sublimate their envy, it is more intense than that of women, which is indicated by the fact that they need to devalue women more than women need to depreciate them.

Horney has, in effect, psychoanalyzed both cultural and analytic attitudes toward women and found them to originate in male envy and feelings of inferiority. Made to feel inferior in childhood because she was a girl, in this essay she proclaims the biological superiority of females, which arouses male envy, hostility, and need to devalue women. That Horney had been brooding on these ideas for some time is shown by her having copied into her diary Adler's statement that he had "not seen a male neurotic yet who did not in some way emphasize the inferiority of women" (UD, April 1911).

So far Horney has challenged psychoanalysis in a fundamental way by questioning its epistemological basis, seeing it as a product of its culture, and ridiculing its phallocentricity. When she begins to advance her own explanation of female development, however, she reverts to conventional modes of psychoanalytic thought and accounts for the girl's adoption of a male view of herself in psychosexual rather than in cultural terms. Although she offers many new ideas, her version of feminine psychology is not as radical a departure from Freud as she has led us to expect.

Just as she had generated a number of different, sometimes conflicting explanations for her fatigue in the fifth diary, so Horney proposes diverse explanations of the masculinity complex in her writings on feminine psychology. In "The Flight from Womanhood," she traces it to "female genital anxiety, which, like the castration dread of boys," bears "the impress of feelings of guilt" because of its association with onanism and incestuous desires. She thinks it probable that the vagina, as well as the clitoris, plays a role in early sexuality because of "the familiar fantasies that an excessively large penis is effecting forcible penetration, producing pain and hemorrhage, and threatening to destroy something" (see also Horney 1933a). Whereas "the boy can inspect his genital to see whether the dreaded" damage is taking place, the girl remains uncertain on this point. In order to escape her anxiety she "takes refuge in a fictitious male role." Fantasies of being a man secure her "against libidinal wishes in connection with the father" and enable her "to escape from the female role now burdened with guilt" (65–67). Women have castration fantasies because when they adopt a male role their feminine genital anxiety is "translated into male terms—the fear of vaginal injury becomes a fantasy of castration." They wish for the restoration of the penis that they imagine themselves to have lost "as a proof of guiltlessness" (69).

At this point, Horney traces the female sense of inferiority not to the dominance of essentially masculine standards but to the girl's flight from oedipal guilt and genital anxiety into the masculine role. She is bound to feel inadequate when she judges herself by "values that are foreign to her specific biological nature." Although her "sense of inferiority is very tormenting," it is more tolerable "than the sense of guilt

associated with the feminine attitude, and hence it is undoubtedly a gain for the ego
when the girl flees from the Scylla of the sense of guilt to the Charybdis of the sense
of inferiority" (67). Horney has arrived once again at a gloomy view of the female
condition.

Culture exacerbates the difficulties produced by the oedipal stage, especially
the girl's sense of inferiority. The relationship between the sexes is one of "master
and slave"; and Horney quotes Simmel's observation that it is " 'one of the privileges of the master that he has not constantly to think that he is master, while the
position of the slave is such that he can never forget it.' " The "disadvantage under
which women labor in social life" is ignored in male-dominated psychoanalytic theory, but "a girl is exposed from birth onward to the suggestion—inevitable, whether
conveyed brutally or delicately—of her inferiority, an experience that constantly
stimulates her masculinity complex." Because the professions have been filled by
men, women have not been able to display their abilities, and so it has "appeared
that there was a basis in fact for their inferiority." Horney sees women as victims of
both biology and culture. Their "unconscious motives for the flight from womanhood are reinforced" by their "social subordination" (69–70).

In spite of its brilliance, there are inconsistencies in "The Flight from Womanhood" that reflect the ambivalences and perplexities of its author and her conflicting
psychological needs. The first half of the essay contains the seeds of her later emphasis on culture's role in sexual roles, but by the end culture is seen only to reinforce the
unconscious motives for the flight from womanhood. Horney proposes, in effect, two
quite different explanations for women's feelings of inferiority. Although she provides a powerful analysis of their social sources, she ultimately explains them primarily in terms of their sexual etiology. Early in the essay she promises to identify
the point at which the female adaptation to the male structure takes place (58). This
turns out to be the point at which the oedipal girl embraces "the fiction of maleness"
in order escape the guilt and anxiety now associated with the female role (67). Horney has conflated Simmel's cultural explanation with a variation of Freud's biological one without seeming to be aware that she has done so.

Her epistemological critique of psychoanalysis notwithstanding, Horney's argument is based upon Freudian assumptions concerning the role of unconscious sexual
factors. She suggests that the psychoanalytic version of the female unconscious is a
projection of male attitudes, but her model is produced by the same methodology
and may be equally suspect. Although she tries to transcend the brainwashing to
which both males and females have been subjected in their thinking about women,
she is unable to free herself from her indoctrination in the psychoanalytic mode of

thought. We see her beginning to develop a skeptical attitude, however, and starting to explore a different way of thinking. In "The Flight from Womanhood," her belief in Freudian psychoanalysis wins out over her doubts.

The essay reflects ambivalent feelings not only about psychoanalysis but also about being a woman. Horney seems to be struggling with her own sense of inferiority and her wish to be a man—to be trying to convince herself that it is really better to be a woman. She seeks to restore female dignity by celebrating motherhood and by insisting that the clitoris is not simply an undeveloped penis but "legitimately belongs to . . . the female genital apparatus." She posits a specifically "feminine form of onanism" and argues that there are "organic vaginal sensations" in the young girl (65), who is a developing woman, not an incomplete male. And she holds "the mutual attraction of the sexes" to be an "elementary . . . principle of nature," not just, for the girl, a product of penis envy (68). The girl's interest in the penis is, rather, an expression of that attraction. Horney's object is to show that girls and women have intrinsic biological constitutions and patterns of development, which are to be understood in feminine terms and not just as products of their difference from and presumed inferiority to males.

As we have seen, however, the essay is far from being an affirmation of the superiority, or even the equality, of the feminine state. Horney depicts women as inherently worse off than men because of the vicissitudes of their psychosexual development. The masculinity complex is "a secondary formation embodying all that has miscarried in the development toward womanhood"—but the development seems bound to miscarry. Horney discovers regression to penis envy owing to the Oedipus complex "not only in extreme cases . . . , but *regularly*" (64).

"The Flight from Womanhood" serves Horney's psychological needs in a number of ways. It provides an outlet for her considerable irritation with Freud and other male or male-dominated analysts over their phallocentricity and devaluation of women. In addition, it feeds her feminine narcissism and restores her feminine pride. Finally, it enables her to explain her own difficulties with the feminine role in a generalized and depersonalized way, as the inevitable result of the female condition. Women have a masculinity complex because of their need to escape the guilt and anxiety that result from their oedipal situation, and they are alienated from their essential feminine natures because of the overwhelming power of the male-dominated culture.

Chapter 11

The Growing Role of

the Mother

Until the mid-1930s, Horney analyzed her problems largely in terms of the masculinity complex and tried to develop an explanation of the concept that would conform more closely to her personal experience than the one found in contemporary psychoanalytic theory. While continuing to subscribe to analytic ideas about the importance of psychosexual stages in human development, she gave increasing weight to cultural factors and to relationships with family members, especially the mother. Thus her discussions of the masculinity complex increasingly came to reflect her own problems and family history. Her theories about feminine psychology changed in response to her clinical experience, her personal needs, and her evolving self-understanding.

"Inhibited Femininity: Psychoanalytical Contribution to the Problem of Frigidity" (1926–27) is much more autobiographical than "The Genesis of the Castration Complex" or "The Flight from Womanhood." Frigidity, as Horney defines it, always involves an impaired relationship with the male that reveals itself "in indifference or morbid jealousy, in distrust or irritability, in claims or feelings of inferiority, in a need for lovers or for intimate friendships with women," and in the incapacity for a love relationship that includes "both body and soul." Almost all these conditions can be found in Karen's diary accounts of her relationship with Oskar after their marriage.

Given what seems to have been her extremely active sex life, it may be difficult to think of Horney as frigid, but she herself notes that frigid women can be "erotically responsive and sexually demanding." They do not reject sex but are reluctant "to assume the specifically female role" (1926–27, 74).[10] Frigidity may disappear under certain conditions, such as "an atmosphere of the forbidden," "the suffering of some violence," and the exclusion of "all emotional involvement" (81). These factors certainly seem to be present in Horney's experience.

Horney attributes frigidity to the masculinity complex, which she describes quite vividly here. Because of her "bitterness against the male as the privileged one," the woman tries to defeat him "or to weaken him psychologically by the thousand means of daily guerilla warfare." We do not know whether this describes her own marriage, but it perfectly fits the relationship of Sonni and Wackels. The woman both "disparages all men" and "regards them as very much her superior." Because "everything is measured against the masculine," there is "a considerable degree of uncertainty even in gifted women whose achievements are both positive and recognized." This uncertainty "may express itself in excessive sensitivity to criticism or in timidity" (75). The self-reference here is unmistakable: Horney (and Clare, for that matter) was a gifted woman who suffered from timidity and sensitivity to criticism.

By inducing frigidity, the masculinity complex compounds the woman's feeling of inferiority, for "at a deeper level" frigidity "unerringly is experienced as an incapacity for love" (76). The woman therefore feels deficient in relation to feminine standards of lovingness as well as to masculine standards of mastery and achievement. Horney introduces here the concept of the vicious circle, which she will use repeatedly: when the woman flees "from the female role into the fiction of the male one" (79), she reinforces her sense of inferiority by measuring herself "by a yardstick intrinsically alien to her" (75). Anticipating her mature theory, Horney points out that we only intensify our self-contempt when we try to escape it by living up to an unrealistic imaginary version of ourselves. She thus identifies the problem of self-alienation, although at this stage of her thought she sees it as a matter of gender.

In her account of the origin of the masculinity complex, Horney covers the familiar topics of penis envy, disappointment in the father, and "gross favoritism of a brother," but she also observes that the girl may "shrink back from her female role" because she perceives the mother as "being raped, injured, wounded, or made ill" by sexual intercourse. "Real brutality on the part of the father and sickness of the mother" may give the child the idea that "the woman's position is precarious and one of danger" (78–79). A favored brother, a brutal father, and a mother made ill by her marital unhappiness were all prominent features of Horney's own history.

In "Inhibited Femininity" Horney attributes the frequency of the masculinity complex, with its accompanying symptom of frigidity, to the fact that our male-dominated culture is "not favorable to the unfolding of woman and her individuality" (82). But this essay was followed closely by "Der Männlichkeitskomplex der Frau" (The Masculinity Complex of Women, 1927),[11] in which she argues that the masculinity complex is independent of culture and hence is "a piece of specifically female psychology." Given her own increasing emphasis on cultural factors in psychological development, we might have expected her to be sympathetic to Adler's position that the masculinity complex is the result of a social situation in which "we instinctively equate male with superior and female with inferior," but she dismisses Adler because he avoids the strenuous "journey into the depths." "The driving force" behind the masculinity complex is "the fear of female sexual experience that arises from early emotional relationships."

This essay differs from its predecessors in emphasizing the girl's fear of the father as her major reason for seeking to escape her female role. Her oedipal fantasies induce an unconscious dread of the father's sexual aggression, which threatens her with genital injury. Although boys also develop anxieties as a result of child-parent conflicts, for the girl "there is the element of 'real danger'" because she is "in fact physically more endangered than the boy due to the formation of her genital apparatus." In "The Genesis of the Castration Complex" Horney had posited primal fantasies of sexual possession by the father that resulted in castration, but her emphasis was on the girl's sense of betrayal and desertion. Here she incorporates into her theory not only the girl's longing for and disappointment in her father but also her fear of him.

In subsequent discussions, Horney continued to cite a father or brother to whom girls "felt tenderly attached and who disappointed them; or a brother who was preferred to them" (1933b, 167–68); but she increasingly emphasized the importance of the relationship with the mother.[12] In "Psychogenic Factors in Functional Female Disorders" (1933b), she speaks of an "infantile hatred" of the mother as "the agency which forbids sex life and sex pleasure" by prohibiting masturbation. She derives her evidence from the transference situation, describing how one of her patients "trembled with fear in the waiting room and emotionally saw in [Horney] something like a ruthless evil spirit." This patient was able to experience full orgasm with her lover only when her analyst, "the forbidding mother," was away, exclaiming "several times in a sort of triumphant voice, 'I have Horney holidays'" (169–70). We cannot determine whether Sonni in fact chastised her daughter for autoerotic activity, although Horney's frequent references to feminine guilt and anxiety about masturbation suggest that she may have done. In any event, Horney's sense of her mother's inimical influence forces itself into her theory and takes an increasingly prominent place there.

The role of the mother is developed more fully in Horney's next essay, "Maternal Conflicts" (1933c). Competition between a mother and a maturing daughter is natural, but it may "start early in the infancy of the daughter" and "take grotesque forms" if "the mother's own Oedipus situation has caused an excessively strong sense of rivalry." Presumably the mother's rivalry with her own mother for the attention of her father has been transferred to her daughter, whom she seeks to outshine in the competition for men. The mother may then "ridicule and belittle" the child, "prevent her from looking attractive or meeting boys, and so on, always with the secret aim of thwarting the daughter in her female development." Such a mother is suffering from her own masculinity complex, which manifests itself in her "domineering attitude" and "desire to control the children absolutely" (179–80).

Mothers who are fleeing from womanhood induce masculinity complexes in their daughters by communicating their dislike of the female role. They teach their daughters "that men are brutes and women are suffering creatures, that the female role is distasteful and pitiable, that menstruation is a disease ('curse') and sexual intercourse a sacrifice to the lusts of the husband." We can easily imagine that Karen received these messages from Sonni. Horney also mentions that such mothers are "intolerant of any sexual manifestations" (1933c, 180), but the denial of sexual pleasure is only one element in inducing masculinity complexes in the daughters. Although she is still working from Freudian premises, Horney has introduced a number of factors that fit her own experience.

Horney again discussed the masculinity complex in an autobiographical way in a lecture entitled "Common Deviations in Instinct Development" (1933).[13] Here the mother is the central figure in the history of women with a masculinity complex. These women are either afraid that the mother will do "something horrible" to them or they have a "terrific hatred" of her, which may manifest itself in overanxiety, a fear that she "will meet with an accident." This overprotective attitude (like that of Karen toward Sonni) disguises a repressed "death wish" against the mother. When the child is "threatened or thwarted by the mother," she reacts with hostility, and her hostility makes her fear her mother's retaliation. One of Horney's vicious circles has been set in motion in which the child's fear adds to her resentment of the mother, her increased resentment intensifies her fear, her fear intensifies her resentment, and so on. Only in this way can "the immense degree of hostility which comes out" be explained. Is Horney trying to understand the intensity of her anger toward Sonni? The girl's fear and hatred of her mother lead her to disavow her feminine role. Because she hates the mother, she does not want to be like her, and because she fears her, she shrinks from being her rival: "I don't want to compete with you or any other woman. I shall avoid competition on the female line. I withdraw there."

Horney contends that all deviations from normal female development involve withdrawing from the female role and wanting to be a man. Women with a masculinity complex often "resent giving in to authority or anything which is conventional" and dislike being "in a dependent situation." They do not want to become "attached emotionally" because attachment means dependency. When they are involved with males, they "try to be aloof, indifferent and in this way maintain the superior role." This analysis could well be describing Karen Horney, a woman who did not submit to the authority of Freud or Abraham, whose sexual behavior was unconventional, and who seems to have needed to attach men to herself while preserving her independence. As we shall see, she often had relationships with younger men or men in dependent positions, which could have been a manifestation of her need to maintain the superior role.

Horney argues that the father as well as the mother may drive women "to a masculine homosexual attitude," and her discussion of the father-daughter relationship also has autobiographical overtones. Often in her clinical experience there appears to have been "no emotional tie" whatever to the father, who has been the weaker partner in the marriage; but "by and by it comes out that there had originally been a very strong, even passionate attraction to the father" and that the girl "had suffered some disappointment from his side." The disappointment may have been an injustice, such as preference for an older brother, unexpected punishment, or an inconsistent attitude on the part of the father. If Karen did in fact accompany her father on one or more of his voyages, she may have developed a sense of closeness to him that was shattered when they returned or when he was unsupportive of her academic aspirations. The girl's disappointment "is expressed over the whole male sex and it drives her away from a love life." The behavior of Wackels and Berndt did not drive Karen away from a love life, but it may have initiated her lifelong fear of becoming too dependent on a man.

The relationship with the mother plays the central role once again in "Personality Changes in Female Adolescents" (1935), Horney's last published essay on feminine psychology. Here she argues that in adolescence girls may develop either homosexual or "boy-crazy" tendencies or they may become "absorbed in sublimated activities" or be "emotionally detached" (234–35). These four types of girls have in common discomfort with the feminine role, which girls dodge altogether, rebel against, or exaggerate. They may show an antagonistic attitude of varying intensity toward men, but their hostility toward women is "absolutely destructive" and is therefore deeply hidden. They complain of the mother's "lack of warmth, protection, understanding, preference for a brother, over-strict demands as to sexual purity" (237); but the most profound source of hostility toward the mother, and toward the woman analyst in the transference situation, is sexual jealousy deriving from the oedipal situation.

In order to understand Horney's argument, we must also draw upon "The Overvaluation of Love" (1934), which was written around the same time. The scope of the girl's hostility toward the mother is revealed when we uncover her masturbation fantasies, which involve "the infliction of injury . . . upon some woman who is imprisoned or humiliated or degraded or tortured or . . . whose genitalia are mutilated" (198). It is the last fantasy that is most strongly repressed and that is the essential element dynamically. It expresses the desire that the mother not have intercourse with the father or children by him lest she "appear hideous and repulsive to all men" (200). Because of the law of retaliation (*lex talionis*) the girl fears that since she wishes her mother's genitals to be mutilated, she too will be mutilated when she engages in sexual activity. Yet she has been engaging in masturbation and therefore feels that she has already been damaged in the ways she has fantasized and is thus as hideous as the mother she hates.

The girl feels both guilt and fear toward the mother. Her guilt is owing to her sadistic fantasies, and she experiences it in relation to masturbation, during which the fantasies have emerged. Because of her guilt, she has expectations of punishment that she later transfers to the analyst, who, she is convinced, "maliciously and intentionally wants to torment" her (1935b, 239). She wards off the fear connected with her guilt by turning against the analyst as she had previously turned against the mother.

Three of the four types of girls that Horney identifies avoid competition with other females because there has been a particularly strong rivalry with the mother or with an older sister. The "boy-crazy type" does compete, but "with an enormous apprehensiveness." Horney lists the factors that have intensified the natural competition with other females in the family: "premature sexual development and sex-consciousness; early intimidations that prevented the girl from feeling self-confident; marital conflicts between the parents, which forced the daughter to side with one or the other parent; open or disguised rejection on the part of the mother; . . . an over-affectionate attitude on the part of the father." With the possible exception of the last, all these were part of Horney's childhood experience, and all but the last appear in the story of Clare. Convinced of their unattractiveness and feeling inferior to other females, the girls Horney describes turn away from their female role and compete with men in "masculine" fields instead of with women. Because they find the masculine role desirable, "they may develop a strong envy toward men with the tendency to disparage their faculties" (1935b, 239–41).

Horney is now deriving the masculinity complex and all the phenomena traditionally associated with penis envy—such as feelings of inferiority, vindictiveness, and competitiveness toward men—from the girl's relationships with other women in the family, particularly the mother. She still mentions "resentment against men, issuing from old disappointments and resulting in a secret desire for revenge" (240), but the mother has replaced the father as the chief source of developmental difficulties.

The conclusion of "Personality Changes in Female Adolescents" strikingly prefigures Horney's later ideas. The four types of adolescent girls she describes represent different ways of warding off anxiety. Some defend themselves by pursuing sublimated activities, some become absorbed in the erotic sphere, some become detached, and some become homosexual. Horney's discussion of the relations between the various types helps us understand why we recognize her in several of them, despite the fact that they are so different from one other. Both what happens to the girls and how their temperaments lead them to process their experiences determines the outcome. In some cases circumstances are so compelling that "only one solution is possible," and then we see one of the pure types; but many girls are "driven by their experiences during or after adolescence to abandon one way and try another." This is what happened in Horney's own development. Her underlying problems derived from childhood and remained much the same, but her defenses changed. Moreover, "one may find different attempts at solution tried simultaneously," creating a "mixture of typical trends" (244). This, too, describes Horney. We see her personality reflected in different facets of her theory because her problems had many causes, for which she employed a variety of conflicting solutions, both simultaneously and in sequence.

By stressing the autobiographical component of Horney's essays, I do not mean to suggest that she wrote only about herself or that everything she said about women was true of her. Some of her explanations seem applicable to her own situation, while others reflect a mixture of received modes of thought and insights derived from her clinical experience. The more she deviated from orthodox theory, however, the more autobiographical her essays became. She was consistently exploring the same kinds of problems, but her interpretations changed as she freed herself from orthodox thought. Her shift from a father-centered to a mother-centered explanation of the masculinity complex was motivated, I think, by her growing recognition of the importance of her conflicts with Sonni, for which existing analytic theory made little provision. The evolution of her thought went hand in hand with her search for self-understanding.

Chapter 12

Relationships between

the Sexes

In addition to her essays on the masculinity complex, Horney wrote a series of essays on the relationship between the sexes. The earlier essays explained problems in general psychoanalytic terms and the later ones became more specific and personal. At first Horney seemed to be trying to understand why her relationships with men had worked out so poorly and to be protecting her pride by universalizing such failures as inescapable. There is a consolatory pessimism in the three essays she contributed to *Ein biologisches Ehebuch* in 1927 ("Psychic Fitness and Unfitness for Marriage," "On the Psychic Determinants of Choosing a Partner," and "The Psychic Origin of Some Typical Marriage Problems") and in "The Problem of the Monogamous Ideal" (1928). In "The Distrust between the Sexes" (1931) and "Problems of Marriage" (1932), Horney displays a growing awareness of how the psychology of the individual contributes to relational difficulties and holds out some hope for amelioration of these problems. These last two essays are more autobiographical.

In the three essays from the *Ehebuch,* Horney describes marriage as having a basically tragic nature because there must always be a contradiction between what it requires and the psychology of the partners (1927d).[14] Men often feel torn between tender and sensual impulses, women are subject to the masculinity complex, and the partners may have conscious or unconscious homosexual trends (1927c). We develop in different ways after marriage, and marriage itself "inevitably leads to disappointments and conflicts that drive us toward other love objects" (1927b). Because people look to marriage for fulfillment of their oedipal desires, they are bound to be disappointed, for the spouse can be only an imperfect substitute for the parent. The dissatisfaction may lead to Don Juanism—the continuing search for the perfect love object (1927c, d). We also carry the incest taboo into marriage, and it either inhibits us in our sexual relations with our partners or punishes us when we enjoy them. In either case, we withdraw our sexual desires from the spouse as forbidden object, just as we had done in childhood, and sublimate our libidos, either directing them toward other objects or suppressing them (1927d).

In "The Problem of the Monogamous Ideal," Horney again tries to normalize her own marital problems and her polygamous behavior by invoking the Oedipus complex. The problem of monogamy arises from the inevitable alienation attendant upon disillusionment and the incest prohibition, and the need to demonstrate potency or erotic attractiveness—as well as tendencies toward homosexuality and the splitting of tender and erotic feelings—lead the partners "involuntarily to seek for new love objects." The pursuit of other love objects comes into conflict with "the partner's demand for a monogamous relation and with the ideal of faithfulness that we have set up for ourselves" (90–91).

Horney's object in this essay is to show that the monogamous ideal is both primitive and unjustifiable. Our wish to monopolize the partner betrays its oral origin in "the greed of possession that not only grudges the partner any other erotic experience" but is also jealous of friends, work, or other interests (1928, 92). We seek to incorporate the partner so as to make him or her entirely ours. Because of its oral nature, the demand for monopoly is stronger in the male, who at least partially incorporated the mother through suckling, whereas the girl has had no corresponding experience with the father. The monogamous ideal also expresses "an anal-sadistic demand for possession" of the woman, who is thus regarded as chattel. It is a revival of "the infantile wish to monopolize the father or mother," a wish that met with frustration, producing hatred, jealousy, and a universal narcissistic scar. Monogamy might be described as "an insurance against the torments of jealousy." Our pride demands an exclusive relationship "with an imperiousness proportionate to the sensitiveness" of our narcissistic injury. The "claim to permanent monopoly" is unjustifiable, for "it represents the fulfillment of narcissistic and sadistic impulses far more than . . . the wishes of a genuine love" (92–94).

Whereas the demand for faithfulness has an instinctual origin, fidelity "represents a restriction of instinct" and is therefore less primitive. It comes more readily to women, for they have already had to resolve their Oedipus complex by abandoning their sexual role—and frigidity has been a common result. "Genital inhibition," Horney proclaims, is an "essential condition of faithfulness." People whose fidelity is of an obsessional character are often suffering from sexual guilt toward the parent owing both to onanistic fantasies involving other partners and to early sexual experiences with siblings, playmates, or servants. For these people unfaithfulness in marriage "would signify a repetition of the old guilt." Another motive for faithfulness is the desire to ensure the partner's fidelity. This involves "fantasies of omnipotence, according to which one's own renunciation of other relations is like a magic gesture compelling the partner likewise to renounce" (95–97).

In the *Ehebuch* essays and "The Problem of the Monogamous Ideal," Horney uses psychoanalytic theory to explain her problems in relating to the opposite sex as normal, inevitable, and insoluble. Marriage has an inherently tragic character; the monogamous ideal is greedy, sadistic, and unworkable. Those who live up to it are genitally inhibited, obsessional, or given to magic gestures. In "The Distrust between the Sexes," she continues to depersonalize disturbances in love relationships by presenting them as "entirely comprehensible, unmitigatable, and as it were, normal" phenomena (1931a, 118).

More than half of "Distrust between the Sexes" is devoted to examining male devaluation and resentment of women from historical, cultural, and anthropological perspectives. Horney's analysis of male attitudes is part of her ongoing effort to free herself and other women from unwarranted feelings of inferiority by showing that the depreciation of women in the dominant ideology is a product of male insecurity. In

"The Dread of Woman" (1932), she argues that men disparage women as a way of dealing with the narcissistic scar they incur as children when they realize the disparity between the size of their penis and the size of the mother's genital. The "dread of [their] own inadequacy, of being rejected and derided" is kept alive in adulthood by their need "to go on proving [their] manhood to the woman," a form of performance anxiety from which women do not suffer, for they can have intercourse and conceive children without ever being sexually aroused (1932a, 142, 145). The male dread of woman, with all its destructive consequences, is an unavoidable result of anatomy.

In spite of the generality of much of the argument, there are passages in "The Distrust between the Sexes" where Horney seems to be expressing her own deepest feelings. "That many-faceted thing called love," she writes, "succeeds in building bridges from the loneliness on this shore to the loneliness on the other one. These bridges can be of great beauty, but they are rarely built for eternity and frequently they cannot tolerate too heavy a burden without collapsing" (1931a, 117). The very intensity of the affects connected with love makes us afraid of them. They "can lead to ecstasy, to being beside oneself, to surrendering oneself, which means a leap into the unlimited and boundless"; but much as we long for this, "we all have a natural fear of losing ourselves in another person," and so "we are inclined to be reserved and ever ready to retreat" (108). This seems to have been Horney's own pattern: a craving for merger, ecstasy, and self-surrender combined with a fear of losing herself or trusting another person, all leading to a series of intense but unstable relationships.

Horney's description of the contradictory nature of women's wishes also seems self-referential: "The partner is supposed to be strong, and at the same time helpless, to dominate us and be dominated by us, to be ascetic and to be sensuous. He should rape us and be tender, have time for us exclusively and also be intensely involved in creative work." Women's belief that the partner can actually fulfill these expectations leads them to "invest him with the glitter of sexual overestimation," and they confuse "the magnitude of [their] expectations" with the greatness of their love. When the partner disappoints them—as he inevitably must—they become distrustful and angry, just as they did when their parents failed to live up to their unrealistic demands. Horney presents these disappointments as an "almost unavoidable" part of "our normal love life" (109), but readers can recognize the contradictions she describes as having undermined the relationships described in her diaries.

The essay seems most autobiographical when Horney explores the relation of childhood experiences to the distrust between the sexes. Because children are "relatively powerless," they must repress their anger and aggression, which are pent up within them "in the form of extravagant fantasies" that "range from taking by force and stealing" to "killing, burning, cutting to pieces, and choking." As a result of the talion principle, children fear that these very things will be done to them by the adults at whom they are angry. Because later love objects are parent substitutes, "the old childhood fears of a threatening father or mother are reawakened, putting us instinctively on the defensive." We are afraid of "what we might do to the other person, or what the other person might do to us" (110). Hence, we are afraid of love.

Horney goes on to discuss how childhood conflicts affect later relationships with the opposite sex. In the girl who is "badly hurt through some great disappointment by her father," the wish to receive from the man is transformed into a "vindictive" desire to take from him "by force." The repressed drive for power over men may be masked by excessive modesty, so that the woman "shies away from demanding or accepting anything from her husband." She reacts with depression, however, "to the non-fulfillment of her unexpressed, and often unformulated, wishes," and this hits her husband "much harder than direct aggression" (111). In her diary Karen had wondered whether she needed her illness to "avenge [herself] on Oskar" at a time when she seemed to have no reason to be angry with him (AD, 241). "Quite often," she notes now, the woman's "repression of aggression against the male drains all her vital energy." Feeling helpless, she shifts responsibility for her plight onto the male and thereby robs him "of the very breath of life" (1931a, 111).

Here Horney seems to be trying to understand her earlier depression and fatigue as products of a repressed aggression against her partner that originated in the hurt she received from her father. Unlike her previous writings, "Distrust between the Sexes" does not present the problems it discusses as universal and inevitable. Horney is beginning to explore her own contribution to the difficulties she experiences with men (unrealistic and contradictory expectations, repressed vindictiveness, and cravings for power) and to see her partners as in some sense victims of attitudes that she brought into her relationships. While much of the rather disjointed essay depersonalizes the problem of the distrust between the sexes, its conclusion emphasizes that childhood conflicts "can vary greatly in intensity, and will leave behind traces of variable depth." Their destructive effects can be ameliorated by psychoanalysis, which can "also attempt to improve the psychological conditions of childhood and forestall excessive conflicts" (118).

In "Problems of Marriage," Horney begins by wondering whether the failure of marriage is unavoidable or whether we are "subject to forces within us, variable in content and impact, and perhaps recognizable and even avoidable" (1932b, 119). While she continues to present as inevitable conflicts between the demands of marriage and human nature, her emphasis here is on "the unresolved conflicts we bring into the marriage from our own development," and she examines which of the factors leading to dislike of the marriage partner can be avoided, which can be alleviated, and which can be overcome (131). Marriages get into trouble because "we so often select an unsuitable partner" (121). Usually the partner does fulfill some of our needs—hence the initial attraction—but we become frustrated and angry because there are others that he or she cannot meet. This problem is compounded by the fact that we often have inner conflicts that generate contradictory expectations, which no partner could satisfy completely.

Some of the examples of contradictory expectations Horney offers indicate that she is once again referring to herself. She mentions women "who are ambitious for themselves and who always want to be on top" but who do not dare to pursue their dreams and want their husbands to fulfill their expectations by being "accomplished, superior to all others, famous, and admired." Some are content to live through their husbands, but others resent their husbands' success because their "own craving for power does not tolerate being overshadowed" (124). Horney rejoiced in Oskar's success in the early days of their marriage, when she was paralyzed by fatigue, but she seems to have an ambivalent attitude toward it later on and to have found his loss of employment and bankruptcy not altogether unwelcome. After his failure, she left him to pursue her own ambition.

Horney also refers to women who "choose a feminine, delicate" husband because of their own masculine attitude but who harbor at the same time "a desire for a strong brutal male who will take them by force." They blame the husband for his "inability to live up to both sets of expectations" and "secretly despise him for his weakness" (124). Karen admired Oskar for his permissiveness but longed for a masterful male who would not tolerate her infidelity.

Horney has moved a long way from seeing marriage as having a basically tragic nature. The dominant theme of "Problems of Marriage" is that the chances of a marriage succeeding depend on "the degree of emotional stability acquired by both partners before marriage" (131). She now recognizes that she brought problems from her childhood into her marriage, that she blamed Oskar unfairly for failing to satisfy her contradictory needs, and that many of her difficulties in relating to men have nothing to do with her partners: "We are inclined to overlook the fact that the decisive factor may well be our own inner attitude toward the opposite sex and that it may express itself in a similar manner in our relationship with any other partner" (125).

As Horney moved away from received psychoanalytic generalizations and toward ideas rooted in the particularities of her own experience, she also moved toward a fuller awareness of her own contribution to her failed relationships. Her essays show a concomitant shift from the resigned, self-exculpating pessimism that characterized her Freudian phase toward the hopefulness of her later theory. If our difficulties are the result of individual development rather than inevitable features of human nature and the human condition, perhaps there is something we can do about them.

Chapter 13

"The Overvaluation of Love"

In a 1991 essay, Marianne Eckardt describes "The Overvaluation of Love: A Study of a Common Present-Day Feminine Type" (1934) as one of her mother's richest and most powerful essays. Whereas Horney's later books "are detached systematic presentations," this essay "puts one in touch with the raw events": "One feels the suffering of defeat, the deathly competitive rivalry, the struggle to find a way out of the driven dilemma, and the power of anxiety" (242).

I too consider "The Overvaluation of Love" to be one of Horney's most powerful essays. It is the culmination of her attempt to analyze herself in terms of feminine psychology. We have little specific information about her personal life during the years she was writing the essays on feminine psychology, but they became the place where she recorded her struggle to make sense of her experience, and they tell us a great deal about her inner conflicts, her patterns of behavior, and her relationships with men. None reveals more than "The Overvaluation of Love."

Although it begins with a sociological emphasis on the conflict in contemporary women between their desire for independent development and a "patriarchal ideal of womanhood," the essay quickly "enters the domain of individual psychology." What, Horney asks, are the predisposing factors that lead *some* women to fall ill from this conflict? (1934, 182, 184). The remainder of the essay focuses on the specific factors in their family histories that are responsible for the problems of the seven patients who constitute Horney's clinical sample, and she seems to recognize by the essay's end that these problems are not as common as her subtitle suggests. Because the essay is devoted to the analysis of women whose family histories, symptoms, and social backgrounds are similar to her own, I suspect that Horney herself is one of the seven women. Perhaps it comforted her to have found patients who resembled her.

All the women in Horney's sample have difficulties in relation to men and to work. They are obsessed by the thought that they must have a lover, but either they cannot connect with men or they engage in "a series of merely evanescent relationships" that show a lack of selectivity. If they achieve a relationship of greater duration, they inevitably undermine it through their attitudes or behavior. They also have serious difficulties in the sphere of work and accomplishment. Although highly ambitious, they are inhibited in using their abilities, which they underestimate, and lack perseverance in pursuing their goals. Their problems in love and work derive from similar psychic sources and are connected because inhibitions in work result in part from the overvaluation of love.

Most of the essay is devoted to trying to explain why its subjects have an obsessive need for a male but are unable to form satisfactory relationships. Their obsession is traced to a childhood situation in which each "had come off second best in competition for a man" (193). It is the typical fate of the girl to be frustrated in her love for her father, but for these women the consequences are unusually severe because of the presence of a mother or a sister who dominates the situation erotically. In most of these cases sexual development is intensified by "exaggerated early experience of sexual excitation" that lays the "foundation for instinctively appreciating . . . the importance of the struggle for the possession of a man" (195).

The girl's awareness of the significance of the struggle, combined with her sense of defeat, generates "a permanent and destructive attitude of rivalry with women." She develops "a feeling of being downtrodden, a permanent feeling of insecurity with regard to feminine self-esteem, and a profound anger with [her] more fortunate rivals." The anger can be so intense that it leads to death wishes and to the masturbation fantasies discussed above involving genital mutilation of the mother. The girl responds to her sense of defeat either by withdrawing from competition with women or by developing "a compulsive rivalry of exaggerated proportions," in which she tries to demonstrate her erotic appeal (195).

The conquest of men provides not only what Horney would later call a "vindictive triumph" but also a way of coping with anxiety and self-hate. The insecure girl develops an anxiety about being abnormal that often manifests itself as a fear that something is wrong with her genitals or that she is ugly and therefore cannot possibly be attractive to men. Such fears have little or nothing to do with reality but are associated with a deep feeling of shame and result in hypersensitivity to any real or imagined defects. As a defense, she may pay an inordinate amount of attention to dress or may wish to be a male. The most important defense is proving that, despite her disadvantages, she can attract a man. To be without a man is a disgrace, but having one proves that she is "normal": "Hence the frantic pursuit." This pursuit is unselective, since "*au fond*, he need fulfill only the single requirement of being a man" (196–98). Horney rejects some of her earlier explanations of the unselective need to conquer a man—homosexual trends, father fixation, and the masculinity complex— in favor of "wounded self-esteem" and rivalry with women as sources of this behavior.

Up to this point, Horney has not traced "the overvaluation of relationships with men" (the true topic of the essay) to unusually strong sexual impulses, but the women in question do display "an excess of desire" for heterosexual intercourse. They often feel that "they cannot be healthy or efficient in their work without it" (202). They assure themselves of the availability of intercourse through "prostitution fantasies" and the wish to be a man—both features of Horney's inner life. Marriage also provides such assurance.

These women are sexually driven, notes Horney, because they have taboos against other kinds of satisfaction, because promiscuous sex proves their attractiveness, and because childhood sexual excitation has left traces of "a pleasure far in excess of that from any other source, and of something strangely vitalizing to the whole organism." They "conceive of sexual gratification as a kind of elixir of life that only men are able to provide and without which one must dry up and waste away." The "lack of it makes achievement in any other direction impossible" (204).

The situation of these women is sad because although their relationships with men are paramount, these liaisons are never satisfactory. They fail because the women are competitive with other women, insecure about themselves, afraid of becoming emotionally dependent, and vengeful toward men as a result of childhood humiliations.

The women's "embittered attitude of rivalry" with other women simultaneously forces them to demonstrate their erotic superiority and causes anxiety at the prospect of doing so. Because they experience "destructive impulses" toward the women who have triumphed over them, they expect those over whom they triumph to harbor similar impulses toward them and are afraid of retaliation. The results of such rivalry run the gamut from women whose anxiety makes them extremely inhibited to those whose need for vindictive triumph turns them into "veritable Don Juan type[s]" (204–05).

Because of the damage to their self-esteem at the hands of mother or sister, even women who seem to have proven their erotic superiority are unable to view themselves as successful. Their triumphs are never "emotionally esteemed as such" (205). Even when "one man after another [falls] in love with them, they are able to conjure up reasons for depreciating their success" (198). This leads to "a rapid change from one relationship to another" (205), as they keep hoping that the next relationship will provide the feeling of worth they seek.

Horney gives a good deal of attention to the phenomenon of rapid change of partners. The women she describes often have the "illusion of being tremendously in love," but they tend to lose interest in a man "as soon as he is 'conquered'—that is, as soon as he has become emotionally dependent on them." They share "a profound fear of the disappointments and humiliations that they expect to result from falling in love," and hence they are afraid of becoming emotionally dependent. Because they have experienced "humiliations" in childhood at the hands of father or brother, they want to make themselves "invulnerable" by avoiding deep emotional bonds. They strive to make men fall in love with them as a way of avenging their earlier rejection. They want "to get the better of a man, to cast him aside, to reject him just as [they themselves] once felt cast aside and rejected" (205–06). Does this help to explain Karen's need to cast Oskar aside early in their marriage?

The only escape from this unsatisfactory situation is through achievement in some other sphere. But the women in Horney's sample, although capable of productive work, are "foredoomed to failure along this path as well": the same problems that undermine their relationships with men prevent them from living up to their potential. They are as pathologically competitive in work as in the erotic sphere. But they are discouraged by both criticism and praise. Criticism touches off their fear of failure, and praise activates their dread of success, which might bring on retaliation from their defeated rivals. Productive activity requires a certain self-confidence, but their "broken morale" has a "paralyzing effect" and deprives them of the courage to pursue their objectives. Because of the conflict between their need to achieve and their lack of self-confidence, they labor under tremendous tension (207–09).

These women turn to work in order to compensate for their sense of failure in the erotic sphere, but work for them becomes so painful that they "are thrust back with redoubled force . . . into the erotic sphere." They dream of obtaining a man's love "by the device of being helpless," through "a magic appeal to [his] pity" (211). If they marry, their own repressed ambition may be transferred to the husband, "so that with the whole momentum of their own ambition they demand that he be successful." At the same time, however, they may regard him as a rival, "in relation to whom they fall into an abyss of feelings of incompetence, accompanied by the deepest feelings of resentment toward him." As a consequence they may be "unconsciously lying in wait" for his failure (208).

Horney's account of problems in work does not seem to fit the productive woman close to fifty years old who wrote the essay, but it fits the Karen of the fifth diary and seems to be yet another effort to make sense of her earlier difficulties. Her tremendous ambition helped her to compensate for her sense of rejection by father and brother and to overcome the damage to her self-esteem inflicted by her mother.

Because she needed to achieve great things but lacked self-confidence, she worked under tremendous tension and was often paralyzed. When she married Oskar, she was extremely proud of his accomplishments, yet her own difficulties worsened as she compared herself with him, and she felt increasingly incompetent. Like her patients, she controlled her partner through her suffering and behaved in ways that undermined him psychologically while lying in wait for his failure.

Horney's prognosis for the women she is describing is very dark. The prospects for a satisfactory relationship diminish because of their emotional difficulties, and they come to regard continued failure in love as inevitable. They feel the "emptiness" pervading their sphere of work more and more acutely, for both economic and psychological reasons. Life lacks meaning for them, and they become bitter as their frustrations mount: "They think that they can be happy only through love, whereas constituted as they are, they can never be, while on the other hand they have an ever-diminishing faith in the worth of their abilities" (212).

Only half of this description fits Karen Horney. What evidence we have suggests that she struggled lifelong with the problems in love that she describes. She was successful in the sphere of achievement, however. In this essay she seems to be presenting the fate of many women and what could have been her own had she not somehow overcome her difficulties in relation to work. But she gives no indication here how these problems can be resolved—indeed, she suggests that they cannot. Her account of the Clare case, as we shall see, is more optimistic.

It is important to recognize that when Horney says that achievement is the only way out of an unsatisfactory erotic situation, she is describing what she would later call a compensatory neurotic strategy rather than a healthy resolution involving self-realization. Here she notes that if one *could* accomplish great things, thereby triumphing over all rivals, that achievement would "build up one's self-esteem" (207). The problem for these patients is that they cannot achieve the necessary triumphs. But Horney will later observe that such victories do not repair damaged self-esteem (any more than do conquests of men). Great accomplishments can leave one still feeling insecure. At this point in her life she wanted to believe in the reparative quality of achievement, perhaps because she was herself pursuing that solution. She argues that "the struggle for achievement" is a far more "trustworthy" source of satisfaction than relationships with men (187).

"The Overvaluation of Love" concludes with an attempt to connect the body of the essay with the social issues raised in the introduction. After having repudiated the idea that the problems she has described result from "the social narrowing of women's sphere of work," Horney endeavors to reinstate the importance of social forces in inhibiting women by a repetition of her formula that "the *frequency* of the type" she has described is explained by social factors, although the type does not seem very common. She may have intended to describe a rather broad phenomenon when she started to write, but the essay turned into a narrow exploration of cases like her own. Here Horney is neither generalizing nor normalizing her problems nor attributing them to social conditions. The "neurotic entanglement" she describes "arises clearly," she insists, "from an unfortunate individual development" (212).

Chapter 14

"We Should Stop Bothering
about What Is Feminine"

As we have seen, when Karen Horney came to the United States in 1932 she identified her given task as a woman psychologist as working out "a fuller understanding for specifically female trends and attitudes in life." She had devoted herself to this effort over the previous decade, and she continued to write essays about feminine psychology for the next several years. In the mid-1930s, however, she stopped writing on this topic and never resumed. Horney's apparent loss of interest in feminine psychology has led some to contend that she was never really a feminist, despite the fact that she was far ahead of her time in her trenchant critique of the patriarchal ideology of her culture and the phallocentricity of psychoanalysis. Janet Sayers argues that although Horney's "rejection of Freud's work in the name of women's self-esteem has certainly inspired many feminists," she herself "was far too much of an individualist ever to engage in collective political struggle—feminist or otherwise" (1991, 93).

Among the unpublished Horney material that I found in Harold Kelman's papers at the Postgraduate Center for Mental Health in New York is a talk she gave to the National Federation of Professional and Business Women's Clubs in July 1935 entitled "Woman's Fear of Action" (see Appendix B). It provides the best explanation of why she stopped "bothering about what is feminine." She was opposed to a continued emphasis on the distinctively feminine because she *was* a feminist and wanted to promote the emancipation of women. She had reached the conclusion that all "we definitely know at present about sex differences is that we do not know what they are." Why we do not know had already been spelled out in "The Flight from Womanhood" and "The Problem of Feminine Masochism" (1935), which emphasize the role of culture in shaping the feminine psyche.

While recognizing the impact of culture, Horney had difficulty integrating it into her thinking. She was increasingly impressed by the writings of sociologists, anthropologists, and ethnologists concerning cultural variation and the role of social forces in the formation of gender identity, but it was not until "The Problem of Feminine Masochism" that she consistently employed a social-psychological perspective. A brief look at this essay will help us to appreciate the significance of "Woman's Fear of Action."

In "The Overvaluation of Love," Horney asks whether the patriarchal ideal of woman "as one whose only longing is to love a man and be loved by him" corresponds to "her inherent character" (1934, 182). That women so often behave in accordance with this ideal has led many people to infer "an innate instinctual disposition," but Horney points out that "biological factors never manifest themselves in pure and undisguised form, but always as modified by tradition and environment." In support of her position, she cites Robert Briffault's contention in *The Mothers* (1927) that "the modifying influence of 'inherited tradition,' not only upon ideals and beliefs but also upon emotional attitudes and so-called instincts, cannot possibly be overestimated" (182–83).

This line of thought is central to her argument in "The Problem of Feminine Masochism," which challenges the idea that "masochistic trends are inherent in, or akin to, the very essence of female nature." This is the position of psychoanalysis, which "has lent its scientific tools to support the theory of a given kinship between masochism and female biology." Horney's object is to refute the arguments of psychoanalysis, especially as developed by Sandor Rado and Helene Deutsch, and to insist on the importance of "social conditioning" (1935a, 214).

Horney's attack on Rado and Deutsch is savagely brilliant, but more important to our present concerns is her critique of both the overgeneralization and the neglect of cultural factors that characterizes psychoanalysis. The conclusion that "women must be almost universally masochistic" because of analysts' experiences with their patients is an "unwarranted generalization from limited data." It follows from Freud's hypothesis that "pathologic phenomena merely show more distinctly as through a magnifying glass the processes going on in all human beings." Because analysts have regularly found the Oedipus complex in patients, they have inferred that it is a ubiquitous phenomenon. This has not been confirmed by the study of "normal" people, and it conflicts with ethnological studies, which "have shown that the peculiar configuration denoted by the term Oedipus complex is probably nonexistent under widely different cultural conditions." We are led to conclude that "this peculiar emotional pattern in the relations between parents and children arises only under certain cultural conditions" (222–23). The same considerations apply to feminine masochism: it is a pathological condition that is not necessarily part of normal femininity, and the frequency of its occurrence is probably the result of social and cultural factors. It has not been established as a universal phenomenon belonging to woman's essential nature.

Horney identifies a number of social and cultural conditions that tend to make women more masochistic than men, but comparative studies show that these conditions have not been universal and that some societies have been more unfavorable to women's development than others. In cultures where the conditions conducive to feminine masochism are present, ideologies develop concerning "the 'nature' of women; such as the doctrines that woman is innately weak, emotional, enjoys dependence, is limited in capacities for independent work and autonomous thinking." Horney includes among these ideologies "the psychoanalytic belief that woman is masochistic by nature." These ideologies "reconcile women to their subordinate role" by presenting it as unalterable and thus lead them to seek fulfillment in the expected ways. In our society, says Horney, "it is hard to see how any woman can escape becoming masochistic in some degree, from the effects of the culture alone" (231).

Writers like Deutsch see cultural complexes as products of the anatomical-physiological characteristics of women and their psychic effects, but Horney disputes this, although she does not deny that there are physiological factors "that may prepare the soil for the growth of masochistic phenomena" in women. These include inferior physical strength; the possibility of being raped; menstruation, defloration, and childbirth; and the female role in intercourse, which is to be penetrated. These biological factors "have in themselves no masochistic connotation for women, and do not lead to masochistic reactions." They may become involved in women's masochistic fantasies, however, and lead to masochistic gratifications "if masochistic needs of other origin are present" (232). Biological factors are secondary and reinforcing rather than determinative. How women experience their physiology is profoundly affected by culture.

Turning to "Woman's Fear of Action," we find Horney reporting that she is frequently asked to identify "the specific trends of female psychology." She can reply only that she hopes one day to be able to do so, for after all the speculation of psychologists we have not moved beyond "the biological differences." Horney feels that there are important differences between the sexes, but she contends that "we shall never be able to discover what they are until we have first developed our potentiali-

ties as human beings. Paradoxical as it may sound, we shall find out about these differences only if we forget about them." Only when women have been freed from the
conceptions of femininity fostered by male-dominated cultures can we discover how
they differ from men psychologically. Our primary objective must not be to identify
what is distinctively feminine but to foster "the full development of the human personalities of all for the sake of general welfare."

Horney argues that emphasizing sexual differences is a political act that has
deleterious effects upon women. In cultures where "women were seriously granted all
opportunities" for development, "there was no interest in special features of feminine psychology." An increasing interest in sexual differences "must be regarded as
a danger signal for women, particularly in a patriarchal society where men find it
advantageous to prove on biologic premises that women should not take part in shaping the economy and the political order." When jobs are scarce, as they were in the
mid-1930s, men contend that "it is in absolute accord with woman's 'nature' that she
keep out of competitive fields of work and remain restricted to emotional fields of
life, concerning herself with charity, sexuality, and child bearing."

Most of "Woman's Fear of Action" is devoted to the effects these views of the
woman's nature have on women themselves. They become "leaning and dependent"
and "often regard professional pursuits as secondary to love and marriage." Such
behavior tends to confirm the male ideology; yet, Horney points out, individuals in
any group that has been suppressed for a long time undergo "a psychic adaptation
which brings them to accept the limitations which the dominant group finds it
advantageous to impose." Although "great changes have come about" in recent
years, "psychic effects of the long history of restriction linger." These effects
include the overvaluation of home, children, sexuality, and love; the cult of beauty
and charm; and the fear of losing erotic attractiveness through age. As in "The
Problem of Feminine Masochism," Horney here explains in cultural terms many of
the phenomena she had attributed to individual psychology in "The Overvaluation
of Love."

The central point of the essay is that the psychic effects of cultural attitudes
toward woman's nature keep her from "becoming genuinely and actively concerned
with the great economic and political questions of our time, even when these broader
interests concern woman's own position in the world and should be of vital interest
to her." Women have not been more active in improving conditions for themselves
because "such action was outside the magic circle into which [their] existence was
confined." The cult of beauty and charm has induced a "fear of being 'unfeminine,'"
that is, of holding "any attitude or belief that [stands] in opposition to masculine
ideas about the divine order of things." This often unconscious fear has led to a lack

of interest in important social movements, including the "struggle for improvement in the position of women."

The "restriction of women to a private emotional sphere" has fostered feelings of inferiority: women have not been able to earn self-respect through achievement, and "self-confidence built on success in giving and receiving love is built on a foundation too small and shaky." Given the cultural climate, "every woman who fights for the opportunity to realize her potentialities as a person exposes herself to all kinds of insinuations and ridicule," which threaten her self-esteem. It is true that American women have greater opportunities to play important social roles than Europeans, but the "general self-confidence which is the psychic capital for achievement is not won because a few women have achieved success in competition with men."

Horney is saying, in effect, that the success of individual women—like herself—is not enough to counteract the undermining effects of the culture as a whole. Women need to cooperate, to join in a common cause. Another tenet of male ideology is that there is "something innate in women" that makes it impossible for them to work together; and in fact, women's "long restriction to the emotional sphere" has "made action in solidarity more difficult." They have experienced a "great deal of anxiety and insecurity" in the competition for men, and the resulting hostility has made them wary of each other. Even "the greatest psychologists" have believed that "women were more jealous than men on biological grounds." Although women often have the limitations ascribed to them, these are not "unalterable qualities . . . due to laws of God or of nature" but are, for the most part, "culturally and socially conditioned."

"Woman's Fear of Action" concludes with two appeals. The first is to stop bothering about what is feminine and to focus on developing "our potentialities as human beings." The other is a call for solidarity, "the necessary prerequisite for any great action." It is my belief that Karen Horney could have become a feminist leader had she found a receptive audience, but she was too far ahead of her time.

Part 3

The Break with Freud and the

Development of a New Paradigm

For the decade after her analysis with Abraham, Horney had been a conventional Freudian, but in the early 1920s she began to quarrel with her mentors on the issue of feminine psychology. At first she simply wanted to revise the Freudian version of feminine development, but as she dug deeper into her own experience and responded to new intellectual influences, she moved away from instinct theory and toward an emphasis on family dynamics and culture. Instead of universalizing her problems, she increasingly focused on the specific conditions that she believed had produced them—her relationships with her mother, father, and brother. While recognizing the importance of culture, she had difficulty combining a sociological perspective with the insight into individual psychology to which she had been led by her search for self-understanding. In the mid-1930s, at the end of her Freudian phase, she adopted a more consistent social perspective. She criticized psychoanalysis for emphasizing biology to the exclusion of culture and abandoned her effort to define the "feminine" because she considered how we experience and think about gender to be products of social conditioning.

In the 1930s, Horney published two books that led to her virtual excommunication from the psychoanalytic community, *The Neurotic Personality of Our Time* (1937) and *New Ways in Psychoanalysis* (1939). There she developed her own version of psychoanalysis and subjected Freud's theories to a systematic critique. One of the leading features of Horney's new version of psychoanalysis was its emphasis on the role of culture in the formation of neurotic defenses and conflicts. This was in part a continuation of the sociological orientation that first appeared in her work during the mid-1920s and in part the result of her encounter with different social conditions and patients after she moved to the United States in 1932. It also reflected her receptivity to the work being done in the social sciences. While still in Germany, Horney had begun to cite ethnographic and anthropological studies, as well as the writings of the philosopher and sociologist Georg Simmel, with whom she developed a friendship. As the associate director of the Chicago Psychoanalytic Institute from 1932–34, she met the social scientists Harold Lasswell, Edward Sapir, and John Dollard, and in New York she exchanged ideas with the anthropologists Margaret Mead and Ruth Benedict. The most powerful influence upon her was that of Erich Fromm, whom she had known in Berlin and saw again in Chicago. She began an intimate relationship with Fromm, probably when they both moved to New York in 1934, that was to last for a number of years. One of their mutual friends observed that Horney "learned sociology from Fromm and he psychoanalysis from her" (Rubins 1978, 195).

Horney was a leading figure in what came to be known as the cultural school of psychoanalysis (see Thompson and Mullahy 1957; Mullahy 1948), which included

Erich Fromm, Clara Thompson, and Harry Stack Sullivan. But the emphasis on culture was a passing phase for her. A more important feature of her work of the 1930s was her new version of the structure of neurosis. Horney did not reject the significance of childhood in emotional development, as is sometimes thought, but she emphasized the pathogenic conditions in the family that made the child feel unsafe, unloved, and unvalued rather than the frustration of libidinal desires.

She had been moving in this direction in her essays on feminine psychology. The big leap she made in *The Neurotic Personality of Our Time* was to posit "basic anxiety" as the consequence of pathogenic conditions and to focus on the defenses employed to cope with this anxiety. Because she made basic anxiety rather than the specific conditions that had produced it her starting point, her insights could be applied to a great many people, male and female, with quite different individual histories, not just to women whose backgrounds resembled her own. I believe that this is one of the reasons for her popularity during the last fifteen years of her life and for the continuing appeal of her books.

Horney's increased emphasis on culture also had the effect of making her theory more general, but it was limiting as well, since cultures differ from each other and constantly change. The structure of neurosis as she describes it tends to remain the same in different cultures, however, even though the forms of the defenses and the relations between them vary.

Perhaps the most significant feature of Horney's thought in the 1930s was her focus on the present structure of the psyche. She felt that trying to understand symptoms in terms of their infantile origins was "an endeavor to explain one unknown . . . by something still less known" (*NW*, 146). Instead of interpreting the present in terms of the past, she sought to account for behavior in terms of its function within the existing structure of defenses. She acknowledged that the structure had grown out of the past, but she pointed out that it now had a logic of its own that made it inwardly intelligible, whatever its origin. Although she was building on some of Freud's basic insights, Horney's emphasis on present structure made her theory incompatible with his, and her contribution to psychoanalysis has been undervalued as a result.

In her essays on feminine psychology, the development of Horney's thought seemed to be driven predominantly by her effort to comprehend the genesis of her own difficulties. *The Neurotic Personality of Our Time* and *New Ways in Psychoanalysis* were more influenced by intellectual and clinical considerations, but they still drew on her own experience and reflect a good deal of self-exploration. Her third book, *Self-Analysis,* brings together her search for self-understanding and her new paradigm in a systematic way, as she employs her conception of the structure of neurosis and her synchronic approach in the autobiographical case of Clare.

Chapter 15

The Role of Culture

In the fall of 1935 Horney began teaching at the New School for Social Research, a practice she continued for the rest of her life. Her first course was entitled "Culture and Neurosis." Invited by the publisher W. W. Norton to expand her ideas into a book, she responded with alacrity and submitted a draft at the end of June 1936. She revised the manuscript during her summer holiday in Mexico and put it in the hands of an editor when she returned to New York in the fall. The editing was finished by early December, and by February 1937 Horney was at work on her next book.[1]

Horney and Norton settled on *The Neurotic Personality of Our Time* for the title, although at one point Norton proposed changing it to *The Neurotic Personality* in *Our Time*. Horney resisted, arguing that "neuroses are generated not only by incidental individual experiences, but also by the specific cultural conditions under which we live" and that these conditions determine the "particular form" of individual experiences (*NP*, viii). A person may have "a domineering or a 'self-sacrificing mother,'" but she is the product of specific cultural conditions that determine her effect on her offspring (viii). She later observed that a girl may be adversely affected by her family's preference for a brother, but that this is not merely an accident of her individual lot because "a preference for male children belongs to the pattern of a patriarchal society" (*NW*, 170). Neuroses do not simply occur *in* our time but are consequences *of* it. There is a "neurotic personality of our time" in the sense that many of the problems people have in common are a result of the "specific life conditions" found in our culture. Different "motivating forces and conflicts" will produce different neurotic personalities in other cultures (*NP*, 34).

Horney stressed the importance of culture—not, I think, because of a need to rebel against Freud but because as a woman she had long been conscious of its role in shaping our conceptions of gender. In addition, she had been profoundly impressed by the differences between central Europe and America, and she was thus receptive to the work of such sociologists, anthropologists, and culturally oriented psychoanalysts as Erich Fromm, Max Horkheimer, John Dollard, Harold Lasswell, Edward Sapir, Ruth Benedict, Ralph Linton, Margaret Mead, Alfred Adler, Abraham Kardiner, and Harry Stack Sullivan. In response to these influences, Horney argued that culture is more important than biology in the generation of psychological characteristics and that pathogenic conflict between the individual and society is not inevitable but is rather the product of a bad society.

According to Horney, Freud overemphasized the biological sources of human behavior, assuming that the feelings, attitudes, and kinds of relationships that are common in our culture are universal. Not recognizing the importance of social factors, he attributed neurotic egocentricity to a narcissistic libido, hostility to a destruction instinct, an obsession with money to an anal libido, and acquisitiveness to orality. But anthropology shows that cultures vary widely in their tendency to generate these characteristics. Once we stop regarding culturally conditioned behavior as biologically given, we shall no longer be inclined "to regard the masochistic trends frequent in modern neurotic women as akin to feminine nature, or to infer that a specific behavior in present-day neurotic children represents a universal stage in human development" (*NW*, 169).

The specific behavior Horney has in mind, of course, is the Oedipus complex. Following Bronislaw Malinowski, Felix Boehm, and Erich Fromm, she regarded the Oedipus complex as a culturally conditioned phenomenon. The "destructive and lasting jealousy reactions" described by Freud are the product of "neurotic parents who by terror and tenderness forced the child into these passionate attachments" (*NP*, 84). These parents in turn are the products of their culture, which influenced their upbringing and attitudes toward child rearing. The healthier members of our culture have not suffered from an Oedipus complex, and its incidence can be reduced through social modifications.

For Freud, notes Horney, culture is at once the product and cause of the repression of instincts. Differences among cultures are determined by which instinctual drives are expressed or repressed. Thus capitalism is "an anal-erotic culture," wars are the expression of "an inherent destruction instinct," and cultural achievements in general are "sublimations of libido" (*NW*, 169). Horney sees cultural phenomena as the result of "a complex social process" rather than of repressed or sublimated instincts, and she claims that "historical and anthropological findings" do not support Freud's idea that the more complete the repression of biological drives the higher the culture (*NP*, 283).

Horney did not elaborate a theory of cultural development to set against Freud's. She left that to the social scientists, and after *New Ways* she had little to say about culture. What remained an issue for her was Freud's derivation of neurosis from the clash between culture and instinct. In Freud's view, we must have culture in order to survive, and we must repress or sublimate our instincts in order to have culture. Since happiness lies in the full and immediate gratification of our instincts, we must choose between survival and happiness. Sublimation gives us a measure of satisfaction, but our capacity for it is limited. Because "the suppression of primitive drives without sublimation" leads to neurosis, neurosis is the price we have to pay for cultural development (*NP,* 283). The inevitable clash between instinct and culture is internalized and becomes an unresolvable conflict between "untamed passions" and "moral standards." Horney does not believe that we collide with our environment as inevitably as Freud assumes. When there is a collision, "it is not because of [our] instincts but because the environment inspires fears and hostilities" (*NW,* 191).

For Horney, then, there is no necessary conflict between civilization and human nature. In her critique of *Civilization and Its Discontents* she argued that there is no "innate destructive instinct"; rather, "analytic examination" shows "thoroughly adequate grounds for overt and covert hostility," which "disappears when these grounds are removed" (1931b, 136). In *Neurotic Personality* and *New Ways* she contends that we are not inherently insatiable, destructive, or antisocial; these are neurotic responses engendered by bad conditions. Later, in *Our Inner Conflicts* and *Neurosis and Human Growth,* she proclaims that we have the capacity for benign self-fulfillment, given a nurturing environment. If our reasonable needs for safety and satisfaction are frustrated, we become unhappy, defensive, and destructive, with the severity of our neurosis depending upon the extent of our deprivation.

Chapter 16

The Structure of Neurosis

In *The Neurotic Personality of Our Time,* Horney develops a new paradigm for the structure of neurosis. She is not concerned with neuroses caused by particularly stressful situations but with those in which "the main disturbance lies in the deformations of the character." The term *neurosis* having been abandoned by the *Diagnostic and Statistical Manual of Mental Disorders* of the American Psychiatric Association (DSM-III) in 1980, Horney's use of it has become outdated. Readers who prefer the current terminology can think of Horney as describing personality disorders of the type discussed in DSM-III, Axis II (see Millon 1981).

As we have seen, Horney traces neuroses (or personality disorders) to pathogenic conditions in the family that make the child feel unloved, unvalued, and insecure. These disturbances in human relationships generate "basic anxiety," a feeling of being helpless in a potentially hostile world, as a result of which children develop overwhelming needs for safety and reassurance. They try to satisfy these needs by adopting such defensive strategies as the pursuit of love, power, or detachment; but the strategies initiate vicious circles that intensify rather than reduce anxiety. The strategies are incompatible with each other, moreover, and create painful inner conflicts that generate new difficulties. Horney developed and refined this model of neurosis in her subsequent books but did not alter its basic features.

Although Horney's primary focus is on "the actual structure of the neurotic personality" rather than on the individual experiences leading up to it, she pays a good deal of attention to childhood as the source of basic anxiety. She does not believe that neurosis is bound to develop, for the child's needs are not inherently insatiable or in conflict with reality. They become so only in the absence of loving parents and a fostering environment. Often parents lack warmth and affection because of their own neuroses, which lead them to act in ways that impair the child's development and arouse great hostility. Their behavior might include "preference for other children, unjust reproaches, unpredictable changes between overindulgence and scornful rejection, unfulfilled promises," and lack of respect for the child's needs and preferences (NP, 79–80). Frustration of the child's sexual desires may be a factor in arousing hostility, but Horney feels that this has been overemphasized in psychoanalysis and that, in general, "the spirit in which frustrations are imposed" matters more "than the frustrations themselves." Children can accept a good deal of frustration if there is an overall atmosphere of love. The Oedipus complex is a product of the anxiety aroused by neurotic parents rather than of libidinal attachment (NW, 82–84).

In New Ways in Psychoanalysis Horney introduced the idea of "the spontaneous individual self," later called the "real self," and began to see as perhaps the greatest tragedy of childhood the loss of contact with this self as a result of parental oppression. Authoritarian or self-righteous parents create a situation in which children feel "compelled to adopt their standards for the sake of peace"; self-sacrificing parents make children feel they have no rights of their own and should live only for their parents' sake; ambitious parents make children believe themselves to be loved for imaginary qualities rather than for their true selves. Other self-alienating conditions include "direct blows to the self-esteem, derogatory attitudes of parents who miss no opportunity to make a child feel that he is no good, [and] the parents' preference for other siblings, which undermines his security and makes him concentrate on outshining them." This list reminds us of the conditions of Horney's own childhood. The child comes to feel that in order to be accepted and liked he must live up to the expectations of others. The parents "have so thoroughly superimposed themselves" on his mind that "he complies through fear, thus gradually losing what [William]

James calls the 'real me.' His own will, his own wishes, his own feelings, his own likes and dislikes, his own grievances, become paralyzed" (91–92).

As a result of adverse conditions, the child comes to dread the environment as a whole, which he feels to be "a menace to his entire development and to his most legitimate wishes and strivings. He feels in danger of his individuality being obliterated, his freedom taken away, his happiness prevented" (75). This is not an imaginary danger, says Horney, like the fear of castration, but a threat that is based in reality. Feeling so menaced, the child develops a basic distrust of the environment and a basic hostility toward it.

Horney places a great deal of emphasis not only on children's hostility but on the pressure they are under to repress that hostility and on the consequences of the repression. Psychologically endangered children deeply resent the way they are treated but are afraid to express their outrage because they desperately need their parents and fear retaliation. Moreover, in a culture in which parents are invested with great authority, there is a powerful taboo against breaking their rules or criticizing them, and children are forced to feel guilty for either feeling or expressing anger. It may be unfortunate when children have to battle their parents, but not fighting means living a life of pretense and reinforces children's feelings of helplessness.

Repressed hostility does not disappear but is "split off": it becomes "highly explosive and eruptive, and therefore tends to be discharged" (67)—as was Karen's anger toward Sonni in her twenty-first year. We "register" our rage, knowing that "it is there without being consciously aware of it," and repress it all the more because it feels dangerous (68). To deal with this frightening affect, we project it outward, imagining that "the destructive impulses come . . . from someone or something outside." When we project our hostility onto those with whom we are angry, imagining that they want to do to us what we want to do to them, they assume "formidable proportions" in our minds, increasing our sense of defenselessness and rage (70). Our projection not only increases but also justifies our anger, for we have a right to be vindictive toward those who have ill-will toward us. Horney still seems to be trying to understand the intensity of her dread of and animosity toward Sonni.

The most serious consequence of repressed hostility is an intensification of anxiety. Freud thought that sexual impulses were the dynamic force behind anxiety, but Horney contends that hostile impulses are "the main source from which neurotic anxiety springs" (63). Children become anxious because their needs are not being met and they feel menaced in their development. This provokes a reactive hostility that, when repressed and projected, increases their sense of inner weakness and external threat, thereby intensifying anxiety. As they become more afraid of themselves and others, angrier with those by whom they feel threatened, and more anxious because of their anger, a vicious circle develops of ever-increasing anxiety and hostility. In view of these dynamics, we do not need the hypothesis of a death instinct to explain why "we find in neuroses such an enormous amount of relentless hostility" (74).

The child's reactions to provocations crystallize into a feeling that Horney calls basic anxiety. It is "a feeling of being small, insignificant, helpless, deserted, endangered, in a world that is out to abuse, cheat, attack, humiliate, betray, envy" (92). Basic anxiety may be "divested of its personal character and transformed into a feeling of being endangered by thunderstorms, political events, germs, accidents, canned food, or [this applies to Horney] to a feeling of being doomed by fate" (94). In the grip of basic anxiety, people are caught between a desire to escape emotional isolation by getting close to others and a fear of betrayal that makes it impossible to do so. They want "to be protected and taken care of" (96), but their hostility and distrust make them afraid to rely on anyone else.

Basic anxiety resembles "normal" kinds of anxiety, but it is essentially different from them. After disillusioning experiences, "normal" people will become "reserved" and "cautious," but they will not feel helpless and begin mistrusting others indiscriminately. Basic anxiety differs from *Angst der Kreatur,* the anxiety caused by being at the mercy of "forces more powerful than ourselves, such as death, illness, old age, catastrophes of nature, political events, accidents" (94), which shares the element of helplessness but does not attribute hostility to the more powerful forces. In basic anxiety "the helplessness is largely provoked by repressed hostility, and what is felt as the source of dangers is primarily the anticipated hostility of others" (203).

In order to deal with basic anxiety, we develop methods of coping designed to provide safety and reassurance. Horney calls them "protective devices" and "neurotic trends" in *Neurotic Personality* and "defensive strategies" in *New Ways*. In our culture, she says, there are four principal ways in which people try to protect themselves: "affection, submissiveness, power, withdrawal" (*NP,* 96). She identifies the two drives that "factually play the greatest role in neuroses" as "the craving for affection and the craving for power and control" (105), and she devotes most of *Neurotic Personality* to a discussion of them.

Horney is careful from the beginning to distinguish between "normal" and neurotic forms of the wish for love, the tendency to comply, the striving for success, and the tendency to withdraw. These tendencies "are present in all of us in various combinations, without being in the least indicative of a neurosis," and one or another may predominate in a culture: "mothering care and compliance" characterize the Arapesh, for example, while striving for prestige distinguishes the Kwakiutl, and withdrawal from the world is a dominant trend in the Buddhist religion. When motivated by a direct wish for satisfaction, we will display "spontaneity and discrimination" in relating to others, but if we are driven by anxiety, our behavior will be "compulsory and indiscriminate" (*NP*, 102–04).

Searching for affection is "the most logical and direct way" of coping with the feeling of being alone and helpless in a menacing world (106). In the neurotic search for affection—as distinct from love—people cling to others to satisfy their own needs. There is no reliability or steadiness to their feeling, and they experience a ready revulsion when their wishes are not fulfilled. Unaware of their incapacity for love, they have the illusion of being loving people. Giving up this illusion "would mean uncovering the dilemma of feeling at once basically hostile toward people and nevertheless wanting their affection" (110–11).

The neurotic need for affection is also characterized by compulsiveness, indiscriminateness, an overvaluation of being liked, and an incapacity to be alone. People in the grip of this need "have the feeling of drifting forlornly in the universe, and any human contact is a relief to them" (117). They are excessively compliant, self-abnegating, and emotionally dependent. They blame their enslaved condition on others, but their hostility increases their anxiety, causing them to cling to others all the more. The fear of being rebuffed may lead them to avoid exposing themselves "to any possibility of denial," from which excessive timidity (one of Horney's early traits) often results (136). The insatiability of the neurotic need for affection leads to jealousy and the demand for unconditional love. Whereas a healthy child, growing up in an atmosphere of warmth and reliability, does not require "constant proof of the fact" that he or she is wanted, the neurotic need for affection can never be assuaged (123).

Horney insists that the characteristics of the neurotic need for affection are not childish traits that the adult has failed to outgrow but pathological states brought on by adverse conditions in his or her environment. When we find such traits in children we know they have been made anxious by a lack of love in the family and are seeking security and reassurance. When we find them in adults it is because they have developed character neuroses as a result of being unloved as children.

The defenses Horney describes are doomed to failure. The frustration of the need for love makes the desire insatiable, and the demandingness and jealousy that follow make it less likely than ever that the person will receive affection. People who have not been loved develop an irreversible feeling of being unlovable because they discount any evidence to the contrary and assume that any offer of affection comes from ulterior motives. Being deprived of affection has made them dependent on others, but they are afraid of that dependency, which makes them too vulnerable.

"The situation created in this way is similar to that of a person who is starving for food yet does not dare to take any for fear that it might be poisoned" (114). This was Horney's dilemma, I think.

The search for affection cannot succeed because, as with the other protective devices, "the very means which serve to reassure against anxiety create in turn new hostility and new anxiety." According to Horney, these vicious circles represent "one of the most important processes in neuroses," as well as the main reason why "severe neuroses are bound to become worse, even though there is no change in external conditions." The individual cannot grasp their dynamics but "notices their results in the form of a feeling that he is trapped in a hopeless situation" (138). Uncovering patterns of self-defeating behavior is one of the main goals of analysis.

Although the neurotic need for affection often takes the form of an insatiable sexual hunger, it is also present in people whose sex lives are satisfactory from a physical point of view. Frustrated libido cannot account for such symptoms as possessiveness, the demand for unconditional love, and sensitivity to rejection. Horney believes that "a great deal of what appears as sexuality has in reality very little to do with it, but is an expression of the desire for reassurance" that springs from basic anxiety (157–58). To a person hungry for love, sexual relations might seem "the only way of getting human contact" (153). This is especially true for people who have despaired of obtaining genuine affection.

In spite of her own drivenness in relating to the opposite sex, Horney took a strong stand against ascribing a sexual etiology to neurosis. She stated her position most succinctly in *New Ways in Psychoanalysis,* where, repudiating the idea that sexual problems are "the dynamic center of neuroses," she proclaimed that they "are the effect rather than the cause of the neurotic character structure" (10). This is how Horney had come to see her own difficulties. Neuroses are "the ultimate outcome of disturbances in human relationships," disturbances that "must of necessity appear in every relationship, sexual or non-sexual" (65).

Horney devotes most of *The Neurotic Personality of Our Time* to the neurotic need for love, no doubt because she had been wrestling vigorously with this problem for some time. She also focuses on the quest for power, prestige, and possession that develops "only when it has proved impossible to find reassurance for the underlying anxiety through affection" (*NP,* 163–64). The quest for power seeks reassurance against helplessness and expresses hostility in a tendency to domineer; the quest for prestige seeks reassurance against humiliation and expresses hostility in a tendency to humiliate; and the quest for possession seeks reassurance against destitution and expresses hostility in a tendency to deprive. Each of these quests sets in motion a vicious circle. Freud and Adler had discussed these trends, but neither had recognized the role that anxiety plays in bringing them about or the "cultural implications" of the forms in which they are expressed (187).

Power, prestige, and possession can be pursued in ways that issue from strength and a normal desire to have some control over one's life, but the neurotic strivings for these objectives are "born out of anxiety, hatred and feelings of inferiority" (163). Neurotically aggressive people constantly measure themselves "against others, even in situations which do not call for it." They need to outstrip everyone else, "to be unique and exceptional"; "it is more important for [them] to see others defeated than to succeed" themselves (189, 192–93). The normal striving for power, prestige, and possession can bring some measure of satisfaction, but the neurotic quest is insatiable, like the neurotic need for affection. No amount of success can make neurotically aggressive people feel safe, secure, or happy about themselves.

The destructive impulses involved in the neurotic pursuit of power, prestige, and possession also operate in the relationship between the sexes, where the "tendencies to defeat, subdue, and humiliate the partner play an enormous role." Horney now attributes the split in the love life of the male to the boy's humiliation by the mother, whom he wants to humiliate in return, but whom he fears, so that he hides his hostility "behind an exaggerated devotion." Since intercourse is coupled in his mind with his desire to humiliate, he represses his sexual desires toward women he loves, although he is free to express them with women he does not respect. He shows his hostility toward women he loves by "frustrating them" (197–98).

A woman, too, may have an "unconscious tendency to degrade the partner." The reasons Horney cites all seem autobiographical: "resentment toward a preferred brother, contempt for a weak father, conviction of not being attractive and hence anticipating rejection from men." A girl who is intent upon subduing and humiliating men may start a love affaire "with the frank motivation of getting the man under her thumb," or she may "attract men and drop them as soon as they respond with affection" (199).

Both men and women may cover up their "disparaging or defeating drives" with "an attitude of admiration." Men who secretly want to hurt and spurn women might put them on a pedestal, while women who try to defeat and humiliate men "may be given to hero worship." In the hero worship of the neurotic woman there is "blind adoration of success," because she longs for it herself, although that wish is combined with a desire to destroy the successful person (201–02).

In showing how this explains some typical marriage conflicts, Horney describes, I think, her relationship with Oskar. If a woman marries a man "because his existing or potential success appeals to her," she may be gratified as long as the success lasts; but she is full of conflict, for she also hates him for his achievement and wants to subvert it. She may betray her resentment by destroying her husband's equanimity through enervating quarrels and by undermining his self-confidence through an insidiously disparaging attitude. Her resentment will become more manifest at any sign of failure. Although she may have appeared a loving wife while he was successful, "she will now turn against her husband instead of helping and encouraging him, because the vindictiveness that was covered up as long as she could participate in his success emerges into the open as soon as he shows signs of defeat" (202–03). Hence Karen's callousness toward Oskar when he lost his position and almost died of meningitis. Horney seems once again to be assessing her own contribution to the failure of her marriage.

A further discussion of hero worship in *Neurotic Personality* adds to our sense of Horney's contradictory needs and helps explain why she never found a man who could satisfy them. In women who need to dominate, there is often "a queer contradiction" that "may considerably frustrate any love relationships." They cannot love a "weak" man because they despise weakness, but they cannot "cope with a 'strong' man because they expect their partner always to give in." What they "secretly look for is the hero, the superstrong man, who at the same time is so weak that he will bend to all their wishes" (170).

An important part of Horney's conception of the structure of neurosis is that conflict occurs not only within but between defensive strategies. Usually people try to cope with basic anxiety in several incompatible ways. They may "at the same time be driven imperatively toward dominating everyone and wanting to be loved by everyone, toward complying with others and imposing [their] will on them, toward detachment from people and a craving for their affection." This generates "insoluble conflicts which are most often the dynamic center of neuroses" (100–101).

Neurotic people are often compulsively competitive, yet they frequently recoil from competition because it arouses tremendous anxiety. The anxiety has several sources, including fear of retaliation and fear of losing affection. Being caught between ambition and affection is "one of the central conflicts in neuroses"—Horney will later call it the "basic conflict"—and it leads to both "a fear of failure and a fear of success" (208, 210). Some people respond to this dilemma by justifying their drive for dominance and redoubling their efforts to succeed, while others check their ambition, withdrawing from effort so that they will neither fail nor risk rejection. Approaching an anxiety-arousing examination, a person may "work very little and . . . perhaps conspicuously indulge in social activities or hobbies, thus showing to the world his lack of interest in the task" (212). Again, this sounds like Karen.

Compulsively inhibited people "may do excellent work but shrink from evidence of success" (216). They tend to belittle themselves, taking their feelings of inferiority at face value and insisting on their validity. Horney describes, for example, the girl who develops an inordinate ambition at school after humiliating experiences with her brother: she was "always first in her class and was regarded by everyone as a brilliant student, but was still convinced in her own mind that she was stupid." A woman to whom much attention has been paid by men "may still cling with an iron conviction to the belief that she is unattractive" (218). The function of these feelings of inferiority is to curb ambition and thereby allay the anxiety connected with competitiveness.

Another source of these feelings in ambitious people is their exaggerated notion of their own value and importance. Because their real achievements can never measure up to their "notions of being a genius or a perfect human being," they feel inadequate (221). The discrepancy becomes so unbearable that they take refuge in grandiose fantasies that cover up "unendurable feelings of nothingness" and allow them "to feel important without . . . incurring the risk of failure or success" (223). Their fantasies make them all the more vulnerable to feelings of inferiority, however, since, unlike psychotics, they "cannot help registering with painful accuracy all the thousand little incidents of real life which do not fit in with [their] conscious illusion." They easily feel slighted or hurt, react with vindictive resentment, and waver between "feeling great and feeling worthless" (225). All this contributes to yet another vicious circle (see 227).

The basic features of Horney's mature theory are present in the paradigm for the structure of neurosis that she developed in her first book. Disturbances in human relationships generate a basic anxiety that leads to the development of strategies of defense. Horney concentrates on the pursuit of love and mastery here, but she also mentions detachment, and in *New Ways* she adds narcissism and perfectionism to her taxonomy of interpersonal strategies. In her first two books, she also introduces intrapsychic strategies, such as self-inflation, self-recrimination, neurotic suffering and guilt, and overconformity to standards. These will be more fully developed later. Her early paradigm for the structure of neurosis includes the self-defeating character of the defensive strategies and the clash of the solutions with each other, which results in insoluble conflicts. These conflicts are especially important in her analysis of the relation between culture and neurosis.

Chapter 17

Culture and Neurosis

Although she begins by emphasizing the importance of culture, Horney devotes most of *The Neurotic Personality of Our Time* to developing her paradigm for the structure of neurosis. Not until the final chapter does she discuss how culture produces neurotic personalities. She is also concerned with the impact of culture upon our conceptions of what is "normal" and what is "neurotic." Is there a universal human nature and a standard of mental health that can be derived from it, or should our conception of normality vary with culture? By *normal* do we mean what is desirable or what is typical in a given culture? Horney establishes a culturally relativistic position in *Neurotic Personality,* but in *New Ways* and "What Is a Neurosis?" (1939c), she begins to develop a conception of psychological health in terms of which cultures can themselves be evaluated.

In *Neurotic Personality* the feature of American culture that Horney holds most responsible for generating neurotic trends is its emphasis on competition. In the economic sphere the individual has to fight with others, to surpass them, and frequently to thrust them aside. Competitiveness pervades interpersonal relationships as well. Women compete with each other for the attention of men, and men and women seek mates who will enhance their wealth, power, or prestige. Once married, they engage in a struggle for dominance. There is culturally induced rivalry "between father and son, mother and daughter, one child and another" (*NP,* 285). Because of the competitive atmosphere in which we live, we are constantly in fear—of the hostility of others and of our own hostility, which will provoke their retaliation. We dread failure and feel that we amount to something only when we are "successful."

The combination of competitiveness, hostility, strained human relationships, and shaky self-esteem creates both an exaggerated need for love and great difficulty in giving and obtaining it. Love becomes "a phantom—like success—carrying with it the illusion that it is a solution for all problems" (287). We expect so much from love that we are bound to be disappointed.

There are contradictions in our culture that engender neurotic conflicts, like the one between "competition and success on the one hand, and brotherly love and humility on the other." Because of our need for success, we are driven to push others out of the way, but we are also deeply imbued with "ideals which declare that it is selfish to want anything for ourselves." As a result of this contradiction, we tend to be "seriously inhibited in both directions." Through advertising and an ideology of conspicuous consumption, the culture stimulates our economic appetites, but most of us are unable to satisfy our cravings. This produces a constant discrepancy between desire and fulfillment. There is also a contradiction between "the alleged freedom of the individual and all his factual limitations." We are given the message that we can achieve what we want through efficiency and energy, but in reality we are subject to restraints and contingencies. As a result, we waver between "a feeling of boundless power" and "a feeling of entire helplessness" (288–89).

The contradictions in our culture correspond exactly to the conflicts characteristic of the neurotic personality of our time: "tendencies toward aggressiveness" and "tendencies toward yielding," "excessive demands" and the "fear of not getting anything," strivings toward "self-aggrandizement" and "feeling[s] of personal helplessness" (289). Horney thus connects culture to the account of neurosis developed in the body of *Neurotic Personality,* but with a major inconsistency. She observes early in the text that the quest for power, prestige, and possession usually results from the frustration of the need for affection, and she traces that need to disturbances in family relationships (163–64). In her analysis of the contribution of culture to neurosis, however, she reverses the causal relationship, presenting the need for affection as a product of the feelings of isolation, insecurity, and shaky self-esteem induced by a competitive society. There is confusion as to whether the need for affection or competition is primary.

Horney's examination of the relation between culture and neurosis is suggestive but underdeveloped (see Young 1938; Brown 1937). She claims that pathogenic conditions in the family are reflections of the culture but does not show how they are connected (see Green 1946). Franz Alexander noted the lack of precision and detail in Horney's analysis but argued that she should not be blamed for it because "sufficient observations" regarding the topic "do not exist" (1937, 536–37). We must remember that Horney was in the vanguard of those who wanted to bring a cultural perspective into psychoanalysis. She denied a wish "to trespass on the sociological domain" (*NW*, 173) and looked to others to flesh out her ideas.[2] As Ruth Benedict observed in her review of *Neurotic Personality,* Horney raised a number of fruitful issues "demanding the cooperation of students of social problems and of individual psychology" (1938, 135).

Horney herself did not contribute much more to this cooperative venture. Her great gift was not for exploring the relations between cultural conditions and individual psychology but for analyzing the intricacies of interpersonal and intrapsychic dynamics. Perhaps it was because she recognized this that she had little to say about culture in her later books.

In *The Neurotic Personality of Our Time* Horney defines neurosis as relative to culture. The normal, she initially argues, is that which conforms to patterns of behavior that are usual and accepted in a given society; the neurotic is what deviates from those patterns. Since what is normal in one culture may be neurotic in another, "there is no such thing as a normal psychology, which holds for all mankind" (19). Thus it is normal to be competitive in mainstream American culture, but competitiveness would be abnormal for a Pueblo Indian, an artist living in a village in southern Italy or Mexico, or an ancient Greek (14). There are variations within cultures as well, in different time periods and social classes. And there are gender variations, since men and women in the same culture are often judged differently for similar behavior.

In addition to being deviations from patterns of behavior regarded as normal, neuroses have distinguishing features, such as a "lack of that flexibility which enables us to react differently to different situations." Rigidity is indicative of a neurosis, however, "only when it deviates from the cultural patterns," for there can be a "normal rigidity," like the European peasant's suspicion of anything new, or the bourgeois emphasis on thrift. The "essential factor common to all neuroses" is "anxieties and the defenses built up against them," but not all fears and defenses are neurotic, and every culture has fears and accepted ways of coping with them, such as rituals (22–23). In spite of sharing in the fears and defenses of their culture, normal people can make "the best of the possibilities" available to them; but because of conditions in their individual lives neurotic people have to pay "an exorbitant price for [their] defenses," consisting in "an impairment of [their] capacities for achievement and enjoyment" (25–26).

Horney seems to be describing a society that damages all of its members and to be classifying the less severely impaired as normal. "Practically everyone," she claims in *New Ways*, develops defenses and inner conflicts, though not with the same degree of compulsiveness and rigidity (59). Everyone suffers from competitiveness, as well as from the isolation and compensatory need for love that it engenders. Most people in our society are "incapable of true friendship and love" and "tend to overrate their personal significance." These characteristics are the product of a culture that creates "fears and hostile tensions among people," that curtails "individual spontaneity," that values people "for what they appear to be rather than for what they are," and that prescribes "the striving for prestige as a means of overcoming fears and inner emptiness" (*NW*, 98).

Lacking a basis upon which to judge cultures, Horney regards the average damaged member of society as normal and sees neurosis as deviation from the average, the difference being one of degree rather than of kind. Social conditions create "a fertile ground for the development of neuroses" (*NP*, 287), but whether a person

becomes neurotic depends on how "severely" he or she was "hit by the existing difficulties" in his or her early family experience (*NW*, 178). The important role Horney
assigns to culture as a determinant of neuroses notwithstanding, she places more
responsibility on the family, which she is able to evaluate in a way that she cannot
assess culture. A family situation is bad that produces a greater-than-average degree
of disturbance, but each culture is in a class by itself and cannot be judged by norms
other than its own.

Although she has sometimes been identified with this initial position, Horney
quickly moved away from cultural relativism, with its implied advocacy of adaptation
to a pathogenic society and acceptance of the status quo. In *New Ways in Psychoanalysis,* she distinguishes between "psychic normality and psychic health" (182)
and argues that cultures as well as individuals should be evaluated in terms of psychic
health. Frequent neuroses and psychoses indicate that "something is seriously wrong
with the conditions under which people live" (179–80).

Horney begins to develop her definition of psychic health in *New Ways*. Drawing upon W. Trotter's *Instincts of the Herd in Peace and War* (1916), she describes
psychic health as "a state of inner freedom in which 'the full capacities are available
for use'" (182). Free of the compulsiveness and rigidity that characterize neurosis,
the individual is able to actualize his or her potentialities. The central feature of neurosis is now self-alienation, loss of contact with "the spontaneous individual self"
(11). Health is equivalent to self-realization (although Horney does not use this term
as yet), and the objective of therapy is to "restore the individual to himself, to help
him regain his spontaneity and find his center of gravity in himself" (11). Horney
cites Otto Rank's concept of will and William James's idea of the spiritual self as
sources of inspiration, but it is Erich Fromm to whom she is primarily indebted for
the new direction in her thinking. Fromm has given her, she says, a new perspective
on "the central significance which the loss of self entails for neurosis" (13). The
spontaneous individual self—which she later calls the "real self"—becomes the
foundation of Horney's understanding of both health and neurosis.

The conception of health as self-realization, the free and full use of our capacities, is not relative to culture. Self-alienated people are neurotic even when they conform to the values of their culture, since those values may reflect the self-alienated
condition of its members. Cultures can be evaluated in terms of the degree to which
they foster or thwart self-realization, and such evaluation provides a basis for social
criticism.[3] Becoming well adjusted to a sick society perpetuates neurosis, and there
are many situations in which it is better not to adapt to the existing conditions,
although this creates its own problems. Misfits or rebels are abnormal in sociological
terms, but they may be standing up for values superior to those of their culture. Ana-

lysts need to be culture-conscious so as to avoid endorsing unhealthy behavior. Those familiar with Erich Fromm's early books—*Escape from Freedom* (1941), *Man for Himself* (1947), and *The Sane Society* (1955)—will recognize that Horney antici-pated him in *New Ways in Psychoanalysis*. Although she was the first to publish, they no doubt worked out many ideas together.[4]

In her essay entitled "What Is a Neurosis?" Horney took up the question of absolute versus relative definitions. We can define neurosis in a way that is univer-sally valid if we use basic anxiety and neurotic trends, rather than deviations from the norm, as the distinguishing characteristics. A valid standard for psychic health would be having "a good attitude toward self and others" and "the free use of one's ener-gies." Horney recognizes the subjective character of such a standard, however: even if it were acceptable as a general formulation, "we could hardly avoid making our-selves the judge as to what is a 'good' attitude toward self and others or as to what is a 'free' use of energy" (1939c, 431–32).

As a solution, Horney falls back upon "practical criteria, such as the degree of being handicapped or the degree of suffering." This resembles the relativism of *Neu-rotic Personality,* but Horney tries to combine the two positions by agreeing that neurosis is "a deviation from the average" while insisting that the deviation con-cerns not manifest behavior but the amount of basic anxiety and the quality of the defensive strategies (1939c, 432).

In spite of her vacillations and uncertainties, Horney moved steadily toward conceptions of health and neurosis that could hold for all cultures. Indeed, even in *Neurotic Personality* she acknowledges that some people may deviate from the norm without being neurotic while others may have a severe neurosis who appear to have "adapted to existing patterns of life" (21). Most of the characteristics she ascribes to neurosis are neither relative to culture nor culturally determined, although they are culturally mediated.

Although Horney set out to describe the neurotic personality of her time, she developed a paradigm for the structure of neurosis that transcends culture. Indeed, one reviewer wondered why the book was limited to "our time" since its account of neurosis "is applicable to any culture, any period, class and sex" (Lowrey 1937, 434). Going a step farther, Horney noted that the reactions of anxiety and defense "are not restricted to human beings. If an animal, frightened by some danger, either makes a counter-attack or takes flight, we have exactly the same situation of fear and defense" (*NP,* 24). Different cultures may favor different defenses and provide vari-ations of them, but the basic patterns of defense are found in the animal kingdom as well and may be said to have a biological basis. Possibly because it subverted her attack on Freud's biologism and her emphasis on culture, Horney did not recognize the implications of her invocation of animal behavior. She thought she was con-structing an account of human behavior as it has been conditioned by a particular society, but she actually built a paradigm with unacknowledged biological elements and species-wide applicability.

Chapter 18

Structure versus Genesis:

Horney's Synchronic Paradigm

In her review of Otto Rank's *Modern Education,* Horney calls for "a critical review of the body of knowledge which is embraced by psychoanalysis" (1932c, 349), and in *New Ways in Psychoanalysis* she undertakes that task. She identifies Freud's "imperishable" contributions (*NW,* 18), attacks his "debatable premises" (8), and devotes the remaining chapters to a consideration of separate aspects of Freudian theory and practice. Her usual procedure is to begin with an exposition and evalua-tion of Freud's views and then to state her own position. Although she professes great respect for Freud, she is often critical, and many reviewers complained of her polemical tactics. In *The Nation,* J. F. Brown observed that "the book turns into a fourteen-round ring battle between the 'new ways' (Horney) and the 'old ways' (Freud)," with Horney winning three rounds (feminine psychology, death instinct, and culture and neurosis), Freud winning seven, and four a draw (1939, 328; see also Fenichel 1940, 114–15).

According to Horney, Freud's enduring contributions to psychoanalysis are the doctrines "that psychic processes are strictly determined, that actions and feelings may be determined by unconscious motivations and that the motivations driving us are emotional forces" (*NW,* 18). She is grateful for his account of repression, reaction formation, projection, displacement, rationalization, and dreams. And she believes that Freud has given us indispensable tools for therapy in the concepts of transfer-ence, resistance, and free association.

One of Horney's main objections to Freudian psychoanalysis is that it is "a genetic psychology" that focuses too much on infantile origins (8). It is difficult to determine why Horney shifted from an emphasis on the past to one on the present, both in theory and clinical practice. She acknowledges the influence of Harald Schultz-Hencke and Wilhelm Reich, analysts whom she knew from her days in Berlin. In a review of *New Ways* Franz Alexander cites himself, Ferenczi, and Rank as other analysts who emphasized current emotional problems (1940, 11–12). Although this emphasis was not original with Horney, she was the first, I think, to explore its implications seriously.

Horney began to articulate her new position in the early to mid-1930s, first in lectures to the Baltimore-Washington group of analysts, led by Harry Stack Sullivan,[5] and then in "Conceptions and Misconceptions of the Analytical Method" (1935c) and in "The Problem of the Negative Therapeutic Reaction" (1936), where she argues that *"the attitudes we see in the adult patient are not direct repetitions of infantile attitudes, but have been changed in quality and quantity by the consequences which have developed out of the early experiences"* (43–44, emphasis Horney). In *Neurotic Personality,* published the next year, she insists that she is not discarding the idea that neuroses develop out of early childhood experiences but wants to show the relation between past and present to be "much more intricate than is assumed" by those who "proclaim a simple cause and effect" connection (vii–viii).

In *New Ways in Psychoanalysis,* Horney distinguishes between her "evolutionistic" and Freud's "mechanistic-evolutionistic" thinking. Evolutionistic thinking presupposes "that things which exist today have not existed in the same form from the very beginning, but have developed out of previous stages. These preceding stages may have little resemblance to the present forms, but the present forms would be unthinkable without the preceding ones." Mechanistic-evolutionistic thinking holds that "nothing really new is created in the process of development," that "what we see today is only the old in a changed form" (42). For Horney, the profound influence of early experiences does not preclude continued development, whereas for Freud "nothing much new" happens after the age of five, and "later reactions or experiences are to be considered as a repetition of past ones." Freud's mechanistic-evolutionistic thinking is manifested in his ideas about the timelessness of the unconscious, repetition compulsion, fixation, regression, and transference. It "accounts for the extent to which trends are designated as infantile and for the tendency to explain the present by the past" (44–45).

At the heart of Freud's conception of the relation between childhood experiences and adult behavior is the doctrine of the timelessness of the unconscious. Fears and desires—even entire experiences—that are repressed in childhood "remain uninfluenced by further experiences or growth." This gives rise to the concept of fixation, which may pertain to a person in the early environment or to a stage of libidinal development. While developing in other respects, the child may be fixated on the mother, or his or her "'sexual' wishes" may "remain concentrated on some pre-genital striving" (133–34). Through the concept of fixation, it is possible to regard later attachments or other behaviors as repetitions of the past, which has remained encapsulated and unchanged in the unconscious. Behaviors "not fitting the rational picture of what the average adult is supposed to feel, to think or to do are designated as infantile" and are to be understood and treated by connecting them with their early origins. "If it were not for the assumption of repetition compulsion," says Horney, "it would be difficult to realize why a destructive ambition, . . . or miserliness or inordinate demands made upon the environment should be considered infantile trends. They are alien to a healthy child and are found only in children who are already neurotic" (139).

Horney attempts to refute neither the doctrine of the timelessness of the unconscious nor its related concepts but instead builds her theory on a different set of premises. The "non-mechanistic viewpoint is that in organic development there can never be a simple repetition or regression to former stages" (NW, 44). The past is always "in some way or other . . . contained in the present," but through a developmental process rather than through repetition (NW, 153). If we tell a patient that he does not want to have anything to do with women because he was disappointed by his mother, we will be "giving him the first and the last link in a chain with all the intermediate links missing." The way personalities "really develop" is through "each step condition[ing] the next one." Thus "interpretations which connect the present difficulties immediately with influences in childhood are . . . practically useless" (1935c, 404–05).

In Horney's model early experiences affect us profoundly not by producing fixations that cause us to repeat earlier patterns but by conditioning the ways in which we respond to the world. These in turn are influenced by subsequent experiences and eventually evolve into our adult patterns of response. Early experiences may have a greater impact than later ones because "they determine the direction of the individual's development" (1936, 44), but their ultimate effect is the product of how subsequent experiences interact with and modify the attitudes and modes of response they have initiated. The psyche of the adult is the *evolved product* of all previous interactions between psychic structure and environment.

Whereas for Freud the determining experiences in childhood are relatively few in number and mostly of a sexual nature, for Horney "the sum total of childhood experiences" is responsible for neurotic development (NW, 153). Neuroses arise because of all the factors in the culture, in relationships with peers, and especially in the family that make the child feel unsafe, unloved, and unvalued and that give rise to basic anxiety. These adverse conditions initiate the development of the neurotic character structure, and "it is this structure from which later difficulties emanate" (9). The development of the character structure may stop at any time—at the age of five, in adolescence, at the age of thirty—or continue all through life (153).

Because the connection between past and present is so difficult to trace, it is more profitable to focus on "the forces which actually drive and inhibit a person; there is a reasonable chance of understanding these, even without much knowledge of childhood" (146). When analyzing "the immediate motives for the observable attitudes of the patient," we often "trace the emotional causal chains which lead from the present symptoms to the earliest shaping influences" (1935c, 406). We recover the past layer by layer, working back from the present, rather than by immediately pursuing infantile origins. Recovery of the past is useful, however, "only as long as it helps the functional understanding" (NP, 33).

Horney distinguishes between explanation in terms of genesis and explanation in terms of structure. This corresponds to the distinction between diachronic and synchronic modes of understanding that originated with Ferdinand de Saussure and that has become a commonplace of twentieth-century thought. Diachronic approaches, in which the present is explained in terms of the past, were dominant in the nineteenth century, resulting in remarkable findings in such fields as linguistics and biology (the theory of evolution, for example). Freud grew up in a climate of diachronic thought and constructed his theory accordingly. In synchronic thought, which has been dominant in the twentieth century, theorists try to explain phenomena in terms of their function within an existing system. We can account for a feature of a language diachronically, by showing where it came from, or synchronically, by analyzing how it fits into the current linguistic system. Similarly, we can explain a feature of a culture, an organism, or a literary work either diachronically or synchronically, in terms of history or of function. Neither mode of understanding excludes the other, and they can be used together, of course.

Horney advocates using the two together, but she feels that a knowledge of the past is valuable mainly for its contribution to an understanding of the present character structure. Freud's approach leads "to a neglect of the actually existing unconscious tendencies and their functions and interactions with other tendencies" (NP, 33). In a passage in New Ways, Horney distinguishes between "structural" and "vertical" interpretations. In structural interpretation, instead of drawing "vertical lines from the trends a, b, c, to the factors a-1, b-1, c-1 in childhood," we draw "horizontal lines," trying "to understand how a, b, and c are actually interrelated" (160–61). Being aware of "the historical source of an attitude is not sufficient to explain it" (NP, 250). What we most need to understand is the function of the attitude in the constellation of defenses that constitutes the present character structure. That character structure has evolved out of the past, but it is now an autonomous system with an inner logic of its own.

Horney's objections to Freud's explanatory method are fourfold: not only does it oversimplify the relation between past and present but it is based on a mechanistic view of the psyche, it has a narrow view of what constitutes "deep" analysis, and it converts analogies into causes. With her holistic view of the psyche, Horney contends that no change can occur "in any part of a living organism which does not influence the entire organism" (1939c, 429), whereas in Freud the neurotic components of the psyche do not necessarily affect the personality as a whole. Libido theory tempts us to "understand a whole machine out of one wheel, instead of trying to understand how the interrelation of all parts brings about certain effects, and in the process to understand also why one wheel is located where it is and why it has to function as it does." Masochistic trends are explained as "the result of the individual having been sexually excited in painful situations, such as being beaten" instead of being seen as "one expression of a whole character structure." And many different traits in women are regarded as "the outcome of one allegedly biological source: penis-envy" (*NW*, 70–71).

Because it posits libidinal manifestations as the ultimate source of all trends, Freudian theory fosters the impression that "only such interpretations are 'deep' which show presumably biological roots"; but this is "an illusion born of theoretical preconceptions" (*NW*, 70). Deep interpretation is an important issue for Horney since she was frequently accused of superficiality, a charge that she in turn had leveled against Adler during her Freudian phase. She considers her interpretations "deep" even though they do not trace current problems to early fixations on forbidden sexual objects or bodily orifices but rather explore unconscious anxieties and hostilities, defenses and inner conflicts.

Horney argues that libido theory is unsubstantiated in "all its contentions." What Freudians have offered as evidence is often a form of analogical reasoning that turns similarities into causes: "Similarities existing between physiological functions and mental behavior or . . . strivings are used to demonstrate that the former determine the latter. Peculiarities in the sexual sphere are off-hand assumed to engender similar coexisting peculiarities in character traits" (*NW*, 68). Instead of explaining greediness or possessiveness as a result of fixation at an oral or anal stage of development, Horney understands them as "a response to the sum total of experiences in the early environment" (62). Freud was right to point to similarities in many aspects of a person's behavior and to call our attention to patterns of repetition, but these phenomena are products of character structure.

Horney's most fully developed example of structural interpretation is the case of Clare, which I shall examine after considering the implications of her new paradigm for the psychoanalytic process.

Chapter 19

The New Paradigm and the

Psychoanalytic Process

Horney claimed that her desire to reevaluate psychoanalytic theory had its origin in "a dissatisfaction with therapeutic results" (*NW*, 7). In *New Ways in Psychoanalysis* she redefines transference, countertransference, and the goals of therapy, and in *Self-Analysis* she develops an account of the analytic process in accordance with her new paradigm. She refined her ideas about psychoanalytic therapy in subsequent writings, but the focus on structure rather than genesis remained the same.[6]

According to Freud, analysis fosters regressive reactions, leading the patient to transfer onto the analyst feelings that derive from childhood. Horney's view of transference was that patients behave toward analysts in accordance with their character structure; the analyst can therefore use the transference to understand the patient's defenses and inner conflicts. Like transference, countertransference is a manifestation not of infantile reactions but of character structure—in this case that of the analyst. Analysts must understand their own defenses lest they be blind to or indulgent of similar defenses in their patients. Hence the importance of a good didactic analysis and of "never-ending self-analysis" (*NW*, 303).

Horney focused on recognizing patients' defenses and discovering the functions and consequences of those strategies. The purpose of therapy is "not to help the patient to gain mastery over his instincts but to lessen his anxiety to such an extent that he can dispense with his 'neurotic trends.'" The patient's defenses not only distort relationships with others but lead to a loss of contact with the spontaneous individual self. The ultimate goal of therapy is "to restore the individual to himself, to help him regain his spontaneity and find his center of gravity in himself" (*NW*, 11).

Self-Analysis contains Horney's fullest account of the analytic techniques she developed on the basis of her new paradigm. In order to relinquish our neurotic trends and achieve self-realizing growth, we must recognize our defenses, explore their implications, and see how they are interrelated. Success in this painful and difficult process requires powerful incentives and ruthless self-honesty. It also requires both patient and analyst to assume specific roles and responsibilities. In self-analysis, the individual must try, as far as possible, to be both patient and analyst.

Horney's analytic procedure is to begin with the patient's most conspicuous neurotic trend. Some patients begin by presenting their "need for absolute independence," others their "need to be loved and approved of," and yet others their "highly developed power drive." The trend that appears first is not necessarily the strongest or the most influential, but it will be the least repressed and the one that "jibes best with the person's conscious or semi-conscious image of himself" (*SA*, 74–75). The more repressed trends will emerge later. The analysis must go through three stages: recognition of the neurotic trend; "discovery of its causes, manifestations, and consequences"; and "discovery of its interrelations with other parts of the personality, especially with other neurotic trends" (89).

These steps must be taken for each neurotic trend, although they are not always taken in the same order, and each has "a particular therapeutic value" (89). Recognition of a neurotic trend does not usually produce radical change, but it diminishes people's sense of being powerless or at the mercy of intangible forces, and it gives them hope that they can alleviate their suffering. Exploring the unfortunate consequences of the trend leads them to an appreciation of the "necessity for change" (92). Because each trend is bound up with other, often contradictory, trends, patients cannot work on one without taking up the others and trying to understand how they are related. They must face the fact that their conflicts are either paralyzing them or tearing them apart.

Incentive is crucial in analytic therapy, for patients must be strongly motivated if they are to endure the pain and struggle involved in working through their trends and changing their personality. Incentive is even more important in self-analysis, where one has no help in overcoming resistances. There are two sources of incentive, the desire to suffer less from one's problems and the desire to unfold one's potentialities, "to live as full a life as given circumstances permit." Horney posits "an incentive to grow" that motivates a person "to come to grips with himself despite all the ordeals he may have to go through" (22–23).

For Freud, urges toward self-development emanate from narcissistic self-inflation. For Horney, narcissistic impulses are not primary but neurotic. They lead us to abandon our real selves and to try to actualize a "phony self." As the phony self "evaporates" through the process of analysis, we get in touch with our real self, which "is, or should be, the most alive center of psychic life. It is this psychic center to which appeal is made in analytical work" (291). The desire to find ourselves, to develop ourselves, to realize our potentialities "belongs among those strivings that defy further analysis" (23). It is a given of human nature.

Horney presents the psychoanalytic process as a cooperative enterprise in which "both analyst and patient work actively toward the same goal." If the analyst assumes "an authoritative attitude," patients may develop "the paralyzing feeling that [they are] more or less helpless," whereas the object is to foster their "initiative and resourcefulness" (301). In Horney's model, both patients and analysts have responsibilities. The three main tasks of patients are to express themselves as completely as possible—mainly through free association—to become aware of their unconscious driving forces and the effects of those forces on their lives, and to change the patterns of behavior that disturb their relationships to self and others.

Horney has often been accused of having discarded psychoanalytic conceptions of the unconscious; it is therefore important to understand what she means by unconscious driving forces. By and large, she is not referring to drives that were repressed in early childhood and are still pressing for fulfillment. For Horney, the repressed early affect with which we most need to get in touch—and which we may still be afraid to acknowledge—is hostility. The repressed material that primarily concerns her derives from neurotic trends that are either in conflict with our predominant trend or our conscious conception of ourselves or whose full implications we do not wish to recognize.

When we gain insight into an unconscious component of our personality, we may recognize something that has been entirely repressed, as when "compulsively modest or benevolent" people discover that they actually have "a diffuse contempt" for others. Or we may recognize the extent and intensity of a trend that we acknowledge only dimly, as when consciously ambitious people realize that their ambition "is an all-devouring passion," which dominates their lives and contains "the destructive element of wanting a vindictive triumph over others." Or we may discover a relation between seemingly unconnected factors, as did the patient who was preoccupied with impending disaster because his "grandiose expectations" had been thwarted and he had "an underlying wish to die" (111–12). In each of these examples the unconscious factors are part of the current character structure.

Because of our resistance, insight into unconscious factors is difficult to achieve. Part of us wishes to maintain "the illusions and the safety afforded by the neurotic structure," while another part seeks to change and grow (267). The part attempting to maintain the status quo is threatened by every self-insight and seeks to block the analytic process. This is why incentive is so crucial. Horney advocates developing an accepting attitude toward our resistances, for we are not responsible for the forces behind their development, and the defenses they are protecting have given us "a means of dealing with life when all other means have failed." Resistances should be regarded as "given factors," "organic developments" (284–85). An understanding of genesis can help us to achieve such self-acceptance. We must recognize that there are reasons beyond our control for why we are as we are and that our parents were also "caught in conflicts and could not help harming" us (*NW*, 284). Accepting the inevitability of our neuroses does not mean approving of them, however, or giving up the effort to change.

Horney believed that if we can overcome our resistances, the insight we gain can have a therapeutic effect, especially if it is not merely intellectual but is felt "in our 'guts'" (111). Facing the truth of our feelings liberates the energy that had been expended on repression and opens the way for action. Once we achieve a fuller self-understanding, we can envision a "way out of [our] distress." This possibility is a source of hope, even if our initial reaction to insight was "one of hurt or fright" and we are not immediately able to change (114).

The patient's third task is to change the internal factors that interfere with development. Horney does not provide a precise account of the mechanics of change, but she is quite clear on what she wants to see come about. She hopes that patients will gain "a more realistic attitude" toward themselves "instead of wavering between self-aggrandizement and self-degradation"; that they will develop "a spirit of activity, assertion, and courage" instead of being paralyzed by "inertia and fears"; that they will become "able to plan instead of drifting"; that they will find "the center of gravity" in themselves "instead of hanging onto others with excessive expectations and excessive accusations"; and that they will develop a "greater friendliness and understanding for people instead of harboring a defensive . . . hostility" (118).

Analysts contribute five components to the psychoanalytic process: observation, understanding, interpretation, help with resistances, and "general human help" (123). In observing, they try not to select "any one element prematurely" (126) but to pay equal attention to everything the patient presents. They then try "to grasp the red thread that passes through the apparently amorphous mass of material." They interpret repetitive themes, overreactions, dreams and fantasies, resistances, evasions and omissions, and transferences (127, 134–137). They solicit the patient's free associations as an aid to interpretation, which is a cooperative process. When the patient is ready, the analyst makes "suggestions as to possible meanings" of the various trends, and the two of them "try to test out the validity of the suggestions" (138).

As we have seen, in Horney's conception of transference, patients unconsciously display in analysis "the same irrational emotional factors, the same strivings and reactions" that they manifest in other relationships (136–37). Since (ideally) the analyst has been well analyzed and also engages in continuous self-analysis, the patient's patterns of behavior will not develop in response to peculiarities in the analyst and thus can be more readily traced to the patient's character structure. "By his very presence," therefore, the analyst "gives the patient a unique opportunity to become aware of his behavior toward people" (142–43).

Horney assigns an active role to analysts in dealing with resistances. They must recognize them, help the patient to recognize them, and try to find out, "with or without the patient's help, what it is that the latter is warding off" (139–40). They can help patients overcome their resistances by providing encouragement and emotional support.

For Horney, providing "human help" is a major part of the analyst's role. When the analysis is conducted in an atmosphere of "constructive friendliness" (NW, 299), anxiety is reduced and patients become better able to recognize and relinquish their defenses. Because they are self-alienated, patients have trouble taking themselves seriously—their real selves, that is, rather than their "inflated image[s]" of themselves, which they take too seriously. The analyst's friendly, serious interest helps them to regard their growth as important and gives them the courage to be on friendly terms with themselves. If the analyst proves reliable as a friend, "this good experience may help the patient also retrieve his faith in others" (SA, 144–45).

The analyst's support is particularly valuable in helping patients deal with discouragement, anxiety, and the realization of painful truths about themselves. The analyst assists them in overcoming fear or hopelessness, giving them a sense that their problems can be resolved. Patients will feel profoundly threatened when, "bereft of glory," they realize they are "not as saintly, as loving, as powerful, as independent as [they] had believed." At this point, they need "someone who does not lose faith" in them, even though their "own faith is gone." In the course of analysis, patients must confront not only their loss of glory, but also their unsavory characteristics, which are destructive to themselves and to others. They tend to react with unconstructive self-hate, rather than with the self-acceptance that will enable them to grow. The analyst perceives that they are "striving and struggling human being[s]" and "still likes and respects" them as a result (145). This encouragement counteracts patients' self-hate and helps them to like and respect themselves.

Self-analysis is much more difficult than analysis because the analysand must play not only the patient's role but also that of the analyst. It is harder to understand our behavior toward others without the well-analyzed analyst on whom to play out our neurotic patterns of interaction, but we can develop "an amazing faculty of keen self-observation," says Horney, if we are bent on understanding our problems (146).

The biggest problems in self-analysis are overcoming resistances and maintaining a hopeful and constructive attitude toward ourselves in the absence of human help. In spite of these difficulties, Horney feels that self-analysis can be successful if the person has had previous analytic experience. Her prime example is herself in the guise of Clare.

Chapter 20

Clare, the New Paradigm, and

the Psychoanalytic Process

The Clare case, as presented in *Self-Analysis,* is Horney's most fully developed illustration of the paradigm developed in *Neurotic Personality* and *New Ways* and of the psychoanalytic process based on that paradigm. Because it is so autobiographical, it enables us to see how Horney understood her earlier self in light of her later ideas. She here simplified the case to fit her illustrative purposes and presented only a selection of her problems and insights into herself.

When first we meet Clare we discover that as a result of conditions in her family, she has developed three neurotic trends: compulsive modesty, the need for a partner, and neurotic ambition. Her analysis accordingly goes through three phases, as she recognizes each of these trends in herself. During each phase, she must work through the three stages of understanding—recognizing a neurotic trend, exploring its origins and implications, and understanding its relation to other trends.

Clare begins by recognizing that she minimizes her own value and capacities. She feels inferior to others and believes that they are in the right when they wrong her. Although she holds an executive position, she either cannot give orders at all or is apologetic when she does so. She lives "beneath her means" in every way, "socially, economically, professionally, spiritually." Her self-minimization results in "a progressive lowering of self-confidence and a diffuse discontentment with life." Without explaining how it is accomplished, Horney reports that the first phase of Clare's work results in "a beginning of faith in herself and a beginning of courage to feel and assert her wishes and opinions" (76–80).

In the second phase, conducted largely through self-analysis, Clare becomes aware of a yet more deeply repressed trend, her dependency on a partner. She recognizes that she feels completely lost when a love relationship ends, that nothing but the relationship matters to her during the affaire, and that she harbors a fantasy of "a great and masterful man whose willing slave" she is and who gives her everything she wants. The consequences of her compulsive dependency are a "repressed parasitic attitude," coupled with the expectation that her problems will be solved and she will be transformed into a wonderful person without any efforts of her own, followed by severe disappointment when the partner fails to fulfill her expectations. Because of her dependency, her relationships make her still more passive and insecure and "breed self-contempt" (82).

In the course of exploring her dependency, Clare becomes aware of its connection to her compulsive modesty. She needs someone to fulfill her wishes because she cannot pursue them herself; she needs someone to defend her because she cannot defend herself; she needs someone to affirm her worth because she cannot appreciate her own value. Because of an unconscious conflict between her compulsive modesty and her excessive expectations of her partner, she needs to see herself as "the victim of intolerably harsh and abusive treatment." It would clash too much with her modesty for her to be aware of the unreasonableness of her demands on her partner. She becomes miserable and angry at the way she feels herself to be treated but has to repress her hostility because of her dread of desertion. "The resulting upsets," notes Horney, "proved to have a great bearing on her fatigue and her inhibition toward productive work" (83).

As a result of the second phase of her analysis, Clare overcomes her "parasitic helplessness," becoming capable of greater activity and gaining relief from her fatigue, which is now intermittent rather than continual. Whereas before she had been unable to work productively, she now begins to write although she still has to struggle against resistances. Her relationships with people improve, but they are "still far from being spontaneous"; she impresses others as "haughty" while still feeling "quite timid" (83).

During the third phase of the analysis, Clare deals with her repressed ambitious strivings, the presence of which are suggested not only by her elation at any form of recognition but "by her dread of failure, and by the anxiety involved in any attempt at independent work." In contrast to her other trends, Clare's ambition constitutes "an attempt to master life actively," and she therefore sees it as having a positive value. It is also an expression of her need to regain her self-esteem and to triumph vindictively "over all those who had humiliated her" (84).

Clare comes to realize in analysis that her ambition has undergone a series of changes in the course of her development. Her aggressiveness had subsided when she lost the "fight for her place in the sun," but had reemerged at the age of eleven, after a series of unhappy experiences, in the form of "a fierce ambition at school." Clare remained first in her class through high school, but she did not make the effort to meet tougher competition in college. She lacked the courage to compete both because of doubts about her intelligence and because her need to triumph over others was so great that she dared not risk failure. Clare's ambition now manifests itself not directly, as in her academic strivings, but in a devious compromise, through erotic conquest, particularly of a masterful man who would make her great by "giving her the chance to indulge vicariously in his success" (85–86).

Clare must now recognize how her ambition is related to her other trends. It intensifies her need for a partner, since having a partner becomes a mark of success and the partner's triumphs can restore her injured pride. But her dependency on the partner further mortifies her pride, which increases her vindictiveness and reinforces her need for triumph. Her "compulsion to assume a humble place" and her need to triumph over others are clearly in conflict. The stronger her need for triumph, the more modest she must be in order to disguise her ambition. Each need threatens the other, causing anxiety and paralysis. "This paralyzing effect," observes Horney, "proved to be one of the deepest sources of the fatigue as well as of the inhibitions toward work" (87).

Clare's task in the third phase of her analysis involves recognizing her repressed ambition and examining its consequences. Her examination results in a lessening of her inhibitions toward work, but Horney never accounts for how the change came about. What is missing in the Clare case, as in Horney's theoretical writing, is a precise explanation of how going through the stages of understanding leads to insight that frees us, in some measure, from our neurotic trends. Horney says only that "working at the implications" of a neurotic trend loosens a person's "illusions, fears, vulnerabilities, and inhibitions" from "their entrenchments," leading the person to become "less insecure, less isolated, less hostile." The "resultant improvement in his relationships with others, and with himself, in turn makes the neurotic trend less necessary and increases his capacity to deal with it" (93). Her description of Clare's self-analysis, however, may help us better to understand this process.

Clare's effort at self-analysis is triggered by her dissatisfaction in her relationship with Peter, who I think is a fictionalized version of Karen's lover Erich Fromm. At first Clare hopes that understanding how she contributes to the relationship's difficulties will improve it, but then Peter leaves her, and she must cope with this psychological blow. That she does so successfully is owing to her prior self-analytic work, which had led her to recognize many of the reasons for Peter's overwhelming importance to her. Chief of these is her morbid dependency, a problem that Horney discussed in earlier works under such names as the overvaluation of love and the neurotic need for affection. Clare's self-analysis can be divided into two main parts, before and after Peter leaves.

Initially, Clare is unhappy about aspects of her relationship but is unaware of the force of her resentment, of her desire to break away, or of her desperate need for Peter. She uncovers these feelings through a series of episodes in which a particular event will trigger emotions, memories, and dreams that she will then try to interpret. Although her associations sometimes take her into the past, she tries to focus on current needs. The process unfolds slowly, as insight is stimulated by pain but impeded by resistance. Horney evaluates Clare's self-analytical work, telling us what she has understood correctly and what she has missed or cannot yet afford to see. An episode of self-analysis initiated by a sudden sharp mood swing that occurs one evening when Peter unexpectedly gives Clare a pretty scarf will give us a clear idea of how the process works.

When she first receives the present, Clare is delighted, but when Peter subsequently proves reluctant to make summer plans, she becomes tired and frigid. That night she has a dream in which a large, gloriously colored bird is flying away. When she awakens "with anxiety and a sensation of falling," she realizes at once that the dream expresses a fear of losing Peter. The beauty of the bird causes her to wonder whether she has glorified Peter, a good-looking man, as she earlier had glorified others, but she is not ready to delve into this. She connects her recollection of a song from Sunday school in which children ask Jesus to take them under his wing to the falling sensation with which she awoke and to the need for protection of which she has recently become aware. She realizes that the many times when she had become tired, depressed, or frigid all occurred when Peter's behavior had aroused her fear of desertion. Horney observes that this part of Clare's analysis "illustrates the astonishing fact that a person can be entirely unaware of a fear that actually is all consuming" (210). Clare is still far from fully comprehending the nature of her fear, but she understands that she was elated at receiving the scarf because it temporarily allayed that fear and that Peter's lack of interest in summer plans aroused it again.

Clare understands her mood swing more fully a week later, after crying while at a movie when the situation of a wretched girl takes an unexpected turn for the better. She remembers that she always cries on such occasions. In addition, she recalls two aspects of her great-man fantasy: her joyful surprise when the man singles her out for his favors and his anticipation of her desire for luxuries that makes it unnecessary for her to ask him for anything. This leads to the startling realization that she is an exploiter of men, that "her love was at bottom no more than a sponging on somebody else" (212). Although Horney does not dissent from this view, Clare seems to me to be a bit hard on herself. She may also have been longing for evidence that she was worthy of being prized by a man she valued.

Clare's tears at the movie heroine's good fortune and her joy at Peter's present are a response to the unexpected fulfillment of her "most secret and most ardent wishes" without effort on her part. Because she grew up repressing her own wishes, "she needed somebody who wished for her, or who guessed her secret wishes and fulfilled them without her having to do anything about them herself." She feels "quite taken aback, almost like a criminal who is confronted with overwhelming evidence," when she realizes this, but she soon feels "greatly relieved" at having "uncovered her share in what made her love relationships difficult" (212–13). She sees that the depression on the evening of her mood swing was a result not only of anxiety about losing Peter but also of repressed anger because her wishes had been frustrated. She recognizes that she has an unconscious insistence on her wishes being complied with, on others honoring her magical claims.

Clare has made a number of self-discoveries, including intimations of her disappointment in, resentment at, and desire to break away from Peter. She is becoming aware of her need for protection and her fear of losing Peter, whom she senses she may be overrating. She has also seen that she mistook her expectations and demands for love and that she needs so much from others because of her inhibitions about "wishing or doing anything for herself" (215). She has recognized that her "sponging attitude" has led her to give little to her partner. And she has realized that she becomes offended and depressed when her expectations are not met. As a result of her self-analytical work, Clare's "sudden eruptions of irritation" stop; she tries to share Peter's interests, consider his wishes, and give him more; and she moderates her demands (214). She feels happier because her new understanding gives her a sense of control and because her relationship with Peter improves.

A little later, when Peter cancels their summer trip and scolds her for becoming distraught about it, Clare realizes more clearly how much she has been overrating him. By impressing on her that "everything was her fault," he has acted like her mother and brother, "first stepping on her feelings and then making her feel guilty." He is a phony, and she has again allowed herself to be deceived. She has taken so long to see through Peter's facade of righteousness, devotion, and generosity because she needed him to be "the great man of her daydream" (218–19).

But Clare is unable to see that Peter is determined to leave her, and because of her dependency, she cannot fully face her own desire to break away from him. She expects less of Peter and is more resigned to his deficiencies, but she still centers her life around him. Three weeks after Peter cancels the summer trip, she thinks suddenly of Margaret, a married friend whom she has not seen for a long time who was "pitifully dependent on her husband despite the fact that he ruthlessly trampled on her dignity." Although Clare had "felt contemptuous of Margaret's lack of pride," she had tried to help her friend find ways of saving her marriage. What startles her now is the similarity between herself and Margaret. She "had never thought of herself as dependent," but she realizes "with frightening clarity" that she, too, has "lost her dignity in clinging to a man who did not really want her and whose value she doubted" (221–22).

Having recognized her dependency, Clare now begins to understand its implications. It is largely responsible for her fear of desertion and for her hero-worship, for she turns people into figures who can give her what she needs. It damages her self-esteem: "injuries to her dignity" become less important than holding onto the other person. And it makes her "a threat and a burden" to others—an insight that results in "a sharp drop in her hostility" toward Peter. Clare sees the compulsive character of her dependency and the damage it does to her relationships, but she is "far from recognizing its formidable strength." She overrates her progress and succumbs to "the common self-deception that to recognize a problem is to solve it" (222–23).

Clare is forced to face the full extent of her dependency and the need to free herself of it only when Peter, who is having an affaire, suggests they separate. She is "thrown into a turmoil of wild despair" in which "the idea of suicide [keeps] recurring to her," as it had done on similar occasions. She feels now "the unmitigated power of her need to merge with another person," which is not love but is "like a drug addiction." She has only two alternatives: to succumb to the dependency and find another partner or to overcome it. Although afraid that life will never seem worth living without a lover, she begins to feel hopeful when she realizes that her absorption with one person has led her to devalue everything else. She accepts the need to "do something about her bondage" (227–29).

Clare's previous self-analytical work makes it possible for her to deal with her crisis in a constructive way, for without it she would probably "have reached out for a new partner as soon as possible, and thus perpetuated the same pattern of experience" (232). But analytical work alone might never have forced her to confront the fact "that her dependency was like a cancerous growth" that had to be "eradicated" (230). It is a combination of analysis and experience that leads Clare to fight her dependency.

There are "still powerful unconscious forces" blocking Clare's progress, however. She discovers that she has "an active defiance against living her own life, feeling her own feelings, thinking her own thoughts, having her own interests and plans, in short against being herself and finding the center of gravity within herself" (232). She has no inkling of the source of this defiance; she simply feels its existence.

The analysis of an incident in which she complains that everyone is better off than she gives her a new insight into her resistance. She realizes that she has a tendency to "talk herself into an exaggerated misery," and she remembers crying in bed as a child and feeling it "unthinkable that her mother would not come and console her." Among her associations is a Sunday school song that promises divine comfort "no matter how great our sorrow, if we pray to God." She recognizes a pattern of "exaggerated misery" along with "an expectation of help, consolation, encouragement." Her playing the martyr role in childhood "must have been also an unconscious plea for help" (234–35).

Clare is on the verge of understanding one of the major reasons for her resistance to being centered in herself, but it is difficult for her to believe that she can be so irrational as to expect "magic help" because of her suffering. But she must accept that she does and that as a result she tends "to make a major catastrophe out of every difficulty, . . . collapsing into a state of complete helplessness." That helplessness is actually a source of power, for she has "a kind of private religion" in which her dependency will bring about the fulfillment of her wishes. Clare has made a bargain with fate in which if she remains "humble and self-effacing all happiness, all triumph" will be hers. Greater self-reliance or self-assertion would "jeopardize these expectations of a heaven on earth." Hence her "active defiance" against throwing off her dependency and taking her life into her own hands. Because she has ascribed "the godlike role of magic helper" to the male partner, he becomes all important to her, and she wants only to be wanted and loved by him (237–38).

Now that she has lost Peter and uncovered some of the deeper sources of her dependency, Clare really wants to learn how to fend for herself, but she still cannot bear to be alone and develops an obsessive craving for a close friend. She realizes that one reason for her intolerance of solitude is that the attitude of others entirely determines her evaluation of herself. Solitude not of her own choosing makes her feel "disgraced, unwanted, excluded, ostracized." Her problem, then, is not so much an incapacity to be alone, but "a hypersensitivity to being rejected" (242). When others are not giving her attention, she feels that she has been "thrown to the dogs" (242). Clare connects this with her earlier sense of exclusion from the community between mother and brother and her fear that "in their eyes she was only a nuisance." The defense she adopted to cope with that exclusion further undermined her self-confidence. By acquiescing in her family's evaluation of her as inferior and admiring them as superior, she "had dealt the first blow to her human dignity" (243).

Horney endorses this part of Clare's self-analysis, but it seems problematic to me. According to Clare, she was all right as long as she was "rebelling against discriminatory treatment" (243), but she lost her self-esteem when she knuckled under. Although rebellion may have been better than submission, it too was a defensive response that damaged her personality and used up energy she needed for growth. She had to keep insisting on her worth because she lived in a threatening environment and felt insecure, but she did so indirectly, by becoming a difficult child. This compounded her problem by provoking further rejection, which finally became more than she could bear. I attribute Clare's (and Horney's) faulty interpretation to contempt for the humble, self-effacing side of herself and to an admiration for her earlier aggressive behavior.

According to Horney, Clare's self-knowledge has a highly beneficial effect. Once she realizes that the loss of Peter had been such a shock because it "left her with a feeling of utter worthlessness" and that because of this feeling she could not bear to be alone, her wish for a lover loses its "compulsive character" and she can tolerate solitude, even enjoying it at times (244). She now sees that she had "blinded herself to the evidence" that Peter wanted to get away and had made frantic efforts to keep him simply to restore her self-regard. These efforts had involved not only "an uncritical bending to Peter's wishes," but also "an unconscious inflation of her feeling for him," which ensnared her "still more deeply in her bondage." Her insights "into the needs that constituted this 'love'" show her that in fact she feels very little for Peter. She can thus regard him calmly, instead of wavering between longing and a desire for revenge. She appreciates his good qualities but knows that she will never want to be "closely associated with him again" (244–45).

Horney's account of the Clare case ends optimistically. Clare returns to analysis to work on inhibitions when attempting creative writing that are related to "her repressed aggressive and vindictive trends." Her earlier insight into her dread of being alone helps her to understand her repressed ambition, for triumphing over others is another way of "lifting her crushed self-regard." The analysis of her repressed aggressive trends contributes to her understanding of her dependency (she needs someone else through whom to experience these trends vicariously), and the lifting of her inhibitions against self-assertion removes any danger that she will "relapse into another morbidly dependent relationship." "But the power exercised on her by her need to merge with a partner was essentially broken," Horney assures us, "by the analytical work that she had done alone" (246).

Clothilde Marie ("Sonni") Danielsen, Karen's mother (Courtesy Karen Horney Papers, Manuscripts and Archives, Sterling Memorial Library, Yale University)

Berndt Henrick Wackels Danielsen, Karen's father (Courtesy Karen Horney Papers, Manuscripts and Archives, Sterling Memorial Library, Yale University)

Karen Clementina Theodora Danielsen, around age 3 ½ (Courtesy Karen
Horney Papers, Manuscripts and Archives, Sterling Memorial Library,
Yale University)

Karen and her brother, Berndt, around the ages of 7 and 11 (Courtesy Karen Horney Papers, Manuscripts and Archives, Sterling Memorial Library, Yale University)

Karen, age 10 (Courtesy M. Eckardt and R. Patterson)

Sketch of Karen at age 15 (Courtesy Karen Horney Papers, Manuscripts and Archives, Sterling Memorial Library, Yale University)

From left: Ida Behrman (Idchen), Sonni, Louis Grote (Losch), and Karen in Freiburg, 1907 (Courtesy M. Eckardt and R. Patterson)

Karen and Losch, 1907 (Courtesy M. Eckardt and R. Patterson)

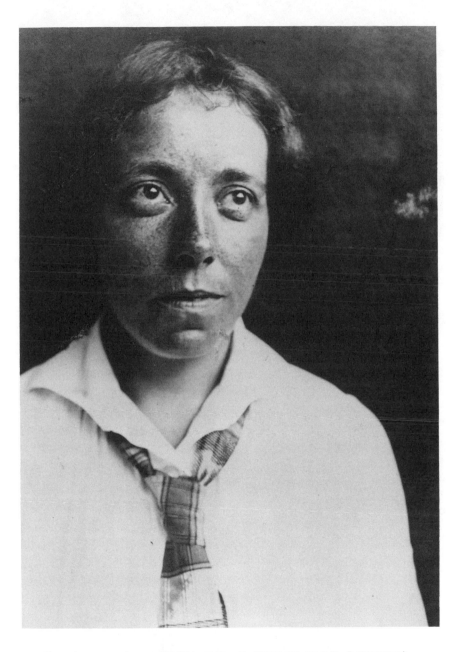

Karen, around age 22 (Courtesy M. Eckardt and R. Patterson)

Oskar Horney and his parents (Courtesy M. Eckardt and R. Patterson)

Karl Abraham, Karen's analyst, around 1912

Part 4

Horney as an Adult

Apart from the diaries, *Self-Analysis* is the most revealing of Horney's writings. The process of self-discovery and growth through which Clare goes over the course of approximately five years, however, took almost three decades of Karen Horney's life. Despite the omissions, simplifications, and fictionalizations, the Clare case gives us a good idea of how Horney perceived her own development and helps us fill in our picture not only of her life but also of her personality. Horney probably perceived herself as having discovered and tackled her trends in very much the sequence she attributes to Clare and as having made similar progress.

In 1942, Horney had good reason to feel that she had overcome many of her difficulties. When she ended her last diary, in July 1912, her psychological state was practically the same as when she had begun analysis with Karl Abraham. We have little detailed personal information about the next twenty years, but what we know suggests significant progress combined with continuing problems. In the ten years between her arrival in the United States and the publication of *Self-Analysis*, Horney became a major figure in psychoanalysis and developed a wide circle of friends. She described the young adult Clare as having "inhibitions concerning expansive plans," while her later life showed that she could be liked, look attractive, and write something valuable and original (*SA*, 78). This assessment expresses, I think, Horney's sense of self-vindication.

Although the years between 1912 and 1932 were marked by a number of professional achievements, Horney's personal life was troubled. She enjoyed being a mother but was so preoccupied with her work that she had little time for her daughters. According to Harold Kelman, she had "basic feelings of ugliness, unfemininity, unlovability" and was therefore deeply hurt by Oskar's "interest in other more attractive and glamorous women."[1] She consoled herself with affaires of her own, but they probably had the same desperate character that we saw toward the end of her diary. Her distress at her compulsive need for men and her inability to form and maintain satisfactory relationships is recorded in her essays on feminine psychology.

I think that Horney's description of Clare's professional career as "rather successful" is a reflection of the way she felt about her own career before she left Germany. Her moderate success did not fully reflect what she sensed to be her capabilities. She had begun to assert herself by taking issue with Freud and Abraham on the topic of feminine psychology, and after her separation from Oskar had published a steady stream of essays; but her work did not receive the attention for which she had hoped, and it made little impact on the psychoanalytic community. Margaret Mead reports that Horney "was very bitter about Freud" because "he had never recognized her work on feminine psychology." Horney was well-regarded at the Berlin Psychoanalytic Institute, but according to Abraham Kardiner, she was "not of the inner council" in that bastion of classical theory.[2]

The picture we receive from the few available accounts of Horney at this time is of a rather subdued person. The psychoanalyst G. H. Graeber, who knew her as a seminar instructor and supervising analyst in 1931–32, wrote to Jack Rubins that he could not "imagine that she could have had any enemies—very likely not even enviers or rivals among her colleagues." Although she was admired by her students, there was no "particular radiation. She did not appear very dynamic. I have never heard her laugh out loud or seen her get excited or even combative in discussions or debates." This is quite unlike the Karen Horney who wrote *Self-Analysis*. In Berlin, however, according to her colleague Edith Weigert, Horney was not "outgoing" at professional meetings: "I think she more and more withdrew. I was at the meeting when Schulze-Hencke was excluded. He protested. Karen Horney never protested." Although Horney was quite assertive—even at times polemical—in her essays, Weigert felt that "in the society there were signs of reluctance, reservations on her part; she held back and sometimes I felt she was afraid of expressing herself, maybe of disagreeing. I don't remember her ever doing it openly."[3] There seems to have been a conflict in Horney between a desire to express her controversial ideas, as she did in her essays, and a fear of rejection—a wish to retain the approval of her colleagues— that made her reticent at meetings of the society.

In 1932 Horney accepted Franz Alexander's invitation to become the founding associate director of the Chicago Psychoanalytic Institute, in part because she was intrigued by the possibility of expressing herself more freely. But she soon found herself at odds with Alexander and realized that she would not have the opportunity to follow her own ideas at the institute. Coming to the United States seems to have liberated her expansiveness, and she now found it intolerable to be in a subordinate position (especially to a man who had been her junior in Berlin) and to have to repress her thoughts and feelings.

Horney moved to New York in 1934, where her fortunes rose rapidly. She joined the New York Psychoanalytic Institute, despite opposition from Sandor Rado, whom she had ridiculed in "The Problem of Feminine Masochism," and she was appointed to the faculty of the Washington-Baltimore Institute, where she lectured periodically. She began a rewarding relationship with Erich Fromm and became a member of the informal group of analysts known as the Zodiac Club formed by Harry Stack Sullivan in the mid-1930s. At the invitation of Clara Mayer, the future dean of the New School for Social Research, she began offering courses at the school that attracted large audiences and that led to her association with W. W. Norton. Through the New School, she also enlarged her circle of friends, which already included many well-known refugees and social scientists. Between 1937 and 1942 she published three books that were widely discussed and gave her great prominence. As her importance grew, she became more assertive, more combative, and more charismatic. Although her unorthodox ideas led to her forced resignation from the New York Psychoanalytic Institute, Horney had really wanted an institute of her own, and in 1941 she established one.

It is not difficult to see why the autobiographical Clare case ends on such a positive note. Horney's relationship with Fromm had broken up, but she felt that she had recovered from it and freed herself from the dependency on a partner. Lack of self-confidence, fatigue, and inhibitions in work were no longer the problems they had been. She had become much more self-assured and assertive, she was a marvel of energy, and she produced an impressive amount of creative work, especially when we consider how busy she was teaching, analyzing, supervising, lecturing, administering her institute, reading, traveling, and socializing. She is described frequently as having a zest for life and a wonderful capacity for enjoyment. Horney must have felt that she had transformed herself through the thirty years of analytical work she had done alone. It is no wonder that *Self-Analysis* and Horney's subsequent books are informed by an optimistic belief in change.

Throughout this book I have argued that Horney's psychoanalytic writings were to a large extent inspired by her effort to comprehend and resolve her own problems and that her theory kept evolving not only because she was exposed to new clinical, cultural, and intellectual experiences but also because she felt the need to continue her self-exploration. The sense of Horney that we get from the Clare case is of a person who has worked through her major difficulties and anticipates few problems in the future. This is not confirmed by other biographical data and subsequent developments in Horney's life. *Self-Analysis* may convey how Horney felt about herself in 1942, but her problems were far from resolved. There were some areas in which she had been unable to change and others where she was experiencing new difficulties. Both her self-analysis and the evolution of her theory continued.

As I mentioned in the introduction, my discussion of Horney's mature theory will ignore its autobiographical character, for I do not wish to distract from the presentation of it as an intellectual system that makes sense in itself and is an important contribution to human thought. Before looking at that theory, however, I shall complete my portrait of its creator with the testimony of those who knew her in the last two decades of her life and her letters to her daughter Brigitte.[4] After examining Horney's relationships with men, her experiences in psychoanalytic institutes, and her interactions with her daughters, we shall readily understand how the insights contained in her last two books grew out of her continued search for self-understanding.

Chapter 21

Relationships with Men

Although Horney had made great psychological progress between the time she kept her diaries and the time she wrote *Self-Analysis*, her relationships with men had not changed much. Problematic from the start, they remained so throughout her life. As we have seen, there was a major dichotomy in young Karen's love life. She wanted a man who would provide emotional rapport, intellectual stimulation, and moral elevation, but when she found someone—like Oskar or Rolf—he did not appeal to her sexually because he lacked the crude force she also craved. Along with her desire for a mentor and soul mate, she had fantasies of sexual degradation that expressed a masochistic wish to relinquish her personality, to let herself be used by the other. She hoped to resolve her conflict by finding a great man who could satisfy all her cravings. The typical pattern of her relationships was first idealization of a male as "the one," followed by disappointment, depression, and efforts to relieve her pain through analysis of the reasons for the failure of the relationship. Because of her disappointments, she moved from lover to lover, often trying to hold on to several at once, since each satisfied different demands.

The pattern of multiple relationships was established early, and Karen recognized its compulsiveness even before she became an analyst. She felt that she had to have sex in order to be able to work, but she worried that her dependency on it would jeopardize her ambitions and prevent her from doing justice to her abilities. She frequently lamented her lack of self-control. When she did not have a lover or a relationship was breaking down, she felt lost, lonely, desperate, and sometimes suicidal. When she was involved in a morbidly dependent relationship, she hated herself for her inability to break free. She attributed her desperate need for a man and her lack of selectivity to her unhappy childhood.

Horney's essays on feminine psychology suggest that the early patterns continued, with some variations. She took and discarded lovers in an effort to find her ideal. She continually hoped that her next relationship would provide the reassurance she craved, but her need could be satisfied only by continual conquests. Winning a man, rejecting him, and conquering another was a way of proving her attractiveness without risking abandonment. It also allowed her to avoid emotional dependency, and to gain revenge on a whole sex by which she felt injured.

Horney was torn between fear of men and a compulsive need for them. Because of her disappointments at the hands of her father and brother, she tried to make her-

self invulnerable by avoiding deep emotional bonds, even as she craved them. Sometimes she clung to men who were indifferent or rejecting and sometimes she dropped
them before they could hurt her. Her Don Juanism gave her a sense of human contact
without commitment. Her compulsive need for men derived in part from her wish
to compensate for her defeat in the competition for father and brother by her erotically dominant mother. Her mother had made her feel like a failure as a female,
which drove her to demonstrate repeatedly that she could attract men. Her conquests
provided vindictive triumphs and a way of coping with anxiety and self-hate. Yet
they also stimulated self-hate, because while she longed for a deep and meaningful
relationship, she was able to have only evanescent and unselective ones. In her writings, Horney portrayed this kind of behavior as neurotic.

Horney devoted most of *The Neurotic Personality of Our Time* to the compulsive need for love because this was the problem that most haunted her. As she
saw it, she was caught because of her basic anxiety between a desire to escape her
emotional isolation by getting close to people and a fear of betrayal that made it
impossible for her to do so. Being deprived of affection had made her dependent on
others, but she was afraid of dependency because it made her vulnerable, and so
she could not accept affection when she found it. Once again we get the impression
of a person whose need for affection was compulsive, indiscriminate, and incapable of fulfillment. She now saw her need for intercourse not as a sexual problem
but as a product of her neurotic character structure. It served as "a substitute for
emotional relationships" (153). Her Don Juanism was also in part the product of
her vindictive feelings toward men. She began some love affaires simply to humiliate the man, to gain control over him and then to drop him as soon as he
responded with affection.

What we know about Horney's actual relationships after she stopped keeping a
diary accords with the picture of her as both a clinging, dependent, hero-worshiping
woman who stayed in failing relationships too long and a female Don Juan who
needed to feed her pride, act out her aggression, and preserve her invulnerability by
seducing men and then leaving them. Her contradictory needs were so strong that
she seems to have engaged in both kinds of behavior simultaneously.

From the early days of their marriage both Karen and Oskar had indulged in
numerous affaires. Among Karen's lovers in the 1920s were Hans Lieberman, Karl
Müller-Braunschweig, and possibly Max Eitingon, all colleagues at the Berlin Psychoanalytic Institute. Renate Patterson vividly remembers one evening when her
father was not at home and Karl Müller-Braunschweig "was there for dinner, teasing
[Karen] and laughing. She laughed so much and was so happy, happy in a way I had
never seen her before." This anecdote suggests the misery of Karen's marriage and

her subdued demeanor at home. According to Gertrude Weiss, Horney left Germany in part because "her practice was shaken by [her] divorce [she was only separated at that time], and things she did (boyfriends) were brought out." Gertrude Lederer-Eckardt, Marianne's mother-in-law and Karen's companion in the 1940s, also reported that Horney's "practice wasn't good" before she left Germany.[5] If she behaved in Berlin as she did after she came to the United States, lovers may have been part of the problem.

In both Chicago and New York there were stories of Horney's having affaires with candidates at the institutes with which she was associated, including supervisees and analysands. Roy Grinker described Horney as "a very seductive woman" who was having sexual relations with the younger analysts at the Chicago Institute, including Leon Saul, who was traumatized by the experience. Lawrence Kubie told Jack Rubins similar stories of Horney's behavior at the New York Psychoanalytic Institute and said that "this was why Franz Alexander got her out of Chicago; she was disrupting analytic relationships." According to Kubie, Horney was a seductress who made passes at younger men, thereby doing them emotional "damage." She had affaires with some of them but did not succeed with others, whom she then hated.[6]

It should be noted that Kubie was Horney's great enemy at the New York Psychoanalytic Institute, and his account of her is not necessarily to be trusted. He claimed that Horney employed her followers as ghost writers, for example, but there is no evidence of this. There is other testimony, however, about her behavior toward candidates. Marie Levy, who was Horney's secretary while she was at the New York Psychoanalytic, reported that Horney "was involved with these disciples at the Institute": "It wasn't only sex. I'm not sure it was only physical; younger men made her feel younger, rejuvenated; she seemed to need the disciple aspect." Perhaps, Levy speculated, "the disciple aspect kept her from getting too involved." Horney's "drive toward younger men" continued to manifest itself when she was head of her own institute in the 1940s. According to Lederer-Eckardt, Horney had many lovers. And Frances Arkin observed that she was always with younger men, "all of them in psychiatry," thereby "proving her sexual attractiveness despite her lack of beauty."[7]

Many have attested to Horney's ability to attract men, even in her later years (she was forty-seven when she came to the United States, sixty in 1945). She was described by other women as being "very feminine and seductive," as having "a way with men that was terrific," and as having a "light from within" that attracted men despite the fact that she was considered plain. According to Gertrude Weiss, "she never flirted openly; it was just there." Rollo May confessed that he had "always had the secret question in [his] mind as to how a woman with so few physical assets, so far as beauty and charm, could be so attractive." We know from her writings how important it was for her to be attractive to men and to make sexual conquests. Wanda Willig felt that Horney was not driven simply by sex but that she needed to be wanted "to prove she was still desirable." She was engaged in an "endless search for reassurance" that led her to "use men," to "love them and leave them."[8]

The compulsiveness of Horney's behavior is evident from its lack of professional decorum: the young men with whom she was involved were often candidates in training analysis or supervision with her. (The rules against such behavior are far more strict nowadays.) Horney's lovers sometimes became favorites to whom she gave power until, to their pain and bewilderment, she turned against them. She then replaced them with other favorites.

Why the drive toward *younger* men? We have already seen that Horney wanted to prove her sexual attractiveness and had a "desire to remain eternally young."[9] A case described in "Maternal Conflicts" may shed additional light. There, a forty-year-old teacher is uncomfortable because some of her male students have fallen passionately in love with her, and she wonders whether she has unwittingly encouraged them. During the course of analysis it comes out that she has actually fallen in love with one of the students, a twenty-year-old, and that she is strongly tempted to have an affaire with him. Her love is not for the young man himself, however, but for her father, whom he represents in her mind. All the students have, in fact, physical and mental characteristics that remind her of her father, and they often appear as her father in her dreams. In analysis she becomes aware that "behind rather bitter opposition toward her father in her adolescent years, a deep, passionate love for him was concealed." A woman afflicted with father fixation usually prefers older men, but in this case "the infantile age relationships were reversed. Her attempts to solve the problem had taken this form in fantasy: 'I am not the small child who cannot get the love of my unattainable father, but I am big, then he will be small, then I shall be the mother, and my father will be my son" (1933c, 177).

Was Horney attracted to younger, dependent men because her position of power in relation to them made her feel less likely to be rebuffed or deserted, as she had been by her father? They were attracted by her fame, as well as by her personal qualities; having an affaire with Karen Horney "fed their pride." It is interesting that Horney, like the woman in her case, discovered warmer feelings toward her father behind the bitter opposition of adolescence. Renate Patterson writes that "as a young child, Karen had a great admiration for her father," and according to Harold Kelman, "she talked about him with awe, regard, even a kind of fondness" despite her "deep feelings of having been deserted and abandoned by a father who had failed her" (Academy). Valer Barbu reported that Horney referred to her father as "a great person who took her around places." It is also noteworthy that Kelman, Horney's protégé and lover, was described as behaving at Horney's funeral as if he had lost his mother.[10] If Horney wanted to be the all-conquering mother in this scenario, some of her lovers may have wanted to be the son.

Horney's most sustained relationships were with Erich Fromm in the 1930s and Harold Kelman in the 1940s, both of them men considerably younger than she. We recall that in her discussion of hero-worship in *Neurotic Personality,* Horney described "a queer contradiction" in women who need to dominate. They cannot love a weak man because they despise weakness, but they cannot "cope with a 'strong' man because they expect their partner always to give in." What they "secretly look for is the hero, the superstrong man, who at the same time is so weak that he will bend to all their wishes without hesitation" (170). Horney may have felt that Fromm and Kelman were bright, strong men whom she could respect and who would at the same time bend to her wishes because she was older than they. Perhaps she hoped that she could both lean on and dominate them.

Fromm struck Abraham Kardiner as a man of "great pretensions" and "insufferable arrogance," while Ruth Moulton saw him as "autocratic, shy, and brilliant," a "power-driven prima donna." (Kelman has been described in similar terms.) These characteristics would have appealed to Horney's need for a superstrong man. While Horney sought a maternal control in relationships, Fromm "had some kind of attachment to older women, mother-figures." Karen was fifteen years his senior; his first wife, Frieda Fromm-Reichmann, had been ten years older than he. Erich's father is reported to have told Frieda on her wedding day, "I'm glad you're going to be in charge of him now." Having been his mother's darling, Erich was "very dependent, a prince who needed to be catered to," who "may have been drawn to older women for mothering."[11]

Horney's relationship with Fromm extended over a period of about twenty years. Born in Frankfurt in 1900, Fromm received his doctorate from Heidelberg in 1922 and went to the Berlin Institute for psychoanalytic training in 1923. There he met Horney and, according to Jack Rubins, they "felt a mutual attraction," although he was married to Frieda at the time (1978, 121). Renate remembers Fromm as a friend and frequent visitor in Berlin. The romantic relationship began either when Fromm came to Chicago in 1933 or when Horney and Fromm both moved to New York in 1934. It flourished over the next four or five years. Fromm profoundly influenced Horney's first two books, and Horney likewise inspired him. According to Kardiner, "he took her ideas and used them." In the summer of 1937, Horney's daughter Marianne entered the Payne-Whitney Clinic as a psychiatric resident and, at the suggestion of her mother, Fromm became Marianne's training analyst. Marianne testifies: "I went to Erich Fromm when their relationship was very good and she trusted him most. I was with him while the relationship deteriorated."[12] The breakup occurred in part because Horney blamed Fromm for Marianne's emerging resentment toward her.

By the time Marianne's analysis ended, in 1940, the romance between Horney and Fromm was probably over, although they continued social and professional relations for the next several years. Fromm taught courses for the American Institute for Psychoanalysis that Horney helped to found in 1941, and Horney spent part of that summer with him and mutual friends on Monhegan Island in Maine. Their relationship became increasingly strained, however, and by April 1943 Fromm had been driven to resign from the American Institute in a dispute that ostensibly concerned his status as a lay (nonmedical) analyst.

The Clare-Peter story could well be a fictionalized account of Horney's breakup with Fromm. Certainly the chronology fits. Kelman notes that Horney was engaged in painful self-analysis between 1938 and 1942. It was the deterioration of her relationship with Fromm, I suspect, that triggered this self-analysis, just as problems in her relationship with Peter led Clare to analyze herself. Horney sent her first plan for *Self-Analysis* to Norton in June 1940. According to Jack Rubins' notes, Horney was seeing a man named Hans Baumgartner in 1940–41. One day she confessed to Marie Levy, "I don't know whether to marry Hans or get a cocker spaniel."[13] She got the cocker spaniel, the famous (or infamous) Butschi. Presumably she began working on *Self-Analysis* and seeing Hans after her liaison with Fromm ended.

Clare sounds very much like Karen Horney, but does Peter sound like Erich Fromm? The evidence is weaker here since there are no biographical studies of Fromm, and the picture I have of him emerges only from interviews with people who knew both him and Horney at this time. Clare's version of Peter is not incompatible with that picture. Fromm has been described as "messianic," and Peter was "the savior type" (*SA*, 238). Peter was usually "sympathetic and helpful" (235), willing "to give advice and to console [Clare] when she was in distress" (205). According to Rainer Funk, this fits Erich, "who could impress you by his concentration on you and his empathy. This holds true for all relationships he had, but especially for his relation to women." Peter gave Clare much-needed support, but she later came to feel that he was "wrapped up in himself" and that there was something fraudulent about him: "He could not help playing the role of one who was always right, always superior, always generous" (217). Peter sounds not unlike the pretentious, arrogant person described by Kardiner. Fromm struck Hannah Tillich as well as being "very authoritarian" beneath "his gentle surface."[14]

According to Ruth Moulton, there "was something quite remote" about Fromm. This is the keynote of Clare's portrait of Peter. He created the illusion of a "deep and everlasting love, and yet was anxious to keep himself apart" (*SA*, 218). He was "an aloof person, hypersensitive to any demands upon him." Because of this hypersensitivity, Clare "refrained from mentioning the possibility of marriage, though she often thought of it" (200–201). Horney finally filed for divorce from Oskar in December 1936 when she returned to Germany (it came through in 1938), perhaps because her relationship with Fromm was flourishing and she hoped he would marry her. When the affaire was over, Horney told Marie Levy that Fromm was a "Peer Gynt type," by which Levy thought "she meant he wasn't loyal."[15] She also probably meant that Fromm was overly detached. Horney later discussed Peer Gynt in the chapter "Moving away from People" in *Our Inner Conflicts* (1945). For the Peer Gynt type, "any close and lasting relation would be bound to jeopardize his detachment and hence would likely be disastrous." His ideal partner would be a Solveig, who expected "nothing from him. Expectations on her part would frighten him as much as would loss of control over his own feelings" (85).

Susan Quinn feels that "Horney's version of Peer Gynt/Erich Fromm suggests that the relationship with Fromm may have ended because she wanted more from him than he was willing to give" (1987, 367). In fact, the Horney-Fromm relationship was probably similar to that of Clare and Peter, an unworkable combination of a dependent woman and a man hypersensitive to any demands upon him.

We may be getting Horney's version of this relationship in *Self-Analysis* and Fromm's in *Escape from Freedom*. Clare ascribes to her partner "the godlike role of magic helper" (*SA*, 238). The term "magic helper" is Fromm's, as Horney acknowledges, and his discussion of dependent people who crave such a helper could be a description of Karen or Clare. Dependent people want someone who will "protect, help, and develop" them, who will be with them constantly (Fromm 1941, 175). If the helpers are also dependent, it strengthens "the impression that this relationship is one of 'real love.'" People are bound to magic helpers because of "an inability to stand alone." Having no faith in their own efforts, they hope to satisfy all their wishes through the magic helper. Their object is not to live their own lives but to manipulate their partners, making the partners responsible for their well-being. Their dependency "results in a feeling of weakness and bondage" and a resentment that must be suppressed because it "threatens the security sought for in the relationship." Such relationships often end with separation, "which is usually followed by the choice of another object who is expected to fulfill all hopes connected with the magic helper" (175–77).

That Fromm's account resembles Horney's picture of Clare's morbid dependency on Peter so closely suggests that they may have been writing about the same relationship. Not surprisingly, Horney was more sympathetic toward Clare, while

Fromm shows an underlying irritation toward the dependent partners and sympathy with those who are supposed to protect, develop, and stick with them. Fromm acknowledges the possibility that both parties may be dependent, and Clare realizes that Peter yielded to her wishes "not because of love and generosity but because of his own weakness" (*SA*, 217). There is a suggestion here of a mutual morbid dependency, although one of the partners is far more enslaved than the other. I cannot help wondering whether Fromm and Horney were writing in part for each other, each trying to show the other how much he or she understood.

There are parallels in the course taken by the Clare-Peter and Horney-Fromm relationships as well. Clare is more interested in the affaire than Peter, and she does not realize for a long time that he wants a separation. According to Marianne Eckardt, it was Fromm's pulling away from Horney that "generated the heat"; she was "eager to talk with him, but he was withdrawing." Clare is crushed when she hears of Peter's affaire with another woman. Horney was equally upset when she learned of Fromm's involvement with the dancer Katherine Dunham. Frances Arkin remembers that she "blurted . . . out" news of Fromm's affaire to Horney, who "probably wanted to kill me."[16]

When Peter broke off their relationship, Clare was "thrown into a turmoil of wild despair" (*SA*, 227). There is evidence that Horney was extremely hurt by Fromm's behavior. The most vivid account of this has been given by Ernst Schachtel, a friend of Fromm's with whom Horney had a close connection, who reported that "our relationship stopped after she broke with Erich Fromm. She shocked me by saying that she didn't want to go on with me unless I stopped seeing Fromm. I was surprised she'd make such a condition. I think she was deeply hurt by Erich Fromm. I continued to see him because we were old friends." Schachtel "never saw [Horney] again. My wife died of cancer and she never came to the funeral."[17]

After her love affaire with Fromm was over, Horney continued social and professional relations with him, much as she had maintained a relationship with Oskar long after the romantic side of their marriage was dead. In both cases, the man was successful and still had something to offer. Horney initially wanted Fromm to teach at her institute, and she "spoke highly" of his first book, *Escape from Freedom*. Horney broke with Oskar when he was no longer successful, and she broke with Fromm when he became so successful as to pose a challenge to her preeminence. There was a widespread perception among the American Institute faculty that she drove him away because she was threatened by the success of his book and his popularity with students. The issue of lay analysis was seen as merely a pretext for getting rid of him. Her professional resentment and jealousy were undoubtedly important, but I doubt that she would have behaved as she did had the pain of her rejection by

Fromm not still been rankling. Renate was "puzzled by the violence of the break-up, which made many enemies" for her mother, and felt that there was an "underly-ing viciousness on her part."[18] Fromm confided to Paul Lussheimer the evening before Fromm's status as a training analyst was revoked that "there were personal rela-tionships involved" (Rubins 1978, 265).

Horney's behavior was foreshadowed, I think, by a passage in *Self-Analysis,* written more than a year before the final break with Fromm. After Clare allowed herself to see Peter's faults, she was able to take "a calm stand toward him. She still appreciated his good qualities but she knew that it would be impossible for her ever to be closely associated with him again" (245). When I first began to ponder the Clare case, I was startled by the word *associated,* which sounds more like a refer-ence to a colleague than to a lover. It indicates, I think, a determination on Horney's part—of which she may not have been fully aware—to sever her professional rela-tions with Fromm. After his rejection of her, she tried to understand his faults, to appreciate his good qualities, and to maintain their professional contact, but she felt an underlying anger that made her want to keep Fromm at a distance. It was this that made his threat to her status, and indeed his very presence, intolerable.

Although the Clare case enables us to infer a good deal about Karen Horney and her relationships with men—particularly her relationship with Erich Fromm—it does not show the polygamous side of her nature. Peter cheats on Clare, but she remains devoted to him; however, Horney's relationship with Fromm did not pre-clude other liaisons. It was not only Erich who was having affaires. Horney's inti-macies with her young disciples at the New York Psychoanalytic Institute occurred while she was involved with Fromm, and during this period she also had affaires that we know of with Paul Tillich and Erich Maria Remarque. According to Paul's wife, Hannah, Remarque "treated her like a little girl. He was tough. He called her 'you little goose.' And she loved that; she wanted someone strong." This was only part of what she wanted, but it seems to have been a persistent craving. Gertrude Lederer-Eckardt claims that Horney was "masochistic" and was often involved with "aggressive men."[19]

Horney never freed herself from her compulsive needs in relation to men, as she seems to have thought she had done in 1942. Clare came to feel that her need to merge with another person was like a drug addiction or cancerous growth. If we look at Horney's relationships with men for the next decade, we do not find her to have escaped her addiction. She turned quickly to Hans, and several sources affirm that she had numerous affaires in the forties. Louis De Rosis has described her as a "Rabelais in quality" who "liked boys" and "seemed to need a man around." According to Richard Hulbeck, a Dadaist artist turned analyst who gave Karen painting lessons in the early 1940s, "she was someone who badly needed to have a man with her." She was not interested in the "average citizen" but was looking for someone "up to her intellectual level," and such a man was hard to find. Hulbeck felt that he could have married her had he wished to, but he did not want to leave his wife and children. He thought that the "whole art business was an attempt to get closer" to him. Horney had "great sexual desire without being obscene and was frustrated. It was hard for men to approach her. She felt men like Tillich and Niebuhr to be old and weak."[20]

Horney's series of liaisons culminated in an affaire with a candidate twenty-five years younger than she. This candidate was her analysand, as Harold Kelman had been. I think she knew that her behavior was compulsive but could not help herself. Renate remembers her mother saying late in life that "even self-analysis does not work,"[21] a remark suggestive of continued struggle and disappointment. Her claims for self-analysis were more modest in *Neurosis and Human Growth* (238).

Horney never found another lover of the stature of Erich Fromm, nor did she expose herself again to the kind of disappointment she had experienced with him. In *Neurosis and Human Growth* she wrote of the morbidly dependent woman. "Assuming that she does manage to struggle out of her involvement, the value of her action would depend upon these questions: did she, by hook or crook, get out of the one dependency only sooner or later to rush into another one? Or did she get so wary of her feelings that she tended to deaden all of them? . . . Or has she changed in a more radical way and come out a really stronger person?" (257). When she was writing *Self-Analysis,* Horney thought she had achieved a radical change, but the first two alternatives are more descriptive of her actual condition. She rushed from one relationship into another, but she protected herself by not investing her feelings as deeply as she had done with Fromm.

As Susan Quinn has noted, "Horney herself possessed many of the attributes of the Peer Gynt type" (1987, 367), whose chief characteristic is what Horney defined as a need for "emotional distance": "He may be capable of having intense short-lived relationships . . . in which he appears and vanishes. They are brittle, and any number of factors may hasten his withdrawal. Sexual relationships may mean inordinately much to him as a bridge to others. He will enjoy them if they are transitory and do not interfere with his life. They should be confined, as it were, to the compartment set aside for such affairs" (*OIC*, 86–87). Horney's relationships do seem to have been set aside in a compartment. They were conducted with such discretion that many people did not know about them at the time. They were not, however, the main focus of Horney's life; her need for men was compulsive but not all-consuming. It did not interfere with her creative work but rather fueled her continuing search for psychological insight. Yet it did blemish her conduct as training and supervising analyst, and her favoritism toward her lovers and her quarrels with them had a disruptive effect on her institute.

Chapter 22

Schisms and Problems of Leadership

Karen Horney left the Berlin Psychoanalytic Institute in 1932, the Chicago Psychoanalytic Institute in 1934, and the New York Psychoanalytic Institute in 1941. In each place she had wanted more freedom to teach her own ideas, a desire that led her to offer courses at the Washington-Baltimore Institute and at the New School for Social Research. In spite of her statement in *New Ways in Psychoanalysis* that her formulations were not "meant to be the beginning of a new psychoanalytical 'school'" (11), she did want to lead a new movement, and she hoped that the formation of her own association and institute would promote this objective.

Founded in the spring of 1941, the American Institute for Psychoanalysis got off to a strong start, but two years later some of its leading faculty—Erich Fromm, Clara Thompson, Harry Stack Sullivan, Janet Rioch—along with eight others, resigned and formed the William Alanson White Institute. In February 1944, a second split occurred, as William Silverberg, Bernard Robbins, Judd Marmor, Harmon Ephron, Frances Arkin, and Isabel Beaumont resigned to join Stephen Jewett in founding the Comprehensive Course in Psychoanalysis at the New York Medical College. These schisms within Horney's own organization, which weakened it greatly, were the result of both personal and professional conflicts. Tensions continued at the American Institute even after Horney had warded off threats to her dominance and made the institute completely her own.

The first schism in which Horney was involved occurred when she resigned from the New York Psychoanalytic Institute and took with her a number of faculty members and candidates. When she first came to the New York Psychoanalytic, such colleagues as Adolph Stern, Lawrence Kubie, Fritz Wittels, and Gregory Zilboorg perceived her as a threat to classical theory. They also feared such other "dissidents" as Sandor Rado, Abraham Kardiner, David Levy, and Clara Thompson. In 1939, therefore, the Educational Committee of the institute revised the curriculum to ensure that candidates were well-grounded in Freud before being exposed to unorthodox teachers. According to the dissidents, candidates who were working with them were subjected to discrimination, and other candidates were discouraged from taking their courses or choosing them as training or supervising analysts.

Horney became a particular target because of her critique of Freud in *New Ways in Psychoanalysis*—which was acrimoniously discussed at two meetings in 1939— and because she wanted to teach courses that would evaluate psychoanalytic concepts from her point of view. There had already been conflict about her teaching. In 1937 her request to teach a technical course had been denied on the ground that beginning "students this year should first get acquainted with Freud's views." When the unorthodox Rado was then allowed to teach a technical course, Horney protested, refusing to accept the explanation that her proposal had been "forgotten": "I do not doubt that that is so, but as an analyst, I must ask for the reasons of such a collective amnesia."[22] On being demoted from instructor to lecturer in 1941, Horney was told that she could still offer elective courses but could no longer teach the basic curriculum.

As a result of her demotion, Horney resigned from the New York Psychoanalytic Institute, taking with her Clara Thompson, Bernard Robbins, Harmon Ephron, and Sarah Kelman. Soon thereafter, fourteen candidates also withdrew, proclaiming their action to be "the inevitable result of the unscientific spirit and undemocratic attitude of the Educational Committee." Those who resigned formed the Association for the Advancement of Psychoanalysis (AAP) and issued a highly publicized letter explaining their actions.[23] The central issue, they claimed, was the institute's decision to designate courses offered by "deviating" analysts electives, to be taken only after the required courses in "classical" theory. This presupposed classical theory to be the incontrovertible ground of all further investigation.

The AAP's position was that psychoanalytic theory "is still in an experimental stage," that candidates must not be misled by "the illusion of certainty, where none actually exists," and that a candidate at the beginning of training should be able to "choose whether he will first be exposed to 'classical' or to 'deviating' or 'nonclassical' concepts." A candidate who is analyzed by a "non-classicist" should also be trained in classical concepts, and vice versa. Unlike the New York Psychoanalytic Institute, where scientific issues were "decided through the possession of political power," the new institute, the defectors affirmed, would be "devoted to truly liberal and scientific principles, in psychoanalytic training, investigation, and discussion."

The AAP letter provoked a furious counterattack, led by Lawrence Kubie. A "Statement on Behalf of the New York Psychoanalytic Society and Institute" was widely distributed, and Kubie and a colleague traveled around the country presenting their case. In its statement and in an even more combative preliminary version (now in the Brill Archive), the remaining members of the New York Psychoanalytic not only denied all the charges against the institution but made charges of their own.[24] They charged that as training analysts the dissidents had enlisted candidates as allies and projected them into the midst of "heated scientific controversies." These troublemakers were using their position as teachers "to gather together a band of disciples, under the pretext of 'academic freedom.'"

In order to prevent students from becoming "indoctrinated with a one-sided viewpoint," the Educational Committee had asked "the most outstanding instructor" in the dissident group "to limit her teaching to lecturing," a decision that was ratified by a democratic vote of the society. The society did not thereby violate any principles of academic freedom, but the "divergent group" was aggrieved because it thus "lost the opportunity to maintain exclusive control over a small band of disciples."

It is not difficult for a dispassionate observer to sympathize with both sides of this dispute. The institute naturally wanted to curb the influence of Horney and other divergent instructors, and the dissidents naturally resented this. When Rado, Kardiner, and Levy split off to form the Columbia Psychoanalytic Clinic about a year later, their complaints echoed those of the people who had left with Horney (see Rubins 1971, 243–44). The leaders of the New York Psychoanalytic Society fought to preserve the classical character of their institute while the dissidents wished to cultivate their own disciples and to see their ideas taken as seriously as Freud's. Each side wanted to expose candidates to its point of view from the beginning of their training, and each accused the other of seeking to brainwash candidates by being the first to indoctrinate them. Although the outrage of the dissidents is understandable, they lost sight of the fact that the New York Psychoanalytic was not a university committed to the free play of ideas but a training institute devoted to the teaching of Freudian theory.

Separate institutes was the ideal solution, but the warring factions continued their dispute. Each side felt threatened and tried to discredit the other. Kubie was outraged by Horney's charges of unfair treatment and annoyed by her subsequent success. He collected the proclamations and announcements of the AAP and the American Institute as well as press reports about them. In March 1942 he sent Adolph Stern a series of clippings, "one from the 'Post,' one from 'PM,' one from the

'A.M.A.,' all glorifying that well known American girl, Karen Horney" (Brill Archive). Horney was at last free to teach her own ideas, but Kubie's propagandizing ensured that she and her associates were excluded from mainstream national and international psychoanalytic organizations and journals. She was much vilified and her later books were not reviewed in establishment journals.

The conflict between Horney and the New York Psychoanalytic Institute was even more bitter than the public documents indicate. Horney was not simply demoted from instructor to lecturer and denied access to required courses; she was deprived of her status as training and supervising analyst. This was an enormous insult. One of the complaints leading to this step was that she misused her position "to build little bands of neophytes and proselytes around her, and to keep them from having contact with any other points of view." Another was that "she had a tendency to become involved in serious counter-transference relationships with some of her young male students." Not only did she lure some of them into her bed, but she did not make it possible for them "to work out the negative aspects of their transference relationships to her." She had a tendency to build "closely dependent relationships in which all hostile elements had to be bottled up and never expressed."[25] We know from other testimony that Horney was not good at allowing other people to express anger or criticism toward her.

Horney had charged that Freud was inhospitable to other people's ideas, but Kubie felt that she "suffered from the same myopia," since she kept changing her own theory but could not allow anyone else to challenge or modify it. The dissenting Horney could not tolerate dissent. She had hoped that those who later left for Columbia would join her, but they did not. She was most disappointed in the loss of Kardiner, who explained that Rado, the Columbia clinic's head, "gave me complete liberty to go any way I wanted; I think I couldn't have done it with her."[26]

Within three weeks of the resignations from the New York Psychoanalytic Institute, the Association for the Advancement of Psychoanalysis was formed, with William Silverberg as president, Clara Thompson as vice-president, Harold Kelman as secretary, and Stephen P. Jewett as treasurer. The AAP then launched *The American Journal of Psychoanalysis* and founded the American Institute for Psychoanalysis with Karen Horney as dean.

Neither the association nor the institute was originally devoted to Horney's theory, although she now had many more opportunities to work with candidates and to promulgate her ideas. Silverberg, who had been a member of Sullivan's Zodiac group, was sufficiently classical in outlook to come within one vote of being elected president of the American Psychoanalytic Association in 1941—his defeat by Karl Menninger sealed the exclusion of the AAP from the APA. Erich Fromm and Harry

Stack Sullivan each had a distinctive viewpoint, and a variety of other positions were represented by the members. In his presidential address of September 1941, Silverberg stressed the eclectic nature of the association. It was unified only by its devotion to "the principle of complete scientific freedom," he asserted; otherwise "we represent as a group . . . many differences of opinion." He criticized those who "use available power to silence those who dissent"—an obvious reference to the New York Psychoanalytic Institute—and stood up for mutual respect and "the freedom to think as our experience dictates" (1941, 21–23).

There were signs of conflict from the beginning. Soon after the association was organized, Fromm and Sullivan were elected honorary members, but Fromm was at first unwilling to accept honorary status because it did not constitute "adequate recognition of his standing as a psychoanalyst." He demanded the privilege of being able to train and supervise candidates. This was conferred at a special meeting on 2 November 1941, but "a minority strongly opposed . . . this step on the grounds that it committed the Association to the acceptance of the principle of lay-analysis and thus set a dangerous precedent."[27] Fromm was allowed to teach, but because he was not an M.D., he could not offer courses in analytic technique. Candidates were not sent to him for training analysis, which made him feel excluded and unappreciated. It is impossible to determine Horney's role in all this, but I suspect that she wanted to draw upon Fromm's reputation and talent while keeping him in a peripheral role. She may have had a conflict between her desire not to associate with Fromm after the breakup of their affaire and a reluctance to sever their professional relationship.

In January 1943, students petitioned for Fromm to offer a seminar on technique as part of the program. The faculty council rejected the petition "on the grounds that this would be a further sanctioning of lay-analysis" and proposed that Fromm give a course at the New School on theoretical fundamentals. Fromm rejected their compromise because "it impugned his standing as a psychoanalyst" and announced that "either he would have to be permitted to teach technical seminars on a par with other faculty members or he would withdraw from all connection with the Association and the Institute."[28] When the association voted to revoke Fromm's training and supervising privileges, Fromm withdrew, accompanied by Clara Thompson, Janet Rioch, Harry Stack Sullivan, and candidates who were in analysis with them.

There has been a good deal of debate over whether this conflict was really about lay analysis. In the early years of the American Institute, classes were held in homes and offices, at the New School, and at the New York Medical College, where Stephen Jewett was chair of the department of psychiatry. Almost from the beginning there was talk of having the institute join the college, which would give it a base and enhance its stature in the medical community. Some feared that because Fromm was a lay analyst, his presence on the institute's faculty would weaken its chances of becoming part of a medical school, while others felt that all analysts should have medical degrees—as Horney herself had argued in 1927 (1927e). Clara Thompson contended, however, that the issue of lay analysis was a false one. True, Jewett had affirmed that the medical school "would not sponsor a layman on their own faculty," but he had not said that a layman on the faculty of the institute would be a bar to a merger.[29] Moreover, having a distinguished lay member does not constitute an endorsement of lay analysis, as the practice of other societies had demonstrated.

Thompson felt that the real issue was power: that although the Horney group was in control, it felt itself "threatened politically by the increasing strength of another point of view." Because of his popularity with students and the success of *Escape from Freedom,* Fromm had become a formidable rival to Horney. There was a widespread perception that despite her stated commitment to the free play of ideas, Horney wanted "to have her own institute and to run it in her own way" and that the fight over lay analysis was "an excuse for getting rid of Fromm."[30] After all, Horney had seen a lay analyst herself (Hanns Sachs), she had sent Marianne to Fromm for her training analysis, and she had "joked about" her previous opposition to lay analysis (Rubins 1978, 248).

The rivalry between Horney and Fromm was personal as well as political. There is much testimony that Horney envied Fromm's new fame and his success as a teacher and wanted "to be the one and only star" at the institute. "I don't know of any two people with such a strong will as those two," observed Gertrude Lederer-Eckardt. "They both wanted to dominate; they were bound to clash. Both had the feeling they were predestined to be leaders." According to Ruth Moulton, Fromm and Horney were both "messiahs who knew all the answers" and hence were engaged "in bitter rivalry," with Horney having "more chutzpa." She was "terrifying in attacking Clara Thompson and Erich Fromm."[31] Horney's desire to get rid of Fromm was also fueled, of course, by her resentment at his having broken off their romantic relationship and her need to distance herself from him.

Thus, as a result of both political and personal factors, a "situation painfully similar" to the one at the New York Psychoanalytic Institute had developed, leading to another split. In his letter of resignation, Ralph Crowley charged that the same tactics that had "instigated the organization of the Association for the Advancement of Psychoanalysis" had now been used "by this very association supposedly dedicated to an opposite principle." Horney did to Fromm what the New York Psychoanalytic Institute had done to her. The AAP was not devoted to democratic principles, he complained, "but is founded basically on the idea that purge and punishment should be outlawed if done to Horney, while they are all right if done to someone else."[32] To many of those who remained, the "original idealism" of the institute "seemed to have been tarnished" (Marmor 1964, 6). Academic freedom had once again proven to be an unattainable objective at an institute in which the most politically powerful group was committed to ensuring the dominance of its own ideology.

In February 1944, negotiations for an affiliation between the American Institute and the New York Medical College broke down. Jewett wanted to establish a psychoanalytic training program under the aegis of his department and looked to the American Institute for staff. The central issue from the institute's point of view was preserving its autonomy if it became part of the Medical College. Those who wished to affiliate for the sake of enhancing the prestige of psychoanalytic training and gaining access to a larger constituency were opposed by those who distrusted Jewett and feared that the institute might lose control over its program, its standards, and its identity. The conflict was not bitter, but the hesitancy and dissension were enough to make Jewett realize the difficulty of "working out satisfactory arrangements with a group as a whole which is already organized into an Institute." He decided to develop his plan "independent of an already existing organization" and to deal directly with individuals.[33] He informed the AAP of this on 18 February 1944, and the next day six members of the association resigned and joined the Medical College.

Horney had effectively blocked affiliation of the institute with the Medical College after she had purged Erich Fromm on the ground that he would endanger that affiliation. She was motivated once again by a fear of diminished status and loss of political and intellectual dominance. She "wanted to be the big shot" and was "hurt" and "furious" if she was "overlooked," noted Marianne Eckardt. As head of her own institute she could not be ignored, but as part of the Medical College she might be. It was clear that "she didn't want anyone else to have control."[34]

Those who did join the college wanted the medical affiliation, but they also craved a freer atmosphere. According to Judd Marmor, there was "a growing concern" that the institute was becoming "a Horney group" rather than an organization "in which varying points of view . . . would be freely taught" (1964, 6). Horney's reluctance to affiliate with the Medical College seemed to confirm these fears. It was no secret that Horney "demanded disciples and did not encourage creative thought" that disagreed with hers.[35] She was a rebellious fighter for freedom who became an autocrat after gaining power—an all-too-familiar story.

The second schism was a great blow to Horney, for it not only deprived the association of more talented people but left it with only thirteen members (there had been thirty-four a year earlier). According to Harold Kelman, Horney "wanted to give up the AAP and to withdraw from all organizations. It required considerable support and encouragement from those who remained to help her through this difficult period" (1971, 21). The institute recovered, however, helped by the boom in psychoanalysis following World War II, when many people sought treatment and a large influx of physicians eager for analytic training returned from military service.

But although it prospered during the remainder of Horney's life, the institute suffered from a lack of gifted intellectuals who could continue to develop her theory. In the short run Horney got what she wanted, but in the end her needs for dominance, conformity, and preeminence diminished her influence, for they drove away many talented colleagues and fostered an environment in which she alone could be highly creative. Without others to engage it with succeeding developments, Horney's mature theory has not continued to develop in the forty years since her death. This is partly responsible for its lack of cultural presence.

Horney received much of the support she needed after the second split from Harold Kelman. Born in 1906, Kelman was a Harvard M.D. who had had Horney for three supervisions at the New York Psychoanalytic, where Kardiner had been his training analyst. He resigned along with Horney, went into analysis with her, and quickly became a mainstay of the AAP. He supported Horney in her opposition to Fromm, to whom he was hostile, and in her reluctance to affiliate with Jewett.[36] Kelman filled the void left by the departure of Bernard Robbins, at that time president of the association, for the Medical College. Kelman was a powerful figure at the institute—until Horney turned against him in 1951.

Kelman and Horney have often been described as having had a symbiotic relationship in which "they used each other" to accomplish their objectives. Kelman, say various observers, was a "power-hungry, manipulative" man who "wanted importance." He was "pushy even as a student" and used his connection with Horney to further his ambitions. Harmon Ephron remembered "this strange, uptight, frantic guy. He was a student, then all of a sudden he became a *macher*, a big shot, teaching, writing, talking." According to Wanda Willig, "at first he was a big help; then he wanted too much power." His power, claimed others, "went to his head" and he became increasingly obnoxious: "He was a bastard, a slave driver; no one liked him." While being difficult with others, he "placated" Horney, lent himself to her purposes, and "seemed interested in being her son."[37]

Kelman himself has explained what Horney derived from their relationship: "Horney [had been] placed in a leadership role she neither wanted nor found congenial. Characteristically, she tried to delegate the organizational tasks as quickly as she could" (1971, 19). Whereas Horney was "oblivious to organizational matters" (Eckardt 1978a, 159), Kelman was a gifted organizer, and because Horney "relied on him terrifically," he became "the power behind the throne."[38] According to Kelman, Horney did not like the leadership role because of her self-effacing tendencies (1971, 28). The expansive Kelman was happy to fight her battles, and she was glad to have him do so. (We remember that Clare, too, had difficulty exercising authority.)

In spite of her aversion to the leadership role, Horney did want to be boss, to dictate policy, to be in control. Kelman became her enforcer. Because she "had difficulty dealing with hostility," she ensured that it was "directed at Kelman" rather than at her.[39] As can be imagined, morale at the institute was low. Kelman felt empowered to be ruthless because he had Horney's approval, while those who resented his behavior had no one to whom to appeal. Jack Rubins reports that when Muriel Ivimey, "the rather quiet and unassuming assistant dean, complained in a letter to Karen that Kelman was exceeding his authority, she replied protectively that if he was, . . . it was no doubt for the good of the Institute" (1978, 291).

As dean, Horney fostered an atmosphere of anxiety, insecurity, and contentiousness. Marianne has observed that she "was in a leadership role but was not a leader"; she had power but "no political awareness." She "brushed aside rules which facilitate organizational work" (1978a, 159) and shunned "parliamentary procedures" (Kelman 1971, 18). She delegated responsibilities but then failed to exercise oversight. In Marianne's words, Horney was "not a team person" but was "totally erratic" and felt that she "could do whatever she pleased." She was, said Frances Arkin, "very moody and self-centered"; she "measured everything in terms of how it would affect her." Her shyness and aversion to open conflict notwithstanding, she could be ruthless and vindictive and was a formidable opponent. In his biography of Horney Rubins characterized her as the "gentle rebel" of psychoanalysis, but in a letter to Susan Quinn he wrote that "she was willful, emotionally cold, dominating and out to get her own way—whatever she wanted—regardless of the cost or whoever stood in her way." Arkin observed that "no man or woman with any aggressivity would stick around. She was not a nice soft female. She made a statement and God spoke." According to Marianne, she was "friendly but not a good friend."[40] She made many enemies by her habit of using people and then dropping them.

Thus the divisiveness and tension at the institute were the product not only of Horney's leadership style but also of her manner of relating to people. She had "difficulty getting along with anyone unless she got her way in what mattered to her" (Harry Gershman, Academy). According to Wanda Willig, in close relationships she was "difficult, stubborn, not likable"; she "did what she wanted to." Her immoderate likes and dislikes caused a good deal of discomfort. She could react to individuals with a "complete, total, and immediate rejection that took one by surprise" (Alexander Martin, Academy). She "had a biting tongue," "put people down," and treated "people whose ideas differed from hers" with "contempt and derision." While she disparaged some people, she celebrated others as "wonderful," often placing them in positions of power. In Marianne's view, one of her mother's worst traits as a leader was her "totally unconscious" tendency "to create jealousies and rivalries by a very marked play of favoritism." Horney seems to have become like her mother, "a pushover for people who adored her."[41] They became the wonderful disciples of a wonderful leader.

Being Horney's favorite was an insecure position, for her "feelings were fickle" and it "took very little to lose her friendship." She would often "hurt people's feelings and not be aware of it," but she was hypersensitive to "minor slights to her self-esteem." Like Sonni, she demanded adulation and could not endure complaints. There was a great deal of insecurity beneath her sense of importance. She seemed to shrug off her former friends, but Kelman tells us that "although she did not talk about her former friends," he gradually realized "from occasional remarks, over the years" that "the pain of such breaks healed very slowly" (1971, 24). In spite of her wisdom as an analyst, Horney rarely tried to work out the difficulties in her own relationships. She seemed to rely on her power and eminence to acquire new people as replacements for the ones she had lost. The pattern in these relationships is the same as in her love affaires: high hopes fed by need, idealization, disappointment, rejection of the other, and a search for a new person to fulfill her expectations. She may have turned against people for no discernible reason because the combination of high demands and insecurity led her to anticipate that they would injure her.

The most striking instance of Horney's rejection of a favorite was her treatment of Kelman, who had devoted himself to her. It is difficult to say exactly when the change in her feelings occurred, but in 1951 she began attacking him in public. During a discussion of his paper "Rational and Irrational Authority," she is reported to have said, "What are you doing? You are out of it." One of the people who spoke to him afterward described him as "crushed, bewildered, almost in tears." In her most shocking attack she denounced him in front of his students. Sara Sheiner, Kelman's analysand, described his course on "Process" as "remarkable," "revolutionary," "electrifying." But Horney "did not approve." She once interrupted a lecture, proclaiming, "I don't understand a word you are saying; this is all nonsense." In addition to these open assaults, Horney avoided Kelman socially, was unduly critical of his students, and encouraged his archrival Frederick Weiss's long-standing animosity toward him.[42]

Many explanations have been offered for Horney's turnabout. Kelman "got too big for his britches and she had to cut him down," suggests Arkin. Rubins reports that letters addressed to Horney were intercepted, opened in the institute office, and "forwarded directly to Kelman for his action," a practice to which Horney objected in a "scathing letter" to the secretary (1978, 319). According to Lederer-Eckardt, Horney "hated Kelman violently" because she "seemed to have realized he was exploiting her." The most frequent explanation has been that Horney turned against Kelman because he began to develop ideas of his own that she considered a challenge to hers. "My uncle was insufferable," says Norman Kelman, "but he was brilliant, devoted, and original. Karen couldn't stand his originality." Abe Pinsky felt that Horney was doing to Harold Kelman what had earlier been done to her; she was "attacking him for his independent thinking." Horney, note others, "respected what other people said if she wasn't challenged," but Kelman "began to contradict her," and when challenged "she was ruthless, like a man with a woman's wiles."[43]

Another factor in the rift may have been a breakdown in Horney's romantic relationship with Kelman. Just as the aggressiveness of her behavior toward Fromm is in part attributable to her anger at having been spurned, so the vehemence of her attacks on Kelman may have been partly the result of a lover's quarrel. Observers differ about whether Kelman and Horney were in fact lovers, but there is a great deal of testimony from good sources to support the theory. Beginning in the mid-1940s they vacationed together in Mexico, the Caribbean, and Guatemala. Kelman's remarks at the American Academy's historical session on Horney show that she would talk to him about her life and her feelings in an unusually intimate way. He clearly thought about her a great deal, perhaps because she had hurt him so deeply. According to Gertrude Weiss, on one occasion he said to Horney, "You are without human emotions. How can you get people healthy without feeling for them?" This could well have been a reaction to her coldness toward him after many years of intimacy. And, as we have seen, at Horney's funeral, Kelman "bawled like a baby"; "he reacted like his mother had died."[44]

Horney's having been in part a mother figure for Kelman put them at cross-purposes, since she seemed more motherly than she was. According to Gertrude Weiss, Horney "hated it when someone would say, 'you are motherly.'" She craved adulation and was ready to give approval in exchange for it, but she was not eager to see her young admirers develop minds of their own. Kelman adored Horney, but he wanted her to approve of his thinking, to "take over his ideas, quote him,"[45] and that she was not prepared to do. He was profoundly influenced by her, as he readily acknowledged, but he sought to influence her too. He wished her to be proud of him, the way a mother is of a son, but his independent ideas aroused her competitiveness instead, and she belittled him. She needed intellectual autonomy for herself, but she had difficulty granting it to others, especially those she expected to be her followers and to feed her pride.

Chapter 23

Karen and Her Daughters

Karen Horney had three daughters. Brigitte, born in 1911, became a star of German film, theater, and television. When Karen moved to America, Brigitte remained in Germany in order to pursue her career and escaped to Switzerland barely ahead of the Soviets toward the end of World War II. After the war, Karen visited her every summer, beginning in 1948, and in December 1951 Brigitte moved to the United States to be with her mother. Karen and Brigitte admired each other immensely and had an exceptionally close relationship. Marianne, born in 1913, studied medicine at the universities of Freiburg, Berlin, and Chicago and graduated from the American Institute for Psychoanalysis in 1944. She followed in her mother's professional footsteps, but their relationship became strained after she entered analysis with Erich Fromm in the late 1930s. Renate, born in 1916, came to the United States with her mother in 1932, returned to Germany in order to marry in 1935, and settled in Mexico in 1939, where her husband worked as a film director and she reared a family. Karen visited Renate in Mexico once or twice a year, sometimes staying for much of the summer, and provided both emotional and financial support to her unhappily married daughter.

Karen had markedly different relationships with each of her daughters, and each has given a different account of her. The variations reflect not only the divergent personalities of the daughters but also the many-sidedness of Karen Horney. She was empathetic and nurturing toward Renate, defensive and distant toward Marianne, and adoring toward Brigitte, in whom she may have found at last a great person with whom to merge. Karen's interactions with her daughters, both as they were growing up and in adulthood, reveal many facets of her personality.

Marianne's problems in childhood were partly the result of her position in the birth order. Brigitte resented her new sister and was hostile from the outset. Karen recorded Brigitte's jealousy in a notebook she kept about her children: "Bigge [Brigitte's nickname] was decidedly hostile towards Marianne initially; in the first few days she told her very crossly, 'Go away, you.' A few days later she even wanted to hit her in the face." As the girls grew older, the fact that Marianne was more beautiful and charming than Brigitte exacerbated the situation. They fought constantly, with Brigitte often hitting Marianne. When Brigitte took up dancing, she thought Marianne's quiet yoga exercises "ridiculous" and teased her "mercilessly." Renate often cried out "in anger and outrage at this unfair treatment," but Marianne would just smile and declare that it did "not really matter," since Brigitte did not understand her. Marianne later described herself as having become quite detached, and we can see here how she employed this defense as a way of coping with Brigitte. Of course, despite Marianne's disclaimer, Brigitte's assaults did matter. Describing the childhood strife to Jack Rubins, she characterized her sister as "impossible, ruthless," a "beast." Renate notes, "It was terrible, what Marianne went through."[46]

One of Marianne's complaints was that her mother did not protect her from Brigitte, which Renate confirms. Both Marianne and Renate explain their mother's behavior as the result of her identification with Brigitte, a difficult child like herself who was not pretty when she was young. Karen, they say, saw Marianne being favored by others, as Berndt had been, and sided with the child who felt left out. Karen may indeed have identified with the less attractive and popular Brigitte, but we get a different picture from her notebook. The descriptions of Marianne are warmly affectionate and the comparisons with Bigge are almost always in Marianne's favor. Marianne is "a little rogue," "a clown," a generous, good-natured child, in contrast to the jealous, demanding Bigge, who always wants the largest share. The leading motifs in the notebook are Bigge's jealousy, Bigge's illnesses, and Marianne's cuteness. If Karen came to favor Bigge, her preference seems to have been a later development. Perhaps she remembered her own difficulties as a child and overcompensated for her greater fondness for Marianne, or perhaps Marianne's change of personality made her less appealing.

In 1918 Karen sent Marianne to the town of Zuoz, in Switzerland, a few months after Brigitte had gone there for treatment of tuberculosis. Brigitte made a good adjustment (Heyerdahl 1992, 18), but the experience was traumatic for Marianne. She was beset by shyness and fear of her teachers. She experienced learning difficulties after her return; it took three years of special tutoring to help her catch up in school. The sunny, trusting, friendly child seems to have disappeared after this experience. Marianne has always resented having been sent away from her parents and into a foreign environment at so young an age.

Another mistake of Karen's, though far less serious, was to try sending her daughters to Melanie Klein for prophylactic analysis in 1925. The strong-willed Brigitte refused to go, but Marianne went for two years. She feels that the analysis "doesn't seem to have hurt," although it could not possibly have helped because, being focused on libidinal issues, it did not deal with any of her real problems (Maeder 1989, 217). The nine-year-old Renate, on the other hand, had a distinctly negative reaction to her experience with Klein. She began having nightmares and finally vented her anger by writing letters to the neighbors telling them "all [she] had learned from [her] analysis," signed "Greetings from your Fart." Karen later told

Renate that the analysis had been "her biggest mistake and she was sorry she had exposed us to that torture."[47]

That Karen would send her children to Melanie Klein was understandable in view of the analytic ideas of the day, but it was inconsistent with her overall approach to child rearing, which was "letting children grow" and not interfering with them. Marianne came to feel that her mother's philosophy was a "rationalization" for her neglect of her daughters (Academy). Renate remembers her mother's approach in the same way, but feels more positively about it: "Looking back, I find it remarkable that she never interfered or lectured and seldom gave any advice. . . . She knew she had to release us completely and let us make our own mistakes."[48]

Karen's philosophy of parenting may have been inspired by her reading of Ellen Key, a Swedish feminist whose progressive ideas about love, marriage, and motherhood she admired. In her early diaries she had celebrated Key as "a great person" whose "high idealism finds an echo deep in my nature" (AD, 91). Key strongly opposed the idea that children have a natural depravity that needed to be "bridled, tamed, [and] suppressed" (1888, 2). In The Education of the Child she claims that the chief evil of present-day methods of child rearing is "not leaving the child in peace" (5). The object of education must not be to supplant the personality of the child with another personality that conforms to social norms and resembles that of everyone else, but to strengthen the child's "natural disposition to become an individual human being" (14). Children are entirely new souls who need to "choose for themselves the path they must tread." A "hard or even mild pressure towards uniformity can make the whole of childhood a torment" (11). The secret of education, therefore, is "do not educate" (4). Children are unique beings with purposes of their own and are not here "only for the pleasure, pride, and comfort of their parents" (13). Parents should encourage their children to be independent, she concludes, and not keep them from becoming strong, competent adults by overprotecting or spoiling them.

These ideas had a tremendous appeal to the nineteen-year-old Karen: they helped her to formulate what was wrong with her own upbringing, and they continued to influence her after she became a mother. Although incompatible with the Freudian view of the child, they perfectly anticipate Horney's later emphasis on self-realization. Marianne has described Karen's mothering style as one of "benign neglect": "no pressure; we could be anything we wanted" (Academy). According to Renate, Karen wanted to give her children the freedom she had missed and taught them "to be true to ourselves and also respectful of others."[49] This was Ellen Key's formula.

Horney's works contain many passages about childhood that are reminiscent of

Key. In *Neurotic Personality* she writes: "It all depends on what the parents try to achieve in the education of their offspring: whether the tendency is to make a child strong, courageous, independent, capable of dealing with all sorts of situations, or whether the main tendency is to shelter the child, to make it obedient, to keep it ignorant of life as it is, or in short to infantilize it" (85). In her own parenting Karen may have carried her philosophy too far, with sending Marianne to Switzerland being the most striking example. It is understandable that Marianne later felt that "too much independence was expected of them too soon" (Quinn 1987, 179). Karen's noninterference in the conflicts between Brigitte and Marianne may also have been a misapplication of the hands-off policy recommended by Key. Her children needed more nurturing and protection than she supplied.

That Karen had a philosophy of parenting which she tried to follow in raising her children does not negate Marianne's idea that her mother's belief in noninterference was a rationalization of her neglect. In *Neurotic Personality,* Horney notes that "the basic evil" in an unfavorable environment is parents' inability to give "genuine warmth and affection" because of "their own neuroses." Usually "the essential lack of warmth is camouflaged," and the parents, sometimes citing "educational theories," "claim to have in mind the child's best interest" (80). Horney was probably thinking of Sonni and Wackels when she wrote this passage, but it also describes her own conduct as a parent.

All the daughters have reported that their mother was preoccupied with her profession, even on weekends, and that aside from Christmas, summer holidays, and the cook's night off, she spent little time with them. She was not entirely free even on vacations, for she took patients and writing projects with her. Although the children were looked after by servants and governesses, Marianne asserts that they were "always neglected": "Dresses too long or short; stockings didn't fit; nails dirty." As far as she was concerned, the neglect was also emotional: "We'd go on a school excursion every year, one week. When I'd come back, [Karen would] say, 'you are back already,' as if I could have come back five days later without any difference."[50] Karen tried to find schools that suited her daughters' interests and temperaments, but, being preoccupied with her work and her love life, she was unable to give them much of herself.

Brigitte's and Renate's accounts of their childhood are similar in many respects to Marianne's but have a different emotional tone. Brigitte told Gerd Høst Heyerdahl, a long-time friend, that she could not have chosen better parents (Heyerdahl 1992, 11). Her mother was beautiful, healthy, and clear-minded and provided a modern education for the girls (13). Because her parents were unhappily married and her mother was always busy, nobody really took care of the children; there were governesses and housekeepers, but these servants did not provide love (19). Her mother would compensate by taking the children on long summer vacations, which were happy times (21). When money became short after her separation from Oskar, Karen worked hard and was always tired. Brigitte did the shopping and housekeeping: "I couldn't ask Mutti so many things which had to do with everyday life—she was so busy and when she was done with her work, she was tired and I put her to bed" (28). Brigitte found a substitute family in the home of her best friend, Inga (20).

Karen's youngest daughter, Renate, entitles the opening chapter of her memoir "A Happy Childhood." She describes periods when she cried frequently or acted out, but she feels that her "family life was a happy, united one" and that she "was a happy child." She "loved [her] mother very much" and "wanted to be with her as much as possible and to take care of her." Renate felt that "in spite of her busy and often unhappy life, Mother surrounded us with warm family feeling." Her memoir is full of glowing memories of the "really wonderful years of my childhood."[51]

The differing relationships between Karen and her daughters continued into adulthood. Perhaps as a defense against Brigitte's abuse and her mother's absorption in her work, Marianne, by her own account, became "very detached." Karen was also reserved, leading to "an absence of relationship" on both sides.[52] There was a void, not only in her relationship with her mother, but in her life as a whole: "Outwardly I was pleasant, conscientious, even-tempered, liked, yet without close friends and very detached. I was neither happy nor unhappy" (Eckardt 1980).

Marianne's life changed when she went into analysis with Erich Fromm. There surfaced "an incredible degree of irritation" at her "lack of genuine contact" with her mother. Marianne feels that Fromm "was the only person who could have helped" her because his validation of her mother's "aloofness" and "alienation in personal relationships" allowed her to recognize her "needs for love."[53] As a result, she developed "a readiness for making warm responsive contacts" (Eckardt 1980).

Marianne's desire for a closer, more affectionate relationship with her mother coexisted with an "antagonism" that she "expressed by aloofness." Karen "felt it," Marianne observed, but did not try to reach her. Instead, Karen blamed the change in her daughter on Fromm and thought it was the product of "his antagonism to her." Marianne tried to get her mother to discuss their problems but met with "a stone wall."[54] Instead of understanding what her daughter was going through in analysis and responding to her need to express her feelings—as someone with her analytic experience might have done—Karen seems to have reacted defensively.

Her letters to Brigitte indicate that Karen was sensitive to Marianne's withdrawal and frustrated by it: "She has something of the porcupine; if you want to get close to her she puts up her pricks."[55] Karen complains that "one never has the feeling she is there." The worst thing is not Marianne's "occasional eruptions or her snide remarks" but the fact that Karen cannot "figure her out" (9 December 1946). On 21 October 1947 she confides: "I have tried for years to get close to her. It's not possible. And—just when you think the atmosphere is at least peaceful, there is a new vitriolic outburst from her. I finally gave up. It is very sad." Each woman longed for emotional contact but felt that the other could not be reached; both gave up on the relationship and grieved over its loss. The irreconcilable differences between them were partly the result of similarities in temperament, since both became withdrawn when they felt threatened. In spite of her hurt and disappointment, Karen was proud of Marianne's professional accomplishments and felt that her daughter was "a *very* good mother": "Really, 100 times better than I am. She treats me like a broomstick but with her children she is loving and friendly" (8 October 1947).

After Karen's death, Marianne continued to be critical of her as a mother, a leader, and a theorist, but at a special session of the American Academy on Horney (1975), she confessed that "over the past ten years, through the diaries and conversations with my sisters and colleagues, a person has emerged, attractive and admirable, but whom I did not have the privilege of knowing." She told Jack Rubins that the diaries opened up a "Karen Horney I never knew—emotional, intense, full of ups and downs," engaged in a "vivid dialogue" with herself. Her mother was "afraid to reach out to other people" as "a warm, vulnerable human being," "yet there was a genuine spontaneous core" and "she had a great deal of joy and enthusiasm." In her conversations with me, Marianne observed that her mother's "way of adapting to her childhood situation was remarkable" and urged me not to portray her as a "self-tortured individual" without also depicting her as an "intense, questioning, creative, exploring person."[56]

Renate also saw her mother as both a tortured person and a remarkable human being whose childhood problems, deep depressions, and neurotic trends enabled her to develop a profound understanding of human psychology. And, like Marianne, Renate urged me to remember that despite her difficulties, her mother "was always positive and full of the joy of life," a person who "loved adventure, travel and learning anything new."[57]

Both Marianne and Renate insist that because of their mother's reserve, they did not know her very well. "Mother loved me and liked me," says Renate, "but we were never close." Mother and daughter were miserable their first year in Chicago, but "instead of sitting down and talking it out, we made the big mistake of keeping our frustrations to ourselves." During their "many long summers" together in Mexico, Karen gave Renate moral support, but "she talked little about herself and never about her own emotional problems." Karen's reserve was so great that Renate had

not been "aware of the tension" between her mother and father during her childhood—"they carried it off well."[58] She was surprised to learn of her mother's
affaires—even those with Fromm and Kelman, both of whom she had seen with her
mother many times.

In spite of her reserve, Karen was warm and supportive toward Renate. She
made great efforts to help Renate and her family get out of Germany in 1938 and
sympathized with her daughter's marriage problems. Renate's husband, Fredy, was
given to "biting, sadistic, and violent tempers," and Renate was often "crushed" by
his anger. She felt that her mother understood her situation completely, in part
because she saw a repetition of her own morbid dependency. Karen let Renate talk
freely, urged her not to lose her spontaneity, and tried to make her feel "that I was
still 'I.' "[59] She also tried to counsel Fredy during her visits to Mexico.

Karen came to Mexico not only to play but to work and established a regular
schedule of writing in the morning and painting, exploring, and family activity in
the afternoon. *Our Inner Conflicts* was largely written during her visits. In 1949
Karen bought a house for Renate in Cuernavaca where she could have quarters of
her own. Unfortunately, she did not get much pleasure from this house, visiting it
only once, at Christmas in 1950. After Karen's death, Renate's possession of the
house and the money she inherited from her mother facilitated her decision to seek
a divorce.

Renate claims that she and her mother "had a good but not an intimate relationship. She helped me when I needed help and was always concerned." Karen
"came to appreciate Marianne as quite a person in later life" but "never understood
her." Renate and Marianne both grew up believing that Brigitte was their mother's
favorite, and Karen's fondness for her eldest daughter intensified after the war.
Renate has described her mother's later relationship with Brigitte as an "infatua-
tion,"[60] and there is testimony from those who saw them together in New York that
Karen adored Brigitte and delighted in being with her. The letters she wrote to
Brigitte between 1945 and 1951 show a passionate attachment between mother and
daughter.

After Karen left Germany, she and Brigitte saw each other on Karen's frequent
trips to Europe, but during the war they could neither visit nor correspond. In 1942 or
1943 Brigitte developed tuberculosis of the knee and went to Switzerland for treatment. After about a year she was sufficiently recovered to return to Berlin, but near
the end of the war she returned to Switzerland to escape the oncoming Soviets.
When her correspondence with her mother resumed in 1945, she was at the Shatzalp
Sanatorium in Davos. Karen's early letters are full of concern for Brigitte's health,
sympathy with her trials, and offers of financial assistance. She expresses great long-

ing for Brigitte, but they were not to see each other again until April 1948, when Karen flew to Switzerland and spent three weeks in Chardonne.

Karen's letters to Brigitte were always affectionate, but there is a marked escalation of warmth after Brigitte's successful return to acting in 1946: "You are just a spectacular person!! I am terribly proud of you" (22 February). Karen inquires about Brigitte's career, wants to see reviews, and admires her "wonderful gift" as an actress (5 December). She goes to see Brigitte's movies and writes appreciatively of her art.

Before their reunion, Karen's letters are filled with longing to see Brigitte. She has a vision of herself and Brigitte "flying into each other's arms" when she gets off the plane in Geneva. According to Gerd Heyerdahl, there was equal anticipation on Brigitte's side. Apparently they found their reunion everything they had dreamed of: "It was one of the most beautiful summers for both" (1992, 176).

Renate feels that Brigitte was her mother's "one great love,"[61] and after the first reunion, Karen's letters often have a loverlike quality. She longs "indescribably" for Brigitte: "With each curler I am thinking of you. And with the simmering pot! And with the beautiful blue scarf. And with gymnastics" (8 June 1948). She tries to thrive on having been "really happy" when they were together. When Brigitte is slow in writing, Karen pleads with her: "You know I am not complaining—but sometimes one is cruelly lonely—and a letter from you now and then would mean so much. Please, please write more often" (30 October 1948).

After Karen does hear from Brigitte, she is all praise and fondness—"How wonderful that you are acting and happy with it. You are a quite marvelous person"—and she begins planning their next summer meeting. They will get a house on the water, she muses, Kostja (Brigitte's husband) can go fishing, "and you and I can make ourselves beautiful and go swimming. And we will cook the most wonderful things!! What do you think about that?!! For me it would be like heaven. Kiss, my sweety" (31 October 1948). Karen spent at least part of the summer of 1949 with Brigitte in a village near Lake Maggiore. In January 1950, she writes that she is out of her "mind with excitement because of Ascona," and we know that she spent the summers of 1950 and 1951 there, with Brigitte joining her when her work schedule permitted.

The loverlike quality persists in the letters of these years. Bigge is Karen's "sweet, beautiful, beloved Alpaca" (11 January 1950)—"Alpaca" being a pet name derived from a sweater Karen gave to Brigitte (there was much exchanging of gifts). On 1 August 1950 Karen hopes to see her "dear one" again before she leaves Switzerland and finds it "indescribably wonderful" that her "beloved" will "be able to come after all!!!" (16 August). After her return to New York Karen writes, "My beloved Bigge darling, ah my life, how I long for you!" (22 September). She is "beside [herself] with joy" at the thought of seeing Brigitte again (27 December), and as the time for her departure for Europe approaches she asks for reassurance: *"Do you love me?"* (28 June 1951).

In the summer of 1950 Karen renewed her friendship with Erich Maria Remarque, also a friend of Brigitte's, who had been a patient and lover of hers more than ten years earlier. He lived near the house that she and Brigitte had rented on Lake Maggiore and came to visit while Brigitte was away. Remarque seems to have had love affaires with both women, each of whom was ready to relinquish him to the other. Karen felt that Remarque "probably couldn't do anything better than marry" Brigitte and that it was "wonderful that the three of us get along so easily" (1 October 1950). When Remarque came to New York in late 1950, Brigitte was upset at his not writing but decided that he probably loved Karen best. She could understand that, for who would not. Karen was such a "heavenly person" (Heyerdahl 1992, 192).

Brigitte was with her mother for the last year of her life, having arrived in New York on 10 December 1951. This was something that both women had desired. According to Heyerdahl, after Brigitte and Kostja divorced one love remained, the love for her mother (1992, 183). She had friends, but her relationship with Karen was unique. "You know what good friends we were, Mochen and I. Besides that, there was also the great love. Also, I was so proud of her, this heavenly person. It was so sad for me whenever she left. We would just stand there and stare at each other—and she would disappear. She felt the same way. And so I went over to see her. I had the feeling it was about time. And we spent a wonderful year together" (190). Karen and Brigitte bought a house in Rye, New York, where they spent weekends, and they traveled to Japan in the summer of 1952.

"Mother and Brigitte were a happy couple," writes Renate. "No one could have been better to look after her and endlessly fuss over her than Brigitte, who loved to play the role of the mother hen." They "both enjoyed good food and wines, sparkling company, and both had the same kind of sardonic humor." Karen's year with her daughter was a "most marvelous time" for her.[62] After Karen's death, Brigitte missed her mother terribly, feeling that she had lost her best friend. Heyerdahl reports that when Brigitte came to Norway for a visit, she carried with her the letters of condolence she had received at her mother's death and would often read them before she went to sleep (1992, 215).

How are we to account for the intensity of this relationship? The two women seem to have been similar in character. Heyerdahl describes Brigitte as a proud, sensitive woman who seldom confided in anyone and never forgot an injustice. A temperamental person, she could explode at people and hurt them, after which she was often sorry and asked for forgiveness. She was a romantic who was always looking for ideal happiness and an everlasting love (1992, 35). She could be generous, helpful, caring, and full of understanding for the weakness and difficulties of others. Although Karen does not seem to have acknowledged her faults by asking forgiveness, the rest of the description of Brigitte fits her well.

As Brigitte's close friend and admirer, Heyerdahl provides an admittedly partial account. She portrays Brigitte as a modest, amiable, charming person who was concerned for the happiness of others. Brigitte has also been described, however, as "difficult, willful, and stubborn," a "very hard, tough person" who was given to sarcasm. Gertrude Lederer-Eckardt, whom Brigitte displaced as Karen's companion, characterized her as "a devil, very self-willed, strong, domineering." Karen has been described in similar terms, especially in relation to institute politics. Brigitte "rolled over you," says Renate, "destroyed you, like a tank." This side of her personality showed itself early, in her behavior toward Marianne. After she came to the United States, she displayed a fierce possessiveness toward her mother that led her to push Karen's friends away and to prevent them from seeing her mother at the hospital. According to Katie Sugarman, when Karen was dying, Brigitte tried to deny even the doctors access. She allowed the candidate who was Karen's current lover to visit but was, reports Renate, "angry about the situation,"[63] perhaps because she felt him to be a rival.

Both Brigitte and Karen had complex personalities with similar traits and conflicts, and their psychological affinity had much to do, I think, with the intensity of their relationship. They entered into each other's feelings and had a profound and effortless rapport. They were both reserved women who rarely shared their feelings, but they opened themselves to each other—more, perhaps, than to anyone else. Being adored by her wonderful daughter allayed Karen's fears of disappointment, desertion, or injury to her pride, and she could allow Brigitte into her inner life. Brigitte cherished her privileged position and did not want to share it with anyone else. Karen wrote from Cuernavaca in 1950 that although everything was going well at Renate's, "It just isn't the same as with you and me. I mean there isn't a genuine immediate relationship. Well, that is actually quite rare" (27 December).

Karen found in Brigitte not merely a reflection of herself but also a complement. Through Brigitte she vicariously fulfilled her early dream of having an acting career, and there were other facets of Brigitte's personality that Karen prized. As Renate has observed, Karen always felt insecure and unlovable, while the self-assured Brigitte was widely adored. Karen admired Brigitte's "charm, wit, and ruthlessness," her "overpowering personality." Her mother "would have liked," says Renate, "to have been [as] openly assertive" as Brigitte, and she speculates that Brigitte was Karen's "idealized image."[64]

Perhaps Brigitte was for Karen the great person with whom she longed to merge and by whom she wished to be validated. She looked up to Brigitte, deferred to her, and happily allowed herself to be dominated by her daughter, who was, we must remember, of an age with some of Karen's lovers. Karen's "self-effacing side came out with Brigitte; she did what Brigitte wanted."[65] According to Heyerdahl, Brigitte sometimes felt that her mother was the child in the relationship (1992, 272). In her letters to Brigitte, Karen often sounds like a clinging, pining lover. Brigitte's success as an actress at once gave her an exalted glamour and fed Karen's pride, for this celebrity was the woman who loved her and was her daughter. I detect no sense of envy or competitiveness in Karen's letters to Brigitte but only great joy in her accomplishments. Karen's response is partly the mother's pride in a child whose glory redounds on her and partly the lover's delight in the greatness of the beloved.

Although Karen seems at times to be the more emotionally dependent partner, we must keep in mind that she and Brigitte shared a reciprocal relationship in which each adored and pined for the other and in which each fed the other's pride through her admiration. With her weakness for adoration, Karen was no doubt intoxicated by her daughter's praise. Brigitte's veneration was all the more meaningful because Karen held her in such high esteem. They were two gifted, ambitious, charismatic women, each of whom saw the other as she wished to be seen. "Praise from her 'Mutti,'" reports Heyerdahl, "always made Brigitte very happy" (1992, 76). Perhaps Karen enjoyed being dominated by her daughter because it showed how much she meant to her, while Brigitte fulfilled a long-harbored desire to be the center of Karen's attention. Each seems to have found in the other the soul mate for whom she was searching.

Renate feels that Karen's letters to Brigitte show that she and Marianne were regarded as "intruders into the close community" between their mother and sister,[66] just as Karen had felt excluded from the community of Sonni and Berndt. In fact, Brigitte admired Sonni, whom she described as "vivacious, bright, beautiful, and witty" (Heyerdahl 1992, 13). Grandmother and granddaughter had much in common; they were both beautiful, domineering, and self-dramatizing women. Was Karen happy with Brigitte because in her she had finally found a Sonni to admire her, one to whom she alone was important and with whom she could be intimate? Perhaps Brigitte counteracted Sonni's rejection and validated Karen as the extraordinary person she needed to be to escape her self-hate. That was the role of the great man in her earlier fantasies, of course.

Chapter 24

The Many Sides of Karen Horney

At the age of twenty-one Karen pleaded with Oskar to help her because she was "wandering in a special labyrinth" in which she saw her "own picture everywhere, but always so extremely different" (*AD*, 187). Two months later she complained that "there are such awfully different sides to me, equally strong," that "a peaceful straightforward development was precluded from the start" (199). Our image of Horney in her later years suggests that although she became happier and more productive, she was still full of contradictions and conflicts that disturbed her relationships with others and prevented her from achieving inner peace.

Karen reported to Oskar that despite her suffering she could "dance nights through in self-forgetful joy" (*AD*, 186). She was much the same way in her later years. Friends and colleagues describe her as "gay," "jovial," "bubbly," "glowing," "ebullient," and possessed of "colossal vitality." Rita Honroth-Welte writes that Karen was full of a "singular breathless, child-like wondering quality and of what at least appeared as a thorough enjoyment of life."[67] Honroth-Welte seems somewhat doubtful about that appearance, and, indeed, there is evidence that Karen's joie de vivre coexisted with a good deal of malaise, as in earlier years.

In spite of her success and her gaiety, Horney still suffered from depression, although it was not as severe as it had been in her youth and it did not disable her. According to Harold Kelman, she endured considerable mental distress and was frequently in "anguish and pain" (Academy). Marianne observes that her mother's "poised appearance of gracious warmth often belied her inner turmoil" (Academy) and that she "didn't enjoy her life as she might have" because "she judged herself too adversely." She "felt grandiose and lousy."[68]

The observations of the people around her reveal many contradictions in Horney. Some characterize her as "ruthless, cynical, vulnerable," as a woman with strong needs for "sex and tenderness" who required "a dynamic man with whom she would clash." Although she was often arrogant, "there was hollowness behind the arrogance," for she was insecure and "needed people around her." "She could be haughty and aloof but also very warm, spontaneous, and direct." While some assert that she was "really quite shy," others report that she had a satirical wit, a "caustic tongue," and was often combative. She was "a tough cookie" with "tremendous ambition" and an "enormous need to be a star,"[69] but she shrank from the direct exercise of power and chose surrogates to absorb hostility that might otherwise be directed at her. Although her work seemed paramount, she was also engaged in a desperate search for reassurance and love and behaved in sometimes extreme ways in order to get them. She needed friends and lovers but often treated them cruelly.

Margaret Mead described Horney as having "a therapeutic personality," but others felt that she was "cold, detached, preoccupied with herself" (Harry Gershman, Academy) and complained that she gave the "impression of having much more compassion than she had."[70] Although self-centered and self-indulgent, Horney could be generous with both financial and emotional support. In addition to spending money liberally on houses, fine dining, and travel, she helped many people, including her daughters, Oskar, Berndt's widow, and Rita Honroth-Welte, to whom she gave an allowance of seventy dollars a month when she first arrived in the United States.

Although the various sides of Horney's personality are bewildering in their profusion, her writings can help us to organize our perceptions of the woman. (I am not suggesting, of course, that Horney or anyone else can be fitted neatly into her clinical categories.) In both *Neurotic Personality* and *Self-Analysis,* she focused on the neurotic need for affection, neurotic ambition, and the conflict between the two. Biographical material suggests that this was Horney's own basic conflict. She also mentioned withdrawal but provided no extended discussion of this defense. But a tendency toward detachment was also one of the strongest sides of her personality, one to which she gave considerable attention in her later books. We have seen evidence of her needs for love and mastery, but her detachment requires further discussion.

"What was my mother like?" asks Renate in her memoir. "The diaries have let us take a first hand look inside herself. From the outside she would remain the ever enigmatic, aloof and often sarcastic personality. She stayed true to the poem she wrote at the age of 17 in which she said: 'I lay my fingers on my lips and stay silent, silent, silent. For what can strangers be to you that our inner self be shown to them?'"[71] Karen kept her inner self hidden not only from strangers but also from those who were close to her. Marianne thought that she had "an incredible inner independence" and that "her general reserve probably increased with adulthood" (Academy).

Many others have commented on Horney's detachment. Gertrude Lederer-Eckardt felt that "she lived in a kind of shell; there was something unapproachable about her," and Lederer-Eckardt's predecessor as Karen's companion, Marie Levy, "always felt the sense of detachment." She observed that Horney did not want to become "too involved" with her young lovers. According to Wanda Willig, Horney "didn't want people to get close," and Medard Boss remembered her as "a full blos-somed woman, charming, but always aloof."[72] Horney had a great need for friends and lovers and dreaded being alone, but she was an intensely private person who needed to maintain distance in her relationships. Jack Rubins sees her tendency to "drop friends for some slight, without remorse or regret and without looking back," as a detached defense against "easily hurt pride or loneliness felt after separation" (1978, 267).

Marianne observes that her mother was "her own best friend": "She didn't really interact with other people so much as engage in internal dialogue, first in her diaries, then in her letters to Oskar, then in her essays and books." Her writing was "the place where she felt most herself and most alive." Everyone has "doubts and insecurities," notes Renate; "Mother was more honest about them than most, with herself. She was honest when she wrote about them, but hid them from other people." Marianne has consistently discouraged people from writing biographies of her mother on the ground that there was little information, since few people "knew her beyond the public or outer image."[73] As she has suggested, however, her mother's writings are a dialogue with herself, and I have tried to show that we can learn a great deal about Karen Horney from her essays and books.

In a videotaped oral-history portrait of Horney, Harold Kelman describes her as having a "most powerful inwardness." According to Kelman, her "early life cir-cumstances forced her to turn inward and develop her own resources." A "deter-mined, intelligent child," she increasingly lived in an inner world, a world of books, of study, and eventually of creative activity. It was also a world of imagination where she told herself stories and played with dolls, which she continued to collect as an adult. "Dolls, animals, and imagination were okay," Kelman observes, because "they won't hurt you" (Academy). Horney's attachment to and indulgence of her dog, Butschi, have been widely noted. She fed him steaks and allowed him to urinate and defecate on the floor, even when she had visitors. "She never punished him; her apartment smelled of dog; he was her constant companion," complains Gertrude Weiss.[74] When we recall that Karen wondered whether she should marry Hans or get a dog, Kelman's comments suggest that Butschi was a substitute for a more threatening relationship with a human being.

According to Kelman, it was Horney's inwardness that resulted in the coldness, detachment, and secretiveness so many observed. "What pained her deeply she kept within herself and did not communicate"—except, as we have seen, in the disguised form of her psychoanalytic writings. There has been much speculation about the interest in Zen that Horney developed late in life, which led her to travel to Japan in 1952 under the tutelage of Daisetz Suzuki. Kelman thinks that she was "deeply moved by her visit to the [Zen] monasteries" because of "their thousand year old tradition of support for dedication to inwardness and silence" (Academy).

It was Horney's detachment, I think, that drew her to psychoanalysis. Her introspective temperament and passion for self-observation were evident in her diaries. At the age of seventeen, she composed a lengthy entry entitled "I Myself." "I really should not read anything," she began, "but only myself. For only one half of my being lives, the other observes, criticizes, is given to irony" (*AD,* 57). On the next page she reports having been denied admission to a class in animal dissection: "*Et Viola* a substitute: I shall take myself to pieces. That will probably be more difficult, but also more interesting." Her writings are the record of her lifelong self-dissection. Her troubled childhood forced her to adopt detachment as a defense, and that defense both damaged her relationships and facilitated her insights. She took pride in seeing not only through others but also through herself. As her analysis of the detached person shows, she also saw through her pride in her insight.

Chapter 25

"Great Gifts, Great Shortcomings"

Harold Kelman has described Karen Horney as a person who had "great vitality, great intelligence, great gifts, great shortcomings" (Academy). Reading her books over the years, I had formed an image of her as a wise, benign, supportive woman who, having worked through her own problems, was now free to help others. Her concept of self-realization had an authority that seemed to derive from experience. First Jack Rubins' biography, then Susan Quinn's, and now my own research have changed my image of Horney. She was a tormented woman with many compulsions and conflicts who violated professional ethics and had difficulties in her relationships.

In a review of Susan Quinn's biography, the psychoanalyst Edward Clemmens worried that those to whom Horney's conduct seems "scandalous" might "wish to discard her ideas." Describing people who are disturbed by Horney's conduct as puritans, he argued that it is inappropriate to call such behavior pathological when we are dealing with "a person of Horney's rank" (1988, 283). In my view, being disturbed by Horney's behavior—and even considering it pathological—need not mean discarding her ideas. Yet I share Clemmens' concern. Horney's contribution to psychoanalytic theory has too long been unfairly dismissed, and I am concerned that only the more sensational aspects of her story will stick in people's minds and will be used to dismiss her again. Although she was a tormented person with significant character flaws, Horney was also a rather heroic figure whose courage in seeking the truth about herself enabled her to make a major contribution to human thought. Her strengths and her shortcomings are inseparable. As Kelman has said, "She created in spite of her problems, because of her problems, and through her problems" (Academy).

We do not achieve profound psychological understanding without having had the need to look deeply into ourselves. Where would Horney's insights have come from had she not experienced her difficulties? She was a troubled human being who redeemed the messiness of experience through her ability to create. Damaged by her traumas, she was not an easy person to know or to be, but she would have made a lesser contribution without them—or, at least, a very different one.

Horney could not have achieved her insights without her neuroses, but did her neuroses compromise her insights? There are, to be sure, ways in which her personality disorders threatened to diminish the value of her work. They might have narrowed her focus so much that her perceptions, however acute, would lack broad applicability. Or she might have become fixated on a particular problem and circled around it endlessly. Her problems are indeed recognizable in every phase of her thought, but she continually examined them from different perspectives, and as she persevered, her theory developed greater and greater resonance. Few people have endured a comparable life history, but many have testified that they see themselves described in her pages. Through her determined explorations of herself Horney got in touch with widespread patterns of human behavior. Like all thinkers, she was limited by her temperament, experience, and blind spots, but there is much in human experience that her theory explains remarkably well. The greatest danger Horney's problems posed to her theory was that she would rationalize her neurosis, thereby creating a definition of health that corresponded to her own defensive strategies. In my view, Horney did not do so.

We can readily find the sources of Horney's understanding of neurosis, but it is difficult to see where she acquired her vision of health. I have to assume that among the many sides of Karen Horney there was a self-realizing one, that her analysis and self-analysis helped her not only to overcome some of her blockages but also to have episodes in which she was in touch with what she called "the spontaneous individual self."

Marianne has spoken of her mother's "innate capacity for undaunted grappling with inner problems" (Academy), and Edward Clemmens feels that Horney "was special in that she was so intensely honest with herself."[75] I think that despite her habits of compartmentalization and denial—to say nothing of her blind spots—Horney *was* remarkably honest with herself. She kept analyzing herself and developing her theory because she recognized that she had severe problems and had a vision of health. Marianne felt that her mother tortured herself unnecessarily "because she measured herself against an ideal norm of self-realization" (Academy). This may be true. In *Neurosis and Human Growth,* Horney observed that after one has made a good deal of progress in therapy there is a tendency to form an idealized image of oneself as an entirely healthy person and to hate oneself for failing to live up to it (356–62). She may have been drawing on her own experience, as well as on that of her patients. If so, the value of this neurotic tendency was that it fueled her "undaunted grappling" with her problems and prevented her from normalizing her pathology as she had done in some early essays.

I believe that Horney offers us an admirable vision of health, which becomes pernicious only if we turn it into what she called a "should," a neurotic demand that we live up to our idealized image of ourselves. "An ideal norm of self-realization" is frightening and destructive if it leads us to feel worthless because we fall short of it. Although she may not always have been able to follow her own wisdom, Horney taught the necessity of accepting ourselves—defenses and all—if we are to change.

Even if we grant Horney's vision of health, it still might be argued that a person in such turmoil cannot have been a reliable observer. I do not wish to claim for Horney an impossible objectivity (and she would be the first to say that our defenses influence our perceptions and beliefs), but a distinction found in *Final Lectures* provides a useful perspective. In trying to clarify the concept of resistance, Horney differentiates between "difficulties" and "defenses." The patient comes to the analyst not only with his difficulties, but also with "the defenses he puts up to protect these difficulties" (79). Instead of being willing "to go through all the steps that are necessary to accomplish self-understanding" (70), he usually wishes "to maintain the status quo" or, better yet, "to improve the functioning of his neurosis" so as to be free of the "disturbances arising from it" (73). Horney's "dream of the ideal patient" would be the patient who "comes with all his difficulties" but is eager to learn about them; who "withholds things, consciously or unconsciously," but acknowledges this when it is pointed out; who seeks to understand why he is not happy, productive, or creative and genuinely wants to tackle his problems. The attitude of such a patient is, "Come hell or high water . . . . 'I want to know who I am, . . . what I am doing, and how I can change whatever is not desirable'" (70).

I suspect that Horney was herself this kind of patient, at least some of the time, both with her analysts and when she tried to heal herself. She had her share of "difficulties," but she also had a fierce determination to understand and free herself of them. That determination made for an almost ruthless self-honesty, which she knew to be the price of genuine insight. Of course, her determination to be honest was not always foremost, nor did it give her instant or even ultimate access to the full truth about herself, but I feel that she was less inclined than most of us to defend her difficulties. Her relative freedom from such defensiveness led her to continue her quest for self-understanding in spite of its painfulness and to see much more than she could remedy.

Her persisting difficulties notwithstanding, Horney had a strong belief in the possibility of psychological change and never gave up her struggle for growth. Partly as a defense, perhaps, she celebrated that struggle for its own sake. At the conclusion of *Self-Analysis,* she acknowledges that we will always have unresolved problems, but she does not say this "in a spirit of resignation," for "the idea of a finished human product" is not only "presumptuous" but "lacks any strong appeal. Life is struggle and striving, development and growth." The positive accomplishments of analysis are important, but "the striving itself is of intrinsic value." She closes the book with a quotation from *Faust*: "Whoe'er aspires unweariedly, / Is not beyond redeeming" (303). Her outlook is the mark not of a facile optimism, of which she is sometimes accused, but of a determination to keep trying despite repeated disappointments.

Although Horney fell far short of embodying her own vision of health, she provides an inspiring example of unwearied aspiration. And her striving was not unrewarded. Some problems she could never resolve, but she gained relief from others, and her courage in facing herself was a major source of insight.

There is a wonderful summing up in a statement Marianne made to Jack Rubins: "It is probably fair to say that she poured all her creative energy into work, into search, in part as a genuine creative effort and in part as a rescue, and a creative rescue at that, from interpersonal difficulties. She was a tremendously conflicted person who found a successful, eminently satisfying creative way of life. I think she would always want her books to speak for her, as justifying her existence. That I believe to be totally right."

I also believe that to be right. Let us now look at Horney's most important books.

Karen and Oskar with daughters Brigitte and Marianne, 1913 (Courtesy
M. Eckardt and R. Patterson)

Karen playing the piano, around age 33 (Courtesy Karen
Horney Papers, Manuscripts and Archives, Sterling Memorial Library,
Yale University)

Brigitte, Karen's oldest daughter, in her early 30s (Courtesy M. Eckardt and R. Patterson)

Marianne, Karen's second daughter, in her early 30s (Courtesy M. Eckardt and R. Patterson)

Renate, Karen's youngest daughter, in Mexico, 1944 (Courtesy
M. Eckardt and R. Patterson)

Erich Fromm (Courtesy estate of John Schimel and the William Alanson White Institute)

Karen, October 1938; photo by Fredy Crevenna, Renate's first husband
(Courtesy M. Eckardt and R. Patterson)

Karen in Mexico, 1944; photo by Fredy Crevenna (Courtesy M. Eckardt and R. Patterson)

Karen, around age 61 (Courtesy M. Eckardt and R. Patterson)

Karen in Switzerland, late 1940s; drawing, based on a photograph, by
Arthur Libov (Courtesy M. Eckardt and R. Patterson)

Harold Kelman, in the late 1940s (Courtesy Natalie Jaffe)

Karen, 1950; photo by Brigitte (Courtesy M. Eckardt and R. Patterson)

Part 5

Horney's Mature Theory

Many of the elements of Horney's mature theory are present in her earlier books. In *The Neurotic Personality of Our Time*, she discusses two of the strategies that people employ to cope with basic anxiety—the pursuit of love and of power—and she mentions a third, detachment, which she deals with in detail in *Our Inner Conflicts*. *New Ways in Psychoanalysis* has chapters on narcissism and perfectionism, which reappear as major defenses in *Neurosis and Human Growth*. In *Neurotic Personality* and *New Ways*, Horney also introduces what she later calls intrapsychic strategies, such as self-inflation, self-recrimination, overconformity to inner standards, and neurotic guilt and suffering. Her list of ten neurotic trends in *Self-Analysis* contains an assortment of interpersonal and intrapsychic strategies that are systematized in her mature theory.

The movement of Horney's theory was toward greater inclusiveness, a more sophisticated taxonomy, and a fuller elaboration of each solution. In *Our Inner Conflicts* and *Neurosis and Human Growth*, she organizes strategies into systems of interpersonal and intrapsychic defenses. She also describes the constellations of character traits, behaviors, and beliefs that accompany each strategy, and she shows how defenses and inner conflicts give rise to complex and infinitely variable character structures.

Because Horney's thought was still evolving in its later phases, there are significant differences between her last two books. In *Our Inner Conflicts* her focus is on our relation to others, while in *Neurosis and Human Growth* it is on our relation to ourselves. In *Our Inner Conflicts* she explains how our compulsive moves toward, against, and away from people give rise to inner conflicts that threaten to paralyze or tear us apart. These conflicting defensive strategies generate contradictory character traits, behaviors, and beliefs and contradictory attitudes toward ourselves. In order to cope with our conflicts, we make one of our strategies predominant and repress the others. In addition, we try to distance ourselves from our inner turmoil, we externalize our problems, and we develop an idealized image of ourselves in which contradictory trends are harmonized and glorified as components of a rich personality.

In *Neurosis and Human Growth*, Horney's focus is on the psychological consequences of self-idealization. When we embark on a search for glory in an attempt to actualize our idealized image of ourselves, we develop a set of intrapsychic defenses that Horney calls the pride system. We make neurotic claims upon the world, impose tyrannical shoulds upon ourselves, and take neurotic pride in the imaginary attributes of our idealized selves. Although the pride system is set in motion by disturbances in human relationships, it develops a dynamic of its own. Because we cannot live up to our shoulds and the world does not honor our claims, our feelings of weakness, worthlessness, helplessness, and inadequacy are intensified. To cope with these feelings, we idealize ourselves all the more, resulting in greater self-hate, more self-idealization, and so on. We create not only an idealized but also a despised image of ourselves, and we oscillate between feeling godlike and worthless.

Horney warns against "a one-sided focus on either intrapsychic or interpersonal factors," contending that the dynamics of neurosis can be understood "only as a process in which interpersonal conflicts lead to a peculiar intrapsychic configuration, and this in turn depends on and modifies the old patterns of human relations" (*NHG,* 237). She disregards her own warning by overemphasizing the intrapsychic in *Neurosis and Human Growth,* but she successfully combines the interpersonal and the intrapsychic in her discussions of the major solutions. In my presentation of her theory, I shall follow her most balanced accounts of the relations between the two kinds of defenses.

Horney calls the major solutions compliance, aggression, and detachment in *Our Inner Conflicts,* describing them primarily in interpersonal terms, and self-effacement, expansiveness, and resignation in *Neurosis and Human Growth,* where she combines the interpersonal and the intrapsychic. The two sets of terms clearly overlap and can often be used interchangeably. In *Neurosis and Human Growth,* Horney discusses the typical childhood conditions conducive to the development of each solution, thus anchoring the solutions in disturbed human relationships, and she also specifies the different kinds of idealized images, claims, shoulds, pride, and self-hate to which each solution gives rise. Although *Neurosis and Human Growth* incorporates the major insights of *Our Inner Conflicts,* the earlier book remains indispensable for its detailed descriptions of interpersonal strategies and the conflicts among them.

Horney discusses the kinds of early experiences that lead to the adoption of particular solutions, but her mature theory is predominantly synchronic in nature and is focused on the present. Each aspect of the individual's behavior makes sense in terms of its function within the current structure of the psyche. That structure has an evolutionary history, to be sure, but it can be understood without a knowledge of its genesis by examining the interrelations between its components. Horney's synchronic approach has a wonderful power to explain the behavior of adults about whom we have current information but of whose childhoods we know little or nothing.

In *New Ways in Psychoanalysis,* Horney begins to see the central feature of neurosis as the "warping" of "the spontaneous individual self" because of parental oppression. The object of therapy is to "restore the individual to himself, to help him regain his spontaneity and find his center of gravity in himself" (11). Horney introduces the term "the real self" in "Can You Take a Stand?" (1939a, 130) and uses it again in *Self-Analysis* (22, 290–91), where she first writes of "self-realization" (10). She begins *Neurosis and Human Growth* by distinguishing between healthy development, in which individuals realize their potentialities, and neurotic development, in which they become alienated from their real selves. The subtitle of the book is *The Struggle toward Self-Realization,* and her concept of the real self is now the foundation of her conceptions of both health and neurosis.

But the real self is an elusive concept, as Horney herself acknowledges (*NHG,* 368). There is no sustained discussion of the real self in her writings, although there are a number of useful statements about it, and her conception of self-realization must be largely inferred from her account of self-alienation. Fortunately, a much more complete model of health has been developed by Abraham Maslow, who was significantly influenced by Horney and whose theory perfectly complements hers. He focuses on self-actualization, she on self-alienation, but for both it is the real self that we actualize or from which we become alienated. Combining the theories of Horney and Maslow gives us a more comprehensive account of health and neurosis than either provides by itself.

Chapter 26

The Real Self and

Self-Realization

The real self will seem like "a phantom," Horney writes, unless we are "acquainted with the later phases of analysis" (*NHG,* 175). It is a "possible self," what we would have been had we developed in a nurturing environment, or what we can be when "freed of the crippling shackles of neurosis." The notion of a possible self seems highly speculative, Horney continues, for who, when seeing a patient, "can separate the wheat from the chaff and say: this is his possible self? But while the real or possible self of a neurotic person is in a way an abstraction, it is nevertheless *felt* and we can say that every glimpse we get of it feels more real, more certain, more definite than anything else" (158).

The real self is not a fixed entity but a set of "intrinsic potentialities"—including temperament, talents, capacities, and predispositions—that are part of our genetic makeup and need a favorable environment in which to develop. It is not a product of learning, since one cannot be taught to be oneself; but neither is it impervious to external influence, for it is actualized through interactions with an external world that can provide many paths of development. People can actualize themselves in different ways under different conditions. Certain conditions in childhood, however, are prerequisites for self-realization. These include "an atmosphere of warmth" that enables children to express their own thoughts and feelings, the goodwill of others to supply children's various needs, and a "healthy friction with the wishes and will" of those around them (*NHG*, 17–18).

Other important conditions can be inferred from an autobiographical passage in "Can You Take a Stand?"—an essay containing one of Horney's earliest invocations of the real self:

> A child may feel that he is not wanted or appreciated for his own sake, but
> that he is acceptable only if he lives up to the expectations of others, espe-
> cially those of his parents. He may feel that he is acceptable only if he
> obeys blindly or if he uncritically adores the one or the other parent. Or, the
> child may feel that he is acceptable only if he measures up to the standards
> that are current in the family, or fulfills the ambitions of his parents, or sat-
> isfies their desire for showing off. Again, the child may become subservient
> to the excessive demands of a self-sacrificing mother. Different as these sit-
> uations are, they all result in the child's feeling that he, his real self, is not
> understood or not wanted, and that he, his real self, does not matter, that
> only the others and their expectations are important. (1939a, 130)

As Horney observed in *Neurosis and Human Growth,* when their own neuroses prevent parents from loving the child or even thinking of him "as the particular individual he is," the child develops a feeling of basic anxiety that prevents him "from relating himself to others with the spontaneity of his real feelings, and forces him to find ways to cope with them" (18). The child's feelings and behavior are no longer expressions of a genuine self but are dictated by defensive strategies.

The process of losing the self has been described in similar ways by one of Horney's patients and by Ingmar Bergman in his published version of *Scenes from a Marriage*. In a letter from a patient that Horney published with a commentary, the patient reacts to the analyst's question "What do you really want?" by realizing that for more than forty years she has been "exiled from [her]self without even suspecting it" and that "the secret of wretchedness [is] SELFLESSNESS!" (1949, 3, 5):

> My original life—*what had happened to it?* . . . How is it possible to lose
> a self? The treachery, unknown and unthinkable, begins with our secret

psychic death in childhood—if and when we are not loved and are cut off
from our spontaneous wishes. (Think: What is left?) . . . Oh, they "love"
[the child], but they want him or force him or expect him to be different!
Therefore he must be unacceptable. He himself learns to believe it and at
last even takes it for granted. He has truly given himself up. No matter now
whether he obeys them, whether he clings, rebels or withdraws—his
behavior, his performance is all that matters. His center of gravity is in
"them," not in himself. . . . Everything looks normal; no crime was
intended; there is no corpse, no guilt. All we can see is the sun rising and
setting as usual. But what has happened? He has been rejected, not only by
them, but by himself. (He is actually without a self.) What has he lost? Just
the one true and vital part of himself: his own yes-feeling, which is his very
capacity for growth, his root system. But alas, he is not dead. "Life" goes
on, and so must he. From the moment he gives himself up, and to the
extent that he does so, all unknowingly he sets about to create and maintain
a pseudo-self. But this is an expediency—a "self" without wishes. This
one shall be loved (or feared) where he is despised, strong where he is
weak; it shall go through the motions (Oh, but they are caricatures!) not
for fun or joy but for survival; not simply because it wants to move but
because it has to obey. This necessity is not life—not his life—it is a
defense mechanism against death. It is also the machine of death. (5–6)

Although Horney entitles the published version of this letter "Finding the Real Self,"
what her patient discovers is that she has lost her real self. But she *has* found "something to believe in, not yet in my *own* self perhaps, for to think it is not quite to be
it—but . . . in my *right* . . . to wish, to want, and to live for no other purpose than that
I do" (7).

Bergman's *Scenes from a Marriage* describes self-alienation in a way that could
have been inspired by Horney. The main characters, Johan and Marianne, are dining
together after having been separated for a year, and Marianne reads a passage from
her diary, while Johan falls asleep.

To my surprise I have to admit that *I don't know who I am*. I haven't the
vaguest idea. I have always done what people told me. As far back as I can
remember I've been obedient, adaptable, almost meek. Now that I think
about it, I had one or two violent outbursts of self-assertion as a little girl.
But I remember also that Mother punished all such lapses from convention
with exemplary severity. For my sisters and me our entire upbringing was
aimed at our being *agreeable*. . . . By degrees I found that if I kept my

thoughts to myself and was ingratiating and farsighted, such behavior
brought its rewards. The really big deception, however, occurred during
puberty. All my thoughts, feelings, and actions revolved round sex. I didn't
let on about this to my parents, or to anyone at all for that matter. Then it
became second nature to be deceitful, surreptitious, and secretive. (1974,
125–26)

Marianne had wanted to become an actress, but her father insisted she study law,
and her family had laughed at her aspiration. In her relationships with other people
there was "perpetual dissimulation."

Here Marianne seems to be describing less having lost herself than having hidden herself from others, but as she continues reading her diary it is clear that in the
process of hiding she has become alienated from her own feelings. In her "desperate
attempts to please everybody," especially men, she has "never thought: What do *I*
want? But always: What does *he* want me to want? It's not unselfishness as I used to
think, but sheer cowardice, and what's worse—utter ignorance of who I am." She
has attained "outward security" but at "a high price: the acceptance of a continuous
destruction of the personality." She thinks she can see "what kind of person I would
have been had I not allowed myself to be brainwashed," but now she wonders
whether she is "hopelessly lost. Whether all the potential for joy—joy for myself
and others—that was innate in me is dead or whether it's just asleep and can be
awakened" (126). For Horney, the object of therapy is to reverse the process of self-
alienation: to undo the brainwashing, restore the person to his or her self, and
reawaken the capacity for joy of which Marianne speaks.

Horney describes the real self as "the alive, unique, personal center of ourselves" (*NHG*, 155). Actualization of the real self is the purpose of life, and alienation
from it may be called a "psychic death" (*OIC*, 185). The loss of self produces despair,
but one that "does not clamor or scream. People go on living as if they were still in
immediate contact with this alive center. Any other loss—that of a job, say, or a
leg—arouses far more concern" (*NHG*, 158). "A self," observes Kierkegaard, "is a
thing the world is least apt to inquire about," so that "the greatest danger, that of losing one's own self, may pass off as quietly as if it were nothing" (quoted in *OIC*,
185). The loss of self leaves us without a source of meaning, direction, and value,
and we are governed instead by the conflicting demands of our neurotic solutions.

The real self is "what *I* really feel, what *I* really want, what *I* really believe, what
I really decide" (*SA*, 291). It is Horney's first cause, her prime mover, a source of
motive and direction, meaning and value, that requires no justification or explanation.
Freud, she contends, did not believe in an inherent desire to grow, attributing urges

toward self-development to narcissistic self-inflation and competitiveness (22). In Horney's view these tendencies belong to a "phony self" that "evaporates" as "the real self becomes invested with interest" (23). In Freudian theory all judgments and feelings are "dissolvable into more elemental 'instinctual' units": "There is no liking or disliking of people, no sympathy, no generosity, no feeling of justice, no devotion to a cause, which is not in the last analysis essentially determined by libidinal or destructive drives" (187). For Horney all of these things may be neurotically determined, but they may also be expressions of the real self, in which case they are irreducible.

The real self is the repository of "the healthy conscience," which is "the reaction of our true self to the proper functioning or the malfunctioning of our total personality." The healthy conscience differs from the Freudian superego or the Frommian authoritarian conscience, which are the result of an "unwitting inner submission to external authorities with the concomitant fear of discovery and punishment" (*NHG*, 131–32). It is also different from neurotic self-accusation, which is a product of the pride system and is directed against the true self for not being sufficiently glorious. It is, like Fromm's humanistic conscience, an expression of our essential nature. The real self is "common to all human beings and yet unique in each" (17). It is a source of values that are in the best interest of human development, regardless of culture. Horney believes that there may be genuine moral values that "can be dissolved neither by Freud's resort to instincts nor by the relativist's resort to social valuations and conditioning" (*NW*, 186).

In the introduction to *Neurosis and Human Growth*, "A Morality of Evolution," Horney distinguishes three major concepts of the goal of morality, each resting upon a different interpretation of "essential human nature." If we believe that "man is by nature sinful or ridden by primitive instincts (Freud)," the goal of morality must be "the taming or overcoming of the *status naturae* and not its development." If we believe that human nature is a mixture of good and bad, the goal of morality becomes "the insurance of the eventual victory of the inherent good, as refined, directed, or reinforced by such elements as faith, reason, will, or grace—in accordance with the particular dominating religious or ethical concept" (14).

In contrast to these positions, Horney's concept of the goal of morality rests upon the belief that "inherent in man are evolutionary constructive forces which urge him to realize his given potentialities." Our values evolve from the striving for self-realization; the good is that which fosters growth; the bad, that which obstructs it. For instance, man cannot "develop his full human potentialities unless he is truthful to himself; unless he is active and productive; unless he relates himself to others in the spirit of mutuality." The goal of morality is the "liberation and cultivation of the forces which lead to self-realization." Our prime moral obligation is not to suppress an inherently evil or primitive nature or to drive ourselves to live up to unrealistic ideals or commandments, but "to work at ourselves" in order to outgrow our destructive tendencies, which are reactive rather than inherent, and to realize our potentialities. As we "become free to grow ourselves, we also free ourselves to love and to feel concern for other people," and we spontaneously behave in ways that promote their development (*NHG,* 15–16).

As we have seen, Horney draws upon others to help her formulate her ideas about the real self. She frequently cites William James, who distinguishes between the material self, the social self, the spiritual self, and the pure ego. Although the distinctions she makes are different from his, she seems to equate the real self with James's account of the spiritual self in chapter 10 of his *Principles of Psychology:*

> [The real self] provides the "palpitating inward life"; it engenders the spontaneity of feelings, whether these be joy, yearning, love, anger, fear, despair. It also is the source of spontaneous interest and energies . . . ; it is the part of ourselves that wants to expand and grow and to fulfill itself. It produces the "reactions of spontaneity" . . . "welcoming or opposing, appropriating or disowning, striving with or against, saying yes or no." All this indicates that our real self, when strong and active, enables us to make decisions and assume responsibility for them. It therefore leads to genuine integration and a sound sense of wholeness, oneness. Not merely are body and mind, deed and thought or feeling, consonant and harmonious, but they function without serious inner conflict. (*NHG,* 157)

As the last few sentences suggest, Horney is enamored of the Zen concept of wholeheartedness, the striving for which she defines in *Our Inner Conflicts* as the most comprehensive goal of therapy: "to be without pretense, to be emotionally sincere, to be able to put the whole of oneself into one's feelings, one's work, one's beliefs" (242; see also 162–63).

For Horney, then, the self-realizing person develops "the clarity and depth of his own feelings, thoughts, wishes, interests; the ability to tap his own resources, the strength of his will power; the special capacities or gifts he may have; the faculty to express himself, and to relate himself to others with his spontaneous feelings" (*NHG,* 17). He knows what he really thinks, feels, and believes; he is able to take responsibility for himself and to determine his values and his aims in life. His judgments and decisions are in the best interest both of his own growth and that of other people. He wants to have good relationships with others and cares about their welfare, but he keeps his center of gravity in himself and is able to refuse when others ask him to behave in self-destructive ways.

Horney provides no concrete example of a self-realizing person, but a good illustration of her ideas would be Sir Thomas More in Robert Bolt's *A Man for All Seasons*. As the play opens, the ambitious underling Richard Rich proclaims his belief that "every man has his price," to which Sir Thomas replies, "No no no" (4). More is above all a man with the courage to say "no," despite ever-increasing pressures to comply, in circumstances where saying "yes" means betraying his values, his sense of reality, and his feeling of selfhood. He maneuvers realistically in a dangerous world and bends as much as he can without abandoning his principles. He hopes that by remaining quiet, he will be left alone; but after the king charges him with ingratitude, he acknowledges his danger. Even then, he resists his friend Norfolk's well-meant plea that he submit: "I will not give in because I oppose it—*I* do—not my pride, not my spleen, nor any other of my appetites, but *I* do—*I!* . . . Is there no single sinew in the midst of this that serves no appetite of Norfolk's but is just Norfolk? There is! Give *that* some exercise, my lord!" (71–72).

Sir Thomas resists not only political pressures but pressures from his family as well. The most moving scene between Sir Thomas and his family occurs in prison, where they visit him in order to persuade him to swear to the Act of Succession and thus be free to return home. "Say the words of the oath," pleads his daughter, "and in your heart think otherwise." "When a man take an oath," Sir Thomas replies, "he's holding his own self in his own hands. Like water. *(He cups his hands)* And if he opens his fingers *then*—he needn't hope to find himself again" (81). Most characters in literature who choose death, as Sir Thomas does, do so in an attempt to actualize their idealized selves. Sir Thomas does everything he can to avoid martyrdom, but he is finally forced to choose death because he will not give up his real self (see also Paris 1986, 62–65).

According to Horney, the desire for self-realization is present in everyone, in varying degrees of strength, and is a prime incentive in analysis. To the self-alienated person (like Bergman's Marianne) the real self might seem like "a phantom, desirable to regain but forever elusive"; but "under favorable conditions, such as constructive analytic work, it can again become an alive force." Only because of this, says Horney, can "therapeutic work go beyond symptomatic relief and hope to help the individual in his human growth" (*NHG*, 175).

Chapter 27

The Major Neurotic Solutions

When adverse conditions in the environment lead us to abandon our real selves, we develop interpersonal and intrapsychic strategies of defense. Because they generate inner conflicts and increase self-alienation, these strategies tend to create new problems and to exacerbate the conditions they were devised to remedy. We abandon ourselves in order to protect ourselves, but as the real self becomes weaker the environment seems more threatening, and our basic anxiety increases, making us more defensive. This is a "dismal picture," says Horney, but she insists that hers is a "constructive" theory, unlike Freud's, because she believes that this process is neither inevitable nor irreversible (*OIC*, 18–19).

In adults, interpersonal and intrapsychic strategies are inextricably intertwined, and the major neurotic solutions are a combination of both kinds of defenses. Horney presents the interpersonal strategies as occurring somewhat earlier in human development, however, and as influencing the intrapsychic ones, by which they are influenced in turn. I shall first discuss the major solutions in terms of their interpersonal components and shall show how the interpersonal and the intrapsychic combine when I examine the idealized image and the pride system.

In their efforts to overcome feelings of being unsafe, unloved, and unvalued in a harsh world, people may adopt a compliant or self-effacing solution and move *toward* people; they may develop an aggressive or expansive solution and move *against* people; or they may become detached or resigned and move *away from* people. Healthy people move flexibly in all three directions. Self-alienated people, however, are "driven to comply, to fight, to be aloof, regardless of whether the move is appropriate in the particular instance" (*OIC*, 202). Each solution involves its own constellation of behavior patterns and personality traits, its own conception of justice, and its own set of beliefs about human nature, human values, and the human condition. Each also involves a deal or a bargain with fate in which obedience to the dictates of that solution is expected to be rewarded.

In each defensive move, one of the elements involved in basic anxiety becomes overemphasized: helplessness in the compliant solution, hostility in the aggressive solution, and isolation in the detached solution. Under the conditions that produce basic anxiety all these feelings are bound to arise, however, so individuals will come to make all three defensive moves compulsively; and because the moves involve incompatible character structures and value systems, these individuals will be torn by inner conflicts. To gain some sense of wholeness, they will emphasize one move over the others and will become predominantly self-effacing, expansive, or detached. Which move they emphasize will depend upon the particular combination of temperamental and environmental factors at work in their situation.

The other trends will continue to exist, but they will operate unconsciously and will manifest themselves in disguised and devious ways. The conflict between the moves will not have been resolved but will simply have been repressed. When the submerged trends are for some reason brought closer to the surface, individuals will experience severe inner turmoil and may become paralyzed. Under the impetus of some powerful influence or the dramatic failure of their predominant solution, self-alienated people may embrace one of their repressed defensive strategies. They will experience this as conversion or education, but it will merely be the substitution of one defense for another.

As we examine the major solutions and the personality types to which they give rise, it is important to keep in mind that we shall not find people who correspond exactly to Horney's descriptions. Her types are composites, of course, drawn from her experiences with people who share certain dominant trends but differ from one another in many ways. The Horneyan typology helps us to see how certain traits and behaviors are interrelated within a psychological system, but once we have identified a person's predominant solution, we must not assume that all the characteristics Horney ascribes to that solution will be present. It is important to remember also, as Horney observes, that people tending toward the same main solution "may differ widely with regard to the level of human qualities, gifts, or achievements." The situation is further complicated by the fact that people experience inner conflicts and display behaviors, traits, and beliefs that belong to more than one solution. Quoting William James to the effect that "'most cases are mixed cases'" and that "'we should not treat our classifications with too much respect,'" Horney concludes: "It would be more nearly correct to speak of directions of development than of types" (*NHG*, 191).

If we forget these qualifications, we are liable to put people into categories instead of grasping their individuality, and our analysis will be little more than a reductive labeling. Horney allows for infinite variations and combinations of defenses and recognizes other components of the personality as well. In a brief description, her theory may seem unduly schematic, but when properly employed it is both flexible and complex.

I have already cited many passages describing the childhoods of compliant or self-effacing people because they resemble Karen Horney's. Such people grew up under the shadow of another—perhaps a preferred sibling, a beautiful mother, or an overbearing father—and sought love and protection through pleasing and appeasing, through a self-subordinating devotion. They may have been rebellious at one time, but the need for affection eventually won out and the children "became compliant, learned to like everybody and to lean with a helpless admiration" on those they "feared most" (*NHG*, 222).

The strategies the children adopted evolve into a constellation of adult character traits, behaviors, and beliefs. As adults, compliant people try to overcome their anxiety by gaining affection and approval and by controlling others through dependency on them. They need to feel part of something larger and more powerful than themselves, a need that often manifests itself as religious devotion, identification with a group or cause, or morbid dependency in a love relationship. Because their *"salvation lies in others,"* notes Horney, their need for people "often attains a frantic character" (*NHG*, 226). Love appears "as the ticket to paradise, where all woe ends: no more feeling lost, guilty, and unworthy; no more responsibility for self; no more struggle with a harsh world" for which they feel "hopelessly unequipped" (240).

Horney observes that in our culture the woman is more often the self-effacing partner in a relationship; and, indeed, in her discussion of morbid dependency, she switches to the feminine pronoun. She notes, however, that the greater frequency of this solution in women is a product of culture rather than owing to an essential feminine nature. The major solutions are found in both genders; there are many self-effacing men.

In order to gain the love, approval, and support they need, compliant people develop certain qualities, inhibitions, and ways of relating. They seek to attach others by being good, loving, self-effacing, and weak; and they try to live up to others' expectations, "often to the extent of losing sight of [their] own feelings." They become "'unselfish,' self-sacrificing," "overconsiderate," "overappreciative, overgrateful, generous." They are appeasing and conciliatory and tend to blame themselves whenever they quarrel, experience disappointment, or are criticized. Regarding themselves as worthless or guilty gives them a feeling of security, for this defuses their anger and prevents others from regarding them as a threat. For similar reasons, they are more comfortable subordinating themselves and "leaving the limelight to others" (*OIC*, 51–52). They are severely inhibited in their self-assertive and self-protective activities and have powerful taboos against "all that is presumptuous, selfish, and aggressive" (*NHG*, 219). They embrace weakness and suffering and use them both to control others and to justify themselves. Their motto is: "You must love me, protect me, forgive me, not desert me, *because* I am so weak and helpless" (*OIC*, 53).

The compliant defense brings with it not only certain ways of feeling and behaving, but also a special set of values and beliefs. The values "lie in the direction of goodness, sympathy, love, generosity, unselfishness, humility" (*OIC*, 54). These can be admirable, but compliant people hold them because they are necessary to their defense system rather than as genuine ideals. They must believe in turning the other cheek, and they need to view the world as displaying a providential order in which people like themselves will be rewarded. Their tacit bargain with fate is that if they remain generous, loving people who shun pride and do not seek their own gain or glory, they will be well treated by both fortune and their fellows. If this bargain is not honored, they may despair of divine justice or conclude that they are somehow guilty or take refuge in belief in a higher justice that transcends human understanding. They need to believe not only in the fairness of the world order but also in the goodness of human nature, and here, too, they are liable to disappointment.

In compliant people, says Horney, there are "a variety of aggressive tendencies strongly repressed" (*OIC*, 55) because experiencing them or acting them out would clash violently with such individuals' need to be good and would radically endanger their whole strategy for gaining love, protection, and approval. It would undermine their bargain with fate. Compliant people's strategies increase their hostility by inviting abuse, but they also make them more afraid of being hostile.

Because of their need for surrender and a safe outlet for their aggression, compliant people are often attracted to their opposites: masterful expansive types whose "egotism, ambition, callousness, unscrupulousness" and "wielding of power" they may consciously condemn but "secretly admire" (*OIC*, 54–55). Merging with such people allows compliant people "to participate vicariously in the mastery of life without having to own it" to themselves (*NHG*, 244). This kind of relationship usually develops into a morbid dependency that exacerbates their difficulties. When the love relationship fails them, they will be terribly disillusioned and may feel that they did not find the right person, that something is wrong with them, or that nothing is worth having.[1]

People in whom expansive tendencies are predominant have quite different goals, traits, and values from those of compliant or self-effacing people. Whereas love is the highest value in the self-effacing solution, expansive people "aim at mastering life. This is their way of conquering fears and anxieties; this gives meaning to their lives" (*NHG*, 212). Expansive people abhor helplessness, are ashamed of suffering, and cultivate qualities that will give them a sense of being in control of their own destinies.

The compliant, aggressive, and detached solutions of *Our Inner Conflicts* are renamed self-effacing, expansive, and resigned solutions in *Neurosis and Human*

Growth. Since Horney further divides the expansive solutions into three categories—narcissistic, perfectionistic, and arrogant-vindictive—she now posits five major solutions instead of three. She did not discuss narcissism and perfectionism in *Our Inner Conflicts,* and the aggressive solution there is equivalent to the arrogant-vindictive solution described in *Neurosis and Human Growth.*

The arrogant-vindictive solution is in many ways the opposite of the self-effacing one. Arrogant-vindictive people have usually had a particularly harsh childhood in which they encountered "sheer brutality, humiliations, derision, neglect, and flagrant hypocrisy." Like the survivors of concentration camps, they go through "a hardening process in order to survive." As children, they "may make some pathetic and unsuccessful attempts to win sympathy, interest, or affection but finally choke off all tender needs." Since affection is unattainable, they scorn it or conclude that it does not exist. Thus they have no incentive to please and can give free rein to their bitter resentment. The desire for love is replaced by ambition and a drive toward "vindictive triumph." They live for the "day of reckoning" when they will prove their superiority, put their enemies to shame, and show how they have been wronged. They dream of becoming great heroes: "the persecutor, the leader, the scientist attaining immortal fame" (*NHG,* 202–03).

As adults, arrogant-vindictive people are ferociously competitive: they "cannot tolerate anybody who knows or achieves more . . . , wields more power, or in any way questions [their] superiority" (*NHG,* 198). They have to humiliate or defeat their rivals. They retaliate when injured by hurting their enemies more than they have been hurt. Ruthless and cynical in their relationships, arrogant-vindictive people seek to exploit and outsmart others. They trust no one and are out to get others before they get them. They avoid emotional involvement and dependency, using the relationships of friendship and marriage simply to enhance their social and economic position. Wishing to be hard and tough, they regard all manifestations of feeling as sloppy sentimentality. Since it is important for people "as isolated and as hostile" as they not to need others, they develop "a pronounced pride in a godlike self-sufficiency" (204).

Whereas self-effacing people tend to be masochistic, arrogant-vindictive people are often sadistic. They wish to enslave others, to play on their emotions, to frustrate, disparage, and humiliate them. For Horney this behavior is not sexual, but is in part a way of retaliating for injuries and in part a response to arrogant-vindictive people's sense of the emptiness and futility of their lives. Such people develop a pervasive envy of anyone who seems to possess something they lack, whether it be wealth and prestige, physical attractiveness, or the love of a mate. Because of intense, though unadmitted, frustration, the arrogant-vindictive person hates "life and all that is positive in it": "But he hates it with the burning envy of one who is withheld from something he ardently desires. It is the bitter, begrudging envy of a person who feels that life is passing him by. 'Lebensneid,' Nietzsche called it . . . others sit at the table while he goes hungry; 'they' love, create, enjoy, feel healthy and at ease, belong somewhere. The happiness of others . . . irritates him. If he cannot be happy and free, why should they be so?" He must "trample on the joy of others" because if they "are as defeated and degraded as he, his own misery is tempered in that he no longer feels himself the only one afflicted" (*OIC*, 201–02).

The arrogant-vindictive person believes that "the world is an arena where, in the Darwinian sense, only the fittest survive and the strong annihilate the weak." A "callous pursuit of self-interest is the paramount law" (*OIC*, 64). There are no values inherent in the order of things except that might makes right. Consideration, compassion, loyalty, and unselfishness are scorned as signs of weakness, "as restraints on the path to a sinister glory" (*NHG*, 203). Those who value such qualities are fools asking to be exploited. Arrogant-vindictive people are sometimes drawn toward compliant types, however, despite their contempt, because of those people's submissiveness and malleability—and also because of their own repressed self-effacing tendencies.

Just as self-effacing people must repress their aggressive impulses in order to make their solution work, so for arrogant-vindictive people any "attitude of compliance would be incompatible" with their "whole structure of living" and would "shake its foundations." They need "to fight all softer feelings. . . . Nietzsche gives us a good illustration of these dynamics when he has his superman see any form of sympathy as a sort of fifth column, an enemy operating from within" (*OIC*, 69–70). Arrogant-vindictive people fear the emergence of their compliant trends because this would make them vulnerable in an evil world, would cause them to feel like fools, and would threaten their bargain, which is essentially with themselves. They do not count on the world to give them anything but are convinced they can reach their ambitious goals if they remain true to their vision of life as a battle and refuse to be seduced by traditional morality or their own softer feelings. If their predominant solution collapses, powerful self-effacing trends may emerge.[2]

Predominantly narcissistic people also seek mastery, but their childhoods were quite different from those of arrogant-vindictive people, as are their strategies of defense. Whereas the arrogant-vindictive person has usually been subject to abuse, the narcissistic person was often "the favored and admired child," who, "gifted beyond average, . . . early and easily won distinctions" (*NHG*, 194). The goal of arrogant-vindictive people is to prove their superiority to their detractors through achievement; the goal of narcissistic people, to maintain that sense of being excep-

tional they imbibed from those who spoiled them. "Healthy friction with the wishes
and will of others" (18)—which Horney regards as an essential condition of healthy
development—and the need to earn a sense of worth through achievement are missing in the early experience of narcissists. They develop an unrealistic sense of their
powers and importance, which creates anxiety of a somewhat different kind than the
apprehension experienced by those toward whom the world has been begrudging.
They are afraid of people whose genuine accomplishments or whose refusal to
indulge them call their inflated conception of themselves into question.

As adults, narcissistic people seek to master life "by self-admiration and the
exercise of charm" (*NHG*, 212). They have an "unquestioned belief in [their] greatness and uniqueness," which gives them a "buoyancy and perennial youthfulness."
The narcissist "has (consciously) no doubts; he *is* the anointed, the man of destiny,
the great giver, the benefactor of mankind." He feels that there is "no one he cannot
win" and is adept at charming people "with a scintillating display of feeling, with
flattery, with favors and help—in anticipation of admiration or in return for devotion
received." His insecurity is manifested in the fact that he "may speak incessantly of
his exploits or of his wonderful qualities and needs endless confirmation of his esti-
mate of himself in the form of admiration and devotion" (194).

Like arrogant-vindictive people, narcissists use others and do "not seem to mind
breaking promises, being unfaithful, incurring debts, defrauding." But they are not
"scheming exploiters"; rather, they feel that their needs are "so important that they
entitle [them] to every privilege." They expect unconditional love from others, no
matter how much they "trespass on their rights" (195).

Narcissists believe "there is nothing [they] cannot do" (194). As a result they
often attempt too much and attribute their lack of accomplishment to a superabun-
dance of talents. They may refuse to restrict their activities because accepting human
limitations is "degrading and hence intolerable." Because their imagination is capti-
vated by "the glory of the dramatic," they resent "the humble tasks of daily living" as
"humiliating." They have fantasies of "quick and glamorous achievement," avoid
consistent effort and attention to detail, and, as a face-saving device, quickly lose
interest in a given task once they encounter obstacles (313–15). When disillusioned,
narcissists may give up their ambitions, telling themselves that they would have
accomplished something great had they chosen to try.

On the surface narcissistic people are "rather optimistic" and turn "outward
toward life," but "there are undercurrents of despondency and pessimism" (196).
They see the world as a fostering parent and expect continual good luck, demanding
the fulfillment of their wishes by fate and other people. Their bargain is that if they
hold onto their dreams and their exaggerated claims for themselves, life must give

them what they want. Since life never can match their expectations, narcissistic people believe, in their weaker moments, that it is full of tragic contradictions.[3]

In *Neurosis and Human Growth,* Horney gives the least amount of attention to the perfectionistic solution, but she discusses it at length in *New Ways in Psychoanalysis.* She argues that an adherence to "rigid and high moral standards" and a "drive toward rectitude and perfection" (*NW,* 207) are not products of an instinctually based superego but special needs of individuals who have had a certain kind of childhood. They may have had "self-righteous parents who exercised unquestioned authoritative sway over the children, an authority that may have referred primarily to standards or primarily to a personal autocratic regime." They were made to feel worthless or guilty when they did not live up to their parents' demands, but by conforming to expectations they put themselves beyond reproach and gained a feeling of superiority. Their source of values shifted from themselves to externally imposed standards that told them "what is good or bad, desirable or undesirable, enjoyable or unenjoyable, likable or not." Perfectionists do not revel in a sense of being wonderful, like narcissists, but derive a sadistic satisfaction from their own rectitude because it makes others see "how stupid, worthless, and contemptible they are." They wish to "strike others with righteous indignation from the height of their infallibility," to "inflict the same injury" on others that their parents inflicted on them (218–21).

As adults, perfectionists feel superior because of their "high standards, moral and intellectual, and on this basis look down on others" (*NHG,* 196). They easily feel guilty but regard this as a virtue because it proves their "high sensitivity toward moral requirements." If the analyst points out that their self-recriminations are exaggerated, they may feel that the analyst is an inferior being who "cannot possibly understand" them (*NW,* 220). Unlike narcissists, perfectionists work hard and pay obsessive attention to details. The details themselves are unimportant, however; rather, what matters is "the flawless excellence of the whole conduct of life" (*NHG,* 196). This alone will reduce perfectionists' anxiety, make them feel superior to others, and give them a sense of controlling their own destiny.

Because they are pursuing the impossible, perfectionists must find ways to defend themselves against failure and its consequences. One defense is to equate "standards" with "actualities—*knowing* about moral values and *being* a good person." Even as they deceive themselves, they may insist that others live up to their standards and "despise them for failing to do so. [The perfectionist's] own self-condemnation is thus externalized" (*NHG,* 196). The imposition of their standards on others leads perfectionists to admire a select few and to be critical or condescending toward the majority of humankind. By presenting themselves as righteous and insisting on perfection in others while failing to live up to their own standards, perfectionists often appear to be hypocrites. Horney argues that their need is not so much to be perfect as to maintain an "*appearance* of perfection" in their own eyes and in those of others (*NW*, 215–16).

The bargain of the perfectionist is based on a legalistic conception of the world order: "Because he is fair, just, dutiful, he is entitled to fair treatment by others and by life in general. This conviction an infallible justice operating in life gives him a feeling of mastery." Success is not a matter of luck or being the favorite of fortune, as it is for the narcissist, or of superior shrewdness, talent, and ruthlessness, as it is for the arrogant-vindictive person; rather, it is a proof of virtue. Ill fortune could mean that the perfectionist was not really virtuous or that the world was unjust. Either conclusion shakes him "to the foundations of his psychic existence," invalidating "his whole accounting system" and conjuring up "the ghastly prospect of helplessness." If he recognizes "an error or failure of his own making," self-effacing trends and self-hate may come to the fore (*NHG*, 197).[4]

People who are predominantly resigned or detached usually have had a childhood in which there were "cramping influences" against which they "could not rebel openly, either because [these influences] were too strong or too intangible." Demands were made for love, understanding, conformity, and emotional support that threatened to "engulf" them. As children, detached people felt that they had to submit to those demands in order to be loved, but they longed at the same time to rebel against "the bonds put around" them. They handled the situation by withdrawal. Putting "an emotional distance between [themselves] and others," these children no longer sought affection—nor did they fight. Withdrawal helped them preserve their individuality but it forced them to put a check on their feelings and "retract all those wishes and needs which would require others for their fulfillment." These included "natural needs for understanding, for sharing experiences, for affection, sympathy, protection." They kept their joys, pains, sorrows, and fears to themselves. It was safer "not to let anybody know that anything matters" lest their "wishes either be frustrated or used . . . to make [them] dependent." But although retracting their wishes made detached people more independent, it also sapped their "vitality and maim[ed] their] sense of direction" (*NHG*, 275–76). Their inner emptiness made them all the more afraid of being influenced by others, whose desires were by definition stronger.

Whereas self-effacing people crave love and expansive people seek mastery, detached people worship freedom and independence. They want to be left alone, to have nothing expected of them, to be subject to no restrictions. They have a "*hypersensitivity to influence, pressure, coercion or ties of any kind*" (*NHG*, 266). They may react with anxiety to pressure exerted by anything, ranging from clothing or closed spaces to long-term obligations, the inexorability of time, the laws of cause and effect, or traditional values and rules of behavior. Detached people wish to do what they please when they please, but since they are in fact alienated from their spontaneous desires, this freedom is rather empty. It is a *freedom from* whatever they feel to be coercion rather than a *freedom to* fulfill themselves. Their desire for freedom may take the form of a craving for serenity, which means for them "simply the absence of all troubles, irritations, or upsets" (263).

Detached people disdain the pursuit of worldly success and have a profound aversion to effort. Although they have a strong need for superiority and usually look upon their fellows with condescension, they realize their ambitions only in their imaginations. They make themselves invulnerable by being self-sufficient. This involves not only living in imagination but also restricting their desires. In order to avoid being dependent on the environment, they try to subdue their inner cravings and to be content with little. They cultivate a "don't care" attitude and protect themselves against frustration by believing that "nothing matters."

Detached people withdraw from both other people and themselves. They seek privacy, shroud themselves "in a veil of secrecy," and, in their personal relationships, draw around themselves "a kind of magic circle which no one may penetrate" (*OIC*, 75–76). They may feel an "intolerable strain in associating with people" (73) and "may very readily go to pieces" (90) if that magic circle is entered. Detached people withdraw from themselves by suppressing or denying their feelings. Their resignation from active living gives them an "onlooker" attitude that often enables them to be excellent observers of others, as well as of their own inner processes. With insight divorced from feeling, they look at themselves "with a kind of objective interest, as one would look at a work of art" (74).

Detached people's withdrawal from themselves is in part an effort to resolve their inner conflicts. In this solution, says Horney, the subordinated trends are not deeply repressed; they are visible to the trained observer and are rather easily brought to awareness. Detached people try to resolve their basic conflict by immobilizing both sides of it. This solution through evasion is "the most radical and the most effective" of the defenses against the basic conflict, but "it is no true solution because the compulsive cravings for closeness as well as for aggressive domination, exploitation, and excelling remain, and they keep harassing if not paralyzing their carrier" (*OIC*, 95).

Because detached people are likely to entertain the attitudes of the subordinated solutions, their values are highly contradictory. They have a high regard for what they define as freedom and independence and cultivate individuality, self-reliance, and an indifference to fate. But they may express at one time "an extreme appreciation for human goodness, sympathy, generosity, self-effacing sacrifice, and at another time swing to a complete jungle philosophy of callous self-interest" (*OIC*, 94). In order to reduce their vulnerability, they believe, "consciously or unconsciously, that is it *better* not to wish or expect anything. Sometimes this goes with a conscious pessimistic outlook on life, a sense of its being futile anyhow and of nothing being sufficiently desirable to make an effort for it" (*NHG*, 263). Detached people do not usually rail against life, however, but accept whatever happens to them with ironic humor or stoic dignity. They try to avoid suffering by making themselves independent of external forces, by convincing themselves that nothing matters, and by concerning themselves only with whatever is within their power. Their bargain is that if they ask nothing of others, they will not be bothered; if they try for nothing, they will not fail; and if they expect little of life, they will not be disappointed.[5]

Horney describes childhood experiences that typically lead to each of the major solutions, but most children undergo a combination of these experiences and develop a combination of defenses. Horney's childhood, for example, contained features of the early experiences to which she traces not only the self-effacing but also the perfectionistic, arrogant-vindictive, and detached solutions, and she behaved in ways characteristic of each of these solutions as an adult. Conflicts between the solutions cause oscillations, inconsistencies, and self-hate. One of the most significant features of Horney's theory is that it permits us to make sense of contradictory attitudes, behaviors, and beliefs by seeing them as part of a structure of inner conflicts. Horneyan theory has a dynamic quality: solutions combine, conflict, become stronger or weaker, need to be defended, generate vicious circles, and are replaced by others when they collapse.

Chapter 28

The Idealized Image and the

Pride System

In reviewing the evolution of her theory at the end of *Neurosis and Human Growth*, Horney observes that she first saw neurosis as essentially a disturbance in human relationships. This disturbance creates basic anxiety against which we defend ourselves by moving compulsively toward, against, and away from people. In her earlier books she had been aware of intrapsychic factors such as self-idealization, shoulds, claims, and self-hate, but she had not recognized their extent and importance. After discussing the idealized image in *Our Inner Conflicts,* however, she had come to realize that its formation marks a turning point in our development, as our energies shift from developing our real potentialities to actualizing our grandiose conception of ourselves. The idealized image generates the pride system, which becomes a kind of Frankenstein's monster that hates and seeks to destroy its creator. Neurosis is a disturbance not only in our relationships with others but also in our relationship with ourselves.

The disturbance in the relationship with ourselves makes it nearly impossible for us to form better relationships with others that could undo the original damage. Referring obliquely to the position she took in earlier books, Horney observes that some people assume that because neurosis is primarily the result of bad human relationships it can be remedied by good ones—like those with an analyst—"in which factors that were injurious in childhood are absent." This expectation may be "justified with regard to the child and adolescent," but it may not be with regard to the adult, for good human relationships "do not have the power to uproot a firmly planted pride system" (*NHG,* 306, 308). The pride system is a logical outgrowth of early development and the beginning of a new one. Once in existence it develops a dynamic of its own, which is to a large degree independent of external events. Since the pride system affects how we interact with others, it poisons all our relationships and makes it extremely difficult for them to be a source of healing or growth. To deal successfully with the pride system, analysts must recognize its manifestations in the transference and try to understand it synchronically, in terms of its structure and inner logic.

In *Neurosis and Human Growth* Horney posits a developmental sequence that leads from interpersonal to intrapsychic strategies of defense. Children try to cope with feelings of weakness, inadequacy, and isolation by developing interpersonal strategies. They then must deal with the conflicts between these strategies by making one of them predominant and suppressing the others. The coherence thus achieved is too loose, and the children need "a firmer and more comprehensive *integration*" (20). The original defenses, moreover, do not fully satisfy their psychological needs and exacerbate their sense of weakness by alienating children from their real selves. As a further defense children or adolescents develop an idealized image of themselves, which is "a kind of artistic creation in which opposites appear reconciled" (*OIC,* 104).

The idealized image gives individuals *"a feeling of identity"* that compensates for their self-alienation and inner division and enables them to achieve "a feeling of power and significance." With the help of imagination they endow themselves with exalted faculties. The individual becomes "a hero, a genius, a supreme lover, a saint, a god." Horney calls self-idealization "a *comprehensive neurotic solution.*" It promises to satisfy all needs, to rid people of their "painful and unbearable feelings," and to provide "an ultimately mysterious fulfillment" of themselves and their lives. In the course of neurotic development, the idealized image assumes more and more reality. It becomes the individual's "idealized self," representing to him "what he 'really' is, or potentially is—what he could be, and should be" (*NHG*, 21–24).

The nature of the idealized image depends upon our own experiences: our "earlier fantasies . . . particular needs . . . and given faculties" (*NHG*, 22). Its content is much influenced by our predominant defense and the attributes it exalts. The idealized image of self-effacing people "is a composite of 'lovable' qualities, such as unselfishness, goodness, generosity, humility, saintliness, nobility, sympathy." It also glorifies "helplessness, suffering, and martyrdom" and deep feelings for art, nature, or other people (222). Arrogant-vindictive people see themselves as invincible masters of all situations. They are smarter, tougher, more realistic than other people and can therefore get the better of them. They take pride in their vigilance, foresight, and planning and feel that nothing can hurt them. The narcissistic person is "the anointed, the man of destiny, the prophet, the great giver, the benefactor of mankind" (194). Narcissists see themselves as having unlimited energies and as being capable of unlimited achievements, effortlessly attained. Perfectionists regard themselves as models of rectitude, who achieve a flawless excellence in the whole conduct of life. They do a wonderful job at whatever they undertake, have perfect judgment, and are just and dutiful in their human relationships. The idealized image of detached or resigned people "is a composite of self-sufficiency, independence, self-contained serenity, freedom from desires and passions," and "stoicism" (277). Detached people want to be free from restraint and impervious to pressure. In each solution, the idealized image may be modeled in whole or in part on a religious or cultural ideal or an example from history or personal experience.

Although the idealized image is designed to provide a firmer and more comprehensive integration of the personality it is actually a composite of various solutions, with one solution predominating. The submerged trends may also be glorified, but they remain in the background, or are isolated through compartmentalization, or are seen, somehow, as "compatible aspects of a rich personality." An arrogant-vindictive man "to whom love seems unpermissible softness" may in his idealized image be not only hard and tough but also "a great lover," "a knight in shining armor." One patient who was particularly successful at compartmentalization was, in his idealized image, "a benefactor of mankind, a wise man who had achieved a self-contained serenity, and a person who could without qualms kill his enemies" (*NHG*, 22–23). People who suffer from inner conflicts because they are pursuing incompatible solutions only compound their problems when they develop an idealized image that incorporates these conflicts.

The idealized image is designed to enhance our feeling of worth and to provide a sense of identity, but it leads to increased self-contempt and additional inner conflicts. We cannot live up to our idealized image because it is highly unrealistic and full of contradictions. Since we will feel worthwhile only when we actualize our idealized image, and since everything that falls short of that image is contemptible, we develop a "despised image" of ourselves that is just as unrealistic as its idealized counterpart. We then waver "between self-adoration and self-contempt," "with no solid middle ground to fall back on" (*OIC*, 112).

There are now four selves competing for our allegiance: the real (or possible) self; the idealized (or impossible) self; the despised self; and the actual self, which is "everything that a person is at a given time," healthy and neurotic (*NHG*, 158). The more self-actualizing we are, the greater will be the congruence between the real self and the actual self and the less the likelihood that we shall harbor idealized and despised selves. The more self-alienated we are, the greater will be the distance between the real self and the actual self, the actual self and the idealized self, and the idealized self and its despised counterpart.

The increased self-hate and inner conflict produced by the formation of the idealized image lead to further self-glorification (with its concomitant intensified self-contempt) and to compulsive efforts to actualize the idealized image, either in action or in imagination. Thus begins the search for glory, as "the energies driving toward self-realization are shifted to the aim of actualizing the idealized self" (*NHG*, 24). The search often takes the form of a quest for the absolute: "All the drives for glory have in common the reaching out for greater knowledge, wisdom, virtue, or powers than are given to human beings. . . . Nothing short of absolute fearlessness, mastery, or saintliness has any appeal." What is considered to be glorious depends on the major solution. In the search for glory, "the needs for the *absolute* and the *ultimate* are so stringent that they override the checks which usually prevent our imagination from detaching itself from actuality" (34–35). Imagination is put into the service of neurosis not only in the creation of the idealized self and the formation of lofty dreams but also in the continual falsification of reality that is necessary to protect the precious illusions.

Horney does not see the search for glory, the quest for the absolute, or the need to be godlike as essential ingredients of human nature. Because we have the ability to imagine and plan, we are always reaching beyond ourselves, but healthy people reach for the possible, dream a possible dream, and work to achieve their goals within the context of human limitations. They are able to take satisfaction in their achievements and to sustain frustration without rage, self-hate, or despair. Self-alienated people, however, are, in their own minds, either all or nothing. Indeed, it is because they feel themselves to be nothing that they must claim to be all. If we can be fully human, however, we do not need to be gods.

For self-alienated people, the search for glory is often the most important thing in life. It gives them the sense of meaning and the feeling of superiority they so desperately crave. They may experience depression or despair at the feeling that they can never actualize their idealized image. They fiercely resist all encroachments upon their illusory grandeur and may even prefer death to the shattering of their dreams. More lives have been "sacrificed on the altar of glory," writes Horney, "than for any other reason" (*NHG*, 30). The search for glory constitutes a "private religion" the rules of which are determined by our particular neuroses, but we also may participate in the glory systems that are a prominent feature of every culture. These include organized religions, various forms of group identification, wars and military service, and competitions, honors, and hierarchical arrangements of all kinds.

We pay a heavy price for our sense of exaltation, a price that is symbolized for Horney by the story of the Devil's pact: "The devil, or some other personification of evil, tempts a person who is perplexed by spiritual or material trouble with the offer of unlimited powers. But he can obtain these powers only on the condition of selling his soul or going to hell" (*NHG*, 39; see also 375–76). By making a Faustian bargain, we condemn ourselves to a kind of psychic damnation: "The easy way to infinite glory is inevitably also the way to an inner hell of self-contempt and self-torment. By taking this road, the individual is in fact losing his soul—his real self" (39). For Freud our condition is tragic because the requirements of survival—civilization—prohibit that full and immediate gratification of instinct which is the only source of true happiness. For Horney tragedy is not inherent in the human condition, but our lives become tragic when "under the pressure of inner distress" we try to transcend our condition by reaching out "for the ultimate and the infinite" and in the process destroy the potentialities we actually possess and condemn ourselves to self-hate (377).

The creation of the idealized image produces not only the search for glory but the whole structure of phenomena that Horney calls the pride system. We take an intense pride in the attributes of our idealized selves and on the basis of this pride make neurotic claims on others. At the same time, we feel that we *should* perform in a manner commensurate with our grandiose conception of ourselves. If the world fails to honor our claims or if we fail to live up to our shoulds, we become our despised selves and experience agonizing self-hate. As with our idealized image, the specific nature of our pride, our shoulds, our claims, and our self-hate will be influenced by our predominant solution and by the conflicts between it and subordinate trends.

Our need to actualize our idealized image leads us to impose stringent demands and taboos upon ourselves, a phenomenon Horney calls "the tyranny of the should." The function of the shoulds is to make us over into our idealized self: *"the premise on which they operate is that nothing should be, or is, impossible for oneself"* (NHG, 68). The shoulds are characterized by their coerciveness, their disregard for feasibility, their imperviousness to psychic laws, and their reliance on either willpower for fulfillment or imagination for denial of failure. A good deal of externalization accompanies the shoulds. We often feel our shoulds as the expectations of others, our self-hate as their rejection, and our self-criticism as their unfair judgment. We expect others to live up to our shoulds and displace onto them our rage at our own failure to do so. The chief effects of the shoulds are a pervasive feeling of strain, hypersensitivity to criticism, impairment of spontaneity, and emotional deadness. The shoulds are a defense against self-loathing, but, like other defenses, they aggravate the condition they are employed to cure. Not only do they increase self-alienation, they also intensify self-hate, for they are impossible to live up to. The penalty for failure is a feeling of worthlessness and self-contempt. Thus the shoulds have tyrannical power. "It is the threat of a punitive self-hate" that "truly makes them a regime of terror" (85).

Our shoulds and taboos are generated by our idealized image. Self-effacing people feel that they should be meek, humble, unassuming, generous, helpful, sympathetic, understanding, self-sacrificial, and loving. They should like and trust others, be full of gratitude, count their blessings, and have faith in the benevolence of people and the deity (or the world order to which they subscribe). They have taboos against self-glorification, pride, arrogance, ambition, triumph, and seeking their own advantage. They should not resent injuries and should shun any thought, feeling, or behavior that might be construed as arrogant, conceited, vindictive, or presumptuous.

Arrogant-vindictive people are governed by an opposite set of shoulds and taboos. They should assume the worst of other people, should attack others before they themselves are attacked, be hard and tough, and retaliate against all who offend them. They should be in control of every situation, win every contest, and shun dependency. They should have "invincible strength" and "be inviolable" (204).

Whereas the taboos of self-effacing people largely concern aggression, the taboos of arrogant-vindictive people are against being meek, generous, helpful, sympathetic, loving, or trusting.

Narcissistic people feel that they should be able to do everything and win over everybody, not by virtue of effort but because of who they are. Horney does not say much about the shoulds of this solution, partly because her treatment of it is so brief and partly because narcissists are less driven by shoulds than others. Rather, they are full of claims, and one of their major shoulds is to believe in their destiny, to hold onto their claims even when the claims are being frustrated. If they have not achieved glory as yet, they are convinced that they are bound to sooner or later, as long as they hold to the belief that they are favorites of fortune. They have taboos against doubting their special destiny, accepting limitations, or doing anything that would mark them as ordinary.

Whereas narcissists identify with their claims, perfectionists identify with their shoulds, which are very strong indeed. They make strenuous efforts to measure up to their shoulds "by fulfilling duties and obligations, by polite and orderly manners, by not telling obvious lies." Their "arrogant contempt for others" is hidden behind "polished friendliness" because their shoulds "prohibit such 'irregular feelings" (*NHG*, 196). They think they "should be able to control every anxiety, no matter how deep it is, should never be hurt, and should never make a mistake" (*NW*, 207). Their judgment must always be correct, and they must perform all roles and tasks to perfection. Horney became aware of the power shoulds wield in her examination of perfectionism in *New Ways in Psychoanalysis,* but she later came to see that they exercise a coercive force in every solution.

The shoulds of resigned or detached people are mostly negative in nature. These people should not "get attached to anything to the extent of really needing it." "Anything" includes not only money, power, and prestige, but also other people. Detached people may have "distant or transitory relations" but should not allow themselves to become dependent on others for companionship, help, or emotional support. Sexual relationships should never "degenerate into love." If they do develop lasting relationships, they need to maintain their distance in these relationships as well. They must not show others their feelings, which ought to stay hidden, and they should not expect anything of life or other people lest they be disappointed (*NHG*, 264–66).

All the shoulds are impossible to live up to, in part because they are unrealistic. Self-effacing people cannot help resenting injuries, wanting things for themselves, craving power and prestige. Arrogant-vindictive people do have feelings of compassion, needs for warmth, and desires for approval. Narcissists harbor doubts about their claims, their exalted conception of themselves, and their destiny. Perfectionists cannot be perfect and cannot control their anxieties. Resigned people cannot repress every expectation and desire; they are dependent on external conditions and other people, they need to share their feelings, and they want love. The shoulds always demand the repression of needs, feelings, and wishes that cannot be repressed.

In addition, shoulds reflect our inner conflicts and are therefore at war with each other. They are generated by the idealized image, but the idealized image is a composite of various solutions, each of which produces its own set of demands. As a result, we are often caught in a crossfire of conflicting shoulds. The self-effacing person wants to be good, noble, loving, forgiving, generous; but he has an aggressive side that tells him to "go all out for his advantage" and to "hit back at anybody who offends him. Accordingly he despises himself at bottom for any trace of 'cowardice,' of ineffectualness and compliance. He is thus under a constant cross fire. He is damned if he docs do something, and he is damned if he does not" (NHG, 221).

Shoulds may be combined in various ways, but in each case if we obey one set of shoulds, we violate the others and hate ourselves for not fulfilling them. By trying to implement the new set, we violate the shoulds we initially obeyed and despise ourselves on that account. This process may result in our embracing our predominant solution all the more rigidly or it may produce oscillation, inconsistency, or paralysis. The cross fire of conflicting shoulds is a powerful concept that explains a great deal of inconsistent behavior.

People with different solutions not only pursue different predominant shoulds but hold different attitudes toward their dictates. Self-effacing persons feel that their "shoulds constitute a law not to be questioned," but although they try to measure up to them, they generally feel that they fall "pitiably short of fulfilling them. The foremost element in [their] conscious experience is therefore self-criticism, a feeling of guilt for not being the supreme being" (NHG, 76–77).

Arrogant-vindictive people also accept the validity of their shoulds, but they abhor failure and are determined "to actualize them in one way or another" (76). They cover over their shortcomings with imaginative reconstructions of reality, arrogance, or arbitrary claims that they are in the right. The shoulds of narcissists "are no less inexorable than [those] in other forms of neurosis," but narcissists are able to escape the tyranny of these demands "by the use of a magic wand. [Their] capacity to overlook flaws, or to turn them into virtues, seems unlimited" (195). Perfectionists identify with their shoulds and look down on others from their lofty height. They make strenuous efforts to fulfill the shoulds and deal with their failures by equating standards with performance or by various forms of externalization. Because of the stringency of their inner dictates, perfectionists are often in rebellion against them and experience "listlessness and inertia" in the face of what they are "supposed to do or feel" (222).

Since detached people, with their ideal of freedom and their hypersensitivity to coercion, feel that they should not be controlled by anything outside or inside themselves, they may also rebel against their shoulds, especially those dictated by their aggressive and compliant trends, which can be close to the surface. They may rebel passively, in which case everything they feel they "should do arouses conscious or unconscious resentment, and in consequence makes [them] listless" (77). Or they may rebel actively and behave in ways that defy their inner dictates and violate their taboos.

The idealized image also produces "neurotic claims," which are our demands to be treated in accordance with our grandiose conception of ourselves. Claims also involve the expectation that we will receive whatever we need to make our solution work. Among the things that self-effacing people expect are love, protection, understanding, sympathy, loyalty, and appreciation of their goodness. Arrogant-vindictive people feel entitled to exploit others with impunity and without guilt. Narcissists require unconditional love and adoration from their fellows, easy superiority, and unvarying good luck. Perfectionists demand "respect from others rather than glowing admiration" (*NHG,* 196) and a just reward for their rectitude. Resigned people feel entitled to privacy; no one should expect anything of them and they ought to be "exempt from having to make a living" and assuming responsibilities (271).

Generally speaking, neurotic claims are unrealistic, egocentric, and vindictive. They demand results without effort. Based on an assumption of specialness or superiority, they deny the world of cause and effect and are "pervaded by expectations of magic" (*NHG,* 62). The effects of neurotic claims are "a diffuse sense of frustration," a "chronic discontent," an attitude of envy and insensitivity toward others, an uncertainty about rights, a feeling of inertia, and an intensification of the burdensomeness of any hardship (57).

Neurotic claims do not achieve their objective, which is confirmation of our idealized image and predominant solution. If the world fails to honor our claims, as is often the case, we must doubt whether we are special and our strategy is effective. We may react with rage, despair, or self-hate. But we may also reaffirm our claims, which are extremely tenacious, for we depend on them for self-aggrandizement and a sense of control over our destinies. We may rationalize away disappointments. A person's discovery "that others do not accede to his claims, that laws do apply to him, that he is not above common troubles and failure—all of this is no evidence against his unlimited possibilities. It merely proves that, *as yet,* he has had an unfair deal. But if only he upholds his claims, some day they will come true. *The claims are his guaranty for future glory"* (*NHG*, 62).

The claims are what we feel entitled to according to the conception of justice that is part of our predominant solution. Although specific expectations will vary from solution to solution, the essential conception of justice remains the same. In a just world, our claims will be honored; if they are not, life is absurd. Since our solution will collapse if the universe is not organized as we need it to be, we have a powerful vested interest in preserving our system of belief in the face of contrary evidence. If we become convinced that the world has belied our expectations, we may either become unable to function or switch to a solution with a different conception of the universe.

An important part of the justice system in each solution is what Horney calls a deal and what I have called a bargain with fate. The bargain is that if we obey our shoulds, our claims will be honored, our solution will work, and our idealized conception of ourselves will be confirmed. When events indicate that our bargain has failed, we may be thrown into a state of psychological crisis.[6] The bargain also involves a conviction that we will be punished if we violate our shoulds. The justice system of our solution can turn against us. In some cases, conflicting solutions generate conflicting bargains, ethical codes, and conceptions of justice.

Neurotic pride, asserts Horney, is "the climax and consolidation of the process initiated with the search for glory" (*NHG*, 109). It substitutes for realistic self-confidence and self-esteem a pride in the attributes of the idealized self, in the successful assertion of claims, and in the "loftiness and severity" of the inner dictates. Because pride turns the compulsive behaviors of the various solutions into virtues, anything can be a source of pride: "Thus inconsistency turns into unlimited freedom, blind rebellion against an existing code of morals into being above common prejudice, a taboo on doing anything for oneself into saintly unselfishness, a need to appease into sheer goodness, dependency into love, exploiting others into astuteness. A capacity to assert egocentric claims appears as strength, vindictiveness as justice, frustrating techniques as a most intelligent weapon, aversion to work as 'successfully resisting the deadly habit of work,' and so on." We commonly take great pride in the mental processes of imagination, reason, and will, since "the infinite powers" we ascribe to ourselves "are, after all, powers of the mind." The mind must work incessantly at "maintaining the private fictitious world through rationalizations, justifications, externalizations, reconciling irreconcilables—in short, through finding ways to make things appear different from what they are" (91–94).

Pride is a vitally important defense, but because it is based on illusion and self-deception, it increases our vulnerability. Threats to it produce anxiety and hostility; its collapse results in self-contempt. We are especially subject to feelings of shame (when we violate our own pride) and humiliation (when our pride is violated by others). We react to shame with self-hate and to humiliation with a vindictive hostility ranging "from irritability, to anger, to a blind murderous rage" (*NHG*, 99).

There are various devices for restoring pride. They include retaliation—which reestablishes the superiority of the humiliated person—and loss of interest in whatever threatens or damages pride. They also include various forms of distortion, such as forgetting humiliating episodes, denying responsibility, blaming others, and embellishing. Sometimes "humor is used to take the sting out of an otherwise unbearable shame" (106). We attempt to protect pride by a system of avoidances, like not trying, restricting wishes and activities, and refusing to become involved in any serious pursuit or relationship. "It is safer to renounce, to withdraw, or to resign than to take the risk of exposing one's pride to injury" (108).

Expansive people tend to identify with their pride, whereas self-effacing people are afraid of it. This is one way of distinguishing self-effacing people from perfectionists, with whom they share many values. Both try to be good, dutiful, and loyal; but perfectionists are proud of their virtue, whereas self-effacing people have a taboo against pride and must disclaim special merit. True, they cannot help being proud of their "saintly and lovable qualities," but their "very image of saintliness and lovableness prohibits any *conscious* feeling of pride," and they "must lean over backward to eradicate any trace of it" (*NHG*, 223). Because their pride in their goodness and humility frightens them, they look for ways to disown it. As a way out of their dilemma, self-effacing people often transfer their pride to an expansive person, which allows them to experience a sense of triumph without owning it to themselves. They can feel humble and unselfish while rejoicing in the greatness of another with whom they have identified. Resigned people also have a problem with pride, in that they have given up the active pursuit of glory. They take pride in being free, in being themselves, in resisting coercion, or in seeing through the folly of others, rather than in "attaining or growing" (272). They feel superior to more productive people because they realize the vanity of all human endeavors and the futility of the search for glory.

The pride system is in large measure a defense against the negative feelings about ourselves created by adverse experiences in childhood, but, as we have seen, it generates self-hate and thus exacerbates our problems. As a neurotic phenomenon, self-hate must not be confused with a healthy self-criticism. Self-realizing people may not always like themselves, but they will not hate themselves. They will handle feelings of guilt and inadequacy in a basically self-accepting and constructive way by recognizing their human limitations and trying to repair damage they may have caused and to avoid future mistakes. They will work at themselves patiently, realistically, and without expecting miracles. Self-alienated people will resort to the strategies of self-glorification, tyrannical shoulds, neurotic claims, and neurotic pride in order to blot out their deficiencies and compensate for low self-esteem. These strategies produce self-hate because of the disparity they create between what our pride system compels us to be and who we actually are. "We do not hate ourselves because we are worthless," says Horney, "but because we are driven to reach beyond ourselves" (*NHG*, 114).

For the most part, self-hate is unconscious, since "there is a survival interest in *not* being aware of its impact." The chief defense against awareness is externalization, which may be either active or passive: "The former is an attempt to direct self-hate outward, against life, fate, institutions, or people. In the latter the hate remains directed against the self but is perceived or experienced as coming from the outside." Self-hate operates through "relentless demands on self, merciless self-accusation, self-contempt, self-frustrations, self-tormenting, and self-destruction." We often take a pride in our self-hate that serves to maintain self-glorification: "The very condemnation of imperfection confirms the godlike standards with which the person identifies himself" (114–17).

Self-hate is in large part the rage the idealized self feels toward the actual self for not being what it should be. The actual self "is such an embarrassing sight when viewed from the perspective of a godlike perfection" that we "cannot help but despise it" (110). We lose our ability to perceive our actual self and see only our despised self instead. In addition to the conflicts between the major solutions, a conflict develops within the pride system between our idealized and despised selves, causing us to oscillate between grandiosity and self-contempt.[7]

In the course of successful therapy, an intrapsychic conflict develops between the pride system and the emerging real self, which now becomes an object of self-hate. Horney calls this the "central inner conflict." Living from the real self involves accepting a world of uncertainty, process, and limitation. It means giving up the search for glory and settling for a less exalted existence. The proud self therefore senses the real self as a threat to its very existence and turns upon it with scorn.

Although this central inner conflict occurs at a rather late stage in psychological growth, it is a fierce one. People who have focused their lives on dreams of glory may never be able fully to free themselves from the habit of self-idealization. If they have made progress in therapy, they may seize on their improvement as "the last chance to actualize [their] idealized self in the shining glory of perfect health" (358).

They may look down on others for being neurotic, drive themselves to behave in self-actualizing ways, and rage at themselves when they realize that they will always have problems and imperfections. Horney's hope is that patients will "feel sympathetic" toward themselves and experience themselves "as being neither particularly wonderful nor despicable but as the struggling and often harassed" human beings they are (359). Marcia Westkott describes "the release of the real self from the seesawing of the pride system" as "a triumph of the ordinary" in which we come to realize that we do "not have to be extraordinary in order to be worthwhile" (1986, 211).

Self-hate is the end result of the pride system. Horney sees it as "perhaps the greatest tragedy of the human mind. Man in reaching out for the Infinite and Absolute also starts destroying himself. When he makes a pact with the devil, who promises him glory, he has to go to hell—to the hell within himself." Only when self-hate abates can "unconstructive self-pity turn into a constructive sympathy with self." In order for this to happen a person must have "a beginning feeling for his real self and a beginning wish for inner salvation" (*NHG*, 153–54).

Because I wanted to let Horney's mature theory speak for itself, I have discussed it without connecting it to her life, but there is, of course, a relationship between her theory and her personality. Horney's theory offers, I think, the most cogent explanation of her contradictory behavior and the conflicting testimony about her. The many sides of Karen Horney include a self-effacing shyness and need for love and reassurance; an aggressive ambition, arrogance, and ruthlessness in her dealings with colleagues; and a detached remoteness, secretiveness, and inwardness. Her detachment was the source of a great deal of her psychological insight, since it enabled her to see through her own defenses, as well as through those of others.

There is less direct evidence of the operation of the pride system in Horney, although we can reasonably assume that her account of its dynamics was partly drawn from self-observation. We know that she had an "enormous need to be a star," and behind her ambition, combativeness, and arrogance was no doubt an idealized image of herself as an international figure. She "wanted to push Freud over," says Frances Arkin, "and stand in his place." In spite of a highly successful career, the recognition she received apparently fell short of her dreams. As Wanda Willig has observed, "With all the acclaim, she . . . was discontented; it was not enough." Several people have described her as doing whatever she pleased; Esther Spitzer asserted that "she seemed to feel she could get away with anything."[8] Perhaps Horney's claims, her sense of being above the rules, precipitated her unprofessional behavior toward some of her male analysands, although her compulsive need for reassurance was also a factor.

Like the people she describes, Horney oscillated between pride and self-hate. Although she garnered considerable fame, she felt that the world was not honoring her claims; and although she was enormously productive, she flagellated herself about "her inability to work" (Marianne Eckardt, Academy). Her conflicting shoulds drove her toward vindictive triumphs but also urged her to be the understanding, supportive, highly ethical person she projects in her books. Horney suffered not only from a struggle between pride and self-hate, but also from what she describes as the central inner conflict between the real and the idealized self. When we are in the grip of this conflict, says Horney, we may hold onto our idealized image by seeking to actualize it "in the shining glory of perfect health" (*NHG*, 358). Perhaps one of the sources of the "great anguish and pain" witnessed by Harold Kelman was her self-hate because of her continued neurosis.

Because her thought evolved through several stages, Horney means different things to different people. Some think of her primarily as the first psychoanalytic feminist, the woman whose work so brilliantly anticipated the reaction against Freud's view of feminine psychology. To others, she is one of the major neo-Freudians and a leading member of the cultural school. And some identify her with her mature theory, in which she develops a sophisticated taxonomy of interpersonal and intrapsychic strategies of defense. While each stage of Horney's thought is important, I think that her mature theory represents her most significant contribution. Most of Horney's early ideas have been revised or enriched—by Horney herself or by others—or have been absorbed or discovered anew by later writers. This is not the case with her mature theory. *Our Inner Conflicts* and *Neurosis and Human Growth* provide explanations of human behavior in terms of currently existing constellations of defenses and inner conflicts that we can find nowhere else. These explanations have not only greater value for clinical practice, but also many more interdisciplinary applications than Horney's earlier ideas (see Appendix A).

Chapter 29

Horney and Third Force Psychology

Although her conception of the real self constitutes the foundation of her mature theory, Horney devoted most of her attention to analyzing the defenses we employ to cope with frustration and threat. It remained for subsequent theorists to elaborate her vision of optimal development. Whereas Horney focused on self-alienation, Abraham Maslow focused on self-actualization, providing a fuller picture than she of our basic motivations and the nature of psychological health. Maslow drew on the work of many others as well, whom he described as belonging to the "Third Force" in modern psychology. Horney was a seminal figure in this group, and it is to Third Force psychology that her mature theory most clearly belongs. Before turning to Third Force psychology, however, I shall briefly review the other schools of thought that Horney either anticipated or influenced, or to which her theories are akin.

Horneyan theory deals with many of the issues found in mainstream psycho-analytic theories, although it differs from ego psychology, self-psychology, and object-relations theory in important ways (Danielian 1988; Paul 1989; Ingram and Lerner 1992; Mitchell 1992). Horney's "basic anxiety" is much the same as Erik Erikson's "basic mistrust," and her theory illuminates many of the stages of development Erikson describes. The search for identity often involves the formation of the idealized image, which precipitates a crisis later in life, when we realize that our search for glory is not going to succeed. Horney's work is also relevant to Heinz Lichtenstein's theory of identity: Lichtenstein's identity themes can often be understood in Horneyan terms as constellations of defenses and inner conflicts.

Like Heinz Kohut and his fellows, Horney is interested in problems of the self; and like Harry Guntrip, Ronald Fairbairn, D. W. Winnicott, John Bowlby, and other members of the British Independent School, she sees neurosis as a product of disturbed object-relations, especially in childhood. She differs from self-psychologists in her denial of primary narcissism and from object-relations theorists in her focus on present structure. Horney's ideas can to some extent be integrated with those of Margaret Mahler if we see her defensive strategies as originating in the vicissitudes of the separation/individuation process. Fear of separation generates the movement toward other people, whereas fear of reengulfment (or perhaps lack of adequate initial symbiosis) generates longings for power and independence (Paris 1991a, 184–85; see also Feiring 1983).

Horney's mature theory has parallels with and implications for other schools of thought as well. It anticipates many of the ideas of R. D. Laing (Paris 1982, 1986) and Alice Miller (Westkott 1986). It helped inspire the interpersonal school (Leary 1957; Teyber 1988), and it provided a model for therapies that focus on the current situation of the patient rather than upon the past (Wachtel 1977). Horney's ideas have influenced the DSM-III and its revision, the DSM-III-R, through Theodore Millon (1981), who has served on the DSM-III Task Force and on the Advisory Committee on Personality Disorders of the DSM-III. Indeed, they have made their way, often unacknowledged, into the array of ideas and techniques that most psychotherapists now employ.

The fact that Horneyan theory is based on the idea of a real self makes it incompatible with Lacanian psychoanalysis, deconstruction, and other postmodern theories that deny an authentic personal identity. The idea of a coherent self as the core of our personal identity is out of keeping with the propensity for decentering, deconstructing, and denying the self, which is often seen to be merely the locus of cultural codes and influences. For those who deny a self, Horney's theory is predicated upon an illusion, but from a Horneyan perspective the belief that the self is inevitably derivative, inauthentic, and fragmented is a product of inner conflict and self-alienation, which is then generalized as the human condition.

The late twentieth-century unfashionableness of the idea notwithstanding, Horney is far from alone in positing a real self and in regarding healthy growth as a process of actualizing it. Her position is akin to the developmental, self, and object-relations approach articulated by James Masterson in *The Real Self,* where he observes that "in our daily toil with our patients, our work revolves around a person with a self, not a collection of objects and an ego" (1985, 5; see also Stern 1985). Horney's real self bears some resemblance to Kohut's "nuclear self" (1977, 1984) and even more to Winnicott's "true self" (1965). According to Winnicott, as a result of inadequate nurturing "something that could have become the individual becomes hidden away[,] . . . protected from further impingement" by a "false self" that develops reactively and supersedes "the true impulsive self which might under more favorable circumstances have been gathering strength" (1987, 61).[9] This sounds like Horney, as does much of Alice Miller's discussion of the loss of and search for the true self in childhood (1981, 1983) and R. D. Laing's account of ontological insecurity (which is comparable to basic anxiety) and the development of a false-self system in response to it (1965). I do not, however, insist on a Horneyan influence—although that is a possibility—nor on an exact equivalence of these ideas, since there are many theoretical differences between these thinkers that are too complex to be specified here.

But there is no doubt that Horney influenced Third Force psychology, which shares her vision of human nature and human values and builds on many of her basic premises. Abraham Maslow, the chief spokesman for Third Force psychology, knew Horney, adopted her conception of the real self, and developed a theory that is complementary to hers. Although modern psychology had until Maslow's time been most influenced by the Freudian and the experimental-positivistic-behavioristic schools, Maslow felt that several other groups were "coalescing into a third, increasingly comprehensive theory" (1968, vi)[10] that had a different philosophy of human nature. The difference has been variously defined as greater optimism, a more holistic approach to human behavior, or a richer array of inherent needs and values; but most crucial is the contention that, in addition to tension reduction and conditioning, we are motivated by an evolutionary constructive force that urges us to realize our potentialities. We each have an intrinsic nature that it is our object in life to fulfill. Whether they call it self-actualization, self-realization, integration, psychological health, individuation, autonomy, creativity, or productivity, Third Force psychologists agree that the highest value for human beings is to become "fully human," everything they "*can* become" (Maslow 1968, 145).

One of the benefits of seeing Horney in the context of Third Force psychology is that it supplements her theory of motivation, which never went much beyond the formula of "safety and satisfaction" introduced in *The Neurotic Personality of Our Time*. Horney derived this formula from Harry Stack Sullivan's distinction between the needs for satisfaction (pleasure) and for security (safety, reassurance). For Sullivan, satisfaction consists in the reduction of bodily tensions, while the desire for security is engendered by "noxious emotional states empathized from the personal environment" (1937, 850). The striving for security heightens tension and thus conflicts with the goal of satisfaction, which is to achieve a tensionless state. Horney observes that the striving for security may be as strong as instinctual drives and may yield "an equally strong satisfaction" through the "relief from tension" (*NP*, 105). Although she rejects the instinct theory upon which Freud's tension-reduction system is based, she does not reformulate the needs for safety and satisfaction in other terms, and she often invokes these needs as if they were sufficient to account for human behavior. But "safety and satisfaction" is an inadequate formulation that leaves out needs to which Horney herself gives great importance—such as those for love, respect, esteem, acceptance of one's individuality, and the freedom to express one's thoughts and feelings spontaneously.

Horney never developed an adequate taxonomy of the motivations she actually discussed in her writings, but Maslow's hierarchy of basic needs helps supply this deficiency and clarifies much that is implicit in her work.[11] According to Maslow, people need physiological satisfaction, security, love and belonging, esteem, and self-actualization. These needs are hierarchical: the physiological needs are the most powerful and the needs belonging to a more highly evolved state are progressively weaker. (Maslow also posits basic needs for knowledge and understanding and for beauty but does not integrate them into his hierarchy.) The needs at the upper end of the hierarchy are no less basic than the lower ones, in the sense that they are a function of our biology and must be gratified if we are to develop in an optimal way. The forms in which they are expressed and the possibility of their satisfaction depend upon the environment, but they exist prior to culture as part of our species-wide nature. Although weaker than animal instincts (Maslow calls them "instinctoid"), they are "stubborn, irreducible, final, unanalyzable facts that must be taken as givens" (1968, 125).

People press by nature for the fulfillment of all the basic needs, but at any given time their motivational life will be centered around the lowest unmet need. Those living in an environment favorable to growth will move steadily up the hierarchy until they are free to devote most of their energies to self-actualization. The hierarchy of basic needs establishes the pattern of psychological development. People whose lower needs are not adequately fulfilled may become fixated at an early stage of development or may be subject to frequent regressions. Frustration of a basic need intensifies its strength and ensures its persistence; gratification diminishes it as a motivating force.

Frustration produces pathology; it arrests our development, alienates us from our real selves, and leads us to develop neurotic strategies for making up our deficiencies. Healthy basic needs can be gratified, but they turn into insatiable neurotic needs when unfulfilled. Destructiveness, aggression, and a need to be omnipotent are not part of essential human nature; they are defensive reactions to what Maslow calls "basic threat," that is, to a fear that basic needs will not be fulfilled. There are valuable as well as pathogenic frustrations, however. We must discover not only our potentialities, but also the limitations imposed by our nature, our place in the cosmos, and the social character of our existence. In all of this, Maslow accords completely with Horney.

Third Force psychology seems optimistic as compared with, say, Freud in that it posits the possibility of health and finds the self-actualizing person to be a relatively happy, harmonious, creative being. It must be pointed out, however, that both Horney and Maslow find psychological health to be rare. Because the instinctoid needs are so weak (especially the higher ones) and the voice of the real self so faint, it is extremely difficult to determine how we really feel and what we really want. Because we humans go through a long period of dependency that makes us sensitive to external pressures and influences, we are easily self-alienated. We are sensitive plants whose complex requirements for healthy growth are rarely fulfilled. But, though readily damaged, we are not easily destroyed. We have a remarkable capacity for developing strategies of defense that enable us to function, however destructively, in an inhospitable world.

Each of the major psychological theories of the twentieth century tends to focus on some part of the hierarchy of needs rather than upon the whole. Jungian and

Maslovian theories focus on love, esteem, and self-actualization and are weak in their treatment of the lower needs. Freudian id psychology and behaviorist theories are much stronger in their treatment of the physiological and safety needs than of the higher ones. Neo-Freudians, Rogerians, ego psychologists, existential psychologists, object-relations theorists, and self-psychologists focus on the middle of the hierarchy. Horney is mainly concerned with how we defend ourselves against the frustration of our needs for safety, love and belonging, and esteem. The solutions she describes cannot work in part because the needs have become insatiable.

Third Force psychology helps to clarify some of the questions concerning values that Horney began to explore. Values are derived from human nature and its needs. Those things are good that gratify basic needs and are conducive to healthy growth, and bad that arrest or distort our psychological development. What we value most will be largely determined by the most powerful ungratified needs; if security is threatened, for example, it will seem more important than love or esteem. Just as there are higher and lower needs, there are higher and lower values. A person who has been gratified in both will place a greater value upon a higher need than upon a lower one, choosing love, for example, over security, or self-esteem over love. Values, moreover, can be healthy or neurotic: the basic need for esteem is not the same as the neurotic need for glory. As Horney shows, the values of self-alienated people are determined less by their basic needs than by their defensive strategies, since they tend to value not so much what they need in order to grow as what they need in order to maintain their neurotic solutions. Insofar as their defenses are necessary to their survival, their values have a certain functional legitimacy and must be respected; but they are not normative, as are the values derived from basic needs.

Third Force psychologists agree that the highest value for all human beings, whether they realize it or not, is to realize their potentialities, to actualize themselves. Each person has a different self to actualize, and constitutional differences generate differences in values. People are most alike in their lower needs and most idiosyncratic in their higher ones. Some values are therefore species-wide (although they take different forms in different cultures) and some unique to the individual or shared only by people who are similar. Self-actualization is the raison d'être not only of individuals but also of social institutions, whose worth can be measured by their success or failure in fostering the psychological growth of individuals.

Like Horney, Third Force psychologists reject many of the relativisms characteristic of our time. Anthropology, they claim, did us a service by alerting us to the dangers of ethnocentricity, but it is a mistake to derive all values from culture or to proclaim ourselves unable to distinguish between good and bad cultures. The paths by which we pursue our goals are culturally determined, but insofar as they are healthy, the goals themselves are products of a universal human psychology.[12]

The value theory of Third Force psychology is essentially a hedonistic one that distinguishes between higher and lower pleasures, healthy and sick values. The values of healthy people hold for all individuals, regardless of whether those people accept them, for "good choosers can choose better than bad choosers what is better for the bad choosers themselves" (Maslow 1968, 151). Maslow contends that there is an essential human nature, that we can identify the people in whom this nature has been most fully actualized, and that we can learn from observing them what would be growth-fostering for everyone and what all people would desire were they healthy. This position is adumbrated in Karen Horney's writings.

There are problems in their value theory of which both Horney and Maslow were aware. It is, in fact, impossible to establish conclusively that there is an essential human nature; all theories based on this premise begin with a leap of faith. Assuming that such a nature exists, it is equally impossible to define it authoritatively or to demonstrate that one has actually identified those people in whom it has been most fully realized. Maslow derives his naturalistic value system from the observation of good choosers; but, as he himself recognizes, the good choosers must be chosen, and there is no way to establish the credentials of those doing the choosing. The possibilities of projection are great; they may just be choosing those whose personalities and value systems are like their own or embody a neurotic ideal. These problems are not confined to Horney and Maslow; no theory can validate its criteria of psychological health for people who do not embrace them to begin with.

Maslow has much to add to Horney's conception of the real self and of healthy growth, as do other Third Force psychologists, like Carl Rogers and Horney's colleague Ernst Schachtel. According to Maslow, self-actualization is not "an all-or-none affair" but is "a matter of degree and of frequency." During what he calls "peak experiences," which are moments of complete fulfillment from which no higher strivings emerge, a person temporarily takes on many characteristics of self-actualization. Self-actualization can be defined, then, as "an episode, or a spurt in which the powers of the person come together" in an "intensely enjoyable way" and he is "closer to the core of his Being" (1968, 97). Psychologically healthy people experience these episodes more frequently and intensely than others, but everyone is capable of peak experiences. This may explain why Horney and Maslow, both of whom emerged from unhappy childhoods with many psychological problems, were able to arrive at a vision of health that they themselves did not often approximate (see Hoffman 1988).

For Maslow, the real self includes the basic needs and everything else that makes up our personal biology: "Being oneself, being natural or spontaneous, being authentic, expressing one's identity, all these are also biological statements since they imply the acceptance of one's constitutional, temperamental, anatomical, neurological, hormonal, and instinctoid-motivational nature" (1971, 338). As we have seen, Maslow believes that the choices or values of self-actualizing people (or of all people in their moments of self-actualization) are normative for the species as a whole. He calls these Being-values (1964, 1971) and includes them in the real self, much as Horney did, although she did not give them a name. All human beings have the potentiality for experiencing these as the highest values and cannot violate them without damage to themselves. Like Horney and Fromm, Maslow posits an "intrinsic conscience" that generates "intrinsic guilt" and that is also part of the real self (1968, 5).

For Maslow, as for Horney, the real self is not an entity, a homunculus, a thing-in-itself. Its components "are potentialities, not final actualizations. Therefore they have a life history and must be seen developmentally. They are actualized, shaped or stifled mostly (but not altogether) by extrapsychic determinants (culture, family, environment, learning, etc.)" (1968, 190–91). The real self is actualized only as a self-in-the-world.

People who develop in accordance with their real selves possess a number of characteristics that distinguish them from self-alienated people. Whereas those who feel unsafe, unloved, and unvalued develop a defensiveness that cuts them off both from themselves and from external reality, self-actualizing people are characterized by their openness to their own inner being and to the external world.

As Carl Rogers observes, openness to oneself is manifested in greater congruence, greater transparence, and greater spontaneity (1961). People are congruent when the feeling they are experiencing is matched by their awareness of that feeling. They are transparent (a favorite word of Horney's) when their acts, words, and gestures are an accurate indication of what is going on inside of them. Spontaneity (another Horneyan word) involves an absence of inhibition in both experiencing and expressing the real self. Healthy spontaneity should not be confused with the acting out of neurotic compulsions that often goes on in its name. There is no serious conflict between spontaneity and morality; self-actualizing people "spontaneously tend to do right because that is what they *want* to do, what they *need* to do, what they enjoy" (Maslow 1968, 159). Most Third Force psychologists would agree with Horney (1950) that the way to become good is to work on our mental health.

The world-openness of self-actualizing people is manifested in their ways of perceiving and relating to external reality. In Schachtel's terms, defensive people tend to be autocentric (subject-centered), while self-actualizing people tend to be allocentric (object-centered) in their perceptions. In autocentric perception, the world is divided into "objects-of-use" and "objects-to-be-avoided," and the perceiver focuses not upon "the object in its own right" but upon those aspects of it that relate to his or her own purposes, needs, and fears (1959, 167). The allocentric attitude is "one of profound interest in the object, and complete openness and receptivity toward it" (220). Allocentric perception provides a far richer and more accurate picture of the world, and it permits us to see other people as they are in and for themselves, holistically, "as complicated, unique individuals" (36).

There is a close connection between allocentric perception and what Maslow calls Being-love (see also Fromm 1956). Those who believe that there are only I-it relationships, in which people use each other as objects and in which the subjectivity of the other is threatening and must be denied, are describing as inherent in the human condition relationships as they exist between autocentric people. In Being-love relationships other people are seen allocentrically, are understood in their own terms, and are loved for what they are. Being-love produces a nondefensive, nonclinging relationship in which there is respect for the other's dignity and autonomy and a desire for the other's growth. Being-love is what Horney feels the analyst should give the patient; it is the central feature of what Rogers characterizes as "helping relationships." Being-love is what we most need in order to grow.

Schachtel observes that although allocentric perception has an "enriching, refreshing, vitalizing" effect, it is also frightening because it threatens our defenses and disturbs our "embeddedness" (1959, 177, 193). He sees human development as, in part, a conflict between our tendencies toward embeddedness and our tendencies toward openness and growth. There is in each person's psychic evolution a conflict between "the wish to remain embedded in the womb or in the mother's care," in that to which we become accustomed, "and the wish to encounter the world and to develop and realize, in this encounter, the human capacities" (151).

Schachtel's concept of embeddedness provides a bridge between Freudian and Third Force psychologies, for it allows him to acknowledge that there are states that seem to be governed by the wish to reduce tension while insisting that there are others "where we find a desire for, and enjoyment of, stimulation and activity rather than the wish to get rid of it" (1959, 56). Schachtel would replace the pleasure principle with the "law of embeddedness," which holds that an increase of stimulation is not always unpleasure, "but that the more nearly complete the state of embeddedness" the more negative is our reaction to any change (60). Freud's concept of the pleasure principle accurately describes a certain portion of our experience, but it leaves out "the phenomena, so striking in the growing infant and child, of the pleasure and fulfillment found in the encounter with an expanding reality and in the development, exercise, and realization of his growing capacities, skills, and powers" (9).[13] Empirical studies of infants and children confirm Schachtel's observations (see Kagan 1984; Stern 1985).

In the course of healthy development "the embeddedness principle yields to the transcendence principle of openness toward the world and of self-realization which takes place in the encounter" with it. Under unfavorable conditions, the embeddedness principle remains "pathologically strong, with the result that the encounter with the world is experienced in an autocentric way as an unwelcome impinging of disturbing stimuli" (Schachtel 1959, 157–58). Embeddedness and openness are always matters of degree; the conflict between them is never resolved: "Man always lives somewhere between these two poles of clinging to a rigid attitude with its closed world and of leaping into the stream of life with his senses open toward the inexhaustible, changing, infinite world" (199–200). Self-actualizing people are distinguished not only by their greater courage to be themselves but also by their greater courage to be in the world. They trust their real self enough to follow its promptings without knowing exactly where they will lead, and they have enough confidence in their ability to sustain their encounters with the world to be open to an authentic experience of what is out there.

Third Force psychology provides an account of human nature and human values, of the real self, and of psychological health that is entirely compatible with Karen Horney's theory and that amplifies her ideas. In addition, we find in Horney herself the combination of defensiveness and openness described by Rogers and Schachtel. Her defensiveness showed up in her human relationships, in which she was often compulsive, self-centered, and insensitive—though she could also be caring and generous. Her openness manifested itself in her zest for life, spirit of adventure, and capacity for wonder—and most of all, perhaps, in the accuracy of her observations. There, we see her ability to transcend her defensiveness and achieve allocentric perception.

Appendix A

Interdisciplinary Applications

of Horneyan Theory

Horney's contribution to psychological thought is one measure of her significance. Another, of perhaps equal importance, is the value of her theory to other disciplines. Horneyan theory may be usefully employed in the study of literature, biography, culture, and gender.

I have been developing a Horneyan approach to literature since 1964, when I realized that the thematic contradictions of Thackeray's *Vanity Fair* become intelligible when seen as part of a system of psychological conflicts. William Dobbin and Amelia Sedley appear to be the normative characters in the novel, while Becky Sharp is the chief object of satire. Becky ruthlessly pursues money, power, and prestige, which are shown to be vanities, while Amelia and Dobbin live for love, friendship, and emotional fulfillment, which are glorified by the narrator. But the narrator also satirizes both Dobbin, whom he calls a "spooney" (someone foolishly in love), and Amelia, whom he describes as a "tender little parasite." In spite of the glorification of love and friendship, the action and some of the commentary of the book show these values to be as fleeting or disappointing as social and economic triumphs.

The novel's thematic contradictions make sense, however, as manifestations of a basic conflict in which compliant tendencies predominate but are continually at war with a powerful submerged aggressiveness. I locate this conflict in the implied author of the novel—that is, in the Thackeray we can infer from the text itself. Thackeray's compliant tendencies manifest themselves in his glorification of self-effacing attitudes, values, and characters, in his attacks on worldly, ambitious people and the social system that spawns them, and in his insistence that the pursuit of money, power, and prestige is destructive and unrewarding. His aggressive tendencies appear in his obvious delight in Becky and her triumphs and in the scorn he shares with her for the weakness and folly of the self-effacing characters. Tendencies toward detachment also figure prominently in the psychic structure of *Vanity Fair*. They are manifested in the narrator's conclusion that all is vanity and in his irony, often unfocused, which is the means by which Thackeray negates what he has affirmed and protects himself from the consequences of commitment (see also Paris 1974).

There are many other literary works that do not make thematic sense because they affirm contradictory positions. Critics often defend the artistic unity of such works by suppressing awareness of subversive elements or by rationalizing contradictions as part of a controlled structure of tension, paradox, and irony. More recently they have tended to delight in contradictions as evidence of the tendency of all linguistic structures to deconstruct themselves. With the help of Horney's theory we are often able both to recognize inconsistencies as genuine problems and to make sense of them as parts of an intelligible structure of inner conflicts.

After explaining the thematic contradictions of *Vanity Fair,* I realized that Horney also enables us to recover Thackeray's profound psychological intuitions about his major characters. Other literary works, as well, contain brilliantly realized characters whose motivational systems can be understood in Horneyan terms. One of the chief objections to the psychoanalytic study of character has been its reliance on infantile experience to account for the behavior of the adult. This results in the generation of crucial explanatory material out of the premises of the theory, with no corroborating literary evidence except the supposed results of the invented experiences, which were inferred from these results to begin with. Horney's structural approach is highly suitable for the analysis of literary characters, since we are often supplied with ample information about their existing defenses, however sketchy our knowledge of their childhoods. Because Horneyan theory describes the kinds of phenomena that are actually portrayed, it permits us to stick to the text.

It is important to distinguish between the psychological portrait and the rhetoric by which a character is surrounded. By rhetoric I mean all the devices an author employs to influence readers' moral and intellectual responses, their sympathy and antipathy, their emotional closeness or distance. When we understand realistically drawn characters in psychological terms, we usually find ourselves responding to them in ways that are different from those that the rhetoric seeks to induce (see Paris 1974, 1978b, 1991b, 1991c). Our reaction often points to a tension in the work between rhetoric and mimesis—between authors' interpretations and judgments and the characters they have actually created. Although the rhetoric may tell us little that is reliable about the character, it gives us a great deal of insight into the implied author of the work and perhaps into the real author as well.

The relation between authors and their works is a vexed question, of course. We must always make allowances for artistic motivations, generic requirements, and the inner logic of the individual work. Even so, it is possible to tell a good deal about authors from their works when we examine such things as their recurring preoccupations, the personal element in their fantasies, the kinds of characters and relationships they habitually create, and their rhetorical stance. In this delicate enterprise, Horney's theory is again very helpful.

In the course of artistic creation authors' defensive strategies tend to manifest themselves in a variety of ways. Their works are, among other things, efforts to reinforce their predominant solution and to resolve their inner conflicts by showing themselves, as well as others, the good and evil consequences of the various trends warring within them. Writers will tend to glorify characters whose strategies are similar to their own and to satirize those who embody their repressed solutions. Their rhetoric will affirm the values, attitudes, and personality traits that are demanded by their dominant solution, while rejecting those forbidden by it. Their plots will often be fantasies in which their claims are honored in magical ways, while their repressed strategies are shown to bring misery and retribution. Because they cannot help also expressing their subordinate trends, their works will frequently manifest their inner conflicts. Their attitudes, values, and beliefs will then be inconsistent or self-contradictory. These conflicting trends will lead writers to criticize each solution from the point of view of the other solutions and to show toward their characters the mixed feelings they have toward the aspects of themselves that those characters embody. The relations among the authors' solutions may change in the course of their lives; and this will be reflected in the kinds of characters they portray, in their rhetoric, and in their dominant fantasies (see Paris 1976a, 1978b, 1991a).[1]

A Horneyan approach can also tell us a great deal about reader response and the interpretive process. Just as every analyst has what Horney calls a "personal equation," so too does the reader's constellation of defenses affect how he or she responds to the author's presentation of various defensive strategies. Psychological reasons may easily account for why some readers feel that Thackeray entirely approves of Dobbin and Amelia and dislikes Becky, while others feel that he secretly despises Dobbin and Amelia and admires Becky, while yet others argue that he is a brilliant ironist who sees through everything and takes no position for himself. Through Horneyan analysis we might be able to make sense of the Babel of interpretations and to see them all as responding to specific aspects of the text while suppressing awareness of others.

Horney's synchronic approach has immense potential for psychobiography. Like the literary critic approaching an author or a character, the biographer usually has information about the adulthood of the subject but little or none about early childhood. Horney's theory enables us to explain the character structure and behavior of the adult without relying on infantile origins. Biographical studies of Robert Frost (Thompson 1966, 1970, 1976), Charles Evans Hughes (Glad 1966), the Kennedys (Clinch 1973), Stalin (Tucker, 1973, 1990), Woodrow Wilson (Tucker 1977), Jimmy Carter (Glad 1980; see also 1973), Felix Frankfurter (Hirsch 1981), and Lyndon Johnson (Huffman 1989) have fruitfully employed Horneyan analysis. Here, the biographies of Frost and Stalin will suffice to show how such theories may be used.

Lawrance Thompson accepted Robert Frost's invitation to be his official biographer in 1939, when Frost was sixty-five, with the understanding that nothing was to be published until after Frost's death, which did not occur until 1963. As he collected material in the intervening years, Thompson became aware of Frost's many cruelties, self-contradictions, and inner conflicts, which he set out to describe in his biography. After completing a draft of the first volume, he read *Neurosis and Human Growth* and found in it the analytic concepts he needed to make sense of his bewildering subject. Had Horney's book mentioned Frost on every page, Thompson wrote in his notebook, "it couldn't have come closer to giving a psychological framework to what I've been trying to say" (Sheehy 1986, 398). Thompson's notebook contains 130 pages of notes and excerpts from Horney's writings interspersed with such applications to Frost as the following: "Frost's pattern involved . . . an affectionate clinging to his mother; a fear of beatings (which he got) from his father and a consequent attempt at compliant appeasement; but more than these, his 'conflict' caused him to 'keep aloof.' The first story he ever tried to write, he said, was the story of his running away to the Happy Valley where the Indian tribes were so nice to him" (quoted by Sheehy, 405).

After studying *Neurosis and Human Growth,* Thompson revised the first volume of his biography to reflect a Horneyan interpretation of his subject. He saw Frost as a man who developed a search for glory in response to early humiliations and who longed to triumph over and retaliate against those who had hurt him. Frost's contradictory accounts of his life were a product of both his inner conflicts and his need to confirm his idealized image by mythologizing himself. His poetry reflects these dynamics. Sometimes Frost used his poetry to "escape from his confusions into idealized postures," while at other times it served "as a means of striking back at, or of punishing" those he considered his enemies (Thompson 1966, xix). (Interestingly, we would not know that Thompson had used Horney without the work of Donald Sheehy, who examined the Thompson papers in the University of Virginia library. Although Horney's ideas gave an interpretive structure to Thompson's biography, Horney is mentioned neither in the text, the footnotes, nor the index of the book.)

Neurosis and Human Growth also influenced Robert Tucker, who was serving in the American embassy in Moscow when it was published in 1950. After reading the book, he was suddenly struck by "a momentous thought": "What if the idealized image of Stalin, appearing day after day in the party-controlled, party-supervised Soviet press, were *an idealized image in Horney's sense?*" If so, "the Stalin cult must reflect Stalin's own monstrously inflated vision of himself as the greatest genius of Russian and world history." This Kremlin recluse, "who was publicly so reticent about himself, must be spilling out his innermost thoughts concerning himself in millions of newspapers and journals published throughout Russia." One could psychoanalyze Stalin "by reading *Pravda,* while rereading Horney!" (1985, 251).

Tucker considered books about totalitarianism like Hannah Arendt's *The Origins of Totalitarianism* to be "deeply flawed because the dictator and his psychodynamics were missing from the picture." A dictator can "politically institutionalize the inner defenses of his ever-threatened idealized self" and "mobilize a vast apparatus of repression to visit revenge not only on individuals whom he had come to perceive as enemies but on entire social groups so perceived." The Holocaust "might have been Adolf Hitler's enactment of vindictive hostility stemming from neurotically generated self-hatred projected onto the Jews as a group" (1985, 254; see also Tucker 1965).

Tucker's thesis about the role of Stalin's personality in Soviet policy was confirmed, he thought, by Nikita Khrushchev's secret report "On the Cult of Personality and Its Consequences": "He depicted Stalin as a man of colossal grandiosity, along with profound insecurity that caused him to need constant affirmation of his imagined greatness. Khrushchev portrayed a neurotic personality precisely in Horney's sense, an example of the 'arrogant-vindictive' type described in *Neurosis and Human Growth*. A self-idealizer, insatiably hungry for the glorification that the public cult provided, Stalin was easily aroused to vindictive hostility by whatever appeared to detract from his inflated vision of himself as a leader and teacher of genius. His aggressions, typically expressed in purges . . . were the other side of his self-glorification" (1985, 259). Now confident of his hypothesis, Tucker embarked upon his ambitious study of Stalin, the third and final volume of which is in progress.

Several writers have used Horney's work in the analysis of American culture. In *People of Plenty: Economic Abundance and the American Character* (1954), David M. Potter draws upon Horney, along with Margaret Mead and David Riesman, as a social scientist whose findings support the idea of a national character and help to define the American one. He is particularly struck by her analysis of the character traits, inner conflicts, and vicious circles created by the competitiveness of our culture. He relates it to his concern with the effects of abundance in our society by observing that increased abundance "means increased rewards in the competitive struggle," and increased rewards mean an increased premium on competitive efficiency. This brings about a heightened aggressiveness, which creates inner conflicts and is self-defeating. We trade security for opportunity and then experience the anxieties attendant upon lack of security. We are driven to enter the competitive contest at the price of becoming neurotic "because society itself regards the rewards as irresistible and is determined to compel everyone to strive for them" (71–72).

In *The Poverty of Affluence: A Psychological Portrait of the American Way of Life* (1989), Paul Wachtel also argues that "there is something compulsive, irrational, and self-defeating" in the way Americans pursue an ever-increasing wealth. Although he does not argue that the whole population is neurotically aggressive, Wachtel feels that Horney's "concept of the moving-against . . . trend captures something important about the manifest patterns of behavior that most characterize our public life and the workings of our economic system" (78). We promote competition rather than mutual support, and in our relation to nature and the environment, "we strive for conquest and domination." We are afraid of being perceived as "a 'pitiful helpless giant' and will commit unreasonable acts of aggression to ward off that feared image" (75). Caught in a vicious circle, we anxiously rely "on the production and accumulation of goods" for our sense of security (79), despite the fact that our reliance makes us more insecure. Wachtel develops these ideas further in "The Preoccupation with Economic Growth: An Analysis Informed by Horneyan Theory" (1991).

Potter draws upon *The Neurotic Personality of Our Time* and Wachtel upon *Our Inner Conflicts*. In work that promises to be the most sophisticated application of Horney to the study of American culture, James Huffman is employing her entire mature theory. He articulates some of his main themes in "A Psychological Critique of American Culture" (1982). Instead of stressing affluence like Potter, Huffman emphasizes the senses of threat and of inferiority that have influenced American behavior. In its youth the nation was regarded as culturally and socially inferior by the established European powers, and during its expansion, life on the frontier was hazardous. The cities created a Darwinian environment in which immigrants, usually poor and oppressed in their homelands, were both discriminated against and perceived as threats by their new compatriots.

These pressures produced compensatory defenses. As a result, much of American history reveals a search for glory and for an "idealized image of American character. Americans began to believe that the United States would be the greatest nation on earth, then that it was already the greatest nation, and perhaps that it always would be." Because of an inflated sense of our own importance, "we place exaggerated claims on other nations to defer to our wishes, consult us before making any decisions, and treat us like the rulers and peacemakers of the earth" (1982, 31). Like Potter and Wachtel, Huffman observes that "aggressive competition" marks our economic life far more than cooperation (35). We like our leaders to be belligerent and glorify people who fight their way up. There are other trends in our culture that conflict with the aggressive ones, of course. In future work, Huffman proposes to show how Horneyan patterns manifest themselves in popular culture, politics, religion and business, and American history, from the Revolution to the present.

There have also been Horneyan analyses of aspects of Elizabethan and Victorian culture (Paris 1991a, 1986).

As we have seen, Horney has been rediscovered in recent years by feminists, many of whose positions she anticipated. By and large, those who are interested in feminine psychology or, more broadly, in gender studies have focused on Horney's early essays and paid little attention to her mature theory, which is not specifically directed to their concerns. The mature theory has important implications, however, for our understanding of gender identity and of masculine and feminine psychology in American culture. Impressive work has been done along these lines by Alexandra Symonds, a Horneyan analyst, and Marcia Westkott, a social psychologist. Horney's mature theory has also been used to address gender issues in popular books by Helen De Rosis and Victoria Pellegrino (1976) and by Claudette Dowling (1981). In this, as in the other areas of application I have discussed, much remains to be done.

Symonds' essays are based largely on her clinical experience with women who were suffering from their feminine role, or who were trying to escape from that role but finding it difficult, or who seemed to have escaped but were having trouble dealing with the consequences. In every case the starting point was a culture that conditioned girls to be self-effacing and dependent, while boys were encouraged to be autonomous and aggressive. While focusing on the plight of girls, Symonds recognized that boys develop difficulties of their own "as a result of cultural stereotyping" (1974, 178).

In "Neurotic Dependency in Successful Women" (1976), Symonds analyzes the problems of women who had difficulty taking advantage of new opportunities because of "psychological patterns which were developed for a totally different emotional climate" (98). In "The Psychodynamics of Expansiveness in the Success-Oriented Woman" (1978), she focuses on women who developed a predominantly aggressive personality from an early age. Their problems are partly the result of their inability to escape the gender identity prescribed by their culture. They need to succeed in their careers but also to be nurturers.

In "Gender Issues and Horney Theory" (1991), her last essay, Symonds observes that despite the great changes of the past twenty years, women still have difficulty freeing themselves from compulsive compliance. "In our culture when men are self-effacing it violates their own expectation of what a man should be. They are pleased when as a result of therapy they are able to be more directly assertive, even aggressive. Women do not necessarily welcome this change and each step of the way is much more complicated." Since they have deep conflicts concerning the aggressive pursuit of success, they often "sabotage themselves in various ways to prevent their emerging sense of power and mastery" (305–06).

In *The Feminist Legacy of Karen Horney* (1986), Marcia Westkott explores the implications of Horney's mature theory for feminine psychology, with chapters on the sexualization and devaluation of women and the dependency, anger, and detachment they feel as a result. She also develops a Horneyan critique of a major strand of feminist theory.

Jean Baker Miller, Nancy Chodorow, Carol Gilligan, and the Stone Center group associate an array of personality traits specifically with women. These include a need for affiliation, a nurturing disposition, a sense of responsibility for other people, and a relational sense of identity. Westkott observes that although these traits are regarded in a positive way, they emerged from "a historical setting in which women are less highly valued than men." "This paradox" suggests "an underside to the nurturance and affiliation" that requires exploration (1986, 2). Westkott proposes that these traits are defensive reactions to subordination, devaluation, and powerlessness and that, however desirable they may seem from a social point of view, they do not advance women's self-actualization.

Whereas Chodorow argues that the woman's nurturing disposition derives from an extended attachment between mother and daughter that fosters the development of empathy, Westkott contends that it originates in a "culturally rooted . . . imperative" that enjoins females to take care of others, including their parents (134). Girls receive less nurturing than boys; they are required to grow up more quickly and to make fewer demands for attention. For Westkott, female altruism is "a contradiction in which the undernurtured nurturer gives what she does not have in order to be 'loved' by those who have disregard or even contempt for her true self and needs" (139–40). The girl is "angry at those who deny her true self," but because of her insecurity she turns her anger against herself, admires the denigrating adults, and tries to gain a sense of safety, worth, and belonging by being what they want her to be. Having been undernurtured themselves, mothers look to their daughters for nurturing, thus perpetuating the demand for female self-sacrifice.

In "Female Relationality and the Idealized Self" (1989), Westkott argues that "the self-in-relation is not the authentic self that the Stone Center theorists presume it to be, but the idealized self that Horney associated with self-effacement." The girl develops a set of *shoulds* that involve "doing for others, caring for them, making their needs the sources of her motives, complying with others' demands for recognition." She needs others to validate her idealized image of herself as caring, empathetic, and lovable. The collapse of a relationship or a sense that she has not been caring or sensitive enough makes her identify with her despised self and triggers enormous self-hate. Since she feels angry with herself when she fails to live up to her shoulds and angry with others for having forced her "to repress desires for individual self-fulfillment," the idealized relational self "perpetuates self-criticism and anger as ongoing intrapsychic processes" (247–48).

Westkott thus demythifies the celebration of female relationality, arguing that it has provided "a contemporary theoretical justification for traditionally idealized femininity" (1989, 245), that is, for self-effacing behavior. She contends, with Horney, that being deprived is not ennobling but damaging and that the compliant qualities many women develop in order to cope with devaluation are destructive. The feminist revolt against the role Western culture has imposed upon women is turning into a reinforcement of that role insofar as women are being told that they need "to 'affiliate' with others in order to validate" their "idealized nurturant" selves (1986, 140).

Westkott contends that Horney's mature theory is at bottom about the psychology of women, but I would argue that it describes me, as well as many men I know, and a host of male authors, literary characters, and historical figures. I am thus convinced that the mature theory can be applied in a non–gender-specific fashion to both male and female experience.

Appendix B

Woman's Fear of Action

Karen Horney

Karen Horney delivered the following talk, which I discuss in Chapter 14, to the National Federation of Professional and Business Women's Clubs in July 1935. I discovered it, along with other unpublished material, in Harold Kelman's papers at the Postgraduate Center for Mental Health. It is considerably less polished than Horney's published writings, for it was never revised or edited. I have made a few changes in punctuation and have emended two sentences that did not make sense. In spite of its stylistic imperfections, it is a remarkable statement for its time and helps to explain why Horney stopped focusing on feminine psychology.

Looking back in the history of woman's position in the last centuries, a striking fact appears: in times when women were seriously granted all opportunities for the development of human values, such as the time before the French Revolution—the so-called period of enlightenment—there was no interest in special features of feminine psychology. The ideal was that all human beings should develop their full potentialities regardless of sex. In politically reactionary periods, such as the time after the French Revolution—called the period of romanticism—and also the economic crisis of today, there appears a consuming interest in woman's "nature."

For some time I took this interest in feminine psychology at its face value. I have done some work in the field of feminine psychopathology and am frequently asked what, to my knowledge, are the specific trends of female psychology. The only answer which I can make is that I hope to know at some future time, for after all the speculation of psychologists concerning these possible differences between men and women, we do not appear to have gone far beyond the old, old discussions in the Talmud—namely, that we do not know much about the specific trends beyond the biological differences that women have. Then it occurred to me that it was not so important to try to find the answer to the question about differences as to understand and analyze the real significance of this keen interest in feminine "nature" nowadays.

Why are people so very interested in woman's "nature"? There are vital reasons why, economic reasons based on the highly competitive nature of society. Although many individuals do not realize it, they are not honestly searching for valid answers to the question of differences. What they really want to do is to prove something to their advantage, or what appears to be to their immediate advantage; that it is in absolute accord with woman's "nature" that she keep out of competitive fields of work and remain restricted to emotional fields of life, concerning herself with charity, sexuality, and child bearing. Whether their reasoning is based, as in the Catholic Church, on the sin of Eve, or on the rules laid down by German philosophy with respect to sexual relations, or on Freud's statements of differences in anatomy, the result is the same. Nor does it appear to make any difference, as regards the effect on women, whether there is a scientific detachment or a frankly depreciatory attitude; whether it goes, as in Fascist countries, with a deification of woman's home-making qualities or, as in other countries, with an expression of concern for social justice or woman's happiness. All these attitudes wax and wane with the increase or decrease of economic competition. When jobs are scarce, it becomes necessary to prove in any way possible that woman's "nature" forbids her free admittance to the market.

Any sudden increase in interest over sex differences, therefore, must be regarded as a danger signal for women, particularly in a patriarchal society where men find it advantageous to prove on biologic premises that women should not take part in shaping the economy and the political order. On these premises elaborate convictions serving the interests of masculine ideologies become strategical means of preserving masculine superiority in the economic and political world by convincing woman that innately she is glad to keep out of it.

Very frequently women themselves serve to strengthen these convictions. They often regard professional pursuits as secondary to love and marriage. They become so preoccupied with the emotional side of life that they are little concerned with the great problems which are moving and shaking our time. They become leaning and dependent, developing a predominant need to be taken care of. All these attitudes help to support the theories which men wish to establish as a means of eliminating women from competition.

So far this is fairly transparent, and has been stated from time to time, but we have not always recognized its deeper significance: that any group of the population, restricted in its activities for a long period of time, undergoes certain psychic changes; that within individuals of the suppressed group occurs a psychic adaptation which brings them to accept the limitations which the dominant group finds it advantageous to impose. Thus love and devotion came to be regarded as specifically feminine ideals and virtues; home-making and rearing of children the one possibility for happiness, security, and prestige. Although in recent years great changes have come about, psychic effects of the long history of restriction linger.

Some of the psychic consequences of woman's own attitudes which we can expect to find, and do find, still in existence are the following:

1. Since woman's gateway to happiness, security, and prestige depended on her relations to home and children, these came to be regarded by her as the only real values in life for women. The boy-crazy girl, the woman who is lost and miserable if she is not being continually sought by men, represents the extreme outcome of such an over-evaluation of love and sexuality. These types supply evidence for the psychologists who like to believe that "The essence of woman's being is love" or "Sexuality is for women something central, for men, peripheral," and so on. As a matter of fact, it would be difficult to explain how, with conditions as they are, woman could avoid overrating sexuality and love. The most serious outcome of this emphasis on her part is that she comes to expect far too much from these relations with men and children and is doomed in many cases to bitter disappointment. The woman who concentrates her expectations on relations with husband and children, whether in the form of ambitious aims or of gratitude and attachment toward her, handicaps husband and children as well as herself, and is all too likely, in the end, to render the emotional relationship upon which she relies so heavily completely unsatisfactory.

Another disastrous result of this overrating of love is that it is bound to degrade any pursuits outside this sphere. Thus we see the neurotic attitude of the woman who regards these other pursuits as unsatisfactory substitutes which she views with secret resentment. Her inner attitude is expressed by such phrases as "Because I am not attractive to men I have to be a teacher" or "I wasn't the feminine type, had no sex appeal, and so I had to go into business." Lacking respect for these other pursuits which are to her only poor substitutes for woman's "normal" pre-occupations, she cannot devote all her energies to them. An undercurrent of resistance, which interferes with whole-hearted devotion, mars her satisfaction and success and gives rise to a belief on her own part that she is inferior and incapable. There are many other sources of woman's convictions of inferiority, of course, but this is an important one, because it so often keeps her from becoming genuinely and actively concerned with the great economic and political questions of our time, even when these broader interests concern women's own position in the world and should be of vital interest to her. This is one of the reasons why woman has not been more active in improving conditions for herself; such action was outside the magic circle into which her existence was confined.

2. As fulfillment for woman had come to mean love, sex, home, children, all depending on her relations to man, it became of paramount importance to please man. Thus came about the cult of beauty and charm. And thus came the fear of being "unfeminine." The unfeminine included any attitude or belief which stood in opposition to masculine ideas about the divine order of things. To be "feminine" was to be submissive and devoted regardless of how she was treated. Any struggle for improvement in the position of women was, therefore, "unfeminine," a denial of what had come to be accepted as the "nature" of woman. The residue today of this fear as seen in the lack of interest, in the don't-care attitude, is the outward expression of a subterranean fear which can be best explained by an illustration with which we are all familiar. Here is a girl who does not care for parties. She cannot be persuaded to go to parties because, she says, she prefers reading alone at home. She is quite honest; her lack of interest is genuine; she is interested in other pursuits, but usually this lack of interest is rooted in fear. She is afraid of being neglected or of meeting criticism, but she does not know that she is afraid. She does not know that when she says she doesn't care for parties she is really expressing her unconscious fear.

In the same way we find an undercurrent of fear which prevents women from taking action in economic and social spheres which concern them most vitally. It is important that we recognize this subconscious fear, because it is necessary, if we would change attitudes, to understand the sources of the energy which sustains them.

3. Fear of displeasing men is not the only anxiety created through restriction [to an emotional sphere]. The fear of losing erotic attractiveness through age is a very real and acute anxiety due to the same over-valuation of love life. Except in times when unemployment is widespread, we would consider it definitely neurotic if a man became frightened and depressed as he approached middle age; in a woman it is regarded as natural, and in a way it is natural because physical attractiveness has come to represent the supreme value for women. This age-phobia in itself is pathetic enough, but it has two aspects that are more serious than is generally recognized and which help to account for the inactivity of women in the world's work. This age fear

is not limited to the period when she is no longer in her bloom. It throws its shadow over most of the years after twenty and creates a feeling of insecurity which thwarts the life-rhythm. A woman of thirty-five or forty will say: "Still five years ahead then my life will be declining." She feels that she must crowd a great deal into the short time left. The resultant anxiety and half-despair accounts for the jealousy between mothers and adolescent daughters and frequently spoils their relations as well as leaving a remnant of hostility toward all women.

Age is a problem for everyone, of course, men as well as women, but it becomes a desperate one if the chief values of life are centered in youth and erotic attractiveness. When the center of gravity is youth, women find it difficult to recognize the worth of the qualities of maturity such as poise, independence, autonomy of judgment, wisdom—qualities which have great value for the entire culture. Mature personality should be more secure and stronger than youthful personality for it has the advantage of experience, but how can the maturing woman develop this security and strength if she believes that her very nature demands that love be the center and sole purpose of her being and at the same time she recognizes her mature years as ones of decline in this sphere? This emphasis on erotic values and the preponderant importance of sex results in a great waste of human values for women. The young woman feels a temporary security because of her ability to attract men, but mature women can hardly hope to escape being devalued even in their own eyes. And this feeling of inferiority robs them of the strength for action which rightly belongs to maturity.

Inferiority feelings are the most common evil of our time and our culture. To be sure we do not die of them, but I think they are nevertheless more disastrous to happiness and progress than cancer or tuberculosis. When the subject of inferiority feelings comes up, someone usually remarks, "But, men too have inferiority feelings." True, but there is an important difference: men do not, as a rule, feel inferior just because they are men, but a woman frequently feels inferior because she is a woman. The restriction of woman to a private emotional sphere leads to inferiority feelings because a sound and secure self-confidence must draw upon a broad basis of human qualities such as initiative, courage, independence, capacity for mastering situations, talents, erotic values. As long as home-making was a big task with plenty of responsibilities, as long as the number of children was not restricted because children added to the wealth of the nation, woman knew that she was a constructive factor in the economic process. This conviction gave her a sound basis for self-esteem. As we all know, these values have gradually vanished and woman has lost one important foundation for feeling herself valuable.

As far as the purely sexual side is concerned, the puritanical influences, however one may evaluate them, certainly have added to the debasement of woman by giving sexuality the connotation of something sinful and low. The same attitude toward sexuality in a matriarchal society would have led to disregarding men as animal-like beings. In a patriarchal society it was bound to make woman the symbol of sin as depicted in early Christian literature. Woman does not herself know, as a rule, that the shadow she feels on her self-esteem comes, to some extent, from sexual sources, deeply rooted in Christian culture.

Self-confidence built on success in giving and receiving love is built on a foundation too small and shaky. It is too small because it leaves out many personality values, and it is too shaky because it is too dependent on many external happenings such as finding adequate partners, marriage possibilities, etc. It very frequently leads to dependence on the other person's affection and appreciation, with a deep feeling of unworthiness if one is not loved and appreciated. This emotional dependence also involves fear of criticism and ridicule, which turns us back to the original point; that every woman who fights for the opportunity to realize her potentialities as a person exposes herself to all kinds of insinuations and ridicule. She must recognize this as a technique and be prepared to face it.

I have sometimes been told that, although the picture as I have drawn it may be accurate for European women, it is quite different in this country. To the extent that the American woman has succeeded in important achievements outside of home, that is a valid distinction. She is a great factor in social and cultural life in the United States. Artistic pursuits are regarded as a domain wide open to women here. But, although opportunities for women are certainly wider than in Europe, we must not be blinded by the surface. For the principle is the same here as there. That general self-confidence which is the psychic capital for achievement is not won because a few women have achieved success in competition with men. There are too many neglected tasks which require initiative, creative imagination, courage, planning experience, capacity to stand on one's own feet [that can only be accomplished] by women endowed with this self-confidence or psychic capital.

Since it is impossible to fight successfully without feeling justified, where are we to find justification for this struggle of women for self-confidence? In this thought: as long as women are thwarted in their personalities, men and children are afflicted too. If we fight for the chance to develop our human values, we certainly shall be happier ourselves and men and children will benefit equally. Ultimately it is a joint enterprise, for the well-being of everyone depends on success in this fight against men's prejudices and fears.

Once it was believed that something innate in women made it impossible for them to work together cooperatively. It is true that woman's long restriction to the emotional sphere made action in solidarity more difficult for her. Within her erotic sphere there was only individual competition, and competition has been stronger among women than among men. There was a great deal of anxiety and insecurity which accounted for much of the hostility among women which made it difficult for them to work together. This gave rise, even among the greatest psychologists, to the belief that women were more jealous than men on biological grounds.

Until recently men, and men only, were forced by their own interests to form cooperative groups for economic or political action. This was a basic education for solidarity in a particular field which expanded into a general attitude of solidarity and developed the discipline for united action.

This solidarity is the necessary prerequisite for any great action, and it becomes highly desirable for women because of all the inner insecurity which they feel in common. The more insecure the individual feels, the greater is her need for support from the tie of solidarity.

It is not sufficient to say, as women are frequently saying these days, that we must overcome the delusion of inferiority. It is more than a delusion; there are real handicaps, equal in importance to the external obstacles we have to overcome. First of all we need to understand that there are no unalterable qualities of inferiority of our sex due to laws of God or of nature. Our limitations are, for the greater part, culturally and socially conditioned. Men who have lived under the same conditions for a long time have developed similar attitudes and shortcomings.

Once and for all we should stop bothering about what is feminine and what is not. Such concerns only undermine our energies. Standards of masculinity and femininity are artificial standards. All that we definitely know at present about sex differences is that we do not know what they are. Scientific differences between the two sexes certainly exist, but we shall never be able to discover what they are until we have first developed our potentialities as human beings. Paradoxical as it may sound, we shall find out about these differences only if we forget about them.

In the meantime what we can do is to work together for the full development of the human personalities of all for the sake of general welfare.

Notes

Introduction

1. Renate Patterson, interview with the author, 28 December 1989.
2. Patterson, letter to the author, 12 July 1989.

Part 1

The Making of a Psychoanalyst

1. Renate Patterson, "My Mother as I Remember Her," unpublished memoir (Horney Papers),
5.
2. Patterson, unpublished introduction to Karen Horney's diaries (Horney Papers).
3. Patterson, "My Mother," 27.
4. Ibid., 7.
5. Ibid., 15.
6. Rita Honroth-Welte, "My Recollections of Karen Horney," unpublished memoir (Horney Papers), 1973, 2.
7. Ibid., 5.

Part 2
The Freudian Phase and Feminine Psychology

1. Eitingon's letter was in the Horney material I discovered among Harold Kelman's papers at the Postgraduate Center for Mental Health in New York. It is now in the Karen Horney Papers, located in the Manuscripts and Archives division of the Yale University Library. All material in this collection except for memoirs and Renate Patterson's unpublished introduction to her mother's diaries will henceforth be identified in the text as Horney Papers.

2. Susan Quinn claims that Karen began her analysis with Abraham early in 1910 and terminated it that summer. I believe that she saw Abraham off and on for more than two years, engaging in self-analysis during the intervals and returning to him when she felt that she was making no progress. Horney's membership application for the New York Psychoanalytic Institute gives the dates of her analysis with Abraham as 1911–1913 and 1918 (Brill Archive). The first date is incorrect, since we know she began her analysis in 1910, but perhaps the time span is accurate. The fifth diary provides evidence that Karen saw Abraham intermittently throughout 1910, 1911, and 1912. In January 1911, she was trying to "master [her] illness" through self-analysis (AD, 247) and often raised the question of whether she should return to Abraham. The unsent letter to Abraham (9 July 1911) with which the published version of the diary ends indicates that she had worked with him during the interval and is proposing to begin a third analysis. After 9 July, there are no entries until 2 April 1912, when she wrote that "keeping a diary is undoubtedly symptomatic. Now it is the introduction and help for the treatment with Dr. Abraham" (UD). This suggests that she was going to Abraham again, perhaps for the fourth time.

3. On her Abitur Karen received a grade of *Gut* (Good) in eight areas: Religious Education, Classical Latin, French, English, History, Mathematics, Chemistry, and Nature Description (*Naturbeschreibung*). She received a grade of *Genügend* (Sufficient) in German and Physics (Horney Papers). She was not awarded the highest grade, *Sehr Gut* (Very Good), in any area. This mark was rare, but she surely aimed at it. She did much better on her medical qualifying exams at Freiburg. Her report shows firsts in Anatomy, Physiology, Physics, Chemistry, and Botany, and a second in Zoology. Her overall grade was *Sehr Gut* (Horney Papers).

4. For accounts of Horney's place in the history of feminine psychology and of the importance of her ideas, see Fliegel 1973, 1982, 1986, Moulton 1975, Rubins 1978, O'Connell 1980, Garrison 1981, Buckley 1982, Grossman 1986, Westkott 1986, 1989, Quinn 1987, Kerr 1988, Eckardt 1991, Symonds 1991, and Sayers 1991.

5. William I. Grossman argues that "in the controversy between Horney and Freud, female sexuality was the manifest issue through which more fundamental but latent differences of broad theoretical outlook were argued" (1986, 66). Grossman's comparison of Freud's and Horney's views on feminine psychology is excellent, but his overall thesis is misleading, for Horney's disagreement with Freud's basic model developed quite slowly and did not crystallize until after her move to the United States. Horney's quarrel with Freud in the 1930s *was* about psychoanalytic models; but in the 1920s, it mainly concerned the particulars of feminine psychology. Grossman has conflated two different stages of Horney's thought. He quotes from her essays on feminine psychology and from *New Ways in Psychoanalysis* without seeming to recognize that by 1939 Horney had developed a very different psychoanalytic model from the one she employed in the 1920s, when she still accepted the Freudian paradigm.

6. I found this lecture, along with four others, among Harold Kelman's papers at the Postgraduate Center for Mental Health.

7. About ten years earlier, Karen had explained her compulsive attraction to Walther and Lisa Honroth in terms of a revival of her infantile relationships with her father and mother: "I have jok-

ingly called Walther the 'father-complex,' and was well aware of the meaning of this joke" (UD, 7 April 1912). She feels that she cannot free herself from Walther because he is a father substitute. From a Freudian perspective, the fact that Karen feels bound to Walther by her "dream of a noble man's love" reinforces the concept of a father fixation, since Abraham traces the need for the "greatest" man to "the infantile desire for the father" (1920, 366).

Karen saw her attachment to Lisa as part of the same picture, since Lisa stood for Sonni in the infantile constellation, and Horney argues in "The Genesis of the Castration Complex" that identifying with the father (as a result of oedipal disappointment) "always amounts also to desiring the mother" (49). In her diary entry for 9 January 1911, she writes that her wanting to be a boy "also had to do with my wish to be Sonni's husband" (UD). In "The Genesis of the Castration Complex" she argues that "in every case in which the castration complex predominates" there is a "marked tendency to homosexuality" (49), and in her fifth diary there are numerous references to what she believed to be her homosexual trends. Her dream about Oskar's having a vagina into which she inserted her finger indicated her "desire for homosexuality" (UD, 11 January 1911), as does her attraction to Lisa (23 January), her frigidity (4 May 1912), and her desire for women friends (16 April and 4 May). Three people who knew Horney in the last two decades of her life spoke of her having had at least one lesbian affaire. Each mentioned a different partner.

8. It is largely through Fliegel's work (see also 1982 and 1986) that we have recovered the history of the debate about female psychology in the 1920s and early 1930s. Ernest Jones sided with Horney (1927, 1933, 1935), but Freud had the last word in "Female Sexuality" (1931) and *New Introductory Lectures* (1933). After Otto Fenichel (1930, 1934) described the disagreement as the Freud-Jones debate, Horney's name disappeared from the discussion, and the debate itself faded away when Horney and Jones fell silent on the subject and Freud's point of view prevailed.

9. This may be a covert attack on Helene Deutsch, whose *Psychoanalysis of the Sexual Functions of Women* (1925) Horney takes issue with in her essay. She implies that Deutsch, like most other women, has been brainwashed into adopting the masculine view of femininity. Horney had published a lengthy critique of Deutsch's book in *The International Journal of Psychoanalysis* (see 1926b).

10. Assuming the female role may refer, among other things, to the female role in intercourse. In her diary Karen wonders whether Lisa Honroth has described her special sexual demands "in a harsh light" to Walther and whether he is "scared now" (UD, 2 April 1912). Perhaps Karen wanted to be the active, dominant partner who assumed the superior (masculine) position. In "Psychogenic Factors in Functional Disorders" (1933) Horney describes a patient whose envy of a preferred brother "poisoned her whole life and particularly her relations with men. She wanted to be a man herself and played this role in fantasies and dreams. During intercourse she sometimes quite consciously had the wish to change sex roles" (168).

11. I am using a translation by Andrea Dlaska of "The Masculinity Complex of Women." Because the translation is unpublished, I shall not supply page numbers.

12. In *Mothers of Psychoanalysis*, Janet Sayers notes that Horney was the first to shift the emphasis away from Freud's father-centered account of development to one focused on the girl's relationship with her mother. Sayers is helpful in describing how Horney anticipated later theoretical developments, but her account of Karen's adoration of Sonni is misleading. She sometimes seems to invoke Horney's various experiences of being mothered, of being a mother, and of being regarded as a mother by her patients to explain too much, or to account for aspects of Horney's thought in too general a way.

13. Horney gave seven lectures on female psychology in Chicago in April and May 1933 (see note 6). The first two are missing; "Common Deviations in Instinct Development" is the third. Lecture 4 is entitled "Conflicts in Relations with Men (The Problem of Frigidity)," and lectures 5

and 6 both discuss "Psychogenic Factors in Menstrual Disorders." The title of lecture 7 is "Possibilities and Limitations of Psychotherapy," but the lecture is not on this topic. The lectures exist only as typescripts apparently made from stenographic notes and seem to have been aimed at an audience of obstetricians and gynecologists. Many of their ideas and examples reappear in the essays Horney published between 1933 and 1935. Lecture 3 is the most valuable, since it contains material that we do not find anywhere else.

14. For the essays in *Ein biologisches Ehebuch*, I cite translations by Andrea Dlaska. Since the translations are unpublished, I shall not supply page numbers.

Part 3
The Break with Freud and the Development of a New Paradigm

1. I am drawing on letters Horney wrote to W. W. Norton. Her correspondence with Norton and his associates is in the Rare Book and Manuscript Library of Columbia University, which has kindly provided me with copies. All quotations from letters to Norton are from this collection.

2. In a letter to Norton, Horney wrote: "As far as sociologists and ethnologists are concerned, I think they will welcome [*The Neurotic Personality of Our Time*] because it gives them psychological data to work with. This was at any rate the response I got from Ruth Benedict, Margaret Mead, John Dollard, Harold Lasswell. . . . I do not intend to bring in more references to other cultures because I feel that is up [to] the ethnologists. In this regard it is meant as nothing but a stimulation" (10 August 1936).

3. Horney and other neo-Freudians (the term included Horney, Fromm, Sullivan, and sometimes Franz Alexander and Abraham Kardiner) were attacked by Paul Goodman for propounding "a psychology of non-revolutionary social adjustment" (1945, 197). The neo-Freudians define mental health as the spontaneous development of the free personality, but since they have done away with the id and its powerful instincts, where, asks Goodman, "is the *content* . . . of the spontaneity to come from?" The method of Fromm and Horney, he complains, "is to empty out the soul and then fill it . . . with social unanimity and rational faith." For them, "the aims of the individual and society are identical," whereas for Freud "instinctual deprivation" is present in all civilization (199–200). There is a similar though far more sophisticated critique of neo-Freudianism by Herbert Marcuse in *Eros and Civilization*. According to Marcuse, the neo-Freudians present themselves as more conscious of culture than Freud, but their rejection of his theory of sexuality "must lead to a weakening of the sociological critique" (1955, 243). Although they reject "the therapy of adjustment . . . in the strongest terms" and "claim that their psychoanalysis is in itself a *critique* of society" (260), they have "no other objective standards of value than the prevailing ones" and they operationally identify mental health with "'adjustive success'" (256–57).

By making the core of the psyche the free personality rather than instinct, charges Marcuse, neo-Freudians fail to recognize that "the personality which the individual is to develop" has been "regimented from the very beginning" (1955, 257). For Freud, mental health "is successful, efficient resignation" (246) that enables us to have a proportionate rather than a disproportionate share of "that 'everyday unhappiness' which is the common lot of mankind." This is all we can hope for from therapy. The goal of the neo-Freudians is the "'optimal development of a person's potentialities and the realization of his individuality'" (258), but this is unattainable because the very structure of civilization prevents it. Freud has "demonstrated that constraint, repression, and renunciation are the stuff from which the 'free personality' is made" and that the "'general unhappiness' of society [is] the unsurpassable limit of cure and normality" (238).

Marcuse complains that the neo-Freudians embrace the idealized values of the criticized culture and give the impression that "the 'higher values' can and should be practiced within the very conditions which betray them" (1955, 261). Like Goodman, he can find no inherent psychological reality corresponding to Fromm's "free personality" or Horney's "real self" and sees these as empty constructs (unlike Freud's instincts) that are filled with the sham ideals the culture has developed in order to reconcile its members to the frustrations it imposes upon them.

I make an implicit reply to Marcuse from a neo-Freudian point of view in my discussions of the "real self" and Third Force psychology in Part 5 of this book. For now, I should like to call attention to the work of Martin Birnbach, whose *Neo-Freudian Social Philosophy* provides an excellent account of the contributions of Horney, Fromm, Sullivan, Alexander, Kardiner, and Lasswell and compares their social philosophy to Freud's. Birnbach describes Fromm's humanistic ethics as a psychoanalytic equivalent of natural-rights theory (whereas the other neo-Freudians are utilitarians). There are immutable laws inherent in human nature that are independent of culture and "whose violation inflicts serious damage on the personality" (1961, 84). Much like Goodman and Marcuse, Birnbach feels that "Fromm obtrudes his own philosophical preconceptions of human nature" into what should be an empirical science and complains of "the strange paucity of psychoanalytical case material" in his works (86). Yet scientific evidence can be brought in "to fortify part of Fromm's moral battlements" in that he repeatedly refers to "an 'impulse to achieve psychic health and happiness,' without which therapeutic efforts would be in vain" (89). This is where Karen Horney comes in. Her "belief in man's constructive possibilities is 'not mere speculation' but is based on the evidence of observed childhood development, clinical experience, and the changes that take place in psychoanalytic therapy,' and she provides ample supporting material (90). Horney and Fromm agree that "the individual has an inner capacity for growth" and that "the environment plays a vital part in promoting or impeding that capacity," but "whereas Fromm prescribes a precise end toward which growth *should* tend, in ethical terms, Horney suggests several different ends toward which growth *can* tend, in psychic terms" (95).

4 Horney tried to interest Norton in publishing a book by Erich Fromm that would have been complementary to *The Neurotic Personality of Our Time:* "Dr. Fromm is a distinguished social psychologist whose name you may have noticed in several quotations in my book. Dr. Fromm is writing a book on Character and Culture which deals with the relationships between culture and personality structure. Dealing with the normal personality the book represents in a certain sense a parallel to mine. Dr. Fromm tries to put psychoanalytical theory on a sociological basis in contrast to the physiological and biological foundation which we find with Freud" (30 November 1936) This book was never published and presumably Fromm employed its ideas in *Escape from Freedom* and *Man for Himself.* Horney's letter suggests how similar Fromm's and her interests were at this time.

5. In the Horney Papers there are twenty-four typewritten pages of notes on lectures Horney delivered to the Chicago Analytic Society in 1933 and to the Baltimore-Washington group from 1933 to 1935. Her topics included masochism, interpretation, analytic technique, transference, negative therapeutic reactions, and case seminars.

6. Horney refined her ideas about psychoanalytic therapy in the concluding chapter of *Our Inner Conflicts*, the penultimate chapter of *Neurosis and Human Growth*, and "The Goals of Psychoanalytic Therapy" (1951), her final work on the topic published during her lifetime. There are reports on her teachings in Kelman 1964, 220–50, and Kelman 1965, 191–241. *Final Lectures* contains transcriptions of tapes of her last course. Had she lived, her next book was to have been on analytic technique.

Part 4
Horney as an Adult

1. *Oral History Portrait of Karen Horney,* American Academy of Psychoanalysis, 5 December 1975, videotape. The other participants in the program were Harry Gershman, Marianne Eckardt, and Alexander Martin. Further references will be to this videotape, and "Academy" will appear parenthetically in text.

2. Margaret Mead, interview with Jack Rubins, 20 July 1977; Abraham Kardiner, interview with Rubins, 2 February 1973.

3. G. H. Graeber, letter (in German) to Rubins, 5 June 1973; Edith Weigert, interview with Rubins, 5 May 1973.

4. My sources throughout this section include the published biographical accounts and unpublished memoirs, audio- and videotapes, and interviews. Unless otherwise identified, the people quoted are analysts who were colleagues, students, analysands, or supervisees of Horney. (I have not further identified well-known people like Margaret Mead or Rollo May.) Although interviewees had different experiences with, perceptions of, and judgments about Horney, there is much overlapping and many areas of consensus. This has given me more than one source for every statement I make about Horney. Even the direct quotations usually represent more than one perspective, since I have often had to choose among similar quotations.

5. Renate Patterson, "My Mother as I Remember Her," unpublished memoir (Horney Papers), 21; Gertrude Weiss, wife of Horney's colleague Frederick Weiss, interview with Rubins, 26 May 1973; Gertrude Lederer-Eckardt, interview with Rubins, 8 January 1972.

6. Roy Grinker, of the Chicago Psychoanalytic Institute, interview with Rubins, 9 May 1976; Lawrence Kubie, interview with Rubins, 27 May 1973.

7. Marie Levy, interview with Rubins, 3 October 1972; Lederer-Eckardt, interview with Rubins, 8 January 1972; Frances Arkin, interview with the author, 6 January 1990.

8. Hannah Tillich, wife of Paul Tillich, interview with Rubins, 28 November 1973; Gertrude Weiss, interview with Rubins, 26 May 1973; Wanda Willig, interview with the author, 23 October 1989; Weiss, interview with Rubins, 26 May 1973; Rollo May, letter to Rubins, 19 August 1975; Willig, interview with the author, 23 October 1989; Weiss, interview with Rubins, 26 May 1973.

9. Abe Pinsky, interview with the author, 23 October 1989.

10. Frances Arkin, interview with the author, 6 January 1990; Patterson, unpublished introduction to Horney's adolescent diaries (Horney Papers); Valer Barbu, interview with Rubins, n.d.; Weiss, interview with Rubins, 26 May 1973.

11. Abraham Kardiner, interview with Rubins, 10 February 1973; Ruth Moulton, interview with the author, 20 March 1990; Weigert, interview with Rubins, 5 May 1973; Earl Witenburg, William Alanson White Institute, telephone interview with the author, 9 June 1992.

12. Patterson, telephone interview with the author, 24 July 1992; Kardiner, interview with Rubins, 10 February 1973; Marianne Eckardt, interview with Rubins, n.d.

13. Levy, note to Rubins, n.d. (probably October 1972).

14. Moulton, interview with the author, 20 March 1990; Rainer Funk, letter to the author, 19 July 1990. Funk, who has written several books on Fromm and is his literary executor, observes: "Another description could fit in some way: 'Someone had once called Peter a bird that never settled down; Peter was good looking and a good dancer.' Although Fromm built a house in Vermont (1948) and later (1957) in Cuernavaca, he was never bound to a place in the world. I have no information that he was a good dancer, but I know that he was admiring dancers and had good contacts to well known girl dancers in this time." According to Funk, Fromm's character changed during the 1960s, which makes it difficult for people who knew him later to assess how closely he corre-

sponded to Peter: "He seems to have had a very different radiation in former times"; Hannah Tillich, interview with Rubins, 28 November 1973.

15. Moulton, interview with the author, 20 March 1990; Levy, interview with Rubins, 3 October 1972.

16. Eckardt, interview with the author, 21 March 1990; Arkin, interview with the author, 6 January 1990.

17. Ernst Schachtel, interview with Rubins, 2 April 1972.

18. Valer Barbu, interview with Rubins, n.d.; Patterson, interview with the author, 28 December 1989.

19. Tillich, interview with Rubins, 28 November 1973; Lederer-Eckardt, interview with Rubins, 8 January 1972.

20. Louis De Rosis, interview with Rubins, n.d.; Richard Hulbeck, interview with Rubins, 1 August 1972.

21. Patterson, telephone interview with the author, 24 July 1992.

22. Letters from Horney to Adolph Stern, 4 March and 7 April 1937 (Brill Archive).

23. Letter of resignation, 14 June 1941, published in the first issue of the *American Journal of Psychoanalysis* (1941): 9–10, and signed by Frances Arkin, Eugene Eisner, Muriel Ivimey, Harold Kelman, Elizabeth Kilpatrick, Judah Marmor, Alexander Martin, Meyer Maskin, Janet Rioch, Leopold Rosanes, Herman Selinsky, Edward Tauber, Lewis Wolberg, and Alexander Wolf (Brill Archive). Many of these people became important figures in the Association for the Advancement of Psychoanalysis and the American Institute, and some later joined the William Alanson White Institute or the New York Medical College.

24. This statement, dated 25 November 1941, was published in the *Psychoanalytic Review* 29 (1942): 222–26; I am drawing from both versions of the statement in the following paragraphs.

25. Kubie, letters to Rubins, 9 August and 11 July 1972 (Horney Papers).

26. Ibid., 9 August 1972; Kardiner, interview with Rubins, 10 February 1973.

27. Letter from Frances Arkin, secretary of the AAP, to the members, 5 May 1943 (Horney Papers).

28. Ibid.

29. Clara Thompson, typed account of Fromm's split with the American Institute for Psychoanalysis (Horney Papers).

30. Moulton, interview with the author, 20 March 1990; Sara Sheiner, interview with the author, 22 October 1989.

31. Judd Marmor, telephone interview with the author, 10 August 1992; Lederer-Eckardt, interview with Rubins, 8 January 1972; Moulton, interview with the author, 20 March 1990.

32. Thompson, account of Fromm's split (Horney Papers); Ralph Crowley, letter of resignation addressed to Frances Arkin, 23 April 1943 (Horney Papers).

33. Stephen Jewett, letter to Elizabeth Kilpatrick (secretary of the AAP), 18 February 1944 (Horney Papers). For more details on the end of the proposed merger, see Rubins 1978, 268–70; Quinn 1987, 369–70; and Eckardt 1978, 150–52. There are letters and reports relating to the schism in the Horney Papers.

34. Eckardt, interview with the author, 21 March 1990; Abe Pinsky, interview with the author, 23 October 1989.

35. Eckardt, interview with Rubins, n.d.

36. According to Sara Sheiner, Kelman "repeatedly said that Fromm was a vicious man, not to be trusted, a liar and cheater" (interview with the author, 3 March 1990). Kelman may have been voicing Horney's attitudes, of course.

37. Eckardt, interview with Rubins, n.d.; Eckardt, interview with the author, 21 March 1990;

Karl Kornreich, interview with Rubins, n.d.; Harmon Ephron, interview with Rubins, 28 January 1972; Willig, interview with the author, 23 October 1989; Ephron, interview with Rubins, 28 January 1972; Kornreich, interview with Rubins, n.d.; Moulton, interview with Rubins, n.d.

38. Kornreich, interview with Rubins, n.d.

39. Arkin, interview with the author, 6 January 1990.

40. Eckardt, interview with the author, 21 March 1990; Arkin, interview with the author, 6 January 1990; Rubins, letter to Susan Quinn, 4 May 1982; Arkin, interview with the author, 6 January 1990; Norman Kelman, interview with the author, 19 October 1989.

41. Willig, interview with the author, 23 October 1989; Eckardt, interview with Rubins, n.d.; Arkin, interview with the author, 6 January 1990.

42. Morris Isenberg, interview with Rubins, n.d.; Isidore Portnoy, interview with Rubins, June 1975; Sara Sheiner, interview with the author, 22 October 1989; Sheiner, telephone interview with the author, 16 August 1992; Gertrude Weiss, interview with Rubins, 26 May 1973.

43. Arkin, interview with the author, 6 January 1990; Lederer-Eckardt, interview with Rubins, 8 January 1972; Norman Kelman, interview with the author, 19 October 1989; Pinsky, interview with the author, 23 October 1989; Norman Kelman, interview with Rubins, n.d.; Louis De Rosis, interview with Rubins, n.d.; Norman Kelman, interview with Rubins, n.d.

44. Gertrude Weiss, interview with Rubins, 26 May 1973; Esther Spitzer, interview with Rubins, 20 March 1977; Gertrude Weiss, interview with Jack Rubins, 26 May 1973.

45. Weiss, interview with Rubins, 26 May 1973; Norman Kelman, interview with Rubins, n.d.

46. Karen Horney, notebook entry for 22 October 1914. See also the entries for 2 August 1915, 25 September 1915, and 6 December 1916. This notebook is in the Karen Horney Papers. Further references to this notebook will be given in the text, and the date of the entry noted parenthetically. Patterson, interview with the author, 27 December 1989 (see also Horney's notebook entries for 23 October 1914 and 28 January 1917 and Heyerdahl 1992, 17); Eckardt, interview with Jack Rubin, n.d.; Patterson, "My Mother," 19; Patterson, interview with the author, 2 June 1992.

47. Patterson, "My Mother," 19–20.

48. Eckardt, interview with Rubins, n.d.; Patterson, "My Mother," 59.

49. Patterson, "My Mother," 5.

50. Eckardt, interview with Rubins, n.d.

51. Patterson, "My Mother," 21, 17, 1, 10, 9, 21.

52. Eckardt, interview with Rubins, n.d.; Eckardt, letter to Rubins, 31 October 1971.

53. Eckardt, interview with Rubins, n.d.

54. Ibid.

55. Horney, letter to Brigitte Horney, 14 December 1945. Brigitte gave fifty letters that her mother wrote her from 1945 to 1951 to her friend Gerd Høst Heyerdahl, who has kindly supplied me with copies. Horney used only the month and day in dating these letters; on thirty-five of them the year has been supplied in another hand, and fifteen have no year at all. By employing internal and external evidence, I have tried to provide, correct, or confirm the year for all of the letters. Further citations to these letters will be in text, where I shall give dates parenthetically, but the reader should be aware that these dates are not always certain. The letters were all translated by Christa Zorn-Belde. Photocopies of the letters are available in the Horney Papers.

56. Marianne is uncomfortable with her mother's psychoanalytic theories because she feels that Horney's typology of neuroses and her ideal of self-realization "pathologize ordinary existence" (1983, 397). She prefers a phenomenological approach that sees people's modes of coping as responses that make sense in light of their life situations. Her essays "The Detached Person: A Discussion with a Phenomenological Bias" (1960), "Life Is a Juggling Act: Our Concepts of 'Normal' Development—Myth or Reality?" (1975), and "Beliefs and Reflections of a Therapist"

(1978b) illuminate how her approach differs from her mother's; Eckardt, interview with Rubins, n.d.; Eckardt, interviews with the author, 21 March 1990 and 20 October 1989.

57. Patterson, letter to the author, 22 January 1990.

58. Patterson, telephone interview with the author, 5 June 1992; Patterson, "My Mother," 47, 93; Patterson, interview with the author, 27 December 1989.

59. Patterson, "My Mother," 29, 78, 77.

60. Patterson, telephone interviews with the author, 2 and 5 June 1990.

61. Patterson, letter to the author, June 1992.

62. Patterson, "My Mother," 116–17; Gertrude Weiss, interview with Rubins, 26 May 1973.

63. Rita Honroth-Welte, interview with Rubins, n.d.; Norman Kelman, interview with Rubins, n.d.; Lederer-Eckardt, interview with Rubins, 8 January 1972; Patterson, interview with the author, 27 December 1989; Katie Sugarman, former wife of Norman Kelman, interview with Rubins, n.d.; Patterson, interview with the author, 27 December 1989.

64. Patterson, interviews with the author, 28 December 1989, 2 June 1992, and 27 December 1989

65. Willig, interview with the author, 23 October 1989.

66. Patterson, telephone interview with the author, 2 June 1992.

67. Rita Honroth-Welte, "My Recollections of Karen Horney," unpublished memoir (Horney Papers), 1973, 7.

68. Eckardt, interview with the author, 21 March 1990.

69. Norman Kelman, interview with the author, 19 October 1989; Moulton, interview with the author, 20 March 1990; Dorothy Blitsten, wife of Lionel Blitsten of the Chicago Psychoanalytic Institute, interview with Rubins, n.d.; Walter Bonime, interview with Rubins, n.d.; Edward Clemmens, telephone interview with the author, 5 October 1989; Moulton, interview with the author, 20 March 1990; Arkin, interview with the author, 6 January 1990.

70. Margaret Mead, interview with Rubins, 20 July 1977; Arkin, interview with the author, 6 January 1990.

71. Patterson, "My Mother," 2.

72. Lederer-Eckardt, interview with Rubins, 8 January 1972; Levy, interview with Rubins, 30 October 1972; Willig, interview with the author, 23 October 1989; Medard Boss, Swiss analyst who knew Horney in Berlin, interview with Rubins, n.d.

73. Eckardt, interview with the author, 21 March 1990; Patterson, interview with the author, 28 December 1989; Eckardt, letter to Rubins, 31 October 1971.

74. Gertrude Weiss, interview with Rubins, 26 May 1973.

75. Edward Clemmens, letter to the author, 20 March 1990.

Part 5

Horney's Mature Theory

1. There are any number of predominantly compliant or self-effacing characters in literature, many of whom I—and a few other critics—have analyzed in Horneyan terms. Starting with Shakespeare, some of the prime examples include Hamlet and Desdemona (Paris 1991a), Antonio in *The Merchant of Venice* (Paris 1989), the poet in Shakespeare's sonnets (Lewis 1985; Paris 1991a), and Antony in *Antony and Cleopatra* (Paris 1991b). We can add to the list Fanny Price in Austen's *Mansfield Park* (Paris 1978b); Dobbin and Amelia in Thackeray's *Vanity Fair* (Paris 1974); Esther Summerson in Dickens' *Bleak House* (Eldredge 1986); Maggie Tulliver in Eliot's *The Mill on the Floss* (Paris 1974); Tess in Hardy's *Tess of the D'Urbervilles* (Paris 1976a); Nora

Helmer in Ibsen's *A Doll's House* (Paris 1978a); the priest in Greene's *The Power and the Glory* (Straub 1986); Moses in Bellow's *Herzog* (Paris 1976b); and Alice Mellings in Lessing's *The Good Terrorist* (Eldredge 1989). As is true of characters exemplifying each of the other major solutions, most of these characters experience inner conflicts and manifest other trends as well.

2. Predominantly arrogant-vindictive characters who have been discussed in Horneyan terms include Iago, Lady Macbeth, and Macbeth after the murder of Duncan (Paris 1991a), Richard III (Paris 1991b), and Shylock (Paris 1989) in Shakespeare; Julien Sorel in Stendhal's *The Red and the Black* (Paris 1974); Becky Sharp in Thackeray's *Vanity Fair* (Paris 1974); Heathcliff in Emily Brontë's *Wuthering Heights* (Paris 1982); Count Guido in Browning's *The Ring and the Book* (Lewis 1986); Raskolnikov in Dostoevsky's *Crime and Punishment* (Paris 1991c); and Joe Christmas in Faulkner's *Light in August* (Haselswerdt 1986).

3. Predominantly narcissistic characters whom I have discussed elsewhere in Horneyan terms include King Lear (1991a) and Richard II (1991b) in Shakespeare, Emma in Austen's *Emma* (1978), and Conrad's Lord Jim (1974). Another splendid example is Sir Willoughby in Meredith's *The Egoist,* the novel Horney was reading during her final illness.

4. Predominantly perfectionistic characters who have been discussed in Horneyan terms include Brutus (Paris 1991b), Othello (Paris 1991a), Cordelia (Paris, 1991a), and Coriolanus (Paris 1991b) in Shakespeare, and Macbeth before the murder of Duncan (Paris 1991a); the heroine of Samuel Richardson's *Clarissa* (Eldredge 1982); and three characters in Austen—Elinor Dashwood in *Sense and Sensibility,* Mr. Knightly in *Emma,* and Anne Elliot in *Persuasion* (Paris 1978).

5. Predominantly detached characters who have been discussed in Horneyan terms include Shakespeare's Horatio in *Hamlet* and Thersites in *Troilus and Cressida* (Paris 1991a), Mr. Bennet in Austen's *Pride and Prejudice* (Paris 1978), Dostoevsky's Underground Man (Paris 1974), and Quentin Compson in Faulkner's *Absalom, Absalom!* and *The Sound and the Fury* (Butery 1989). The detached solution is far more prevalent than this short list might suggest. Among the many notable detached characters in twentieth-century literature are Martin Decoud in Conrad's *Nostromo* and Axel Heyst in his *Victory,* Harry Haller in Hesse's *Steppenwolf,* Meursault in Camus's *The Stranger,* and Jake Horner in Barth's *The End of the Road.*

6. I have made a detailed study of this phenomenon in *Bargains with Fate: Psychological Crises and Conflicts in Shakespeare and His Plays* (1991a), where I argue that the leading characters of the major tragedies are thrown into a state of crisis by events that challenge their bargains with fate.

Hamlet's crisis is precipitated when his father's memory is not honored, Hamlet is passed over for the throne, and the evil Claudius gains the rewards that should be bestowed upon goodness. Whereas the self-effacing Hamlet is oppressed by the ascendancy of Claudius, the arrogant-vindictive Iago's bargain is undermined by the success of "direct and honest" people like Cassio, Othello, and Desdemona. If loyalty and love triumph over egoism and deceit, Iago's conception of the world will be shattered. One of the main functions of his scheme is to prove that he was right in his beliefs by using the compliance, hunger for love, and trustfulness of others to destroy them. Othello's narcissistic and perfectionistic bargains collapse when Desdemona, who was to be the confirmation of his greatness and the reward of his virtue, appears to have betrayed him. Desdemona's self-effacing solution is threatened when Othello turns against her. The narcissistic Lear has been encouraged to believe that he is "everything," and his claims are denied when Cordelia refuses to tell him that she loves him "all." He loses his sanity when his bargain is shattered by his treatment at the hands of the vindictive Goneril and Regan.

The bargains of Hamlet, Iago, Othello, Desdemona, and Lear are violated by the behavior of others, by external events. The case of Macbeth is somewhat different. Macbeth is a perfectionist who has always done his duty. His expansiveness has been expressed, like Othello's, through the "big wars that make ambition virtue." He violates his own bargain by sacrificing the virtue, honor, and "golden opinions" he values in order to satisfy his lust for absolute power and to retain the respect of his wife. His inner dictates tell him that the murder of Duncan is bound to bring retribution, and he turns into a bloody tyrant afterward in an attempt to quiet his fear by killing his conscience. His inability to live with his horrible deed leads him to behave in self-defeating ways.

7. Problems arise in Horneyan theory at this point in *Neurosis and Human Growth,* for she now presents the major solutions as ways of dealing with the conflict between pride and self-hate, the idealized and despised selves. She characterizes them as intrapsychic solutions to an intrapsychic conflict and seems to lose sight of the interpersonal defenses and conflicts she described in *Our Inner Conflicts* and at the beginning of *Neurosis and Human Growth.* She appears to have provided two different sets of major solutions, one interpersonal and one intrapsychic, which have different names, functions, and origins.

What happened, I think, is that Horney became so fascinated with intrapsychic phenomena in *Neurosis and Human Growth* that she tried to recast her entire theory in terms of them, despite her warning against "a one-sided focus on either intrapsychic or interpersonal factors" (237). As a result, she does not present a clear and balanced picture of the relation between the interpersonal and the intrapsychic. She does not explain how the conflict between pride and self-hate gives rise to the self-effacing, expansive, and resigned solutions, nor how these solutions address that conflict.

Horney's accounts of the major solutions present them as both interpersonal and intrapsychic in nature. Had she lived to continue working on her theory, she would no doubt have brought the findings of *Our Inner Conflicts* and *Neurosis and Human Growth* more completely into harmony with each other. I have dealt with these problems by ignoring the unpersuasive thesis that the major solutions are produced by the conflict between pride and self-hate and by synthesizing the interpersonal and the intrapsychic in the spirit of Horney's best statements about their relation to each other.

8 Frances Aikin, interview with the author, 6 January 1990; Wanda Willig, interview with the author, 23 October 1989; Esther Spitzer, interview with Jack Rubins, 20 March 1977.

9. While complaining in 1961 that Horney had "lost touch with the deep Freudian uncon scious," Harry Guntrip agreed that "self-realization of the 'real' self—i.e. of the individual's actual 'nature'—is certainly of the greatest importance"; it "is an emphasis now coming more and more to the forefront in psychoanalysis, as for example in the work of Winnicott" (1961, 170, 169).

10. Maslow includes in the Third Force Adlerians; Rankians; Jungians; neo-Freudians like Horney and Fromm; such post-Freudians as Allen Wheelis, Judd Marmor, Thomas Szasz, and Ernst Schachtel; Kurt Goldstein; Gestalt therapists; such personality theorists as Gordon Allport, Gardner Murphy, and Henry Murray; self-psychologists; phenomenological psychologists; growth psychologists; Rogerians; and humanistic psychologists. For a fuller listing, see Maslow 1968, vi. Of course, some of these theorists have more in common than others with Horney and the version of Third Force psychology that Maslow develops.

11. For a full account of the basic needs and the dynamics of the hierarchy, see Maslow's *Motivation and Personality.* There is a fuller discussion of Third Force psychology in my "Horney, Maslow, and the Third Force" (in 1986), on which the present account is partially based.

12. For an application of Maslow's hierarchy to the study of culture, see Aronoff 1967.

13. Compare the Freudian position as articulated by Sandor Ferenczi: "The development of the reality-sense is represented by a succession of repressions, to which mankind was compelled, not through spontaneous 'strivings towards development,' but through necessity, through adjustment to a demanded renunciation. The first great repression is made necessary by the process of birth. . . . The foetus would much rather remain undisturbed longer in the womb, but it is cruelly

turned out into the world, and it has to forget (repress) the kind of satisfaction it had got fond of, and adjust itself to new ones. The same cruel game is repeated with every new stage of development" (1952, 236–37).

Appendix A
Interdisciplinary Applications of Horneyan Theory

1. Horneyan studies have been published on the following authors: Jane Austen (Paris 1978), Honoré de Balzac (Portnoy 1949), Charles Baudelaire (Van Bark 1961), Saul Bellow (Paris 1976b), Charlotte Brontë (Butery 1986; Paris 1993), Emily Brontë (Paris 1982), Robert Browning (Lewis 1986), Pearl S. Buck (Vollmerhausen 1950), Joseph Conrad (Paris 1974), Anita Desai (Bande 1988), Charles Dickens (Eldredge 1986), Fyodor Dostoevsky (Van Bark 1961; Paris 1974, 1991c), George Eliot (Paris 1974, 1986; Butery, 1982; Lauer 1985), William Faulkner (Haselswerdt 1986, Butery 1989), Gustave Flaubert (Paris 1981), Robert Frost (Thompson 1966, 1970; Thompson and Winnick 1976; Sheehy 1986), Graham Greene (Straub 1986), Thomas Hardy (Paris 1976a, Butery 1982), Ernest Hemingway (Yalom and Yalom 1971), Henrik Ibsen (Breitbart 1948; Paris 1978a), Henry James (Butery 1982; Lauer 1985), James Joyce (Bartlett 1993), D. H. Lawrence (Smalley 1986), Doris Lessing (Westkott 1986, Eldredge 1989), C. S. Lewis (Bartlett 1989), Somerset Maugham (Weiss 1973), George Meredith (Watt 1984), Eugene O'Neill (Falk 1958), Samuel Richardson (Eldredge 1982), William Shakespeare (Rosenberg 1961; Rabkin and Brown 1973; Lewis 1985; Paris 1989, 1991a, 1991b), George Bernard Shaw (Bartlett 1991), Mary Shelley (Keyishian 1989), Stendhal (Paris 1974), William Styron (Huffman 1986), William Makepeace Thackeray (Paris 1974), and Richard Wright (Fishburn 1977).

References

Abbreviations

NP   *The Neurotic Personality of Our Time* (1937)

NW   *New Ways in Psychoanalysis* (1939)

SA   *Self-Analysis* (1942)

OIC   *Our Inner Conflicts* (1945)

NHG   *Neurosis and Human Growth* (1950)

FP   *Feminine Psychology* (1967)

AD   *The Adolescent Diaries of Karen Horney* (1980)

UD   Unpublished Diaries

FL   *Final Lectures* (1987)

Abraham, K. 1920. Manifestations of the Female Castration Complex. In *Selected Papers of Karl Abraham*. Trans. D. Bryan and A. Strachey. London: Hogarth Press, 1949.

Alexander, F. 1937. Review of K. Horney, *The Neurotic Personality of Our Time. Psychoanalytic Quarterly* 6:536–40.

———. 1940. The Human Setting of the Development of Ideas [review of K. Horney, *New Ways in Psychoanalysis*]. *Psychoanalytic Quarterly* 9:1–36.

Ansbacher, H. L., and Ansbacher, R. R., eds. 1956. *The Individual Psychology of Alfred Adler*. New York: Harper Torchbook, 1964.

References

Aronoff, J. 1967. *Psychological Needs and Cultural Systems*. Princeton: Van Nostrand.

Azorin, L. A. 1957. Karen Horney on Psychoanalytic Technique: The Analyst's Personal Equation. *American Journal of Psychoanalysis* 17:34–38.

Bande, U. 1988. *The Novels of Anita Desai*. New Delhi: Prestige Press.

Bartlett, S. A. 1989. Humanistic Psychology in C. S. Lewis's *Till We Have Faces:* A Feminist Critique. *Studies in the Literary Imagination* 22:185–98.

———. 1991. Fantasy as Internal Mimesis in Bernard Shaw's *Saint Joan. Notes on Modern Irish Literature* 3:5–12.

———. 1993. Spectral Thought and Psychological Mimesis in *A Portrait of the Artist as a Young Man. Notes on Modern Irish Literature* 5:57–66.

Benedict, R. 1938. Review of K. Horney, *The Neurotic Personality of Our Time. Journal of Abnormal and Social Psychology* 33:133–35.

Bergman, I. 1974. *Scenes from a Marriage*. Trans. A. Blair. New York: Bantam.

Birnbach, M. 1961. *Neo-Freudian Social Philosophy*. Stanford: Stanford University Press.

Bolt, R. n.d. *A Man for All Seasons*. New York: Vintage.

Breitbart, S. 1948. "Hedda Gabler": A Critical Analysis. *American Journal of Psychoanalysis* 8:55–58.

Briffault, R. 1927. *The Mothers*. 3 vols. London: George Allen & Unwin.

Brown, J. F. 1937. Review of K. Horney, *The Neurotic Personality of Our Time. The Nation* 145 (3 July): 21–22.

———. 1939. Review of K. Horney, *New Ways in Psychoanalysis. The Nation* 149 (23 September): 328–29.

Buckley, N. L. 1982. Women Psychoanalysts and the Theory of Feminine Development: A Study of Karen Horney, Helene Deutsch, and Marie Bonaparte. Ph.D. diss., University of California, Los Angeles.

Butery, K. 1982. The Contributions of Horneyan Psychology to the Study of Literature. *American Journal of Psychoanalysis* 42:39–50.

———. 1986. Jane Eyre's Flights from Decision. In *Third Force Psychology and the Study of Literature*. Ed. B. J. Paris. Rutherford, N.J.: Fairleigh Dickinson University Press.

———. 1989. From Conflict to Suicide: The Inner Turmoil of Quentin Compson. *American Journal of Psychoanalysis* 49:211–24.

Chodorow, N. 1978. *The Reproduction of Mothering: Psychoanalysis and the Psychology of Gender*. Berkeley: University of California Press.

———. 1989. *Feminism and Psychoanalytic Theory*. New Haven: Yale University Press.

Clemmens, E. 1988. Review of Susan Quinn, *A Mind of Her Own: The Life of Karen Horney. American Journal of Psychoanalysis* 48:281–84.

Clinch, N. 1973. *The Kennedy Neurosis*. New York: Grosset & Dunlap.

Danielian, J. 1988. Karen Horney and Heinz Kohut: Theory and the Repeat of History. *American Journal of Psychoanalysis* 48:6–24.

De Rosis, H., and V. Pellegrino. 1976. *The Book of Hope: How Women Can Overcome Depression*. New York: Macmillan.

Deutsch, H. 1925. *Psychoanalyse der weiblichen Sexualfunktionen* [Psychoanalysis of the sexual functions of women]. Vienna: Internationaler Psychoanalytischer Verlag.

Dinnage, R. 1987. Review of Susan Quinn, *A Mind of Her Own: The Life of Karen Horney. New York Times Book Review,* 29 November, 10–11.

Dowling, C. 1981. *The Cinderella Complex: Woman's Hidden Fear of Independence*. New York: Summit.

Dworkin, A. 1989. *Letters from a War Zone*. New York: Dutton.

Eckardt, M. H. 1960. The Detached Person: A Discussion with a Phenomenological Bias. *American Journal of Psychoanalysis* 20:139–49.

———. 1975. Life Is a Juggling Act: Our Concepts of "Normal" Development—Myth or Reality? *American Journal of Psychoanalysis* 35:103–13.

———. 1978a. Organizational Schisms in American Psychoanalysis. In *American Psychoanalysis: Origins and Development*. Ed. J. M. Quen and E. T. Carlson. New York: Brunner/Mazel.

———. 1978b. Beliefs and Reflections of a Therapist. In *Interpersonal Psychoanalysis: New Directions*. Ed. E. G. Witenberg. New York: Gardner.

———. 1980. Reflections on "What Helps a Patient?" Talk presented to the Nassau County Psychoanalytic Group, 1980.

———. 1983. The Core Theme of Erich Fromm's Writings and Its Implications for Therapy. *Journal of the American Academy of Psychoanalysis* 11:391–99.

———. 1991. Feminine Psychology Revisited: A Historical Perspective. *American Journal of Psychoanalysis* 51:235–43.

Eldredge, P. R. 1982. Karen Horney and *Clarissa:* The Tragedy of Neurotic Pride. *American Journal of Psychoanalysis* 42:51–59.

———. 1986. The Lost Self of Esther Summerson: A Horneyan Interpretation of *Bleak House*. In *Third Force Psychology and the Study of Literature.* Ed. B. J. Paris. Rutherford, N.J.: Fairleigh Dickinson University Press.

———. 1989. A Granddaughter of Violence: Doris Lessing's Good Girl as Terrorist. *American Journal of Psychoanalysis* 49:225–38.

Falk, D. V. 1958. *Eugene O'Neill and the Tragic Tension*. New Brunswick, N.J.: Rutgers University Press.

Feiring, C. 1983. Behavior Styles in Infancy and Adulthood: The Work of Karen Horney and Attachment Theorists Collaterally Considered. *Journal of the American Academy of Child Psychiatry* 22:1–7.

Fenichel, O. 1930. The Pregenital Antecedents of the Oedipus Complex. In *The Collected Papers of Otto Fenichel*. Ed. H. Fenichel and D. Rapaport. New York: Norton, 1953.

———. 1934. Further Light upon the Preoedipal Phase in Girls. In *The Collected Papers of Otto Fenichel*. Ed. H. Fenichel and D. Rapaport. New York: Norton, 1953.

———. 1940. Review of K. Horney, *New Ways in Psychoanalysis. Psychoanalytic Quarterly* 9:114–21.

Ferenczi, S. 1952. Stages in the Development of the Sense of Reality. In *First Contributions to Psycho-Analysis*. Trans. E. Jones. London: Hogarth.

Fishburn, K. 1977. *Richard Wright's Hero: The Faces of a Rebel-Victim*. Metuchen, N.J.: Scarecrow.

Fliegel, Z. O. 1973. Feminine Psychosexual Development in Freudian Theory: A Historical Reconstruction. *Psychoanalytic Quarterly* 42:385–408.

———. 1982. Half a Century Later: Current Status of Freud's Controversial Views on Women. *Psychoanalytic Review* 69:7–28.

———. 1986. Women's Development in Analytic Theory: Six Decades of Controversy. In *Psychoanalysis and Women: Contemporary Reappraisals*. Ed. J. L. Alpert. Hillsdale, N.J.: Analytic Press.

Freud, S. 1925. Some Psychological Consequences of the Anatomical Distinction between the Sexes. *Collected Papers*. Ed. J. Strachey. New York: Basic Books, 1959. 5:186–97.

———. 1931. Female Sexuality. *Collected Papers*. Ed. J. Strachey. New York: Basic Books, 1959. 5:252–72.

———. 1933. *New Introductory Lectures on Psychoanalysis. Standard Edition of the Complete Psychological Works of Sigmund Freud*. Ed. J. Strachey. London: Hogarth, 1964. 22:5–182.

Fromm, E. 1941. *Escape from Freedom*. New York: Rinehart.

————. 1947. *Man for Himself: An Inquiry into the Psychology of Ethics*. New York: Rinehart.

————. 1955. *The Sane Society*. New York: Holt, Rinehart, & Winston.

————. 1956. *The Art of Loving*. New York: Harper & Row.

Garrison, D. 1981. Karen Horney and Feminism. *Signs* 6:672–91.

Glad, B. 1966. *Charles Evans Hughes and the Illusions of Innocence*. Urbana: University of Illinois Press.

————. 1973. Contributions of Psychobiography. In *Handbook of Political Psychology*. Ed. J. N. Knutson. San Francisco: Jossey-Bass.

————. 1980. *Jimmy Carter*. New York: W. W. Norton.

Goodman, P. 1945. The Political Meaning of Some Recent Revisions of Freud. *Politics* 2:197–203.

Green, A. W. 1946. Sociological Analysis of Horney and Fromm. *American Journal of Sociology* 51:533–40.

Grossman, W. I. 1986. Freud and Horney: A Study of Psychoanalytic Models via the Analysis of a Controversy. In *Psychoanalysis: The Science of Mental Conflict*. Ed. A. D. Richards and M. S. Willick. Hillsdale, N.J.: Analytic Press.

Guntrip, H. 1961. *Personality Structure and Human Interaction*. New York: International Universities Press.

Haselswerdt, M. 1986. "Keep Your Muck": A Horneyan Analysis of Joe Christmas and *Light in August*. In *Third Force Psychology and the Study of Literature*. Ed. B. J. Paris. Rutherford, N.J.: Fairleigh Dickinson University Press.

Heyerdahl, G. H. 1992. *Brigitte Horney: So oder so ist das Leben* [Life is like this or like that]. Berne: Scherz Verlag.

Hillman, J. 1992. Is Therapy Turning Us into Children? *New Age*, May/June, 60–65, 136–41.

Hirsch, H. N. 1981. *The Enigma of Felix Frankfurter*. New York: Basic.

Hoffman, Edward. 1988. *The Right to Be Human: A Biography of Abraham Maslow*. Los Angeles: Jeremy P. Tarcher.

Horney, K. 1917. The Technique of Psychoanalytic Therapy. *American Journal of Psychoanalysis* 28 (1968):3–12.

————. 1923. On the Genesis of the Castration Complex in Women. *FP*, pp. 37–53.

————. 1926a. The Flight from Womanhood: The Masculinity Complex in Women as Viewed by Men and by Women. *FP*, pp. 54–70.

————. 1926b. Review of H. Deutsch, *Zur Psychologie der weiblichen Sexualfunktionen*. *International Journal of Psychoanalysis* 7:92–100.

————. 1926–27. Inhibited Femininity: Psychoanalytical Contribution to the Problem of Frigidity. *FP*, pp. 54–70.

————. 1927a. Der Männlichkeitskomplex der Frau [The masculinity complex in women]. *Archive fur Frauenkunde* 13: 141–54.

————. 1927b. Psychische Eignung und Nichteignung zur Ehe [Psychic fitness and unfitness for marriage]. *Ein biologisches Ehebuch*. Ed. M. Marcuse. Pp. 192–203. Berlin: Marcus & Weber.

————. 1927c. Über die psychischen Bestimmungen der Gattenwahl [On the psychic determinants of choosing a partner]. *Ein biologisches Ehebuch*. Ed. M. Marcuse. Pp. 470–80. Berlin: Marcus & Weber.

————. 1927d. Über die psychischen Wurzeln einiger typischer Ehekonflikte [The psychic origin of some typical marriage problems]. *Ein biologisches Ehebuch*. Ed. M. Marcuse. Pp. 481–91. Berlin: Marcus & Weber.

————. 1927e. Discussion on Lay Analysis. *International Journal of Psychoanalysis* 8:255–59.

————. 1928. The Problem of the Monogamous Ideal. *FP*, pp. 84–88.

————. 1931a. The Distrust between the Sexes. *FP*, pp. 107–18.

————. 1931b. Culture and Aggression: Some Thoughts and Doubts about Freud's Death Drive and Destruction Drive. *American Journal of Psychoanalysis* 20 (1960):130–38.

————. 1932a. The Dread of Woman: Observations on a Specific Difference in the Dread Felt by Men and by Women for the Opposite Sex. *FP*, pp. 133–46.

————. 1932b. Problems of Marriage. *FP*, pp. 119–32.

————. 1932c. Review of O. Rank, *Modern Education. Psychoanalytic Quarterly* 1:349–50.

————. 1933a. The Denial of the Vagina: A Contribution to the Problem of Genital Anxieties in Women. *FP*, pp. 147–61.

————. 1933b. Psychogenic Factors in Functional Female Disorders. *FP*, 162–74.

————. 1933c. Maternal Conflicts. *FP*, pp. 175–81.

————. 1934. The Overvaluation of Love. *FP*, pp. 182–213.

————. 1935a. The Problem of Feminine Masochism. *FP*, pp. 214–33.

————. 1935b. Personality Changes in Female Adolescents. *FP*, pp. 234–44.

————. 1935c. Conceptions and Misconceptions of the Analytical Method. *Journal of Nervous and Mental Disease* 81:399–410.

————. 1936. The Problem of the Negative Therapeutic Reaction. *Psychoanalytic Quarterly* 5:29–44.

————. 1937. *The Neurotic Personality of Our Time.* New York: W. W. Norton.

————. 1939a. Can You Take a Stand? *Journal of Adult Education* 11:129–32.

————. 1939b. *New Ways in Psychoanalysis.* New York: W. W. Norton.

————. 1939c. What Is a Neurosis? *American Journal of Sociology* 45:426–32.

————. 1942. *Self-Analysis.* New York: W. W. Norton.

————. 1945. *Our Inner Conflicts.* New York: W. W. Norton.

————. 1949. Finding the Real Self: A Letter—with a Foreword by Karen Horney. *American Journal of Psychoanalysis* 9:3–7.

————. 1950. *Neurosis and Human Growth: The Struggle toward Self-Realization.* New York: W. W. Norton.

————. 1951. The Goals of Psychoanalytic Therapy. *American Journal of Psychoanalysis* 51 (1991):219–26.

————. 1967. *Feminine Psychology.* Ed. H. Kelman. New York: W. W. Norton.

————. 1980. *The Adolescent Diaries of Karen Horney.* Ed. M. Eckardt. New York: Basic.

————. 1987. *Final Lectures.* Ed. D. H. Ingram. New York: W. W. Norton.

Houghton, W. 1957. *The Victorian Frame of Mind.* New Haven: Yale University Press.

Huffman, James. 1982. A Psychological Critique of American Culture. *American Journal of Psychoanalysis* 42:27–38.

————. 1986. A Psychological Redefinition of William Styron's *Confessions of Nat Turner.* In *Third Force Psychology and the Study of Literature.* Ed. B. J. Paris. Rutherford, N.J.: Fairleigh Dickinson University Press.

————. 1989. Young Man Johnson. *American Journal of Psychoanalysis* 49:251–65.

Ingram, D. H., and J. Lerner. 1992. Horney Theory: An Object Relations Theory. *American Journal of Psychoanalysis* 52:37–44.

James, W. 1890. *The Principles of Psychology.* 2 vols. Cambridge: Harvard University Press, 1981.

Jones, E. 1927. Early Development of Female Sexuality. In *Papers on Psychoanalysis.* Pp. 438–51. Boston: Beacon, 1961.

————. 1933. The Phallic Phase. In *Papers on Psychoanalysis.* Pp. 452–84. Boston: Beacon, 1961.

————. 1935. Early Female Sexuality. In *Papers on Psychoanalysis.* Pp. 485–95. Boston: Beacon, 1961.

Kagan, J. 1984. *The Nature of the Child.* New York: Basic.

Kelman, H. 1971. *Helping People: Karen Horney's Psychoanalytic Approach.* New York: Science House.

Kelman, H., ed. 1964. *Advances in Psychoanalysis: Contributions to Karen Horney's Holistic Approach.* New York: W. W. Norton.

————. 1965. *New Perspectives in Psychoanalysis: Contributions to Karen Horney's Holistic Approach.* New York: W. W. Norton.

Kerr, N. J. 1988. "Wounded Womanhood": An Analysis of Karen Horney's Theory of Feminine Psychology. *Perspectives in Psychiatric Care* 24:132–41.

Key, E. 1888. *The Education of the Child.* New York: G. P. Putnam & Sons.

Keyishian, H. 1989. Vindictiveness and the Search for Glory in Mary Shelley's *Frankenstein. American Journal of Psychoanalysis* 49:201–10.

Kohut, H. 1977. *The Restoration of the Self.* New York: International Universities Press.

————. 1984. *How Does Analysis Cure?* Chicago: University of Chicago Press.

Laing, R. D. 1965. *The Divided Self.* Baltimore: Penguin.

Lauer, K. 1985. His Husband/Her Wife: The Dynamics of the Pride System in Marriage. *Journal of Evolutionary Psychology* 6:329–40.

Leary, T. 1957. *Interpersonal Diagnosis of Personality.* New York: Ronald Press.

Levenson, E. 1980. Review of K. Horney, *The Adolescent Diaries of Karen Horney. New York Times Book Review,* 21 December, 9, 16.

Lewis, C. R. 1985. Poet, Friend, and Poetry: The Idealized Image of Love in Shakespeare's Sonnets. *American Journal of Psychoanalysis* 45:176–90.

————. 1986. Browning's Guido: The Self-Fictionalizing Imagination in Crisis. In *Third Force Psychology and the Study of Literature.* Ed. B. J. Paris. Rutherford, N.J.: Fairleigh Dickinson University Press.

Lowrey, L. G. 1937. Review of K. Horney, *The Neurotic Personality of Our Time. American Journal of Orthopsychiatry* 7:434.

Maeder, Thomas. 1989. *Children of Psychiatrists and Other Psychotherapists.* New York: Harper & Row.

Marcuse, H. 1955. *Eros and Civilization.* Boston: Beacon, 1966.

Marmor, J. 1964. The Pre-History and the Founding of the Comprehensive Course in Psychoanalysis. *Society of Medical Psychoanalysts Newsletter* 5:6, 14.

Maslow, A. 1964. *Religion, Values, and Peak Experiences.* Columbus: Ohio State University Press.

————. 1968. *Toward a Psychology of Being.* 2d ed. Princeton: Van Nostrand.

————. 1970. *Motivation and Personality.* 2d ed. New York: Harper & Row.

————. 1971. *The Farther Reaches of Human Nature.* New York: Viking.

Masterson, J. 1985. *The Real Self.* New York: Brunner/Mazel.

Miller, A. 1981. *Prisoners of Childhood: The Drama of the Gifted Child and the Search for the True Self.* Trans. R. Ward. New York: Basic.

————. 1983. *For Your Own Good: Hidden Cruelty in Child-Rearing and the Roots of Violence.* Trans. H. Hannum and H. Hannum. New York: Farrar, Straus, & Giroux.

Millon, T. 1981. *Disorders of Personality: DSM-III, Axis II.* New York: John Wiley & Sons.

Mindess, H. 1988. *Makers of Psychology: The Personal Factor.* New York: Insight.

Mitchell, A. 1992. A Response to "Horney Theory: An Object Relations Theory." *American Journal of Psychoanalysis* 52:45–49.

Moulton, R. 1975. Early Papers on Women: Horney to Thompson. *American Journal of Psychoanalysis* 35:207–23.

Mullahy, P. 1948. *Oedipus, Myth and Complex.* New York: Hermitage.

Natterson, J. M. 1966. Karen Horney: The Cultural Emphasis. In *Psychoanalytic Pioneers*. Ed. F. Alexander, S. Eisenstein, and M. Grotjahn. New York: Basic.

O'Connell, A. N. 1980. Karen Horney: Theorist in Psychoanalysis and Feminine Psychology. *Psychology of Women Quarterly* 5:81–93.

Paris, B. J. 1974. *A Psychological Approach to Fiction: Studies in Thackeray, Stendhal, George Eliot, Dostoevsky, and Conrad*. Bloomington: Indiana University Press.

———. 1976a. Experiences of Thomas Hardy. In *The Victorian Experience*. Ed. R. A. Levine. Athens: Ohio University Press.

———. 1976b. Herzog the Man: An Analytic View of a Literary Figure. *American Journal of Psychoanalysis* 36:249–60.

———. 1978a. Horney's Theory and the Study of Literature. *American Journal of Psychoanalysis* 38:343–53.

———. 1978b. *Character and Conflict in Jane Austen's Novels: A Psychological Approach*. Detroit: Wayne State University Press.

———. 1981. Third Force Psychology and the Study of Literature, Biography, Criticism, and Culture. *Literary Review* 24:181–221.

———. 1982. "Hush, Hush! He's a human being": A Psychological Approach to Heathcliff. *Women and Literature* 2:101–17.

———. 1988. Review of Susan Quinn, *A Mind of Her Own: The Life of Karen Horney. Contemporary Psychology* 34:568–69.

———. 1989. The Not So Noble Antonio: A Horneyan Analysis of Shakespeare's *Merchant of Venice. American Journal of Psychoanalysis,* 49:189–200.

———. 1991a. *Bargains with Fate: Psychological Crises and Conflicts in Shakespeare and His Plays*. New York: Insight.

———. 1991b. *Character as a Subversive Force in Shakespeare: The History and Roman Plays*. Rutherford, N.J.: Fairleigh Dickinson University Press.

———. 1991c. A Horneyan Approach to Literature. *American Journal of Psychoanalysis* 51:319–37.

———. 1993. "Teaching *Jane Eyre* as a Novel of Vindication." In *Approaches to Teaching* Jane Eyre. Ed. B. Lau and D. Hoeveler. New York: Modern Language Association.

Paris, B. J., ed. 1986. *Third Force Psychology and the Study of Literature*. Rutherford, N.J.: Fairleigh Dickinson University Press.

———. 1989. Special issue of *American Journal of Psychoanalysis* 49, 3, on interdisciplinary applications of Horney.

Paul, H. 1989. Karen Horney's Theory of the Self. In *Self Psychology: Comparisons and Contrasts*. Ed. D. Detrick and S. Detrick. Hillsdale, N.J.: Analytic Press.

Portnoy, I. 1949. "The Magic Skin": A Psychoanalytic Interpretation. *American Journal of Psychoanalysis* 9:67–74.

Potter, D. M. 1954. *People of Plenty: Economic Abundance and the American Character*. Chicago: University of Chicago Press.

Quinn, S. 1987. *A Mind of Her Own: The Life of Karen Horney*. New York: Summit.

Rabkin, L. Y., and J. Brown. 1973. Some Monster in His Thought: Sadism and Tragedy in *Othello. Literature and Psychology* 23:59–67.

Rogers, C. 1961. *On Becoming a Person*. Boston: Houghton Mifflin.

Rosenberg, M. 1961. *The Masks of* Othello. Berkeley: University of California Press.

Rubins, J. L. 1978. *Karen Horney: Gentle Rebel of Psychoanalysis*. New York: Dial.

———. 1980. Discussion of Barry G. Wood, "The Religion of Psychoanalysis." *American Journal of Psychoanalysis* 40:23–26.

Sayers, J. 1991. *Mothers of Psychoanalysis: Helene Deutsch, Karen Horney, Anna Freud, Melanie Klein*. New York: W. W. Norton.

Schachtel, E. 1959. *Metamorphosis: On the Development of Affect, Perception, Attention, and Memory*. New York: Basic.

Sheehy, D. G. 1986. The Poet as Neurotic: The Official Biography of Robert Frost. *American Literature* 58:393–410.

Silverberg, W. V. 1941. Advancement in Psychoanalysis (Presidential Address). *American Journal of Psychoanalysis* 2:21–23.

Smalley, B. 1986. Lawrence's "The Princess" and Horney's "Idealized Self." In *Third Force Psychology and the Study of Literature*. Ed. B. J. Paris. Rutherford, N.J.: Fairleigh Dickinson University Press.

Stern, D. N. 1985. *The Interpersonal World of the Infant*. New York: Basic.

Stolorow, R. D., and G. Atwood. 1979. *Faces in a Cloud: Subjectivity in Personality Theory*. Northvale, N.J.: Jason Aronson.

Straub, J. 1986. A Psychological View of Priesthood, Sin, and Redemption in Graham Greene's *The Power and the Glory*. In *Third Force Psychology and the Study of Literature*. Ed. B. J. Paris. Rutherford, N.J.: Fairleigh Dickinson University Press.

Sullivan, H. S. 1937. A Note on the Implications of Psychiatry, the Study of Interpersonal Relations, for Investigation in the Social Sciences. *American Journal of Sociology* 42:848–61.

Symonds, A. 1974. The Liberated Woman: Healthy and Neurotic. *American Journal of Psychoanalysis* 34:177–83.

———. 1976. Neurotic Dependency in Successful Women. *Journal of the American Academy of Psychoanalysis* 4:95–103.

———. 1978. The Psychodynamics of Expansiveness in the Success-Oriented Woman. *American Journal of Psychoanalysis* 38:195–205.

———. 1991. Gender Issues and Horney Theory. *American Journal of Psychoanalysis* 51:301–12.

Teyber, E. 1988. *Interpersonal Process in Psychotherapy*. Chicago: Dorsey.

Thompson, C., with P. Mullahy. 1957. *Psychoanalysis: Evolution and Development*. New York: Grove.

Thompson, L. 1966. *Robert Frost: The Early Years, 1874–1915*. New York: Holt, Rinehart, & Winston.

———. 1970. *Robert Frost: The Years of Triumph, 1915–1938*. New York: Holt, Rinehart, & Winston.

Thompson, L., and R. H. Winnick. 1976. *Robert Frost: The Later Years, 1938–1963*. New York: Holt, Rinehart, & Winston.

Trotter, W. 1916. *Instincts of the Herd in Peace and War*. London: T. Fisher Unwin.

Tucker, R. 1965. The Dictator and Totalitarianism. *World Politics* 17, 4.

———. 1973. *Stalin as Revolutionary, 1879–1929: A Study in History and Personality*. New York: W. W. Norton.

———. 1977. The Georges' Wilson Reexamined: An Essay on Psychobiography. *American Political Science Review* 71:606–18.

———. 1985. A Stalin Biographer's Memoir. In *Introspection in Biography: The Biographer's Quest for Self-Awareness*. Ed. S. H. Baron and C. Pletsch. Hillsdale, N.J.: Analytic Press.

———. 1990. *Stalin in Power: The Revolution from Above, 1928–1941*. New York: W. W. Norton.

Van Bark, B. S. 1961. The Alienated Person in Literature. *American Journal of Psychoanalysis* 21:183–97.

Vollmerhausen, J. W. 1950. "Pavilion of Women": A Psychoanalytic Interpretation. *American Journal of Psychoanalysis* 10:53–60.

References

Wachtel, P. L. 1977. *Psychoanalysis and Behavior Therapy: Toward an Integration.* New York: Basic.

———. 1989. *The Poverty of Affluence: A Psychological Portrait of the American Way of Life.* Philadelphia: New Society Publishers.

———. 1991. The Preoccupation with Economic Growth: An Analysis Informed by Horneyan Theory. *American Journal of Psychoanalysis* 51:89–103.

Watt, S. 1984. Neurotic Responses to a Failed Marriage: George Meredith's *Modern Love. Mosaic* 17:49–63.

Weinstein, F., and G. M. Platt. 1973. *Psychoanalytic Sociology.* Baltimore: Johns Hopkins University Press.

Weiss, F. 1973. Of Human Bondage. *American Journal of Psychoanalysis* 33:68–76.

Westkott, M. 1986. *The Feminist Legacy of Karen Horney.* New Haven: Yale University Press.

———. 1989. Female Relationality and the Idealized Self. *American Journal of Psychoanalysis* 49:239–50.

Winnicott, D. W. 1965. Ego Distortions in Terms of True and False Self. In *The Maturational Processes and the Facilitating Environment.* New York: International Universities Press.

———. 1987. *The Spontaneous Gesture: Selected Letters of D. W. Winnicott.* Ed. F. R. Rodman. Cambridge: Harvard University Press.

Wood, B. G. 1980. The Religion of Psychoanalysis. *American Journal of Psychoanalysis* 40:13–22.

Yalom, I. D., and M. Yalom. 1971. Ernest Hemingway—A Psychiatric View. *Archives of General Psychiatry* 24:485–94.

Young, K. 1938. Review of *The Neurotic Personality of Our Time. American Journal of Sociology* 43:654–56.

Index